창의성 개발과
활동 중심 독서지도법
개정증보판

개정증보판

창의성 개발과 활동 중심 독서지도법

1판 1쇄 발행 2006년 3월 15일
2판 1쇄 발행 2011년 2월 28일
2판 2쇄 발행 2021년 12월 30일

지 은 이 | 조일제
펴 낸 이 | 김진수
펴 낸 곳 | 한국문화사
등   록 | 제1994-9호
주   소 | 서울시 성동구 아차산로49, 404호(성수동1가, 서울숲코오롱디지털타워3차)
전   화 | 02-464-7708
팩   스 | 02-499-0846
이 메 일 | hkm7708@daum.net
홈페이지 | http://hph.co.kr

ISBN 978-89-5726-853-7 93370

• 이 책의 내용은 저작권법에 따라 보호받고 있습니다.
• 잘못된 책은 구매처에서 바꾸어 드립니다.
• 책값은 뒤표지에 있습니다.

오류를 발견하셨다면 이메일이나 홈페이지를 통해 제보해주세요.
소중한 의견을 모아 더 좋은 책을 만들겠습니다.

창의성 개발과
활동 중심 독서지도법
개정증보판

조일제 지음

한국문화사

|머리말|

　독서의 중요성에 대한 인식의 보급으로 우리나라에도 이제는 독서를 생활화하자는 독서생활운동이 폭넓게 자리 잡았다. 필자가 1980년대 말과 1990년대 중반에 해외파견 연구교수로 영국과 미국에 있었을 때 감명 깊게 눈길을 사로잡았던 풍경이 독서를 즐기는 그들의 문화였다. 몸이 쉬는 곳마다 손길이 닿는 곳마다 책을 비치하여 읽도록 하는 것이었다. 학생들이나 시민들은 도서관뿐만 아니라 학교 기숙사에서, 학생휴게실에서, 공동아파트 휴게실에서, 지하철과 기차에서 손에 책을 집어 들고 읽기를 즐기는 그들의 풍경은 신선한 감응을 주었고 문화와 국력의 원천이 독서애호에서 나온다는 생각이 들었다.
　독서는 왜 하며, 무슨 책을 읽어야 하고, 어떻게 책을 읽을 것인가, 그리고 교사는 학생들에게 어떻게 책을 읽으라고 지도할 것인가? 이러한 문제는 매우 중요한 사항이다. 지식과 정보 입수, 지성과 감성 연마, 창의력 개발 등이 독서의 효용성을 말할 때 일반적으로 제시된다. 특히 문학작품은 당장의 현실적인 실용성 측면에서는 나타나지 않지만 세월이 지나면서 어린시절이나 학창시절에 어떤 책과 만나 그것을 읽었던 계기가 자신의 삶과 운명을 결정하게 되는 영향력으로 작용하는 사례가 적지 않다. 책은 읽는 사람에게는 그 자체가 교사이다. 독서는 지식과 정보의 보물창고에서 보물을 줍는 것과 같으며, 인생의 방향과 운명을 좌우하는 나침반을 손에 쥐는 것과 같다.
　그런데 독서는 어떻게 해야 그 가치와 효용을 극대화할 수 있는가? 오늘날의 학습자관, 교사관, 지식관은 전통적인 개념으로부터 변화되었다. 학생들은 교사가 주입시켜 주는 지식과 정보를 단순히 받아먹는 수동적인 생물이 아니다. 그들은 스스로 책을 읽으면서 그 책의 지적 소유권자가 되며, 그 책의 텍스트나 내재적 저자와 더불어 의사소통을 하고 상호작용을 하며, 그렇게 하는 과정을 통해 텍스트의 의미를 창조적으로 구성한다. 학생이 책읽기 과정에서 상호작용과 상호적 소통의 과정을 통해서 주체적으로 구성한 지식은 교사라는 재판관의 일방적인 재단에 구속될 이유와 필요가 없다. 독자에게 사고의 자율권과 지적 소유권이 부여되어야 한다는 지식 상대주의와 구성주의적 지식관 개념에 기반을 둔 새로운 독서 개념이 이제는 교사들 사이에 폭넓게 자리를 잡았다.

오늘날과 같이 영어가 국제어로서 필수불가결한 의사소통 도구가 되어버린 지구촌 환경에서 외국어로서의 영어는 이제 모국어만큼이나 중요하게 되어버렸다. 이 시대에 적응하고 주도적인 삶을 살아가는 길은 영어로 쓰인 글과 영어로 만들어진 자료를 많이 읽고 듣고 말하고 쓰고 해야만 하는 것이다. 영어로 쓰인 문학작품은 이를 위한 좋은 자료가 된다. 왜냐하면 이야기라는 요소가 재미를 유발하기 때문이다. 여러 인물, 사건, 플롯 등으로 짜인 구성이 흥미를 불러일으키고 재미를 주며 감정이입과 감응작용을 하도록 하여 독자의 인성에 변화를 주는 것이 문학작품이다. 이 책은 중·고등학교에서 학생들의 영어를 지도하는 영어교사 및 사범대학의 예비교사인 학생들에게 도움을 주고자 하는 마음에서 교재로 집필한 것이다. 하지만 이들에게만 국한되지 않고 다른 언어교과 교사들에게도 지침서가 될 수 있을 것이다.

오늘날 우리는 영어를 잘 하는 사람에 대해 부러워하는 시대에 살고 있다. 영어를 잘 한다는 것은 단순히 영어라는 언어만을 기능적으로 잘 하는 것일 수는 없다. 언어는 곧 문화일 뿐만 아니라 사회이자 인간이며, 자연이자 우주이기도 한 것이다. 언어가 언어 자체로만 홀로 있는 것이 아니라 이러한 여러 측면들과 함께 하는 것이다. 영어로 쓰인 진정성 있는 훌륭한 영문학 작품은 활용만 잘 한다면 영어수재와 영어스타가 될 수 있게 할 뿐만 아니라 시대를 선도하는 창의성을 지닌 인재를 배출하는데 큰 역할을 할 수 있다.

이제 교사의 역할은 전통적인 개념의 전지전능한 지식전달자, 지적 우수자, 지식독재자, 해석독점자가 아니라 학생의 책 읽기를 도와주는 안내자, 촉진자, 상담자, 오케스트라의 지휘자 등으로 변화되었다. 이처럼 지식관이 바꿔진 교육자들은 교수학습 과정에서 지식은 텍스트와 독자가 상호작용하고 의사소통하면서 구성된다는 전제를 수용하여 학습자 스스로 구성해내도록 하는 독서훈련이 국가 경쟁력을 견인하고 주체적이고 창조적인 인간을 만들어낸다고 본다. 단순히 전달식으로 주입되는 지식은 살아 움직이는 영양가 있고 맛있는 음식이 될 수 없다. 이 책은 학생 개인별 활동이나(individual work), 짝지 활동이나 (pair work) 집단별 활동으로(group work) 읽기과정의 전, 중, 후에 걸친 다양한 활동들을 실행해봄으로써 학생들 스스로 의견을 표현·발표·문답·토론하고, 의견을 교환하는 활동중심의 독서개념을 강조하였다. 이러한 과정을 통해 의사소통 능력, 발표토론 능력, 창의력을 키울 수 있으며, 읽고, 말하고, 듣고, 쓰고 하는 언어의 네 가지 기능이 통합적으로 작동되게 하고, 이해능력과 표현능력이 함께 향상되게 한다고 보았기 때문이다. 이와 같은 독서방법은 구성주의적 지식관에 기초한 '총체적 언어 접근법'(whole language approach)이라고 할 수 있으며, '활동 중심'의 독서법인 것이다.

독서에서 이러한 접근법과 활동들을 적용하여 학생들의 창의성을 키우도록 돕고, 동시에 국제어로서의 영어를 유창하게 사용하고 표현하는 능력을 지닌 영어영재로 교육시키는 데 도움이 되기를 바라는 소망이 이 책의 의도이다. 이번 개정판에서는 현대의 영미 에세이 작품들을 읽기자료로 추가했다. 그리고 영어문학 텍스트의 언어학적 이해와 독서감상 표현법, 외국어로서의 영어 문학 텍스트의 언어학적 방법의 작품지도법을 보충하였다. 미흡한 점이 많지만 언어(영어)교육과 독서지도를 담당하는 교육자 여러분께 미력이나마 도움이 되기를 바랄 뿐이다.

  이번에도 이 책의 출판을 흔쾌히 수락해주신 김진수 사장님께 깊은 고마움을 전하며, 좋은 책으로 만들기 위해 애쓰신 편집부에 감사를 드린다.

2011. 2. 1
금정산 자락의 연구실에서
저자 조일제 씀

| 차례 |

머리말 / v

1부_창의성 개발과 열린 독서

1. 창의성 개발을 위한 (영)문학작품 활용과 구성주의 지식관 • 3
2. 창의성을 신장시키는 열린 독서지도 • 7
    2.1 열린 독서지도의 필요성 • 7
    2.2 창의적인 독서감상 표현을 통한 열린 독서 지도 방안 • 8
        (1) 독서 감상문 지도의 의의와 필요성 • 8
        (2) 독서감상 표현을 다양화 하기 위한 전제 • 11
        (3) 창의성을 신장시키는 열린 독서지도 사례 • 12
3. 다양한 교실활동을 기반으로 한 영미소설 독서지도 • 15
4. 동화와 창의성 교육 • 25
    4.1 동화의 극화와 창의성 • 25
    4.2 동화교육에 있어 다매체 활용과 창의성 개발 • 26
    4.3 동화와 총체적 언어교육 • 28
5. 인터넷 활동을 통한 영문학 작품 학습과 창의성 신장 • 29

2부_창조적 독서이론과 읽기방법

1. 좋은 독서 습관과 나쁜 독서 습관 • 33
    1.1 좋은 독서 습관 • 33
    1.2 나쁜 독서 습관 • 37
2. 독해에서의 스키마 이론 • 42
3. 의욕적이고 능동적인 독자가 되는 길 • 44
4. 창조적 독서기술과 독서방법 • 47
    4.1 정독과 통독 • 48
    4.2 음독과 묵독 • 59
    4.3 훑어 읽기 • 60
    4.4 찾아 읽기 • 61
    4.5 구연 • 63
    4.6 암시교수법에서 사용되는 독서기법 • 65
    4.7 제한독서 • 67
    4.8 속독 • 69
    4.9 총체적 언어 접근법에서의 독서 모델 • 75
    4.10 버텨읽기와 굽혀읽기 • 78
    4.11 비판적 독서 • 84
5. 독해력의 단계에 따른 읽기방법 • 86
    5.1 줄거리 읽기 • 86
    5.2 요점 읽기 • 87
    5.3 훑어 읽기 • 88
    5.4 뭉뚱그리며 읽기 • 89
    5.5 분석하며 읽기 • 89
    5.6 관계 읽기 • 90
    5.7 구조화하며 읽기 • 90
    5.8 문맥 읽기 • 91

6. 감상의 단계에 따른 읽기방법 • 92
   6.1 느끼며 읽기 • 92
   6.2 상상하며 읽기 • 93
   6.3 추리하며 읽기 • 94
   6.4 문제 해결하며 읽기 • 94
7. 영어문학 텍스트의 언어학적 이해와 독서감상 표현 • 96
   7.1 영어문학 텍스트의 언어학적 이해 • 96
     (1) 텍스트의 통일성과 텍스트 구사 능력 • 96
     (2) 언어의 부각 작용 • 97
     (3) 작품의 내부 구조 • 98
   7.2 영어문학 텍스트의 기능 문체론적 접근 • 99
     (1) 의미와 관련된 객관적 요인 • 100
     (2) 발화 상황과 관련된 객관적 요인 • 100
     (3) 사용된 언어 재료 • 101
   7.3 영어문학 텍스트의 언어학적 방법의 작품지도법 • 102
     (1) 배제되어야 할 접근방법들 • 102
     (2) 주제 • 103
     (3) 물음을 통한 작품 지도 • 104
     (4) 과제 : 다독과 문체적 작업 • 111

3부_읽기 자료 : 영어 문학텍스트

1. 영미 중단편 소설 • 119
   〈영국 편〉
     ◆Youth —by Joseph Conrad • 119
     ◆The Horse Dealer's Daughter —by D.H. Lawrence • 163
     ◆To Please His Wife —by Thomas Hardy • 188

- ◆The Gioconda Smile —by Aldous Huxley • 213
- ◆Kew Gardens —by Virginia Woolf • 255

〈미국편〉

- ◆A Rose for Emily —by William Faulkner • 265
- ◆The Snow of Kilimanjaro —by Earnest Hemingway • 279
- ◆Red —by Somerset Maugham • 313
- ◆The Black Cat —by Adgar Allan Poe • 344
- ◆The Real Thing —by Henry James • 358
- ◆The Lightening-Rod Man —by Herman Melville • 396

2. 현대 영미 에세이 • 406

- ◆What Statesmen Must Know —by Oswald Spengler • 406
- ◆The social Responsibilities of Scientists —by Bertrand Russell • 421
- ◆Six Typical Americans —by Alistair Cooke • 427
- ◆The Present Human Condition —by Erich Fromm • 437
- ◆My View of History —by Arnold Toynbee • 447

참고문헌 • 463

| 제 1 부 |

창의성 개발과 열린 독서

■ ■ ■

1. 창의성 개발을 위한 (영)문학작품 활용과 구성주의 지식관
2. 창의성을 신장시키는 열린 독서지도
3. 다양한 교실활동을 기반으로 한 영미소설 독서지도
4. 동화와 창의성 교육
5. 인터넷 활동을 통한 영문학 작품 학습과 창의성 신장

창의성 개발을 위한 (영)문학작품 활용과 구성주의 지식관

학습자 중심의 자기 주도적 학습과 열린 교육 및 창의성 신장을 뒷받침하는 교육 이념과 원리가 구성주의(constructivism) 지식관이다. 구성주의적 지식관에서는 지식은 절대적인 것이 아니라 상대적인 것이라는 점이다. 객관주의적인 사고가 팽배하던 과거에는 지식을 고정불변의 것으로 생각하여 사람들이 이 지식을 있는 그대로 받아들일 것을 강조했다. 여기에는 절대적인 진리가 존재한다는 전제가 있었다. 하지만 구성주의 관점에서는 지식은 상대적이라는 입장을 취한다. 지식은 시대와 사회에 따라 달라지는 것이며, 또한 개개인에 따라 다르다는 입장을 취한다. 그래서 지식을 있는 그대로 받아들이기보다는 그 지식을 자신의 입장, 또는 자신이 속해있는 집단의 입장에서 어떻게 나름대로 '구성'하느냐에 관심의 초점을 둔다.

독서의 경우를 예를 들어 구성주의적 관점이 실제 교수-학습 현장을 어떻게 파악하고 있는지를 생각해 보자. 구성주의적 관점에서 보면, '독서는 의미를 재구성하는 과정'이라고 말할 수 있다. 여기에는 여러 가지 의미가 내포되어 있다. 독서는 단순하게 지식을 습득하는 행위가 아니라 나름대로 재구성하는 행위라는 것이다. 즉, 자신의 관점이나 지식, 경험 등에 기초해서 나름의 방식대로 이해하고, 구조화하는 행위라는 점이다. 그리고 독서는 독서 후의 결과가 아니라 의미를 구성하는 '과정'이라는 점이다. 어떤 책을 읽고 무엇을 얻었느냐 하는 것 자체보다는 어떤 과정을 거쳐 그러한 것을 얻게 되었느냐에 좀더 관심을 가질 필요가 있다.

구성주의 관점에서는 독자에 대해 적극적인 관점을 취한다. 독자는 텅 빈 곳으로 교사가 이 빈 곳을 가득 채워 넣어 주어야 한다는 관점을 취하지 않는다. 독자는 스스로 이해하고 해석할 수 있는 능력을 가지고 있다는 관점을 취한다.

구성주의적 관점에서 볼 때, 텍스트의 의미는 책 자체에 있는 것이 아니라 개인에게 있다. 이 점은 여러 가지 중요한 의미를 담고 있다. 우선 의미란 고정되어 있는 것이 아니라 변한다는 것을 뜻한다. 즉, 개인에 따라, 집단에 따라 변하며, 개인에 있어서도 상황에 따라 달라진다. 예를 들어 『어린왕자』를 어렸을 때 읽었을 때와 성년이 되어 읽었을 때 그 의미는 상당히 달라진다. 심지어 아침에 읽었을 때와 저녁에 읽었을 때 느낌이 다르기도 하다. 그리고 또 다른 측면에서 이 말은 의미는 다양하다는 점을 내포하고 있다. 개인마다 받아들이는 의미는 다르기 때문에 극단적인 경우에는 개인의 수만큼이나 의미는 다양하다고 할 수 있다. 그러므로 어떤 단일한 의미를 추출하는 것은 불가능한 일이다.

구성주의적 관점에서는 구성 행위의 주체자가 개인이든(개인적 구성주의), 집단이든(사회적 구성주의), 자신의 경험과 지식, 세계관에 비추어 주어진 내용을 새롭게 해석, 재구성하는 과정을 강조한다. 사회적 구성주의는 이런 재구성의 과정에서 사회적인 측면을 강조한다. 그래서 개인간의 상호작용을 최대한 북돋우면서 의미를 만들어가도록 강조한다. 이러한 사고의 바탕에는 상대주의적 지식관이 전제되어 있다. 즉, 지식이란 개인과 개인이 속해있는 사회에 따라 달라질 수 있는 것으로, 지식은 주어지는 것이 아니라 개인이나 사회가 만들어 가는 과정이라는 점을 강조한다.

개인 내에서의 구성 행위든 아니면 개인간의 상호작용을 통한 구성이든 간에 이들 구성을 촉진하기 위해서는 분리보다는 통합이 바람직하다. 예를 들어 듣기, 읽기, 말하기, 쓰기를 별도로 가르치기보다는 그것이 사용되는 상황을 상정하여 통합적으로 가르칠 때 구성행위가 촉진될 가능성이 높아진다. 읽기를 하더라도 그냥 읽는 것으로 끝나지 않고 읽을 것을 드라마 활동으로 엮어보는 과정에서 구성 행위가 좀 더 촉진되고 풍성해 진다(김종문 외, 『구성주의 교육학』. pp. 154-165. 강인애, 『왜 구성주의인가?』. pp. 131-141 참조).

구성주의는 이른바 학습자 중심의 교과 수업의 이론적 단초를 제공해 주고 있다. 구성주의는 학습자에 대한 적극적인 관점을 갖는다. 지식은 교사에게 주어지는 것이 아니라 학습자 내부에서 만들어지는 것이라는 관점을 취한다(신헌재 외, 『학습자 중심의 국어과 수업방안』. pp. 13-18 참조). 구성주의는 주관주의 인식론에 근거하여 학습자들이 자신이 위치한 맥락에서의 능동적인 경험을 통하여 자신에게 적합한 지식을 구성한다는 점을 강조한다. 실재는 구성된 것이며, 실재의 구성은 문화와 전통을 통해 형성된 의미 구성의 산물이다. 이런 의미에서 교육은 학습자들로 하여금 맥락에 적합한 의미를 구성하고 실재를 구성하는 방법을 학습하도록 도와서 자신이 살고 있는 세상에 보다 잘 적응하고, 필요에 따라 세상을 의도한 대로 변화시킬 수 있도록 해 주어야 한다(Bruner, 1996. Von Glasersfeld, 1996). 구성주의적 관점에서 보면 학습은 학습자들이 자신이 위치한 물리적, 사회적 세계와 능동적으로 상호작용하는 해석적, 순환적, 구성적인 의미 만들기의 과정이다(Fosnot, 1996). 학습은 지식의 단순한 획득과 재생산 과정이 아니라 능동적인 구성적 과정이며, 인지적 과정일 뿐만 아니라 사회적, 문화적 과정이다. 요컨대, 주어진 상황에서의 개인의 주관적 경험과 사회적 상호작용을 통한 의미 구성이 곧 학습이다. 학습자들은 마치 빈 그릇과 같아서 그 속에 무언가를 담아 채우기만 하면 되는 것이 아니라, 맥락에 적합한 의미를 탐색, 추구하는 능동적인 유기체이다.

교사는 학생들이 학습자료를 유의미하고 적합하게 잘 다룰 수 있도록 도와주는 역할을 수행하게 된다. 전통적으로 수행하던 역할이 바뀌어진다. 교사는 학습환경의 조성자이자 안내자, 동료 학습자로서 풍부하고 다양한 학습환경을 조성하고, 상황적 맥락에 따라 참 과제(authentic task)를 제시함으로써 의미 구성을 촉진시키는 역할을 한다. 수업은 마치 공장의 생산라인과 같이 교사가 학생에게 구두로 지식을 전달하는 것이 아니라, 학생들에게 복합적인 환경과 다양한 활동을 잘 배합해 주어야 한다(Shuell, 1996). 행동주의나 인지주의처럼 교사가 미리 수업 목표를 제시하고 모든 학습자들이 이를 성취하도록 하는 것이 아니라, 학습자 스스로가 자신이 원하는 목표를 스스로 결정하도록 해 주어야 한다. 추론, 비판적·반성적 사고, 문제해결, 인지적 유연성 획득 등이 구성주의의 주요 목표이다. 이를 뒷받침하기 위해서는 복잡하고 비구조화된 다양한 상황을 제공, 다양한 관점의 제시 및 사회적 협상과 협력적 학습환경의 조성 등이 강조된다(김종문 외, 같은 책. pp. 154-166 참조).

창의성을 신장시키는 열린 독서지도

2.1 열린 독서지도의 필요성

왜 학생들은 학교에서 권장하는 도서는 외면하면서 무협류의 소설을 즐길까? 대답은 간단하다. 재미있기 때문에 관심을 가지고, 몰입도 하게 된다. 이 간단한 논리에도 불구하고 학교현장에서는 이 원리를 따라가지 못하고 있다. 학생의 개성과 창의성을 살리고 흥미를 유발시키는 교육이 이루어져야 하는데, 그러한 지도 방안의 부재로 입시체제라는 벽에 대한 변명으로 일관하고 있는 실정이다.

교육의 모든 분야가 다 그렇지만 독서지도의 방향도 재정립되어야 한다. 독후감 쓰기 형태의 획일적인 독서지도에서 독서 주체의 개성과 창의성을 살리고 흥미를 유발할 수 있는 열린 독서지도 방안이 강구되어야 한다. 사과가 맛이 있어서 먹게 되면 그 사과가 몸 속에서 양분을 제공하고, 알약을 단맛에 먹고 보면 몸 안에서 약효를 발휘하듯이 독서도 즐거움 속에서 출발하여야 그 즐거움 때문에 독서를 하게 되고 이를 통해서 여러 가지 효용에 도달하게 된다. 교사는 학생들에게 책이 재미있고 맛있다는 사실을 실감하도록 인식시켜서 책을 가까지 하지 않을 수 없는 독서습관을 형성하게 하고 개성과 창의성을 개발하는 독서지도법을 구안해야 한다(조영식, 『창조적 독서교육』. p. 20).

2.2 창의적인 독서감상 표현을 통한 열린 독서 지도 방안

(1) 독서 감상문 지도의 의의와 필요성

 독서는 인격 형성에 커다란 영향을 미친다. 그러나 독서라고 하여 모두가 똑같은 영향을 미치는 것은 아니다. 같은 독서라도 목적이 없이 막연하게 읽는 경우나 단순히 시간을 보내게 위한 오락적인 독서는 그 순간에는 기억되지만 시간이 경과하면 그 내용은 물론 읽었다는 사실조차 뇌리에서 잊혀져버리기 마련이다.
 의의 있는 독서는 그것으로부터 얻은 여러 가지의 지식이나 감명이 자신들의 생활에 비추어져 생활 속에 젖어들 때 비로소 그 의의와 가치가 나타난다. 그러한 독서에는 반드시 반성이 필요하며 사고·사색이 필요한 것이다. 즉, 독서를 통하여 스스로의 생활을 반성하고 독서를 통해 얻은 지식과 감명을 사고와 사색의 끝에 정선하고 음미하여 이것을 자신의 생활 속에 베어들게 할 때 풍부하고 행복한 인생이 이룩되는 것이다.
 독서 감상문 지도의 의의란 바로 책을 읽은 뒤의 느낌, 의견, 비평, 인상 등을 자신의 생활 및 사고와 결부시켜 글로 표현하는 습관을 길러 줌으로써 그와 같은 올바른 사고·사색의 능력과 습관을 길러 주고 비판적인 독서의 태도를 갖게 하는 데 있다. 즉, 단순히 누가, 언제, 어디서, 무엇을, 어떻게 했는가를 중심으로 행한 줄거리 파악과 같은 형식적인 독서가 아니라 읽은 내용을 자신의 생활 경험과 비교하여 비슷한 점과 다른 점이 무엇인가, 등장인물의 행동의 옳고 그름과 그러한 행동의 동기가 무엇이며, 자신이 등장인물이라면 어떻게 행동했을까 등을 깊이 생각하면서 읽도록 지도함으로써 독서를 통하여 받은 강한 인상과 깊은 감명을 오래도록 가슴속에 간직할 수 있게끔 '생각하는 독서'의 태도를 길러 주자는 데 있다고 하겠다.

그러나 이와 같은 사고·사색의 능력과 습관은 짧은 기간 동안에 이루어지는 것이 아니기 때문에 어릴 때부터 독서와 생활을 통하여 서서히 몸에 베일 수 있도록 지도해 나가지 않으면 안 된다. 독서 감상문 지도가 필요한 이유는 보다 구체적으로 보면 다음과 같다(손정표, 『신독서 지도 방법론』. pp. 258-259 참조).

① 독서에 대한 지식과 이해를 심화시킨다.
② 작품을 비판하고 문장을 요약, 정리하는 힘을 길러 준다.
③ 독서의 목표를 확실하게 해주고 보다 발전적으로 읽어갈 수 있는 계획을 세우게 한다.
④ 읽는 과정을 통해서 사고력과 추리력을 증진시킨다.
⑤ 쓰는 과정을 통해서 생각을 확실하게 하고 더욱 깊게 한다.
⑥ 좋은 독서생활을 형성하는 데 자료가 되게 하며, 독서 평가 및 독서 생활을 지도하고, 아동·학생들의 생활환경과 생활감정의 파악을 지도하기 위한 상담표의 역할이 되게 한다.
⑦ 쓰는 작업 중에 보다 향상되고 바르게 읽는 습관이 형성된다.
⑧ 쓴다는 것은 어디까지나 자기표현이므로 틀린 곳이 있어도 소박하고 정직하게 나타내게 한다.
⑨ 아동·학생의 성장 과정에 따른 욕망이 단계적으로 나타나고 스스로의 안내역이 된다.

독서 감상문을 작성할 때 지도해야 할 중요사항에는 다음과 같은 것이 있다.

① 감상의 표현에 들어가기 전에 지도자나 친구들과 이야기를 나눈다거나 감상화 같은 것으로 머리에 떠오르는 것을 잘 이끌어내어 정리하도록 한다.

② 감상문을 쓸 때에는 개개인을 살피고 저항이 될 원인을 되도록 제거시켜 즐거운 마음으로 쓰도록 한다.
③ 표현의 형식에는 여러 가지 유형이 있으나 어떤 형식에 구애됨이 없이 생각한 것을 솔직하게 쓰도록 한다.
④ 다른 사람의 글을 모방하는 것보다는 자기의 경험, 생각, 감상을 가장 소중히 여기도록 지도한다.
⑤ 개성 및 발달 단계에 따라서 쓰기 쉬운 형식을 지도한다.
⑥ 동일한 내용의 읽을 거리를 읽은 아동·학생으로 하여금 좌담형식으로 감상을 얘기할 수 있는 기회를 만들어준다.
⑦ 내용의 기술에 있어 특히 다음 사항을 참고하도록 한다.
- 흥미를 가졌던 점.
- 의문을 품었던 점.
- 문제로 의식했던 점.
- 아주 강하게 느낀 사실.
- 특히 다른 사람에게 전하고 싶은 중심점.
- 마음을 끄는 어휘나 문장의 인용.

다음은 독서 감상문 작성 후에 지도할 중요사항에는 다음과 같은 것이 있다.

① 서로 읽어 보거나 서로의 의견을 통해서 쓰여진 작품을 될 수 있는 대로 넓은 장소에서 객관적으로 보고 고쳐 생각하도록 하는 기회를 마련한다.
② 동일한 작품을 읽고 쓴 몇 개의 감상문을 중심으로 얘기하거나 토론하는 등 집단적인 독서 감상도 한다.
③ 자기만을 주장할 것이 아니라 서로의 의견을 존중하도록 한다.
④ 같은 책을 읽고 그 책의 내용에 비추어 자기와 타인의 감상문 사

이에 틀린 곳이 있을 때는 객관적으로 비판해서 바로 잡는다.
⑤ 무리하게 비약함이 없이 밑바닥에서부터 보고, 느끼고, 생각하도록 지도한다.
⑥ 우수한 감상문은 사람을 감동시키거나 자극시키므로 개별적으로 모아 문집을 만들게 한다든지, 도서관보, 방송, 게시, 학급 독서회 등을 이용하여 발표하도록 한다(손정표, 같은 책. pp. 259-261 참조).

(2) 독서감상 표현을 다양화 하기 위한 전제

독서감상 표현에서도 자신의 개성과 취미에 따른 독서감상 표현을 한다면 그야말로 즐거움을 느끼며 하게 될 것이며, 그 표현의 어려움에 관계없이 신명난 활동이 될 것이다. 실제로 독서감상 표현의 한 가지 방법인 '독서신문'을 제작하는 학생은 토요일에 밤을 꼬박 새웠다고 했다. 그 누가 독서감상 표현 방법으로 독서신문 형태를 강요한 것도 아니다. 자신이 선택한 방법이다. 어느 누구도 밤을 새우라고 하지 않았다. 본인이 몰두하다 보니까 밤이 새워진 것이다. 그 학생이 잠은 좀 못 잤지만 완성된 한 편의 독서신문을 보고서 얻은 보람을 누가 알겠는가? 이렇듯 독서 주체의 내발적 동기에 의한 다양한 독서감상 표현을 통해서 창의성이 꽃피울 수 있을 것이다(조영식, 같은 책. p. 22).

■ 독서신문 제작을 통한 독서 감상의 표현

신문은 우리 일상생활에서 가장 쉽게 접할 수 있는 대량 인쇄매체로서 문자와 그림(사진)을 통해 시각적으로 내용을 전달한다. 신문의 기능은 일반적으로 보도적 기능, 지도적 기능, 오락적 기능, 광고적 기능으로 나뉘는데, 근래에는 신문을 학습자료로 활용하는 신문학습(NIE 학습)이 활발하여 신문이 학습자료적 기능도 가지고 있다고 할 수 있다.

　독서 감상의 표현에 신문형식을 도입하여 나타낸 출판물로는 『삼국지 신문』(나채훈 편집, 실천문학사. 전 3권)과 『역사신문』(역사신문편찬위원회, 사계절. 전 6권)이 있다. 『삼국지 신문』은 삼국지 시리즈 전편에 등장하는 인물과 사건 그리고 당시 사회를 편집자의 입장에서 재조명하여 3권으로 나타내고 있다. 구체적으로 살펴보면 1면은 주요 사건의 보도기사를 비중에 따라서 크기를 달리하여 싣고 있으며, 2면에는 1면의 기사 중 비중을 갖는 사건의 배경과 해설기사, 만평, 사설을 실었고, 3면에 1면 관련기사를 더욱 구체화하고 경제와 생활 기사를 다루고 있으며, 4면에는 문화와 해외 관련기사를 다루고 있다.

　신문 형식의 독서감상 표현은 작품을 현장감 있게 표현하고 작품에 대한 다양한 접근과 해석을 가능하도록 해 준다. 또한 작품을 작품 자체로 해석하는 데 그치지 않고 현실과 관련하여 이해하는 데 크게 기여하게 되며, 작품을 기사화하거나 그에 따른 해설, 사설 등의 표현을 통해서 글 쓰는 능력과 창의력까지 향상하게 되는 이점이 있다(조영식, 같은 책. p. 29).

(3) 창의성을 신장시키는 열린 독서지도 사례

　창의성 개발을 위해서 독서 감상문 위주의 표현에서 탈피하여 독서 주체인 학생들이 가지고 있는 잠재적 능력과 창의성을 활용하여 표현하도록 한다. 예를 들어 학생들 중에는 시를 좋아하는 학생들도 있고 만화를 좋아하는 학생들도 있다. 독서 표현을 할 때 시를 좋아하는 학생은 자신의 잠재적 역량을 살려서 도서의 내용과 감상을 한 편의 시로 표현할 수도 있다. 만화 그리기가 취미인 학생은 만화로서 자신의 감상을 표현하도록 하는 것이다. 학생의 창의성을 인정하는 표현을 수용하여 형식에 구애 없이 독서감상을 할 수 있도록 해야 한다. 자신이 좋아하는 방법을 중심으로 표현을 하게 되면 독서가 더욱 흥미로워지게 되고, 이로 인하여 독서 생활화가 지속될 것이다. 창의적인 독서감상을 표현하는 다양한 사례의 예를 아래에 든다(조영식, 같은 책. pp. 8-26 참조).

> 만화로 그려 표현하기 / 시로 표현하기 / 독서신문 제작을 통해 표현하기 / 논술형식을 통해 표현하기 / 느낌 중심의 감상문 형식 / 독서 게임 만들기 / 개작을 통한 표현 / 광고형식의 표현하기 / 도식화를 통한 표현하기 / 독서퀴즈 문제 제작을 통한 표현하기 / 작품 재구성을 통한 표현 / 퍼즐을 활용한 표현하기 / 자료수집을 통한 표현 / 영작을 통한 표현 / 뒷이야기 쓰기를 통한 표현 / 개사(改詞)를 통한 표현 / 인터뷰 형식의 표현 / 명언, 명구 찾기를 통한 표현 / 시리즈를 통한 표현 / 유머 쓰기를 통한 표현 / 편지 형식을 통한 표현(예: 선생님이나 친구, 또는 등장인물과의 편지 형식) / 작품요약을 통한 표현 / 앙케이트를 통한 표현 / 감상 시작(詩作)을 통한 표현 / 단어 조사를 통한 표현 / 일정한 물음에 대한 대답하기를 통한 표현 / 독후감 쓰기를 통한 표현 / 마인드 맵을 통한 표현 / 다른 작품 인물과의 비교를 통한 표현 / 독서퀴즈 대회를 통한 표현 / 독서 토론회를 통한 표현 / 등장인물과의 대화 형식 / 내가 주인공이라면 표현형식 / 일기를 통한 형식

이러한 창의적인 독서 감상 표현 방안들은 초·중·고 모든 학교에서 적용할 수 있다는 것이 가능하다는 데 이점이 있다. 중·고등학생은 물론 초등학생들도 만화로 표현하기, 시 짓기, 도식화하기, 작품 개작하기, 주장하는 글쓰기, 퍼즐 만들기, 자료 조사하기, 독서 신문 만들기, 도서 광고하기, 자유 연상하기, 앙케이트 조사하기 등 다양한 형태의 표현이 가능하다. 경우에 따라서는 초등학생들이 더욱 신나게 접근하고 있다.

창의적인 독서감상 표현은 국어과만이 아닌 모든 교과에서 적용할

수 있는 방안이다. 이제 독서지도는 어느 특정한 교과의 전유물이 될 수 없다. 독서 감상문 쓰기 위주의 독서지도에서 다양한 독서 감상 표현하기로 전환하면 독서지도에서 특정교과 관련성은 적어진다. '만화로 표현'하거나 '도서를 광고하는' 방법 등은 미술과와의 연관을 맺게 되고, '자료 조사하기', '퍼즐 만들기', '도서내용 요약하기'는 오히려 과학이나 사회교과 등과 밀접한 연관을 지닌다. 이처럼 다양한 독서 감상 표현하기는 모든 교과와 깊게 관련을 맺을 수 있다. 예를 들어 사회교과에서 『조선왕조실록』을 읽도록 권장하였다면, 전 왕조를 왕위 계승 나이, 재임 기간, 업적 등을 하나의 도표로 요약할 수도 있고, 논술 주제를 정해서 논술을 쓰게 할 수도 있으며, 비슷한 군왕-예를 들어 연산군과 광해군-을 비교하는 글을 쓸 수도 있고, 특정의 상황을 그림이나 만화로 표현할 수도 있으며, 특정한 사건에 대한 세밀한 자료를 조사할 수도 있다.

　다양한 독서 감상 표현은 독서지도 교사(독서 지도자)의 몫만은 아니다. 학부모들도 다양한 사례를 자녀들에게 권유할 수 있다. 그러나 다양한 독서감상 표현은 부모와 학생이 함께 할 수 있다. 나아가 다양한 독서감상 표현은 학생끼리 함께 공유할 수도 있다. 자신의 표현을 친구에게 보여줄 수 있으며 친구의 표현을 볼 수도 있다. 친구의 표현과 나의 표현이 방법상 다르기 때문에 얼마든지 보여주고 볼 수 있는 것이다. 예를 들어 퍼즐로 표현한 학생에게 자신의 표현을 보여줄 수 있다. 그리고 만화로 된 표현을 감상할 수도 있다. 그러면서 자신도 만화로 표현해보고 싶은 욕구를 갖게 될 수도 있다(조영식. 같은 책 pp. 21-26).

다양한 교실활동을 기반으로 한 영미소설 독서지도

Joanne Collie & Stephen Slater는 그들의 공동 저서 *Literature in the Language Classroom : A resource book of ideas and activities* (1987)에서 아래와 같은 영소설 읽기 과정을 통해 학생들의 창의성을 개발할 수 있는 재미있고 유용한 학습자 중심의 여러 가지 다양한 교실활동들을 제안하였다. 그 중에서 대표적인 것들을 예시해 본다.

■ 작품의 제목과 표지를 이용하기

읽기 전 활동에 속한다. 교사는 학생들에게 흥미를 불러일으킬 수 있는 표지 디자인이나 제목을 보여주고 작품의 줄거리나 분위기에 대해 생각하여 말해보게 한다.

■ 시각적 자극물 활용하기

로날드 달(Ronald Dahl)이 쓴 '무료승차 도보 여행자'(The Hitchhiker)를 예로 들면, 작품을 읽기 전에 학생들에게 인물 사진이나 잡지의 인물그림을 보여주고 어떤 사람을 차에 태워 주겠는지를 묻고 답하게 한다.

■ 주제를 활용하기

읽기 전 활동으로 교사는 작품에서 하나의 주제를 뽑아 학생들이 그것에 대해 탐구하게 한다. 서머셋 모옴(Somerset Maugham)의 소설 '달과 6펜스'를 예로 들면, 주인공이 갑작스레 그의 가정과 직업을 버리고 집을 떠난다. 학생들에게 그들 자신도 현재 처한 삶의 상황을 포기하기로 결심했다고 상상해 보게 하여 그들이 어떻게 할 것인가를 쓰도록 한다.

■ 핵심 단어와 문장들 이용하기

작품의 첫 번째 장에서 소수의 핵심 단어들을 뽑는다. 단어들을 연결하여 나름대로 좋아하는 이야기가 되도록 글을 쓴다. 또는 핵심적인 문장들을 발췌하여 상상력을 발휘하여 문맥에 맞는 이야기를 만든다.

■ 질문지 사용하기

학생들에게 질문지를 주어서 그 작품의 중심 주제가 야기하는 여러 논쟁에 대해 자신의 태도를 결정하게 한다.

■ 전기 몽타주 작성하기

작품에 들어가기 전에 작가에 관한 이야기를 소개하는 활동의 하나로 전기 몽타주를 만든다. 작가와 관련된 사진, 물건, 지명 등과 같이 작가의 생애와 관련이 있는 것은 무엇이든지 수집한다.

■ 작가에 관해 스케치 하기

작가의 생애를 나타내는, 다른 시기에 걸쳐 찍은 여러 개의 사진을 수집하고 직관으로 작가의 성격을 묘사한다.

■ 별모양 도표 작성하기

다섯 꼭지점이 있는 별모양 도표에다 작품을 읽기 전에 핵심 단어들을 분류하여 일람표를 작성하는 활동이다. 예를 들면 작품의 첫 절에서 핵심 단어들을 꼭지점에 표시한 여러 표제들 밑에 열거한다. 색깔, 분위기, 움직임, 오감 등과 같은 범주로 분류할 수 있다.

■ 타임캡슐을 이용하기

작품의 첫 장을 읽었다고 할 때 이야기가 전개되어 감에 따라 일어날 것 같은 사건들에 대한 예견을 카드에다 적는다. 이 카드를 타임캡슐 봉투에 넣어 봉하고 작품을 끝마칠 때 개봉하여 실제의 작품내용과 비교한다.

■ 다음에 무엇이 일어날까? - 대사 만들기 또는 연기하기

이야기가 계속하여 이어질 수 있는 가능한 형태들을 대사를 만들거나 또는 그것을 연기한다.

■ 제로 챕터 쓰기

시작되는 장의 첫 절 바로 앞에 올 수 있을 장을 상상을 통해 써본다.

■ 편집자로서 제안하기

학생은 출판사의 편집위원이라고 생각한다. 방금 읽은 작품의 첫 문단을 작가가 보내준 초고라고 생각하고 작가를 위한 여러 가지 제안을 작성한다. 예컨대 문체, 플롯, 전개, 성격묘사 등에 관한 견해를 써는 것이다.

■ 스토리 구연하기

(참조하면 좋은 책으로는 Gail Ellis and Jean Brewster, *The Storytelling Handbook for Primary Teachers*. Penguin Books, 1991)

음성언어를 통해 스토리를 구연해보는 것은 어휘 습득, 이야기 구조 이해, 문장력 제고, 문법구조 이해 등에 대해서 뿐만 아니라 작품의 담화적 특성들의 인식에도 영향을 준다. 작품의 언어가 포함하는 사회적, 심리적인 측면까지 이해할 수 있게 된다.

■ 지금까지의 이야기를 다시 말하기

이것은 가치 있는 구두 연습을 제공해주며, 전체의 이야기를 마음속에 기억할 수 있게 도와준다.

■ 계속되는 일기 쓰기

학생들은 자신이 서로 다른 작중인물들이라고 상상하고 새로운 상황이 전개될 때 그들의 인물이 썼을 일기를 쓴다. 작품의 여러 사건과 느낌들을 일기로서 기록하는 것이다. 잘 된 일기의 모델을 제시하여 쓰게 할 수도 있다.

■ 벽 위의 파리로 상상하기

학생들은 어느 등장인물의 역할을 떠맡는 대신에 '벽 위의 파리'로서 행동한다고 상상한다. 파리는 눈에 보이지는 않지만 작품에 날아다니면서 여러 가지를 관찰하고 논평을 한다.

■ 언어 연구과제 수행하기

특별한 언어의 양상이 작품에 있다면 그것을 과제로서 연구한다. 예컨대 『로미오와 줄리엣』을 읽으면서 최대한의 '재담'(pun)을 수집하여 노트에 기록해서 재담의 두 가지 의미와 그 효과가 무엇인지를 결정하라는 연구과제를 수행한다.

■ 연결어를 이용하여 요약문 쓰기

교사는 학생들에게 연결어들의 목록을 제시해주어 그들이 읽은 글의 사건을 연결어들을 이용해서 이야기해 나가도록 한다.

■ 요약문을 다시 요약하기

요약작업의 한 가지 방법으로 단계적으로 줄여가는 것이다. 이를테면 70개의 단어를 가지고 읽은 부분을 요약해서 적는다. 그것을 절반인 35개의 단어로 단축하고 또 다시 그것을 17개의 단어를 사용한 글로 단축한다.

■ 창의적인 대화문 쓰기

작품에서 대화가 사용되지 않은 장면을 선택하여 발생할 수 있었던 대화를 상상하여 쓰는 것이다. 예를 들면 한 등장인물이 어느 장면에 나타나면 그 작품에는 없는 어떠한 대화를 그 이전에 같이 있었던 사람과 했을 것이라고 상상하여 적는다.

■ 등장인물들의 속마음 쓰기

역시 상상력을 동원하는 활동의 하나로 작품에서 행동과 외모의 외부세계와 사상과 감정이라는 내부세계 사이에 존재하는 상호작용을 인식하여 쓰는 것이다. 본문에서 단순하게 제시만 되어있지만 새로운 세계를 창조할 수 있을 추측사항들이 있다. 작품 속에 제시되어있는 외면적 대화에 병행할 내면적 대화를 써보는 것은 하나의 방법이 될 수 있다.

■ TV나 라디오 연속물의 안내글 쓰기

읽고 있는 작품이 라디오나 TV에 연속물로 방송된다고 상상한다. 교사는 학생들에게 신문이나 잡지에 나와 있는 'TV와 라디오 안내' 부분의 한 가지 예를 보여주어 작품의 특정 장면에 대해 아주 간결한 설명문을 쓰게 한다.

■ 신문기사 쓰기

작품 속의 여러 사건들에 대해 여러 가지 신문들 중의 어느 신문을 위해 실제의 기사를 쓰는 것처럼 기사를 쓴다. 하이라이트 장면을 하나 선택하여 특집기사를 쓸 수도 있다. 진짜 신문들의 예를 출판물 형태로 보게 한 후 쓰게 하면 좋다.

■ 보고서 쓰기

교사는 학생들에게 보고서 양식의 여러 관례들을 보여주고 작품의 어느 장면을 중심으로 보고서를 쓰게 한다. 짧은 회의록, 보험계약서, 경찰보고서, 학교의 학생생활보고서 등과 같은 여러 가지 종류의 보고서들이 있다.

■ 실종된 인물의 포스트 쓰기

교사는 학생들에게 실종인물을 찾는 포스터의 예를 보여주고 작품에서 나오는 실종인물에 대한 포스트를 쓰게 한다.

■ 설문지나 과제지에 기초한 토론하기

답을 체크할 난이 있는 간단한 진술문들을 나열한 설문지를 나누어 주어 토론하게 하거나 작중인물들의 성격 발전과 작품 전개에 대한 논쟁적 요소를 결합시킨 과제지를 만들어 나누어주고 토론하게 한다.

■ 설득하기

학생들은 한 쌍식 짝을 지어 각자 상대방에게 작품 속에 나오는 어떤 등장인물의 행동 과정을, 또는 그의 장점과 단점을 설득시키는 역할을 한다. 설득, 비난, 부정 등의 다양한 표현들의 목록을 주어 사용하도록 하면 좋다. 예를 들면, 존 파울즈의 소설 '수집가'에 등장하는 수집가의 친구를 위한 역할이 주어진다. 그의 임무는 패션모델 쇼의 지배인(상대방 학생)에게 그 수집가는 그들이 찾고 있는 이상적인 사진사일 수 있다는 것을 설득시키는 것이다.

■역할극 놀이로 꾸며보기/연극적으로 각색하기

특정 대목을 역할극으로 꾸며서 즉석연기를 하거나, 연극적으로 각색하게 한 다음 촌극으로 공연하게 한다.

■가상적인 상상하기 - 여기서라면 · 거기서라면

'**여기서라면**'은 작품 자체의 일부분이 아닌 가상적인 상황 속에서 작품의 특정 인물들이 처해 있다고 상상하도록 하여 그들이 어떻게 행동하게 될 것이며 무엇을 느끼고 말할 것인가에 대해 생각하게 해서 말하게 한다. '**거기서라면**'은 이와는 역으로 작품 속의 인물이 아닌 어떤 사람을 작품 속의 상황 속으로 끌어들였을 때 있음직한 행동 반응, 영향 등을 토론한다. 예를 들면, 남자 주인공이 나오는 어떤 작품에서 만약 그 주인공과 똑같은 여성을 등장시킨다면 사건과 관계에 대해 어떠한 차이점을 만들게 할 수 있을까에 대해 상상해본다.

■영화 예고편 만들기

읽고 있는 작품의 하이라이트 장면들을 사용하여 작품을 선전하기 위해 2분짜리 영화 예고편을 만든다.

■영화 제작자 되기

작품의 하이라이트 장면을 선택하여 영화나 TV 프로그램의 한 장면으로 각색한다.

■작품의 표지 그림 만들기

작품을 읽은 후 작품에 대한 전체적인 반응을 이끌어내고 구체화하여 표지그림으로 묘사하게 하는 것이다.

■ 작품추천 광고문 만들기

　학생들의 반응에 영향을 끼친 작품의 구성이나 특별한 특징들을 중심으로 짧은 표지용 광고문을 만든다. 서점에서 책을 뒤지고 있는 사람에게 시선을 틀림없이 끌 수 있다고 느끼는 인용어구를 적어도 하나는 작품에서 뽑아내도록 한다.

■ 등장인물들을 몸짓 자세로 조각하기

　한 학생이 조각가로 선정되어진다. 몇몇 학생들을 앞으로 나오게 하여 그들이 작품의 등장인물들이라고 가정된다. 그 조각가는 등장인물을 한 사람씩 선택하여 서거나 앉거나 혹은 인물의 중요한 개인적 특징을 적절히 나타낼 수 있는 어떤 자세나 표정을 짓도록 요구한다. 인물과의 관계를 서로 밀접하다고 여기면 가까이에, 관계가 거의 없다고 여기면 멀리 떨어뜨려 놓는다. 인물들이 서로 얼굴을 맞대게 또는 등을 맞대게 하며, 둥글게 웅크려 모여서 손을 잡고 의논을 하게 하는 등 조각가가 원하는 무엇이든지 조각되어지게 한다.

■ 만약~했더라면 어떻게 되었을까?

　상황이 달라졌더라면 어떻게 되었을까? 인물들은 어떤 대안들을 마련했을까? 작가는 독자들에게 어떤 다른 영향을 끼쳤을까? 등을 상상하여 응답해보는 활동이다.

■ 팀간에 시합하기

　그룹별로 경쟁 팀을 구성하여 팀 사이에 작품에 대해 직접적인 질문을 하거나 또는 인용어구를 사용하여 누가 이것을 했는가, 어디서 했는가, 언제 했는가? 등과 같은 질문을 하여 답변하게 한다. 질문들은 교사 또는 학생들 스스로 만든다. 이것은 작품에 대한 여러 가지 요소들을 상기시켜주는 유용하고 재미있는 활동이다.

■ 1분만 말하기

경쟁자들이 부여받는 화제에 대해 주저하지 말고 빗나가지도 않고 반복도 하지 않으면서 60초 동안 이야기하려고 애쓴다. 교사나 학생대표가 박스(또는 모자)에서 한 개의 화제를 뽑고 나서 60초 동안 그 화제에 대해 말하도록 한다. 초시계를 준비한다.『로미오와 줄리엣』이라면 다음과 같은 화제를 선택하여 할 수 있다 : 사랑, 폭력, 불화, 친구에 대한 충성, 동정, 우정, 분노, 운명, 행복, 한 도시 내에서 시민간의 충돌, 중매결혼, 발코니의 유용성, 젊은이의 맹목성 등등. 경쟁자가 주저하거나 화제를 빗나가거나 주제 어휘를 제외한 어떤 단어를 반복한다면 탈락되게 하며 성공한 경쟁자는 남은 시간 동안 말을 계속하게 한다.

■ 돌아가면서 요약문 완결짓기

그룹을 만든다. 만약 그룹이 5명이라면 읽은 작품에 대해 각자 한 문장씩 적고 그 종이를 오른쪽 학생에게 넘겨준다. 그러면 그 학생은 두 번째 문장을 적고 그것을 똑같이 오른쪽 학생에게 넘겨준다. 이런 방식을 계속하여 결국 다섯 개의 문장으로 된 요약문을 한 그룹에서 공동으로 만든다.

■ 편지 쓰기

작품의 한 등장인물이 다른 사람들에게 편지를 쓴다고 가상한다. 편지를 받는 사람들은 다양하게 한다. 예컨대 학생들은 작품이 다 끝난 후에 등장인물 X가 작품에서 무슨 일이 일어났는지, 어떻게 그런 식으로 일어났는지를 설명하는 편지를 써서 어머니/아내/가장 친한 친구/교장/변호사/사장/의회의 하원의원 등에게 보낸다. 이렇게 하면 여러 가지로 다른 편지글이 연습되며 내용과 문체의 차이점을 이해할 수 있다. 또는 서로 다른 등장인물이 서로에게 자신이 겪은 사건들에 대해 편지를 쓸 수도 있고, 아니면 독자가 주요 등장인물에게 쓸 수도 있다.

■ 작품의 끝에 덧붙여 이어 쓰기

작품의 어떤 연속을 허용하여 후미에 이어질 몇 개의 문단을 쓴다.

■ 다른 청중을 위한 문학작품의 각색하기

다른 청중, 예를 들면, 어린이, 초등학교 학생, 공포영화 감독 등을 위해 읽은 작품을 다시 쓰는 것이다. 이것은 수준에 맞추어 등급에 따라 다시 고쳐 쓴 독본 혹은 쉽게 다시 쓴 어떤 작품의 형태들을 만들게 된다.

■ 신문 보도문으로 만들기

읽은 작품에서 일어난 사건들에 대한 신문 보도문을 쓴다. 써 보내려고 하는 신문이 어떤 종류인지를 결정하여야 하는데, 스캔들 신문 혹은 더 건실한 고급신문인가에 따라 쓰는 글의 어조와 문체가 달라진다.

■ 기자회견 하기

등장인물들이 기자들에게서 질문을 받는다고 가상하고 참여했던 사건들에 대해 의견을 제시한다. 기자회견을 관장하는 기자회견 지휘자는 기자들에게 말을 걸어 달라고 요청하고 순서를 유지하면서 끝날 때까지 진행을 맡는다.

동화와 창의성 교육

　동화는 이미지와 움직임, 음향, 음악, 언어, 학습경험의 다양함 등을 제공하는 자료이다. 그것은 독자로 하여금 정서, 갈등, 의문, 그리고 일상생활의 다의성으로 이끈다. 아이들은 동화로부터 자신의 삶의 경험과 이해를 바탕으로 의미를 창조한다. 독자가 텍스트와 만날 때 새로운 경험은 독자의 전 존재의 부분이 되고 반복해서 반영된다. 창의적 언어활동을 위해서는 동화가 지니고 있는 문자언어 이외의 다양한 매체에 관한 이해와 그것을 활용하여 아이들의 반응을 이끌어 낼 다양한 기법들의 개발이 필요하다. 동화에서 이끌어낼 그들의 반응은 이야기들, 일기, 신문기사, 혹은 편지와 같은 형태로 쓰여질 수 있고, 움직임, 시각예술, 음악, 혹은 연극으로 나타낼 수 있다(황정현,『창의력 계발을 위한 동화교육방법론』. pp. 22-23 참조).

4.1 동화의 극화와 창의성

　교실에서 동화의 극화는 세계와 자기 자신에 대한 효과적이고 즐거운 표현방법을 제공한다. 연극을 통하여 아동들은 자신이 이해한 것을 즉흥극으로 꾸밈으로써 보다 가까이 작품에 다가갈 수 있다. 그들은 창조적으로 생각하도록 격려받으며, 다양한 시점으로부터 삶을 살아봄으로써 그들이 좋아하는 인물이 되어보기도 하는 것이다. 다른 문화와 시대의 문학이 수업에 사용되면 아동들은 세계적이고 역사적인 전망을 얻게 된다. 그리고 연극은 집단예술이기 때문에 아동들은 생산적인 사회관계, 협동학습, 그리고 집단문제 해결을 배우게 된다. 연극은 문학작품을 가지고 놀고자 하는 아동의 자연스런 충동을 이용한다. 예를 들면 아동들은 자신들이 읽고 들은 이야기에 자발적으로 참여한다. 아이들의 이러한 자발성은 창의적 언어활동을 하는 데 있어 가장 기본이 되는 요소이다. 뿐만 아니라 이야기에 대해 민감하게 되고, 사고의 유연성을 키우며, 집중력을 높여 기존의 이야기에서 새로운 이야기로 전환시키는 능력을 개발하기도 한다. 그러므로 보다 깊이 있는 이야기의 본질을 탐구할 뿐만 아니라 창조적으로 사색하게 하고 아이디어를 창안하게 한다. 이러한 전신활동은 자연스럽게 언어활동을 창조적으로 이끌기도 한다.

4.2 동화교육에 있어 다매체 활용과 창의성 개발

동화교육의 본질은 아동들의 잠재된 감수성을 환기시켜 상상력을 개발하는 것이다. 상상력을 개발하기 위해서는 동화에 내재하고 있는 다매체 활용이 필요하다. 다매체는 아동들의 감수성을 활성화하고 나아가 인간의 내적인 삶의 경험을 탐구하고 표현하는 다양한 수단을 제공한다. 시각적 매체, 청각적 매체, 신체적 매체 등 다매체 활용은 의사소통을 하게 된다. 자기표현에 있어 진흙이나 파스텔, 물감, 종이접기 등과 같은 원초적인 시각적 매체는 특별한 기술이나 규칙 및 재능 등이 없어도 사상이나 감정을 쉽게 발견하게 한다. 이미지들의 발생은 단어를 생각나게 하고, 나아가 현재 우리 자신과 우리가 아는 것, 그리고 생각하고 느끼는 방법 등을 의식하게 한다. 이미지 만들기는 상상력과 창조력, 느낌, 생각들을 재발견하는 데에 사용하는 중요한 도구이다. 이것은 아동들의 언어능력 활동의 일환으로 이미지를 만들 때, 이미지 만들기 기술은 동화에 담긴 의미를 밝히거나 하나의 이야기에서 감동적인 부분을 탐구하는 데 사용된다. 이미지는 빨리, 1분 이내에 만들어지며, 특별한 생각이나 경험, 관계를 공부하고 언어적인 표현을 불러일으키고 심화시키는 데에 도움이 되도록 명확하게 고안되어야 한다.

청각적 매체를 활용하는 작업은 리듬이나 소리의 크기, 음색을 사용한다는 점에서 음악과 닮았지만 음악과 달리 악기뿐만 아니라 신체적 도구나 그밖의 도구를 사용하여 생각과 느낌을 표현한다. 그리고 음악처럼 고도의 기능이나 기교를 필요로 하지 않는다. 동화교육에서 청각적 매체를 활용하는 이유는 소리는 아동들의 상상력을 자극하는 데 있어 효과적이기 때문이다. 리듬과 소리는 인간의 두뇌에 직접적인 영향을 준다. 음악이나 어떤 특정한 소리에 의해 우리의 기분이 움직인다. 어떤 소리를 들으면 공포감이 생기고, 또 어떤 소리를 들으면 경건해진다. 그리고 공포감을 만들기 위한 소리나 음악은 특정한 패턴을 가지고 있으며 경건하고 성스러운 감정을 고양하기 위해서는 그것 역시 특정한 패턴을 지닌다. 이처럼 소리표현은 특정한 감정을 나타내는 이미지의 기호화이다. 학습자들은 이런 소리의 기호를 통해 언어로 표현할 수 없는 의미를 탐구하게 된다.

신체적 매체의 움직임 활동은 언어능력을 촉진하고 창의성을 키우며 억눌린 에너지를 풀어주고 신경계통에 영양분을 준다. 그래서 아이들로 하여금 언어 없이도 감정을 개발하고 표현할 수 있게 해준다. 평상시 잘 말하지 않는 아이들은 움직이면서 자기 생각을 발견하고 그런 다음 자신의 경험에 대해 이야기함으로써 움직임을 언어적 표현을 위한 자신의 통로로 사용할 수 있다.

이상과 같은 비언어적 활동을 위한 다매체 활용은 동화가 지니고 있는 환타지들 때문이다. 환타지는 이미지 그 자체이며, 상상력 발현의 기본적 체계를 가지고 있다. 동화에는 수많은 음성상징이나 색채어로 구성된 단순 반복적인 상징적 담론 방식 그리고 움직임을 구체적으로 드러내는 감각어나 환상적 배경과 시각적으로 명확한 인물묘사

등은 문자 매체만을 통해서는 전달할 수 없는 다양한 매체를 내포하고 있기 때문이다(황정현, 같은 책 pp. 23-26. 그리고 황정현 옮김, Nancy King.『창조적인 언어사용 능력을 위한 교육연극방법』. pp. 71-75 참조).

4.3 동화와 총체적 언어교육

총체적 언어교육(whole language education)을 위한 중요한 텍스트로는 동화를 들 수 있다. 동화는 아동들의 잠재된 상상력을 끌어내어 다양한 반응을 하게 하는 중요한 텍스트이며, 동시에 다양한 의사소통을 가능케 하는 매체, 즉 시각적, 청각적, 몸짓 언어 등이 내재되어 있어 총체적 언어 교육을 위한 좋은 자료이다. 교사들은 교실에서 문학작품에 대한 아동들의 반응을 이끌어 낼 다양한 기법들을 개발하여 독후 활동으로 활용하고 있다. 앞에서 이미 보았듯이 어떤 반응은 이야기들, 일기, 신문기사, 혹은 편지와 같이 쓰여지는 것일 수 있고 또 다른 반응은 움직임, 시각예술, 음악, 혹은 연극으로 나타낼 수 있다. 그리고 동화교육에 사용될 수 있는 매체의 활용은 크게 비언어적 활동과 언어적 활동, 관련 활동으로 구분될 수 있다. 비언어적 활동에는 음성언어, 문자언어 등으로 구성되고 관련 활동은 교과 통합적이다.

총체적 언어교육을 구현하는 동화교육방법론은 그 기저 학문으로 연극학을 들 수 있다. 고전적 형식으로서 연극은 한 가지 성격뿐만 아니라 다른 모든 예술의 성격을, 예컨대 언어, 회화, 조각, 춤, 문학, 음악 등을 공유하고 있다. 이러한 연극적 특성은 총체적 언어 철학을 구현하기 위한 방법론으로 적합하다. 연극학의 관점에서 기존의 언어학과 문학을 바라보면 언어와 문학에 대한 인식의 지평을 넓힐 수 있다(황정현, 같은 책 pp. 42-43 참조).

인터넷 활동을 통한 영문학 작품 학습과 창의성 신장

 영어로 된 문학적 텍스트 자료를 모아 만든 학습 사이트들이 상당히 많은데 이것을 활용하는 재미있는 여러 활동들에 따라서 하거나, 아니면 교사가 그러한 인터넷 자료를 활용할 수 있도록 구안한 문제나 과제지를 통해 학생들로 하여금 풀어보게 함으로써 영어 습득 또는 학습에 큰 효과를 올릴 수 있다. 대표적인 학습 사이트와 활용방법을 제시한다.

■ http://www.tellingtales.com

 중고등학생 수준에서 읽기 자료로 사용할 만한 자료들이다. 읽기와 쓰기를 결합한 활동들이 많다. 단순히 읽기 수준에서 끝나는 것이 아니라 직접 이야기를 만들 수 있는 여러 가지 활동들로 구성되어 있다. 그리고 다양한 짧은 이야기들을 직접 오디오 파일로 들을 수 있게 만들어져 있고, 실제로 학생들이 직접 만든 것을 다른 학생들이 쓴 글들을 읽어서 비교할 수 있는 이점이 있다. 또한 교사들에게 수업에 활용할 수 있는 팁들도 있다. 'Things To Do'에서 보면 다음과 같은 활동을 할 수 있다.

① Identikit Stories: 미리 읽은 내용의 이해 여부를 확인하는 것이다. 나머지 부분은 자신이 원하는 내용으로 마무리할 수 있다.
② Story Chains: 이야기를 구성하는 중요한 단어들을 통해 또다시 다른 이야기를 만들어 나가는 활동이다.
③ Characters: 자신이 적고 싶은 짧은 내용의 캐릭터들을 직접 적어 보는 활동이다.

④ Story Skeletons: 이야기의 뼈대(skeleton)를 읽고 난 뒤 친구들에게 다시 자신의 말로 재구성하는 활동이다.
⑤ Story Starters: 이야기의 첫 부분을 제공해줌으로써 나머지는 학생들의 상상력으로 창작할 수 있도록 하는 활동이다.

■ 각국의 동화나 민담 읽기

인터넷에서는 아주 많은 외국의 동화를 구할 수 있고 또 어떤 경우는 학생들이 직접 본국의 전래동화를 영어로 옮긴 것들도 많이 발견할 수가 있는데 이것은 수업에서 귀중한 자료가 된다. 또 외국의 친구나 학급과 동일한 동화를 읽고 느낌을 영어로 적어 교환하기를 해보면 쓰기 공부에도 아주 도움이 된다. 또한 우리와 시차가 별로 없는 나라의 영어교사와 연결해서 학급간 온라인 토론을 할 수도 있다. 대개는 교사가 질문 리스트를 학생들에게 제시하면 시간도 절약하고 단위시간의 학습목표에도 도달할 수 있으며 학생들에게는 굉장한 체험이 될 것이다(부산광역시교육과학연구원, 『인터넷으로 만나는 신나는 영어수업』. 2001. p. 16).

■ 토의주제
- 창의성을 개발할 수 있는 독서 감상 표현 활동들을 세 개 정도 들고 어떤 점에서 창의성이 개발될 수 있는지를 말해보시오.
- 동화교육이 창의성을 개발할 수 있는 좋은 자료가 된다면 어떤 점에서 그런지 말해 보시오.

| 제 2 부 |

창조적 독서이론과 읽기방법

■■■

1. 좋은 독서 습관과 나쁜 독서 습관
2. 독해에서의 스키마 이론
3. 의욕적이고 능동적인 독자가 되는 길
4. 창조적 독서기술과 독서방법
5. 독해력의 단계에 따른 읽기방법
6. 감상의 단계에 따른 읽기방법
7. 영어문학 텍스트의 언어학적 이해와 독서 감상 표현

좋은 독서 습관과 나쁜 독서 습관

레위스(Lewis 1958)에 의하면, 독서는 자동화된 습관이기 때문에 좋은 습관은 효율적이며 빠른 읽기를 가능하게 하고, 반대로 나쁜 습관은 느리고 불만족스러운 읽기를 초래한다.

1.1 좋은 독서 습관

좋은 **독서습관**을 아래에 몇 가지 제안한다.

■ 문맥을 통한 어휘 유추

어휘는 효율적이고 빠른 독해를 위해 중요하다. 독자는 자신이 읽고 있는 단어에 친숙할수록 단어를 덜 의식하고 내용 이해에 더 잘 집중할 수 있게 된다. 반면에 어휘력이 부족한 경우 이해가 잘 안 되고 읽는 속도도 느려지며, 퇴행, 음성화 등의 나쁜 습관이 조장될 수 있다. 그렇다면 모르는 단어가 나올 때 어떻게 해야 할까? 이런 경우 일반적으로 가장 많이 의존하는 것이 사전이다. 그러나 읽기 중 사전 찾기는 읽기 속도를 감소시키고, 집중을 방해하며, 읽기에서의 즐거움을 앗아가는 등 효율적인 독해를 어렵게 한다. 읽기 중 친숙하지 않은 어휘를 접했을 때 읽기 속도를 감소시키지 않으면서 이해에 도움이 되도록 하는 가장 효율적인 대처방법은 바로 문맥을 통해 그 의미를 유추하는 것이다.

문맥을 통해 단어의 의미를 유추하는 습관은 몇 가지 이점을 가지고 있다. 첫째, 중단하지 않고 읽기 때문에 빨리 읽을 수 있다. 둘째, 읽고 있는 내용의 종합적인 의미에 초점을 둘 수 있으므로 이해를 도와준다. 셋째, 단어들을 기억할 가능성이 더 높아지므로 어휘력을 향상시키는 데 도움이 된다. 끝으로, 멈출 필요가 없기 때문에 읽기를 즐길 수 있다(송영희. '속독 훈련이 영어 독해력에 미치는 영향에 대한 연구' pp. 7-9 참조).

어휘력 기르기에 대해 잠간 살펴보자. 책을 좋아하지 않는 아이들의 대부분은 어휘량이 부족한 경우가 많다. 일반적으로 어린 아이들은 몇 가지 특징을 가지고 있다(양재한 외. 『어린이 독서지도론』. pp. 80-81 참조).

- 말을 유창하게 하지 못한다.
- 말하기를 싫어한다.
- 질문을 하면 대충 대답한다.
- 이야기를 하거나 대화를 할 때 내용에 핵심이 없다.
- 이야기를 할 때 부적절한 어휘를 많이 사용한다.
- 이야기를 재미있게 이끌어 가지 못한다.
- 저학년 때는 성적이 좋을 수도 있으나, 고학년으로 올라 갈수록 성적이 점점 떨어진다.
- 대화에 유머나 위트가 부족하다.
- 친구들에게 인기가 없다.

위의 특징들 중에서 4개 이상의 특징을 가진 어린이는 어휘력에 문제가 있는 것으로 볼 수 있다. 이와 같이 독서의 가장 기본적인 기능인 어휘력은 환경의 지배를 받는다. 성별의 차이, 문화의 차이, 부모 직업의 차이에 따라 개인의 어휘력은 영향력을 받는다. 어린이의 어휘력을 기르기 위해서는 다음과 같은 방법이 있다.

첫째로, 폭넓은 독서를 하게 한다. 한국어의 경우에 한국어를 모국어로 하는 보통 사람은 1분간 3백 단어 정도를 읽을 수 있는데, 하루 평균 15분간의 독서를 한다면, 1년이면 150만 단어를 읽을 수 있다. 외국어로서의 영어의 경우에 보통 수준의 영어 학습자는 1분에 175 단어 정도를 읽을 수 있고 그 이하와 이상의 수준을 25 단어씩 가감하여 수준을 매긴다.

둘째로, 많은 사람과 대화를 하게 한다. 사람들과 반복적으로 사용함으로써 새로 배운 어휘들이 기억되러 습관화되어 자기 것으로 된다.

셋째, 무엇이나 말로 지시를 한다.

넷째, 산책하면서 질문하기이다.

다섯째, 어린이의 불완전한 문장을 완전한 문장으로 바꿔준다.

여섯째, 말놀이 게임을 한다. 예를 들면, 뒷말 이어가지, 같은 자로 끝나는 말, 삼행시 짓기 등을 한다.

일곱째, 국어사전, 백과사전을 애용하게 한다.

■ 의미 단위로 끊어 읽기

문법·번역식 교수법이 초래한 읽기에서의 문제의 하나는 단어 중심의 읽기이다. 이러한 문자 또는 단어 중심의 읽기는 이해에 해롭다(Harris 1966; Smith 1971). 왜냐하면 한 단어의 의미는 그 다음 단어가 이해되기 전에 잊혀지며, 그로 인해서 단어들 사이에 의미있는 관계가 형성되지 못하기 때문이다. 뿐만 아니라 읽기 속도도 감소시킨다. 따라서 단어 중심이 아니라 의미 단위로 끊어 읽어야 한다. 의미 단위로 끊어 읽기는 시각훈련과도 관련이 있다. 그렇기 위해서는 단어들을 한 눈에 볼 수 있는 시각 훈련을 해야 한다(송영희. 같은 논문 p. 9 참조. 이하 부분은 pp. 9-13 참조).

■ 통사적 지식

읽기에서의 문자 언어는 음성 언어와는 달리 복잡한 통사구조를 사용하기 때문에 한 눈에 읽기가 어렵다. 의미 단위로 끊어 읽기를 하기 위해서도 통사 지식이 필요하다. 영어를 외국어로 하는 학생들은 보통 단어 중심의 읽기를 하는데, 잘 이해하기 위해서는 통사 구조 중심의 읽기를 해야 하며 읽기 수준이 올라갈수록 복잡한 통사 구조에 대한 학습이 필요하다. 통사 구조를 익히는 실제적인 방법은 영어로 된 자료를 많이 읽는 것이다(Eskey 1970). 통사구조를 모르면 의미 단위로 끊어 읽기가 불가능하다.

■ 독해 기술

읽기 속도를 증가시키기 위해서 학생들에게 필요한 독해 기술로는 위에 제시한 문맥을 통한 어휘 유추, 의미 단위로 끊어 읽기, 통사적 지식 외에 몇 가지를 추가할 수 있다.

첫째, 중심 생각 파악하기는 가장 중요하다고 할 수 있다. 독자는 읽기 자료에 제시된 내용들 중에 작가의 중심 생각을 찾아내고 그에 대한 세부 내용들의 관계를 파악할 수 있어야 하며 중요하지 않은 내용은 무시할 수 있어야 한다. 중심 생각은 대체로(70% 내지 90%) 문단이나 글의 시작이나 끝 부분에 제시된다. 그러므로 중심 생각을 파악하기 위해서는 시작 부분과 끝 부분을 주의해서 읽어야 한다. 중심 생각이 명시되지 않은 경우 독자는 세부 내용이나 논리 전개 구조를 통해서 추론 또는 판단해야 한다.

둘째, 논리 전개 구조를 파악하기이다. 필자가 자신의 중심 생각을 효율적으로 전달하기 위해 어떤 구조로 논리를 전개하고 있는지를 파악하는 것은 사실상 중심 생각을 파악하기 위한 선행조건이라고 할 수 있다. 논리 전개 구조의 종류는 묘사, 공간관계, 과정, 시간 순서,

예시, 분류, 인과관계, 비교와 대조, 유추, 정의 등이다. 독자는 논리 전개 구조를 파악함으로써 필자가 제시하는 내용을 더 빠르고 더 정확하게 이해할 수 있으며, 읽은 내용을 더 잘 기억하고 회상할 수 있다.

셋째, 추론하기이다. 작가는 이야기에 흥미를 더하기 위해 자신이 전달하고자 하는 바를 직접적으로 제시하지 않고 여러 가지 단서들과 우회적인 방법을 사용하여 간접적으로 제시하는 경우가 많다. 이럴 때 독자는 간접적인 진술문을 통해서 작가가 의미하고자 하는 바를 추론해야 할 필요가 있다. 즉 작가는 암시하고 독자는 추론한다. 따라서 독자는 작가가 추론을 조장하는 방법, 예를 들면, 단어의 선택과 배열, 세부 내용의 선택, 주제에 대한 작가의 분명한 태도 등에 주의를 기울이면서 읽어야 한다. 이 때 독자는 어떤 진술문에서 의도되는 것보다 더 많은 것을 읽지 않도록 조심해야 한다.

넷째, 찾아 읽기(scanning)와 훑어 읽기(skimming)이다. 찾아 읽기는 글 전체를 읽지 않고 어떤 특정한 정보를 찾기 위해 선택적으로 건너뛰어 읽는 것이며, 훑어 읽기는 세부 내용이 아닌 종합적인 생각을 찾기 위해 글 이해에 영향이 없는 세부 내용은 무시하면서 선택적으로 빠른 속도로 건너뛰어 읽는 것이다. 보다 더 상세한 것은 나중에 독서법의 종류에서 다룬다.

1.2 나쁜 독서 습관

나쁜 독서습관을 아래에 몇 가지 제시한다(송영희, 같은 논문. pp. 14-16 참조).

▌퇴행

퇴행이란 이미 읽은 내용을 다시 되돌아가 반복해서 읽는 것을 말한다. 내용이 어렵거나 이해하기 힘들 때 의도적으로 하는 의식적 퇴행과, 집중해서 읽지 않아서 자기도 모르게 습관처럼 하는 무의식적 퇴행이 있다. 이러한 퇴행은 독자 자신이 내용의 일부를 놓쳤을지도 모른다는 두려움 때문에 일어나는 것으로, 그 놓친 부분을 명확하게 하지 않고서는 읽기를 계속할 수 없다고 생각한다. 일반적으로 독자는 퇴행을 하는 동안에 이해력이 향상되고 있다고 믿기 쉬우나, 오히려 퇴행은 시간 낭비이고 놓친 부분을 명확하게 하기보다는 읽고 있는 자료의 논리적 연속성을 방해함으로써 혼동을 유발한다. 어려운 자료를 읽을 때의 퇴행은 정상적이지만 모든 자료에 대한 지속적인 퇴행은 속도를 느리게 하고 집중을 떨어뜨리며, 이해력과 자신감을 감소시키고, 불안해하는 습관을 기르게 할 수 있다. 퇴행을 없애는 데 가장 결정적인 것은 독자 자신의 의지이다. 따라서 이를 제거하기 위해서는 어떤 경우에도 퇴행을 하지 않겠다는 단호한 결심으로 지속적으로 노력하고 연습해야 한다.

■ 번역 습관

문법·번역식 교수법에서 오는 폐단 중의 하나가 모국어로 번역하는 습관이다. 이 습관은 읽을 때 단어들을 1:1 대응관계에 의해 우리말로 바꾸어 이해하려는 것으로, 단어 중심의 읽기를 조장할 뿐만 아니라 영어를 영어로 인식하지 않고 우리말로 바꿈으로써 두뇌에서의 이중의 처리 과정을 요구한다. 이러한 번역 습관을 가진 독자는 읽을 때 정보를 처리하는 속도가 떨어지고, 우리말로 자연스럽게 해석되지 않을 때는 이해가 되지 않는 것으로 여기게 된다. 번역은 속독에 장애가 되는 요인이므로 퇴행과 함께 제거되어야 할 습관이다. 영어 텍스트에서는 영어 자체의 코드로 읽고 한국어 텍스트에서는 한국어 자체의 코드로 읽어야만 직독직해 능력을 키울 수 있다.

▎집중력 부족

집중해서 읽기를 하면 이해가 잘 되지만 그렇지 않으면 읽는 내용을 제대로 이해할 수 없다. 집중력 부족은 퇴행의 원인이기도 하다. 읽을 때 읽는 내용에 집중하지 않으면 의미 이해와 함께 읽는 속도도 느려진다. 집중력은 타고나는 것이 아니라 훈련과 의지에 의해 개발될 수 있다. 집중을 위해서는 주위 환경도 중요하지만 무엇보다도 독자 자신의 노력이 중요하다. 마음이 혼란되는 상황에서는 정신집중이 안 되어 독서능률은 저하된다. 원천적으로 안정된 정서 상태를 유지하는 것이 독해력을 기르는 데 필수적이다.

▎지나친 긴장

긴장하지 않고 읽으면 읽는 내용을 잘 이해하지 못하거나 읽었던 내용을 다시 읽게 됨으로써 읽는 속도가 느려진다. 집중력 부족은 위에서 언급한 퇴행의 원인이기도 하다. 그러나 지나친 긴장은 오히려 독자의 이해력과 집중력을 저하시키고 쉽게 피로를 느끼게 하며 심리적 불안감 등을 유발하여 효율적인 독해를 방해할 수 있다. 독해의 효율성을 높이기 위해서는 독자는 읽기 전과 읽기 중에 지나치게 긴장하지 않도록 유의해야 한다.

▎시각 훈련의 부족

독해 지도에서 실제로 가장 무시되어서는 안 될, 주의 깊게 고려해야 할 것이 시각 훈련이다. 단어 중심의 한 단어씩 읽는 것을 당연하게 여기고 있는 경향이 일반적인데 한 단어씩 읽어서는 읽기 속도에 아무런 진전이 없다. Yorkey(1970)는 읽기 속도는 한 번에 눈이 몇 개의 단어를 읽을 수 있는가에 달려있다고 주장하면서 읽기 속도에 따라 독자를 세 가지 유형으로 분류하였다. 느리게 읽는 독자는 한 번에 한 단어씩, 보통의 독자는 한 번에 두 단어씩, 빨리 읽는 독자는 한 번에 약 세 단어 내지 네 단어를 읽는다는 것이다. 가능한 한 빨리 읽기 위해서는 한 번에 많은 수의 단어를 읽을 수 있어야 하는데 이는 훈련을 통해서 가능하다. 속독을 위해서는 많은 수의 단어를 한꺼번에 볼 수 있는 능력과 함께 단어와 구의 형태를 재빨리 정확하게 인지하는 능력도 중요하다. 단어를 잘못 읽으면 읽고 있는 내용의 의미를 놓치게 되므로 그 자료를 다시 읽게 되어 시간을 낭비하게 된다.

책을 읽을 때 일반적으로 글자선(자선)을 따라 움직이는 눈의 행동은 위에서 아래로 또는 좌에서 우로 계속적으로 움직이고 있다고 느낄지 모른다(이하 부분은 손정표, 같은 책. pp. 29-33. 그리고 독고 앤 옮김, 같은 책. pp. 50-51. 또한 이택, "N-R 이론을 이용한 영어독해력 향상방안." 『현장 영어교육의 새로운 방향 모색』. 2003년도 제주대학교 교육대학원 영어교육전공 학술세미나 자료집. pp. 61-62 참조). 그러나 실제는 글자선상에서 순간적인 정지 상태, 즉 의시가 계속 일어나고 있다. 이와 같은 눈동자의 정지 상태에서 글자의 영상을 볼 수 있고 읽을 수 있다. 이것을 바꾸어 말하면 눈동자가 움직일 때는 사물의 영상을 똑바로 볼 수 없다는 뜻이다. 이것은 마치 움직이는 사진기로 찍은 피사체의 윤곽이 흐리게 보이는 것과 같다. 한 줄의 글을 읽을 때 눈동자의 정지 상태가 잦으면 그만큼 독서 속도도 느리게 된다. 따라서 눈동자가 정지 상태에 있을 때 가능한 많은 단어를 동시에 눈에 담도록 하여 눈동자의 움직임을 줄여야 한다. 이를 위해 수개의 단어를 단번에 인지할 수 있는 시폭 확장 훈련이 필요하다. 이러한 시각적 인지작용의 고속화, 능률화를 위해 사용되는 방법과 수단에는 flash cards slide, filmstrip, overhead projector 등이 있으며, 외국에서는 tachistoscope라는 투영기를 이용하여 독서의 자료를 한 토막씩 순간적으로 영사막에 비추어서 시각적 훈련을 하고 있다. 이 투영기에는 속도조절 장치가 되어 있어 같은 자료라도 속도를 달리해서 투영할 수 있게 되어 있다.

그런데 독서의 과정에는 안구를 통한 시각적 인지과정과 뇌를 통한 의미의 해독과정이 따른다. 눈동자를 통해 들어오는 인쇄된 활자의 형태가 망막의 시신경을 통해 뇌에 전달되며, 뇌가 그 의미를 해석하게 된다. 따라서 독서능력을 높이기 위해서는 눈을 통한 시각적 인지과정의 능률화와 함께 뇌에 전달된 시각적 영상의 의미해득의 능률화를 꽤해야 한다. "읽는다"는 것은 눈동자를 통한 글자의 시각적 영상을 뇌가 받아서 그 영상을 분석, 처리하고 뜻을 이해하는 과정이다. 주마간산격으로 아무리 눈이 받아들이더라도 뇌가 이를 처리하지 못하면 뜻의 해석이 불가능하다. 이러한 두 과정은 서로 고립된 관계에 있는 것이 아니라 상호의존 관계에 있다. 뇌의 의미해석이 빠르면 빠를수록 시각적 영상의 수용도 그만큼 빨라지게 된다. 뇌의 작용의 능률화를 위해서는 마음의 민첩성, 사고의 논리성, 비판적 통찰력, 타인의 생각에 대한 명석한 판단, 기억력, 광범위한 지식 등을 필요로 한다. 광범위한 지식에는 많은 어휘의 소유, 문장구조와 문단전개의 이해, 폭넓은 경험과 다양한 관점과 같은 것, 바꿔 말하면 스키마를 포함한다.

▌음성화

소리 내어 읽기가 습관화되어 단계가 올라감에도 불구하고 계속 나타나는 것이 음성화이다. 음성화는 외국어 학습의 측면에서는 새로운 단어들의 올바른 발음 등을 알려준다는 점에서 가치 있는 기능을 할 수도 있지만, 모든 단어들이 형태뿐만 아니라 그것들의 구술적 대응부분인 발음에 의해 이해되기를 요구하므로 읽기 속도가 느려질 수 있다. 게다가 집중력도 떨어지고 피로도 야기한다. 이 습관을 없애기 위해서는 독자는 입술의 어느 부분도 아닌, 눈만 사용하여 읽도록 노력해야 한다.

독해에서의 스키마 이론

　스키마(schema)란(양재한 외,『어린이 독서지도론』. p. 74 참조) 개인이 주위의 환경과 상호작용 할 때 사용하는 일종의 프로그램이나 전략으로서, 어떤 개인이 가지고 있는 지식 구조 또는 우리의 기억 속에 저장되어 있는 경험의 총체를 말한다. 즉 우리가 알고 있는 세상에 대한 인식과 지식을 말한다. 음식점에서는 돈을 내고 음식을 먹어야 하고, 병원에서는 의사의 지시에 따라야 하며, 교실 안에서는 교사에게 허락을 받고 말을 해야 한다는 것도 지식이다. 이러한 모든 종류의 배경적 지식이 스키마이다.
　이와 같이 스키마는 개인적인 경험의 소산이므로 어떤 단어나 개념에 대한 스키마는 사람마다 다르다. 예를 들어, 개에 대한 글이나 국기에 대한 글을 읽을 때 자신의 경험에 따라 다르게 생각하며 이해하게 되는 것은 각자 가진 스키마가 다르기 때문이다.
　앤더슨(Anderson)과 피아트(Pichert)는 다음의 실험을 통하여 스키마가 독서과정에서 하는 일을 증명한 바 있다.
　앤더슨과 피아트는 학생들에게 <집>이라는 제목이 붙여진 글을 두 집단으로 나누어 읽게 하였다. A, B 두 집단을 각각 다른 교실에 나누어 놓고 각 집단의 소년들에게 집을 구경하는 장면이 자세하게 표현된 글을 읽게 하여 집에 대한 한 가지 정보를 주었다.
　A반에 들어가서는 너희들은 이제부터 '나는 복덕방 주인'이라고 생각하면서 이 책을 읽어라. 또 B반에 들어가서는 '나는 도둑'이라고 생각하면서 이 책을 읽으라고 각각 다른 주문을 하였다. 그리고 학생들이 책을 다 읽었을 때 백지를 주고 책의 내용을 자세히 적으라고 하

였다.

 그 결과 두 반 학생들의 답안지에서 서로 다른 사실이 발견되었다. A반의 학생들이 써낸 글에는 못이 빠진 마룻장, 깨어진 유리창의 숫자, 갈라진 벽, 물이 새는 천장 등 주로 복덕방 주인이 알고 있어야 할 정보들이 많은 게 특징이었다. 그러나 도둑이 되어 읽은 B반 아이들은 값나가는 시계, 고대의 골동품, 값나가는 은그릇과 수정 그릇들에 대한 정보와 열려있는 뒷문, 정원에 있는 큰 개 등 도둑에게 필요한 정보가 적혀있었다.

 이 실험을 통해 같은 책을 읽고 얻는 게 적은 사람들은 글자나 단어의 독해에 어려움보다는 그 단어가 지칭하는 사물에 대한 사전지식, 즉 스키마가 부족하기 때문이라는 것을 알 수 있다.

의욕적이고 능동적인 독자가 되는 길

　무엇인가를 얻으려는 분명한 목적의식을 가지고 책을 읽을 때만이 최대한 능동적으로 읽을 수 있고, 보람을 느끼며 책을 읽을 수 있다. 정신적으로 성숙하려고 하거나 어떤 유익을 얻으려는 목적을 가지고 있다면 정신을 차리고 읽어야 한다. 능동적으로 읽는다는 것은 스스로 답을 찾아야 할 질문을 던지며 읽어 내려가는 것이다. 어떤 책을 읽든 다음과 같은 4가지 질문을 던져야 한다(독고 앤 옮김. 모티어 J. 애들러, 찰스 반 도렌 공저, 『생각을 넓혀주는 독서법』. pp. 54-60 참조).

① 전반적으로 무엇에 관한 글인가? 글의 주제를 찾아내고, 저자가 어떻게 더 세분한 주제와 내용으로 전개해나가고 있는가를 살펴보아야 한다.
② 무엇을, 어떻게 자세하게 다루고 있는가? 저자의 글에 나타나 있는 주요사상, 주장, 논점들을 찾아보아야 한다.
③ 전반적으로 또는 부분적으로 이 글은 맞는 이야기인가? 읽는 사람이 그 글을 이해하면서 진지하게 읽으려 한다면 맞는지 틀리는지 스스로 판단할 줄 알아야 한다. 저자의 생각을 아는 것만으로 충분치 않다. 저자의 주장은 올바르고 타당한 근거가 있는가의 여부를 따지고 문제제기를 하면서 읽는다. 바꿔 말해 비판적 읽기를 하라는 것이다.
④ 의의는 무엇인가? 정보를 제공하는 글이라면 그 정보가 어떤 의미가 있는지 질문해야 한다. 저자는 왜 그러한 것을 알아두어야 한다고 생각하는가? 그 정보가 나에게도 중요한가? 그리고 단순

한 정보 외에 어떤 깨달음을 준다면 뒤따라 나오는 내용이 무엇인지 물으며 더 깊은 의미를 찾아야 한다.

글을 읽는다는 것은 저자와 독자 사이에 대화가 되어야 한다. 아마도 그 주제에 대해서는 저자가 더 많은 것을 알고 있을 것이다. 그렇지 않다면 괜히 그런 책을 읽을 필요가 없다. 그런데 이해한다는 것은 상호적인 것이다. 즉 뭔가를 배우려면 자신에게 질문을 던지고 그리고 가르치는 사람에게 질문을 던져야 한다. 가르치는 사람이 하는 이야기를 이해하고 나면 기꺼이 그와 토론을 하고 싶어 할 정도가 되어야 한다. 책에 적는 것은 저자와 다르게 생각하는 점, 또는 동의하는 점 등을 그대로 표현해 보는 것이다. 이는 저자에게 최고의 경의를 표하는 것이다.

지혜롭고 효과적으로 책에 표시나 메모하는 방법은 다양하게 많다 그 중 몇 가지 방법을 소개한다.

① 밑줄 긋기: 요점, 중요하거나 강조하는 문장에 밑줄을 친다.
② 줄치고 싶은 부분이 너무 길 때 그 옆에 수직으로 줄을 친다.
③ 중요표시(※), 별표(☆) 등 표시해 두기: 어느 부분보다도 중요해서 몇 배나 강조하여 표시해두고 싶을 때만 사용한다. 그런 부분은 한 쪽 끝을 접어두거나 종이를 껴두거나 접착표지를 붙여둔다. 나중에 다시 책을 꺼내볼 때 그렇게 표시한 부분을 펼치면 새로이 기억해낼 수 있게 된다.
④ 여백에 숫자 쓰기: 저자가 이야기하는 내용이 연속적으로 전개될 때 표시해둔다.
⑤ 다른 페이지 수 써 넣기: 저자가 같은 내용이나 대조적인 내용 등을 이야기하는 관계된 부분을 표시해둔다. 이렇게 하면 서로 다른 부분에 흩어져있는 내용이라도 연결해 놓을 수 있다. '참조'

를 뜻하는 'cf.' 표시를 하기도 한다.
⑥ 동그라미 치기: 밑줄 긋기와 비슷한 기능으로 주제어나 주요 문단에 동그라미를 친다.
⑦ 여백에 적어넣기: 책을 읽다가 떠오른 질문이나 답, 복잡한 이야기를 쉽게 요약한 것, 또는 주요 내용의 흐름을 파악한 것을 적어둔다. 페이지의 위나 아래의 여백 또는 책 뒤에 있는 면지에 자기만의 색인을 만들어 저자의 요점을 정리할 수도 있다(독고 앤 옮김, 같은 책. pp. 55-60 참조).

창조적 독서기술과 독서방법

양재한 등(『어린이 독서지도론』. pp. 89-90 참조)에 의하면, 읽기라는 것은 원래 창조적인 활동이다. 독자가 글을 읽을 때에는 작가가 써 놓은 뜻을 이해하는 동시에 언제나 그 일반적인 뜻을 넘어서 개성적으로 반응하게 된다. 창의적 독자는 읽은 글을 통하여 자신의 사고와 영역을 끝없이 넓혀간다. 창의성이란 남들이 생각하지 못하는 새로운 생각을 해내고 새로운 대안을 형성하는 정신 과정으로 누구나 가지고 있지만 어른보다는 어린이가 더 많이 가지고 있다. 어린이 중에서도 5-10세 시절이 가장 왕성하다.

창의적 읽기 훈련을 위해 권장할 독서방법에는 다음과 같은 것이 포함될 수 있다.

- 글을 읽으며 궁금한 사항을 메모한다.
- 읽으면서 빠진 사항을 발견하고, 그곳을 적당한 말로 보충하며 읽는다.
- 다음 이야기를 생각해 본다.
- 읽고 대안을 생각한다.
- '만약에', '그와 반대로' 등 반대 상황을 생각하면서 이야기를 전개시켜 본다.
- 그림만 있는 만화를 보고 주인공들의 대화를 써넣어 만화를 완성한다.
- 그림만 있는 포스터, 광고를 보고 제목을 정해본다.

다음은 기본적으로 알아 두어야 할 독서기술과 독서방법들이다.

4.1 정독과 통독

정독(intensive reading)이란 문자 그대로 자세하게 읽는다는 말로서, 중요하지 않거나 미리 알 수 있는 부분을 대강 훑어서 읽는다는 통독(extensive reading)에 대조하는 말이다. 이는 읽기의 기본이 되는 것으로, 곧 문장의 서술 면을 통하여 필자가 이야기하고자 하는 주제나 요지를 정확하게 읽어 파악하기 위한 것이다. 즉 한 작품이나, 문장을 읽은 후 전체의 뜻을 파악하고, 그 의미의 구성과 전개 과정, 어구와 문절의 표현 형태를 깊이 있게 읽어 그러한 과정을 통하여 작품이나 문장 등의 주제와 요지를 파악하는 것이라고 말할 수 있다. 이는 교실에서의 독해 지도란 그의 취급 방법에서 정도의 차이는 있으나 이 과정이 없이는 성립할 수 없다고 할 만큼 아동·학생들의 독서기술 습득을 위한 기초적인 지도로서 중요한 의미를 가지고 있다(손정표, 같은 책. p. 218 참조).

이러한 정독에 대한 지도는 곧 통독의 기초 위에서 이루어질 수 있다. 따라서 통독 지도가 먼저 되어 있지 않으면 정독의 단계로 전진하기가 어렵다. 정독 지도상 고려해야 할 점 몇 가지를 들면 다음과 같다(손정표, 같은 책. pp. 218-219).

① 정독에 필요한 적당한 교재를 선택하여야 한다. 통독으로 한번 읽어 이해할 정도의 도서는 적합하지 않다. 정독에 필요한 도서의 선택은 대체로 아동·학생들의 독서 능력에 맞게 하되 다소 정도가 높은 것을 선택하는 것이 좋다.
② 바람직하고 적합한 분위기를 조성한다. 정독할 수 있는 노력을

집중하고, 진지하게 독서 할 수 있도록 안정되고 조용한 분위기를 만든다.
③ 순서에 따라 한 걸음 한 걸음 독서를 깊이 하도록 한다. 이것은 서술의 순서에 따른다는 뜻은 아니다. 독서를 깊이 있게 하기 위해서는 그 문장에 맞도록 적당한 계획을 세우고 어떤 비약이나 단절된 지도가 되어서는 안 된다는 의미이다. 따라서 가능한 많은 사람들이 이해할 수 있도록 적절한 질문, 조언 등을 신중히 고려하여 준비할 필요가 있다.
④ 연습 문제를 많이 활용하는 것이 좋다. 교과서에 나오는 문제들이나 각종 문제집 등을 이용하여 연습시키거나, 또는 교사가 적당한 문제를 준비하여 시도하는 것은 이 종류의 기능을 길러 주는 데 매우 효과적이다.

애들러(M. J. Adler)와 도렌(C. Van Doren)은 독서의 과정과 수준에 따라 다음과 같이 네 단계로 구분한 바 있다(양재한 외, 같은 책. pp. 75-77 참조).

독서의 제1수준, 즉 최초의 수준은 초급독서이다. 이 초보적인 읽기, 쓰기를 배우는 제 1수준은 기본 독서·기초 독서·초보 독서라고 이름 붙여도 좋은 것이지만, 보통 초등학교에서는 학습하므로 초급독서라고 한다. 초급독서는 읽기·쓰기를 전혀 못하는 어린이가 초보의 읽기·쓰기 기술을 습득하기 위한 것이다. 이 수준의 문제는 '이 문장은 무엇을 말하고 있는가'를 이해하는 것이다.

독서의 제2수준은 점검 독서이다. 시간에 중점을 두는 것이 제2수준의 특징이다. 독자는 일정한 시간 안에 할당된 분량을 읽어야만 한다. 점검 독서의 목적은 주어진 시간 안에 될 수 있는 대로 내용을 충분히 파악하는 데 있다고 할 수 있다. 점검독서는 골라 읽기, 혹은 예비독서라고 해도 되지만, 그냥 띄엄띄엄 골라 읽는다 하더라도 마음

내키는 대로 겉핥기로 읽는 것을 말하는 것이 아니다. 점검독서는 계통을 세워서 띄엄띄엄 골라 읽는 기술이다. 책의 표면을 점검하고, 그 한도에서 알 수 있는 모든 것을 배우는 일이다. 이것은 매우 힘이 드는 일이다. '이 문장은 무엇을 말하고 있는가' 라는 제 1수준의 물음에 대하여, 제2수준의 문제는 '이 책은 무엇에 대하여 쓴 것인가'라는 물음에 답하는 것이다. 구체적으로, '이 책은 어떻게 구성되어 있는가', '어떠한 부분으로 나뉠 수 있는가', '이 책은 어떤 종류의 책인가'의 물음에 답할 수 있어야 한다.

독서의 제 3수준은 분석독서이다. 이것은 제1·2수준보다도 복잡하고 계통적인 독서 활동이다. 읽는 책의 어려움에도 좌우되지만, 독자의 상당한 노력이 필요한 독서법이다. 분석독서란 철저하게 읽는 것을 말한다. 독자로서 가능한 한도의 고도의 독서법이다. 점검독서가 시간의 제약이 있는 경우의 독서법이라면, 분석독서는 시간의 제약이 없는 경우의 독서법이라고 할 수 있다. 분석독서는 아주 적극적인 독서로서, 자기가 맞붙은 책을 완전히 자기 것으로 철저히 소화하여 읽어내는 것이다.

"책은 맛보아야 할 책과 삼켜야 할 책이 있다. 또 약간이긴 하지만 잘 씹어서 소화해야 할 책도 있다"고 프란시스 베이컨도 말했지만, 분석적으로 읽는다는 것은 책을 잘 씹어서 소화하는 것을 말한다. 그런데 정보나 오락을 위한 독서는 분석 독서가 필요하지 않다. 분석독서는 무엇보다 우선 이해를 깊이 하기 위한 것이다. 따라서 독서에 의해서 얕은 이해에서 깊은 이해로 정신을 향상시키려면 분석 독서의 기술을 터득해야 한다.

마지막으로 가장 고도의 독서인 제4수준은 신토피칼 독서이다. 이것은 가장 복잡하고 조직적인 독서법이다. 이는 비교 독서법이라고도 부를 수 있다. 신토피칼로 읽는다는 것은 한 권뿐만 아니라 하나의 주제에 대하여 몇 권의 책을 서로 관련지어서 읽는 것을 말한다. 그러나 단순히 각 텍스트를 비교하는 것만으로는 신토피칼 독서로서 충분하다 할 수 없다. 숙달된 독자는 읽은 책을 실마리로 하여 그러한 책에 확실히 쓰여 있지 않은 주제를 스스로 발견하고 분석할 수 있게 될 것이다. 따라서 신토피칼 독서는 독자에 대한 요구도가 가장 높은 적극적인 독서법이다.

안정효는 그의 저서 『안정효의 영어 길들이기』(1997)에서, '눈뜨기를 위한 문학작품 읽기'를 위해 영어를 배우는 학생들에게 정독보다는 통독/다독을 권하면서 이렇게 말한다(pp. 26-28).

"나는 공부를 위한 책읽기에서는 사전을 찾지 않는 독서를 해야 한다고 믿는다. 사전을 안 찾고 영어소설을 읽기 시작하면 처음에는 내용을 파악하지는 못할지언정 그래도 읽어냈다는 성취감이 만만치 않으며 단어를 찾고 내용을 자세히 이해해야 한다는 부담스러운 의무감도 없어 마음이 홀가분해진다. 사전을 안 찾으면 많은 단어의 의미를 모르기 때문에 소설이 안 읽힐 것 같아서 엄두를 못 낼지 모르지만, 아마도 나 자신만큼은 사전을 안 찾고 많은 책을 읽었기 때문에 영어를 더 쉽게 이해하고 더 빨리 배우지 않았나 생각된다.

나도 고3 때는 남들처럼 무식하게 영어사전을 통째로 외우려고 덤비기까지 했지만, 서강대학교를 다니던 시절 나의 영어 글쓰기를 각별히 돌봐 주시던 번브락 신부(John E. Bernbrock, S.J.)가 가르쳐 준 책읽기 방법이야말로 참으로 효과적인 길잡이였다.

뜻도 모르면서 책을 마구 읽어 나가는 기간이 처음에는 낭비처럼 여겨질지 모르지만, 사실은 그렇지 않다. 그것은 언어 배우기의 터 잡기요 땅 다지기를 위한 기간이며, 나도 모르게 연습을 계속하는 과정이다. 처음 두세 권을 읽어내는 동안은 정말로 도대체 책의 내용이 무슨 얘기인지도 모르겠지만 얼마 안 가서 신기하게도 차차 전체적인 의미가 드러나 보이기 때문이다. 나뭇잎은 잘 안 보여 헤아릴 수가 없어도 어쨌든 나무의 윤곽이 대충 보인다는 뜻이다.

그렇게 책읽기를 계속하면, 네댓 권으로 접어들 무렵부터 어느새 줄거리와 상황의 전개가 조금씩 이해되고, 드디어 눈으로만 익혔던 어휘가 하나 둘 저절로 의미를 드러낸다. 단 한번도 사전에서 찾아보지 않은 단어임에도 불구하고 뜻이 분명해지는 것이다. 그러다가 작품의 이해를 위해서 정말로 중요한 어휘이거나 궁금해서 알아보지 않고는 도저히 견딜 수 없는 단어를 사전에서 하나 찾아볼 때, 그 때는 사전에서 펼쳐 놓은 쪽의 단어를 주욱 훑어 내려가 보라. 그러면 눈으로만 익혔던 수많은 단어가 줄지어 나타나고, "아하, 이런 의미이리라고 막연히 짐작했었는데 역시!"라는 깨침이 온다.

이렇게 '감'으로 익혀 배운 어휘는 그냥 줄줄이 암기해서 배운 단어하고는 달라서 절대로 잊혀지지가 않고, 여기에서부터 어휘력은 기하급수적으로 늘어난다. 단어의 접두어나 접미어 등이 어떤 의미를 가졌는지를 나도 모르게 터득하기 때문이다. 그러다 보면 어느새 책읽기에서 어떤 경지에 이르고, 시야가 훤히 트인다.

대학시절에 내가 실제로 익혔던 이런 독서법은 나에게 부수적인 혜택도 가져다주었다. 영문과의 다른 학생들이 시험 때만 되면 누가 무슨 작품을 썼나 제목을 암기하느라고 바쁜 사이에 나는 아예 작품을 모조리 읽어 버렸기 때문에 "『사랑하는 시바여 돌아오라』(*Come Back, Little Sheba*)는 『피크닉』으로 퓰리처상을 받은 윌리엄 인지의 희곡이다"라는 사실을 암기하느라고 다른 아이들이 애를 먹는 동안 나는 『피크닉』과 『사랑하는 시바여 돌아오라』를 통째로 읽어 버리고는 했으니, 시골에서 가을 벼에 붙은 메뚜기를 잡으러 다닌 아이와 서울에서 처음 내려가 벼를 보고 '쌀나무'라고 그랬다는 아이의 차이가 날 수밖에 없었다.

대부분의 경쟁자가 별로 개인차를 보이지 않는 수준이라면 질보다는 양의 경쟁이기가 쉽고, 어쨌든 이렇게 양적인 책읽기를 하고 나면 언어 연령이 어느새 일곱 살 취학기가 되고, 그러면 이제부터는 체계적인 공부가 필요하다.

언어 배우기는 바둑이나 마찬가지이다. 18급일 때는 아무리 많은 바둑책과 기보를 보고 암기해도 겨우 이해했다가는 곧 잊어버리기가 쉽지만, '싸움바둑'으로 무수한 실전을 거쳐 13급 정도까지 큰 다음 책을 읽으면 모든 얘기가 얼마나 쏙쏙 머리에 잘 들어오는가.

그래서 다음 얘기로 넘어가기 전에 여기서 책읽기에 대한 안내 삼아 일백권의 책을 추천하겠다. 교보문고 외서부에만 가도 읽을 만한 좋은 책이 얼마든지 널렸지만, 여기에 추천한 목록은 내가 직접 읽어 본 책 가운데 사전을 찾지 않고도 읽기에 비교적 수월할 뿐 아니라, 널리 알려진 작품이어서 이미 우리말로 읽어 봤다면 이해가 그만큼 더 쉬우리라는 점도 고려했으며, 또한 문학성이 높고 우리 정서에 잘 맞는 작품을 골랐기 때문에 우리말로 번역이 되지 않은 경우에는 남들이 접하지 못한 숨겨진 작품을 읽어 냈다는 기쁨도 얻게 되리라고 기대한다. 우리말 제목이 붙지 않은 경우는 우리나라에서 아직 번역이 되지 않은 작품임을 의미한다.

만일 사전을 찾지 않으면서 다음에 추천한 책을 1년이나 2년쯤 걸려 모조리 읽어낸다면, 틀림없이 자신의 영어가 두드러지게 달라졌음을 느끼리라고 나는 믿는다. 그리고 이렇게 많은 책을 언제 다 읽느냐고 기가 질리거나 포기하려는 독자라면 그만큼의 노력조차 기울이지 않고 영어로 좋은 글을 쓰고 싶다는 달콤한 결과만 꿈꾼다는 것은 과욕에 지나지 않는다는 사실을 상기시켜 주고 싶다.

마음을 다져 먹고 하루에 한 권씩만 읽기 시작한다면 일백 권을 읽어내는 데 필요한 기간은 3개월밖에 걸리지 않는다. 그리고도 70인생에서는 69년 9개월이 남는다."

안정효가 권장하는 도서 목록 100선은 다음과 같다(pp. 29-34).

① James Agee, *A Death in the Family*.
　제임스 애지는 1955년에 사망했고, 이 소설은 사후에 발표되어

1958년 퓰리처상 수상.
② Richard Bach, *Jonathan Livingston Seagull*(갈매기의 꿈)
③ Richard Bach, *The Bridge Across Forever*(영원을 건너는 다리)
④ Pearl S. Buck, *The Good Earth*(대지)
⑤ Pearl S. Buck, *The Living Reed*(살아있는 갈대)
한국을 무대로 한 흥미있는 소설이며, 장왕록 교수가 처음 번역했고, 최근에 그의 딸 장영희 교수가 다시 번역 발표.
⑥ Pearl S. Buck, *The Hidden Flower*(숨은 꽃)
⑦ Eugene Burdick, *The 480*
유진 버디크는 정치학 교수 출신이며, 이 소설은 케네디가 암살된 후의 대통령 선거를 배경으로 삼은 아주 흥미진진한 정치물.
⑧ Erskine Caldwell, *The Last Night of Summer.*
⑨ Erskine Caldwell, *Place Called Estherville.*
⑩ Erskine Caldwell, *Men and Women.*
⑪ Erskine Caldwell, *Claudelle Inglish.*
⑫ Erskine Caldwell, *Certain Women.*
⑬ Erskine Caldwell, *Gretta.*
이 밖에도 어스킨 콜드웰의 작품은 하나 같이 110쪽에서 130쪽 정도로 짧고 적절히 외설적이기도 하며 재미가 있는 고급 통속 소설.
⑭ John Cheever, *The Stories of John Cheever.*
단편집이기는 하지만 존 치버의 참된 대표작으로서 퓰리처상 수상작.
⑮ John Dos Passos, *Streets of Night.*
⑯~⑱ John Dos Passos, *U.S.A.*
*1919, The 42nd Parallel, The Big Money*로 이어지는 3부작인데 우리나라에서는 1권만 번역되었음. 작가가 되려는 사람에게

는 문체에 대해서 많은 공부가 될 수 있음.
⑰ Michael Crichton, *The Andromeda Stain.*
「쥬라기 공원」의 원작자인 마이클 크라이튼의 뛰어난 공상과학소설.
⑱ Robert Crichton, *The Secret of Santa Vittoria.*
영화도 재미있지만, 소설은 더 재미있음.
⑲ James T. Farrell, *My Days of Anger*(분노하는 젊은 시절)
⑳~㉔ James T. Farrell, *The Studs Lonigan Story.*
*Young Lonigan, The Young Manhood of Studs Lonigan, Judgement Day*로 구성된 삼부작.
㉕ F. Scott Fitgerald, *The Great Gatsby*(위대한 개츠비)
㉖ Kahlil Gibran, *Spiritual Sayings of Kahlil Gibran*(영혼의 소리)
㉗ Kahlil Gibran, *Secrets of The Heart.*
㉘ William Golding, *Lord of the Flies*(파리대왕)
㉙ Graham Greene, *The Power and the Glory*(권력과 영광)
㉚ Graham Greene, *A Burnt-Out Case*(말기환자)
㉛ Alex Haley, *Roots*(뿌리)
㉜ Arthur Hailey, *Airport.* 영화보다 소설이 훨씬 재미있음.
㉝ Arthur Hailey, *Hotel*(호텔)
㉞ Ernest Hemingway, *A Farewell to Arms*(무기여 잘 있거라)
㉟ Ernest Hemingway, *For Whom the Bell Tolls*(누구를 위하여 종은 울리나)
㊱ Ernest Hemingway, *A Movable Feast*(우울한 도시의 축제)
㊲ Ernest Hemingway, *The Old Man and the Sea*(노인과 바다)
㊳ Ernest Hemingway, *By-Line.*
㊴ Jon Hersey, *A Single Pebble*(양자강의 뱃사공)
㊵ John Hersey, *A Bell for Adano.*

1944년 퓰리처상 수상작인데, 로버트 크라이튼의 『산타 비토리아의 비밀』과 분위기와 내용이 비슷함.

㊶ James Joyce, *A Portrait of the Artist as a Young Man*(청년 예술가의 초상)

㊷ Nikos Kazantzakis, *Report to Greco*(영혼의 자서전)

㊸ Milan Kundera, *Life Is Elsewhere*(인생은 다른 곳에)

㊹~㊺ Mary Jutyens, ed., *The Penguin Krishnamurti Reader I, II*(자유인이 되기 위하여)

㊻ Harper Lee, *To Kill a Mockingbird*(앵무새를 죽여라)
우리나라에서도 많은 독자를 확보한 작품이며, 1960년 퓰리처상 수상작.

㊼ Sinclair Lewis, *Elmer Gantry.*

㊽ Anne Morrow Lindbergh, *Gift From the Sea*(바다의 선물)

㊾ John P. Marquand, *H. M. Pulham, Esquire.*

㊿ Gabriel Garcia Marquez, *One Hundred Years of Solitude*(백년 동안의 고독)

(51) Carson McCullers, *Reflection in a Golden Eye*(황금빛 눈동자에 비친 그림자)

(52) Colleen McCullough, *The Thorn Birds*(가시나무새)

(53) Yukio Mishima, *Five No Plays.*

(54) Margaret Mitchell, *Gone With the Wind*(바람과 함께 사라지다)

(55)~(56) Alberto Moravia, *Two Adolescents*(두 청춘)
Agonisto, Luca 두 편으로 이루어졌으며, 사춘기의 심리묘사가 뛰어남.

(57) Iris Murdoch, *The Sea, The Sea*(바다여, 바다여)

(58) John O'Hara, *Appointment in Samarra.*

(59) John O'Hara, *Butterfield 8.*

⑥⓪ John O'Hara, *A Rage to Live*.
⑥① John O'Hara, *Ten North Frederick*.
⑥② John O'Hara, *From the Terrace*.
⑥③ John O'Hara, *Elizabeth Appleton*.
⑥④ John O'Hara, *The Ewings*.
⑥⑤ John O'Hara, *Big Laugh*.
⑥⑥ John O'Hara, *Assembly*.
  마지막은 단편집이지만 어느 장편소설 못지 않게 좋은 작품이다. 존 오하라는 미국에서 그의 작품이 영화로 가장 많이 만들어진 작가 가운데 한 사람으로서, 영어 소설을 처음 읽는 사람이라면 존 오하라부터 시작하도록 권하고 싶다. 그의 문장은 대화체가 많아서 이해가 쉽고, 어스킨 콜드웰보다도 때로는 더 재미있으며, 너무 외설이 심한 *The Ewings* 이외에는 상당한 문학적 수준도 유지함.
⑥⑦ C. Northcote Parkinson, *East and West*(동양과 서양)
  역사책이지만 소설 못지않게 재미있음.
⑥⑧ Boris Pasternack, *Doctor Zhivago*(의사 지바고)
⑥⑨ Boris Pasternack, *Safer Conducta*(어느 시인의 죽음)
⑦⓪ Hugh Prather, *Notes to Myself*(나에게 쓰는 편지)
⑦① Ayn Rand, *The Fountainhead*.
⑦② Erich Maria Remarque, *Three Comrades*.
⑦③ Erich Maria Remarque, *Spark of Life*.
⑦④ Erich Maria Remarque, *All quiet on the Western Front*(서부 전선 이상없다).
⑦⑤ Erich Maria Remarque, *The Night in Lisbon*.
⑦⑥ Erich Maria Remarque, *Heaven Has No Favorites*.
⑦⑦ Antoine de St.-Exupery, *Night Flight*(야간 비행)

⑱ Antoine de St.-Exupery, *The Little Prince*(어린 왕자)
⑲ William Saroyan, *Chance Meetings*(어쩌다 만난 사람들)
⑳ William Saroyan, *The Human Comedy*(인간희극)
㉑ William Saroyan, *The Bicycle Rider in Beverly Hills.*
㉒ Irwin Shaw, *The Young Lions*(젊은 사자들)
㉓ Irwin Shaw, *Rich Man, Poor Man*(야망의 계절)
㉔ Alan Sillitoe, *The Loneliness of the Long-Distance Runner* (장거리 주자의 고독)
㉕ John Steinbeck, *America and Americans*(아메리카와 아메리카인)
㉖ John Steinbeck, *Burning Bright.*
㉗ John Steinbeck, *Cannery Row.*
㉘ John Steinbeck, *Cup of Gold.*
㉙ John Steinbeck, *East of Eden*(에덴의 동쪽)
㉚ John Steinbeck, *The Grapes of Wrath*(분노의 포도)
㉛ John Steinbeck, *The Moon Is Down*(달은 지나)
㉜ John Steinbeck, *Of Mice and Men*(생쥐와 인간)
㉝ John Steinbeck, *The Pearl*(진주)
㉞ John Steinbeck, *The Red Pony*(붉은 망아지)
㉟ John Steinbeck, *Tortilla Flat.*
㊱ John Steinbeck, *Travels With Charley*(아메리카의 초상)
㊲ John Steinbeck, *The Winter of Our Discontent*(불만의 겨울)

존 스타인벡은 문체가 간결하고 감성이 짙은 작품을 주로 썼다. 문장도 쉬운 편이어서 어스킨 콜드웰이나 존 오하라보다 문학적으로 수준이 높은 작가를 찾는 사람은 스타인벡부터 시작하면 좋다. 그리고 처음 책을 읽기 시작하면 한 작가에 한 작품씩 돌아가며 읽지 말고 스타인벡이나 포크너 같은 한 작가의 모든 작품을 읽고 난 다음에야 다른 작가로 넘어가도록 권한다. 그러면

한 작가의 작품 세계와 문체에 익숙해져 접하기가 쉽고, 문학성도 깊이 들여다 볼 수가 있다.
⑱ William Styron, *Lie Down In Darkness*.
⑲ James Thurber, *Fables for Our Times*(우리 시대를 위한 우화).

4.2 음독과 묵독

책을 읽을 때, 초기과정은 대체로 단어를 파악하는 문자 자각의 단계와 그 단어가 어떤 의미를 가지는가에 대한 의미 이해 단계로 나누어진다(양재한 외, 같은 책. pp. 79-80). 음독이란 문자 자각의 단계에 있는 독자가 거치게 되는 초기 독서의 한 형태이다. 즉 독자는 문자의 기호를 안다(문자기호 자각) → 언어를 소리 내어 읽을 수 있다(음성언어 기호) → 자신이 발음한 기호가 어떤 의미인지 안다(소리와 의미 결부) → 종합적으로 문자의 의미를 이해한다(문자의 의미 파악)를 거쳐 글을 읽어 나간다.

음독(reading aloud)은 두 가지 점에서 어린이의 독서 준비도를 높여준다. 하나는 문자 판독을 정확히 할 수 있는 독서 능력을 향상시켜 주고, 다른 하나는 독서흥미 유발에 효과가 큰 것이다. 보통 초등학교 2학년까지는 음독이 독서속도가 빠르지만, 3학년부터는 묵독(silent reading)을 통해 책을 더욱 빨리 읽게 된다.

음독 단계가 끝나면 눈으로 읽게 된다. 음독이 글자 단위의 읽기라면 묵독은 문장 단위의 읽기, 의미 위주의 읽기이다. 묵독은 다음과 같은 효과가 있다.

① 독서속도를 높여준다. 책을 읽을 때 안구는 비약과 정지, 역행운동과 행간운동을 계속하면서 글의 의미를 파악하게 된다. 이때

초보독자는 안구의 정지시간과 횟수, 역행 운동이 많아 독서속도가 느리게 된다. 미숙한 독자는 1행을 읽는데 4-5회 정도 안구가 정지하고, 능숙한 독자는 2-3회 정지한다. 한번 정지할 때 파악하는 문자의 수도 미숙한 독자는 한글 1-2자, 영어 2-3자, 능숙한 독자는 한글 5-6자, 영어 6-7자를 읽게 된다.

초보독자가 안구를 자주 정지하면 자기의 손가락을 통해 독서속도를 증진시키는 훈련을 할 수 있다. 즉 손가락을 글자 밑에 놓고 손가락을 점점 빨리 움직여 안구의 정지 횟수나 시간을 줄여나갈 수 있다.

② 생각하며 읽게 한다. 읽기는 언어적 추측게임이다. 우리는 읽으면서 추측한다. 그리고 자신의 추측이 맞았는지를 순간순간 확인하고 판단한다. 이런 행동을 통해 어린이는 독서의 즐거움을 느끼게 된다.

4.3 훑어 읽기

훑어 읽기(skimming)는 종합적인 생각을 찾기 위해 빠른 속도로 선택적으로 건너뛰어 읽는 것을 말한다. 그런데 특정한 질문에 대한 정확한 답을 찾거나 세부적인 내용을 찾기 위해서 읽는 것이라면 '찾아 읽기' 혹은 '적독'(scanning)라 한다. 훑어 읽기가 가능한 것은 영어로 된 글은 대체로 전체 단어 수의 20% 내지 30%가 없더라도 이해에 아무런 영향을 미치지 않기 때문이다(Lewis 1958). 세부 내용에 너무 주의를 기울이면 읽는 속도가 느려지고 생각의 연결에 방해를 받을 수 있으므로 불필요한 부분들을 미리 생략하고 읽음으로써 읽기 속도를 향상시킬 수 있다. 훑어 읽기를 잘 하기 위해서는 중심 생각과 세부 내용을 구분할 줄 알아야 하고, 작가의 논리전개 구조도 정확하게 알아야 한다. 그러나 레위스가 지적했듯이 작가가 쓴 단어를 하나라도 빠뜨려서는 안 된다는 죄의식과, 만약에 하나라도 빠뜨리면 의미 이해가 제대로 되지 않을 것이라는 선입견 때문에 대부분의 독자들이 실제로 이 기술을 잘 사용하지 않는다는 데 문제가 있다(송영희, 같은 논문. pp. 10-13. 양재한 외, 같은 책. pp. 83-84 참조).

4.4 찾아 읽기

찾아 읽기(scanning) 혹은 적독은 목적을 가지고 빠른 속도로 선택적으로 건너뛰어 읽는다는 면에서는 훑어 읽기(skimming)와 유사하지만 특정한 질문에 대한 정확한 답을 찾거나 세부적인 내용을 찾기 위해서 읽는다는 점에서 다르다. 글 전체를 읽지 않고 선택적으로 어떤 특정한 질문이나 단어 또는 숫자 등을 염두에 두고 원하는 답을 찾을 때까지 빠른 속도로 자료를 훑어보면서 원하는 것을 찾으면 시선을 멈추고 고정한 후 읽는 것이다. 그런데 특정한 정보를 찾기 위해 읽을 경우에도 대부분의 독자들은 그들의 평소 습관에 따라 읽을 필요가 없는 부분들까지도 다 읽기 때문에 효율성이 떨어진다.

Harris(1966: 121-122)에 의하면, 찾아 읽기를 효율적으로 하기 위해서 유념해야 할 사항은 다음과 같다(송영희, 같은 논문. p. 13).

① 찾고자 하는 정보를 명확하게 이해해야 한다.
② 찾고자 하는 정보가 취할 수 있는 형태를 미리 생각해야 한다.
③ 읽기자료를 재빨리 훑어 읽고 직접적으로 관련이 없는 것은 무시해야 한다. 독해를 효율적으로 하기 위해서는 글을 읽는 목적에 따라 자료를 다 읽지 않고 원하는 정보가 있는 위치를 찾아서 읽을 수 있는 능력이 필요하다.

'적독'이란(손정표, 같은 책. pp. 219-220) 필요한 부분만을 골라서 읽는 것을 뜻하는 것으로, 일명 '발췌 독서'라고도 한다. 이는 특히 오늘날과 같이 정보 출판량과 요구량이 급증하고 복잡해진 현실 사회 속에서는 일상생활을 원활히 영위해 나가기 위해서도 그 필요도가 가장 높은 독서 방법이라 하겠다. 이러한 적독의 범위는 필요한 정보를 얻기 위하여 신문 기사의 어떤 면을 골라서 읽는다든지, 학습 독서에서 교과 내용이나 중심 내용에 관계가 있는 참고 도서나 관계 서적 중 필요한 장, 절 등을 선정하여 읽는다든지, 사전, 백과사전, 연감 등을 활용하여 어떤 의문을 해결하는 것 등의 독서가 모두 여기에 해당된다. 따라서 이것을 효과적으로 정확하게 할 수 있는 능력은 현대 생활을 능률적으로 처리하는 중요한 능력이 된다고 할 수 있다.

이러한 적독에 대한 지도는 통독과 정독의 기초 위에서 이루어진다. 적독의 기술을 활용하는 데는 지식과 정보를 제공하는 실용적인 문장을 읽는 경우가 대부분이기 때문에 통독과 정독의 능력이 연마되어 있지 않으면 자신이 원하는 내용을 정확히 파악하거나 그 위치를 확인하기가 어렵다.

적독의 지도상 고려해야 할 점 몇 가지를 들면 다음과 같다.

① 찾고자 하는 내용이 무엇이고, 그것을 찾기 위해서는 어떠한 것에 주의하여 찾아 가면 좋은가 등 적독의 목적을 확립하도록 하여야 한다. 무엇을 찾고자 하는지가 분명하지 않으면 찾는데 시간이 많이 걸리거나 찾지 못하고 마는 예가 생기는 반면, 찾는 목표가 분명하면 정신적인 자세가 확립되고 욕구도 강해지므로 그 부분을 읽는 독서 태도도 효과적인 태도로 나타난다.
② 필요한 내용이 책 속 어디에 있는지, 어떻게 찾는 것이 가장 효과적인지 등 찾는 방법과 기술을 지도하여야 한다. 여기에는 목차, 서문, 색인 등을 이용하여 필요로 하는 내용을 찾아내는 방법

을 지도하여야 한다.
③ 논문이나 설명적인 문장의 경우에는 결론이나 요지 및 요점이 실려 있는 정석적인 위치를, 신문 기사일 때에는 지면의 배당에 관한 상식과 표제를 읽는 방법들을 익히도록 한다.

특히 요점이나 요지의 경우는 대체로 문장 가운데 <중요한 곳을 들어 보면……>, <특히……>, <중요한 것은……>, <요컨대……>나 <……라고 생각한다. 왜냐하면……>, <……가 아니면 안 된다. 그것을 열거하면……>, <……이상에서 설명한 바와 같이 이를 정리해 보면……>, <……했는데 요는……>, 혹은 <……하지 않으면 안 된다>, <따라서 ……하지 않으면 안 된다> 등과 같이 강조된 부분을 유의하여 파악하도록 하여야 한다.
④ 찾는 부분 이외의 것에는 전혀 무관심하도록 지도한다. 이는 시간을 효과적으로 쓰기 위해서도 그렇지만 원하는 부분을 분명히 찾아서 효과적으로 읽도록 하기 위해서는 찾는 내용 이외의 것에는 관심을 두지 않도록 하는 것이 좋다.

4.5 구연

Bruno Bettelheim에 의하면(김옥순, 주옥 옮김, 『옛이야기의 매력 1』. pp. 242-250) 참조), 구연(telling)은 특히 어린이 책에 적용되는 것이지만 반드시 여기에만 제한된다고 할 수 없다. 어린이 책으로서 동화나 옛이야기(Old Tales)는 단순하게 읽기보다는 구연해야 좋다. 구연하는 것은 읽는 것보다 더 큰 융통성을 주기 때문이다. 옛이야기는 매번 어른들이 다른 어른과 다른 어린이들에게 수백만 번 들려줌으로써 형성되고 고쳐진 이야기이자 구연물이다. 구연자는 이야기를 자기 자신과 이미 자기가 잘 아는 듣는 이에게 더욱 의미 있는 쪽으로 덧붙이거나 빼면서 이야기를 한다. 어린이에게 이야기할 때 어른은 어린이의 반응을 추측하여 구연한다. 이렇게 구연자는 어린이가 그 이야기에 영향받는 것을 무의식적으로 이해한다. 성공적인 구연자는 어린이가 그 이야기를 어린이의 질문에 따라, 즉 어른과는 별도로 어린이가 기쁨과 슬픔을 공개적으로 표현하는 데 따라서 그 어린이가 좋아하는 방식으로 이야기를 각색한다. 옛이야기의 활자화된 내용만을 따라가는 것은 이야기의 많은 가치를 잃게 한다. 이야기를 가장 효과적으로 어린이에게 구연하는 것은 그 현장에 참여한 사람들이 상호간의 사건으로 만드는 것이다. 그런데 만약 옛이야기를 읽는다고 한다면 그 이야기가 의미하는 대로 감정을 넣어 듣는 어린이에게 정서적인 몰입을 한 채로 읽어야 한다(p. 242).

옛이야기를 구연하는 목적은 괴테의 어머니의 목적과 같아야 한다. 즉, 이야기의 경험을 함께 즐기는 것이다. 이 즐거움은 어른과 어린이에게는 아주 다를 수도 있다. 어린이는 환상을 즐기는 반면에 어른은 어린이가 즐거워하는 것에서 기쁨을 느낄 수 있다. 어린이는 어떤 것에 대해서 잘 알고 있다고 스스로 생각하기 때문에 기운이 북돋워질 수 있고, 어른은 어린이가 갑자기 깨닫는 충격을 경험하는 데에서 그 이야기를 말하는 즐거움을 느낀다(p. 247).

옛이야기가 단조롭다거나 소중하다고 느끼는 것은 구연자의 감정에 달려있다. 어린이를 사랑하는 할머니가 어린이를 무릎 위에 앉히고 이야기를 구연하여 어린이가 황홀하게 듣도록 하는 것은 지겨워하는 부모가 연령이 다른 여러 명의 아이들에게 의무적으로 읽어주는 것과는 매우 다르다. 이야기를 구연하는 어른이 능동적으로 참여하면 어린이가 그 이야기를 생생하고 풍요롭게 경험하게 된다. 또한 어른임에도 불구하고 어린이의 감정과 반응들을 충분히 헤아릴 수 있는 사람이라면 어린이로 하여금 그 어른과의 공유된 경험은 자신의 인격에 대해 긍정적인 확신을 가지게 한다(p. 250).

옛이야기 구연에서는 개인적인 필요성에 적합하게 이야기를 만들어 이야기에 약간의 왜곡을 가한 사례도 있었다. 개인의 마음속에 받아들여지는 과정에서 내용이 바뀌는 것을 보는 일은 흥미롭다. 이상적으로 옛이야기를 구연하려면 어른과 어린이가 동등한 동반자의 자격을 가진 상호간의 사건으로 경험해야 하며 절대로 옛이야기가 어린이에게 일방적으로 읽혀져서는 안 된다. 괴테의 어린시절 그의 어머니의 구연 사례 이야기가 그것을 잘 설명해 준다(pp. 244-245).

4.6 암시교수법에서 사용되는 독서기법

불가리아의 정신과 의사이며 학자인 Lozanov(1978)가 *Suggestology and Outlines of Suggestopedy*에서 창안한 것이 암시교수법(Suggestopedia)이다(박경수, 『영어교육론』. pp. 300-303 참조). 정확히 말하면 Suggestology는 이론적 접근방법에서 본 명명이고 Suggestopedia는 실제적 방법을 지칭한 것이다. 이 교수법의 기본원리와 교수방법은 무능력이라는 느낌, 과오를 범하게 될까하는 두려운 감, 새롭고 익숙하지 못한 것에 대한 불안감 등 학습의 방해요소로 알려져 있는 여러 가지 부정적인 암시적 요소를 역작용하도록 고안된 것이다. 따라서 학습자에게 천진난만성을 갖게 하여 자신감과 의사소통의 의향을 고취시키고 음악과 미학적 원리를 이용하고 학습자와 교사간의 밀접한 상호작용을 통하면 의사소통능력은 물론 기억력을 증진시킬 수 있다는 것이다. 이러한 수업의 진행을 위해서는 딱딱한 교실환경보다는 편안한 거실분위기에 안락의자와 그림, 음악 등이 준비되어야 하며 학생들은 요가를 하는 기분으로 정신통일과 호흡조정을 한다. 수업시작 전에 학생 개개인에게 학습목표어로 이름이 주어지는데 이것은 학생 본인이 저지르는 실수에 대해 자존심이 손상되지 않게 하기 위함이다. 수업 중 대화과정에서 일어나는 실수는 직접 교정되어서는 안 되며 그와 유사한 내용을 다른 학생들에게 사용하게 함으로써 학생 스스로 실수한 내용을 깨닫게 해 준다. 따라서 오류교정과 과제물은 최소화되어야 한다.

이 교수법에 알맞은 교재는 문장은 주로 긴 대화체로 된 것이며, 내용은 실생활과 연결되어 있다. 교사가 이러한 대화문들을 읽어주는 과정은 세 단계로 제시되며 학생들에게 각각 다른 방식으로 읽어준다. 여기서 교사의 읽기 활동을 학생들로 대체하여 읽을 수 있는 것이라고 필자는 생각한다. 이와 같은 읽기방법을 특히 외국문학작품을 읽는 데 활용한다면 구연 연습과 더불어 독서를 즐기는 멋진 활동이 될 수 있다고 본다.

① '설명적 독서'(explicative reading): 이는 설명이 되는 읽기로서 교사가 읽으면서 필요하면 단어의 뜻이나 문법 등을 설명해 준다. 학생들은 대화를 눈으로 읽어가는데 필요하면 질문도 할 수 있다.
② '음조적 독서'(intonational reading): 이는 억양을 넣는 읽기로써 교사가 세 가지 억양 즉 보통음성, 속삭이는 음성, 그리고 큰 음성으로 섞여가면서 분위기를 살려주는 음악과 함께 다시 읽는다. 대화를 읽고 모국어로 번역하여 낮은 음성으로 들려준다. 학생들은 눈으로 교재를 읽어가며 질문은 하지 않는다.
③ '연주식 독서'(concert reading): 이는 학생들이 대화가 기록된 교재를 옆으로 제쳐두고 편하게 앉아서 눈을 감고 조용히 음악을 들으면서 부담 없이 교사가 읽는 것을 듣는다. 이때에 설명이나 번역 등이 없이 그대로 처음부터 끝까지 읽는다.

4.7 제한독서

일반적으로 영어 실력을 배양하기 위하여 여러 가지로 다양한 내용과 주제에 관한 영문 자료를 읽는다. 이것은 여러 분야의 다양한 영어 텍스트나 서로 다른 주제를 다루는 광범위한 영어책들을 읽는 것이 유익하다고 생각하기 때문이다. 제한독서(narrow reading)는 이와는 반대로 제한된 범위의 영문독서가 더 효과적이라고 보는 것으로서, 동일 작가에 의해 쓰여진 여러 작품을 읽거나 또는 동일 주제에 관한 내용들만으로 된 영문을 읽는 것이다. 예를 들면 헤밍웨이 작품들만 읽거나 추리소설들만을 읽는다. 이것은 "이해도가 높은 영어 독서"를 통하여 단어와 문법 실력을 저절로 향상시킬 수 있다는 이론에 기초한다(이택, "N-R 이론을 이용한 영어독해력 향상방안." 2003년도 제주대학교 교육대학원 영어교육전공 학술세미나 자료집 『현장 영어교육의 새로운 방향 모색』. pp. 166-168 참조).

Krashen & Terrell(1983)의 이론에 따르면, 언어는 오직 한 길을 통해서 획득되며, 이 길은 주어진 메시지를 이해하는 것이라 하였다. 또한 언어발달 과정은 현재 가지고 있는 언어수준보다 약간 높은 정도의 문장구조를 가진 메시지를 이해함으로써 진행된다고 하였다. 비록 잘 모르는 단어나 문법들이 주어진 메시지 속에 가끔 있다 하더라도 현 수준의 언어실력을 바탕으로 그 메시지에 관련된 사전지식, 정보, 문장의 전체의 흐름 등을 통해서 전달된 메시지를 이해하면 그 속에 포함된 단어나 문법들이 저절로 익혀진다고 하였다. 제한독서 방법은 이러한 이해도를 높이는 것을 주목적으로 하며 그러한 과정에서 나타나는 단어나 문법들은 부산물로서 저절로 익히게 하는 학습방법이다.

제한독서 방법이 이렇게 될 수 있는 이유는 무엇인가? 첫째, 문학작품의 작가들은 그들만이 애호하는 표현방식과 독특한 문체를 가지고 있다. 예를 들면 Alexandre Dumas의 *The Three Musketeers*(삼총사. 포켓용 재편집)를 읽다보면 전체 52쪽을 통해 분사형의 문장형태가 60번 이상이 나온다. 읽으면서 60번 이상의 반복을 통하여 분사구문에 저절로 익숙해질 수 있는 것이다. 그리고 무협소설로 분류될 수 있는 이 소설에는 fight란 단어가 16번 이상이나 반복되며 무협소설의 특징과 관련되는 quarrel, attack, surrender, brave, angrily 등의 단어들이 빈번히 사용되고 있다. 따라서 제한독서 방법은 문장을 읽어 내려가는 과정에서 이미 수차례의 반복효과를 얻고 있기 때문에 굳이 별도로 단어와 문법 암기를 위한 노력을 하지 않아도 된다. 둘째, 한 가지 주제나 같은 작가의 작품 내용과의 친근감이나 낯익음은 영문독해력을 높이는 데 강한 활력소가 된다. 한 분야에 관한 내용을 많이 그리고 꾸준히 읽으면 읽을수록 그 분야에 대해 더 잘 알게 되고 따라서 영문독해는 나날이 쉽게 되어감을 알 수 있다.

다양한 문장, 낯설은 내용과 새로운 단어의 공부는 짜증에서 짜증으로 이어질 수 있지만 한 작가나 같은 주제를 다루는 내용의 영문독해는 훨씬 더 효과가 있을 수 있다. 제한 독서 방법으로 자신이 이해하고 있고 재미있다고 생각되는 주제나 작가의 작품들을 읽으면서 점진적으로 범위를 확장하여 나가면 영문독해 실력을 향상시킬 수 있다(이택, 같은 글. pp. 167-168 참조).

이와는 좀 다른 방법이기는 하지만 선택한 특정의 작품을 여러 번 읽는 것도 좋다. 예를 들어, 집중하여 **빠른 속도로** 하루에 8번씩(아침에 두 번, 점심에 두 번, 저녁에 두 번, 잠자기 전에 두 번) 한 달 동안을 읽는다면 그 책을 무의식적으로 외울 수 있을 정도가 될 것이다. 이런 방식으로 한 해에 12권의 소설을 읽는다고 하면 거기서 획득한 어휘, 문장구조, 수사법 등과 같은 지식과 독해능력은 다른 책을 읽는 데에도 전이되어 쉽게 읽을 수 있을 것이다. 다시 말해 전이효과를 통해 독해능력을 크게 향상시킬 수 있다.

조선시대에 한학을 배우는 서당의 서생들이 천자문과 사서삼경을 계속 반복하여 외우고 써보게 하는 훈련을 함으로써 다른 어려운 한문 문장이나 서책을 읽고 쓸 줄 알게 만든 방법도 역시 제한 독서 방법과 같은 이론적 맥락에 속한다고 할 수 있다. 이와는 적용 영역을 달리하는 것으로 읽기가 아닌 쓰기 영역에 속하기는 하지만 불교에서 수행을 위한 한 가지 방편으로 사용되는 사경(寫經)도, 그리고 영어 듣기 훈련을 위해 한 개의 좋은 영어 음성녹음 테이프를 선택하여 계속해서 여러 번 반복적으로 듣는 방법도 역시 이러한 제한 독서의 원리를 원용한 것이라 할 수 있다.

4.8 속독

속독(rapid reading)은 읽기를 처음 배우고 몇 년이 지나면 단어나 문장을 일일이 소리 내어 읽지 않고도 글을 읽을 수 있게 된다는 사실을 보여준다. 애들러와 반 도렌에 의하면(독고 앤 옮김, 같은 책. pp. 50-51), 눈의 움직임을 찍은 영상물을 보면 어린이나 책을 잘 읽지 못하는 사람들의 눈은 한 줄 읽을 때 많으면 대여섯 번 멈춘다. 눈이 움직일 때는 보이지 않는 상태고 멈추어 있을 때만 보인다는 것인데, 결국 한 줄에서 두세 단어로 묶은 구절들만 읽을 수 있다는 말이다. 게다가 두세 줄 읽으면 눈이 역행, 즉 앞에 있었던 곳으로 다시 간다. 이런 습관은 읽는 속도를 떨어뜨린다. 눈과 달리 두뇌는 한 번에 한두 단어 이상을 읽을 수 있다. 두뇌라는 기가 막힌 도구는 "한눈에" 한 문장 또는 한 문단까지 읽을 수가 있다. 눈이 그만큼의 정보를 제공해주기만 하면 말이다. 그러므로 먼저 책 읽는 속도를 떨어뜨리는 눈의 움직임을 교정시켜주어야 한다.

눈의 움직임이 멈추는 습관은 고쳐야 한다. 그것을 고치는 데는 여러 가지 방법이 있는데, 복잡하고 비용이 드는 방법도 있지만 손만 있으면 간단히 할 수 있다. 엄지와 집게 및 가운데 손가락을 붙여 책 위에 올려놓고 책 읽듯이 이쪽 끝에서 저쪽 끝으로 움직인다. 이때 눈으로 따라갈 수 있는 속도보다 약간 빠르게 손을 움직이고 눈은 꼭 손을 따라가도록 한다. 얼마 지나지 않아 손의 움직임만큼 빠르게 읽을 수 있게 된다. 꾸준히 연습하면서 손의 빠르기만큼 속도를 높이면 자신도 모르는 새 두 배, 세 배 빨리 읽을 수 있다.

읽기에서 속도와 이해력은 별개의 요소이지만 상관관계가 있다(이하 부분은 송영희, 같은 논문. pp. 5-6 참조). Ferguson(1973)에 따르면, 독자는 느리게 읽으면 친숙하지 못한 어휘에 겁을 먹어 제대로 읽지 못하게 됨과 동시에 세부사항에 지나치게 주의를 기울임으로써 전체적인 이해에 방해를 받는다. 그러므로 이해를 잘 하기 위해서는 읽는 속도를 증가시킬 필요가 있다.

Nuttal(1996)도 역시 속독이 의미 파악에 기여한다고 하였다. 그는 '약한 독자의 악순환'을 설명하면서 느리게 읽기로부터 기인하는 좌절감을 지적했다. 이해를 못하는 독자는 대개 읽기 속도가 느리고, 따라서 읽는 데 시간이 많이 걸리므로 읽기를 즐기지 못한다. 그 결과 많이 읽지 못함으로써 악순환이 계속된다. 그러나 읽는 속도를 증가시킴으로써 독자는 '훌륭한 독자의 선순환'에 들어 갈 수 있다. 더 빨리 읽음으로써 독자는 더 많이 읽게 되고, 더 많이 읽음으로써 이해력이 향상된다.

영어 속독의 효과는 다음의 다섯 가지로 요약할 수 있다(de Lopez 1993: 50-61).

① 단어 대 단어의 번역하기와 모르는 단어가 나올 때마다 사전 찾기의 습관을 없애는 것을 도와준다.
② 모든 단어들을 이해하지 않고서도 텍스트의 상당한 부분을 이해

할 수 있다는 것을 보여줌으로써 독자의 자신감을 증대시킨다.
③ 독자에게 읽기 전략들을 변화시키고, 사전 지식을 더 효율적으로 활용하여 인쇄된 텍스트에 덜 의존하도록 한다.
④ 독자가 더 적극적으로 정보를 처리하고 통합하기 때문에 집중력을 증대시키는 것을 도와준다.
⑤ 문자나 단어 해독보다는 아이디어와 개념 중심으로 읽기를 촉진한다. 따라서 독자는 속독을 통해 읽는 시간을 절약하고 글의 내용을 원활하게 이해함으로써 독해를 효율적으로 할 수 있다. 뿐만 아니라 독자는 빨리 읽음으로써 많이 읽을 수 있고, 이렇게 하여 언어(영어)에 대한 흥미와 자신감을 증대시킬 수 있다.

독해 훈련의 궁극적인 목적은 짧은 시간 안에 많은 정보를 정확하게 알아내는 것이다(양재한 외, 같은 책. pp. 85-86 참조). 그러기 위해서 속독 훈련이 필요하다. 속독은 눈으로 글자만 빨리 읽는 것이 아니라, 뇌가 빨리 반응한다는 것이다. 아무리 빨리 읽어도 글을 이해하지 못한다면 빨리 읽을 필요가 없다. 대체로 속독을 못하는 아이들은 다음과 같은 특징을 가지고 있다.

- 어휘력이 부족한 경우
- 소리 내어 읽거나(음독), 입술을 달싹거리며 읽거나(순독 脣讀), 마음속으로 읽거나(內語讀), 입속에서 속삭이듯이 읽는 경우.
- 손가락으로 글자를 짚어 가면서 읽거나 는 경우
- 글자를 따라 눈동자만 이동하지 않고 머리까지 이동하며 읽는 경우
- 묵독의 훈련이 안된 경우
- 시력이 나빠 안구 운동이 안 되는 경우
- 사고력이 부족하여 민활한 사고를 할 수 없는 경우
- 심리적 안정이 안 돼 집중력이 떨어지는 경우

그러나 초등학교 시절에는 속독 훈련이 필요하지 않다. 중학교 이상 독자에게 적당하다. 훑어 읽기(skimming), 예견하기, 단어 읽기, 문장 읽기, 건너뛰기(scanning) 등을 하게 되면 1분에 1,800자 정도를 읽을 수 있다.

속독이란 문자 그대로 읽기의 행동을 빨리 한다는 말이다(손정표, 같은 책 pp. 220-221 참조). 독서 속도가 느리면 독서에 권태를 느끼게 되고 독서 정도도 낮아진다. 두뇌의 기능을 느끼는 일, 결정하는 일, 인식하는 일 등 세 가지로 나누어 볼 수 있는데 독서는 인식하는 일에 속한다. 속도가 느리면 권태와 기능 마비를 가져온다는 사실은 독서할 때는 물론이고, 느끼는 일과 결정하는 일에서도 마찬가지이다. 다시 말해 전체적으로 두뇌의 기능은 속도가 느려지면 권태와 기능 부진을 겪게 된다.

그러나 '읽기의 행동을 빨리한다'는 말은 무조건 빨리 읽기만 하면 된다는 말은 아니다. 이는 뇌의 독서 기능이 계속 개발되면서 독서 저력의 확대와 비례하여 빨라져야 비로소 최대의 독서효과를 가져오므로 '독자의 뇌의 생각하는 속도와 비례할 만큼 빨리 읽어야 된다'는 말이다. 즉 이해를 하면서 읽는 행동을 빨리 하는 것으로, 적어도 이해하는 정도는 같고 시간을 단축하여 읽는 법, 또는 이해의 정도도 일단 높이고 읽는 시간도 단축시켜서 읽는 법 등을 말한다. 아무리 빨리 읽더라도 글의 중심 사상이 무엇인지 요점이나 요지가 무엇인지 모른다든지, 또 의미를 이해하는 데 시간이 많이 걸린다든지 하는 독서는 아무런 의의가 없다. 따라서 속독 지도의 근본적 목표는 무엇보다도 글의 중심이 되는 내용과 그들과 얽혀 있는 세부적인 내용들의 관계를 될 수 있는 한 빠를 속도로 파악하여 전체의 짜임새를 한 묶음으로 뭉뚱그려 이해하는 능력을 길러 주자는 데 있다.

속독을 저해하는 요인 중 몇 가지를 들면 다음과 같다.

① 정류수와 정류 시간: 독서 과정 중에 한 행의 정류수가 많다든지 정류수는 적더라도 한 번 정류시 많은 시간을 소비하는 습관이 있는 경우.
② 행간 운동과 역행 운동: 한 줄을 읽고 난 후 다음 줄로 눈동자를 옮길 때 부정확하게 옮기는 습관이 있거나 독서 과정 중 읽었던 부분을 되풀이해서 읽는 습관이 있는 경우. 이러한 경우는 대체로 이미 읽은 부분에 대한 확신이 없거나 주의를 집중하지 않는 습관이 있다든지 어휘력이 부족한 탓으로 그러한 습관이 형성되는 경우가 많다.
③ 음독: 독서 입문기를 벗어났으면서도 소리를 내어 읽는다든지 눈과 뇌로만 읽지 않고 순독(脣讀: 이술을 움직이면서 읽기)을 하거나 내어독(內語讀: 마음속으로 읽기)을 하고 있다든지 또는 입 속에서 속삭이듯이 읽는 습관이 있는 경우.
④ 습관: 문자를 손가락으로 짚으면서 읽는다든지 머리를 움직이면서 읽거나 몸을 움직이면서 읽는 습관이 있는 경우.
⑤ 심리적 안정: 심리적으로 안정되어 있지 않아 정신 집중이 잘 되지 않는 경우 등을 들 수 있다. 속독의 훈련은 바로 그러한 나쁜 버릇을 제거시키고 빨리 읽으면서도 정확히 이해할 수 있는 태도와 습관을 갖게 하는 데 있다.

손정표(같은 책. pp. 222-223)는 속독 훈련을 위해 필요한 안구운동 훈련의 기본자세와 유의점 및 기본요령을 제시했는데, 먼저, 속독력 증진을 위한 기본자세로는 바른 자세를 갖추도록 주의를 환기시킨 후 다음과 같은 훈련을 실시한다.

① 허리를 곧고 바르게 편다.
② 가슴을 펴고 턱을 앞으로 당긴다.

③ 눈을 크게 뜬다.
④ 입은 다물고 이에다 혀를 자연스럽게 붙인 상태를 유지한다.
⑤ 얼굴의 콧날선과 책의 세로 중심선(제본선)을 일치시킨다.
⑥ 책과 눈의 거리는 30-40cm를 유지한다.
⑦ 책상과 몸 사이의 거리는 자기 주먹이 들어갈 정도의 간격을 유지한다.
⑧ 몸과 마음을 평온하게 한다.

그리고 안구운동 훈련시 유의점으로는 다음과 같은 것들이 있다.

① 한 행을 읽어 나갈 때의 정류수
② 한 행을 읽어 나갈 때의 역행수
③ 다음 행의 첫 머리를 찾아내기 위한 눈의 움직임
④ 정류수와 정류수 사이의 거리와 시간
⑤ 두 눈이 함께 행을 따라 움직일 때의 리드미컬한 눈의 움직임

또한 다음과 같은 기본요령을 수시로 주지시킨다.

① 빨리 읽으려는 태도로 읽는다.
② 묵독(목독)을 하도록 한다.
③ 눈동자가 글자 위에서 멈추는 횟수를 되도록 줄이고, 한번 멈출 때마다 한꺼번에 많은 글자를 빨리 보도록 한다.
④ 행간 운동에 시간을 소비하지 않도록 하며, 눈동자는 전진만 하되 되돌아갔다 오는 예가 없도록 한다.
⑤ 손가락으로 짚어가거나 머리를 움직이지 말고 눈동자만 움직여 읽도록 한다.
⑥ 책을 읽을 때는 독서에 정신을 집중하도록 한다.

4.9 총체적 언어 접근법에서의 독서 모델

아동문학 읽기에서 총체적 언어교육 접근법(whole language approach)에 기반을 둔 읽기 모델을 중심으로 살펴보고자 한다(이경우, 『총체적 언어-문학적 접근을 중심으로』. pp. 19-22 참조). 심리 언어학자인 Ken(neth) Goodman(1976)이 공헌한 것은 언어 학습에 있어 조각조각 단편적으로 접근하는 것에 대해 반기를 든 것이다. 그는 학교에서의 언어학습은 가정에서 배우는 것처럼 쉬워야 함을 강조하면서 읽기 발달의 연구에 기반을 둔 읽기 심리 언어적 모델, 즉 '전체에서 부분으로의 접근(top-down model)'을 제안했다.

Goodman(1976)은 읽기란 기존의 읽기에서 정확한 것, 자세한 것, 연속적 개념과 글자, 단어, 언어의 인식을 포함하는 정밀한 과정이라는 관념을 반박하여, 언어란 '그것이 총체적일 때에만 언어일 수 있다'고 보아 언어는 항상 총체적 구조로 유지되어야 한다고 보았다. 따라서 읽기와 쓰기를 위한 총체적 언어 접근은 '이야기→글자'로 향하는 모델을 제시하였다.

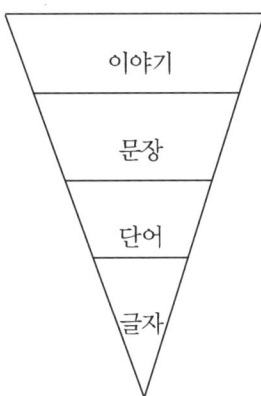

읽기 교수의 심리 언어적 모델: '전체에서 부분으로의 접근(top-down model)'

Goodman에 의하면 총체적 언어 학습은 '확실한 문해 사건'이다. 이 이론에 의하면 언어의 소유권은 어린이에게 있는 것이다. 예를 들어 어린이에게 어떤 단어를 전체 맥락이나 의미가 없는 상황에서 연습하게 한 후 철자법을 아는지 평가한다면 당장은 잘 쓸 수 있을 것이다. 그러나 어린이가 연습한 단어를 다른 맥락에서 이해하고 쓸 수 있는지 살펴본다면 그렇지 못할 것이다. 그렇다면 이러한 현상이 일어나는 이유는 무엇인가? 그것은 어린이에게 소개된 단어는 '확실한 문해 사건'과 연결되지 않았으므로, 어린이는 그 단어를 자기 자신의 것으로 만들지 못했기 때문이다. 즉, 의미 없는 맥락에서 분절되어 소개되었기 때문인 것이다. 전체적 맥락이 없었으며 어린이의 생활이나 흥미와는 동떨어진 것이었기 때문이다.

총체적 언어 학습에서는 언어의 학습과정을 단원이나 주제별로 나누지 않고 통합하여 어린이가 접하는 문맥의 풍부함을 전체적으로 유지하도록 하는 데 중점을 둔다. 통합적 접근은 언어 과정을 자연스럽게 유지하는 데 치중하면서 개념학습을 가능하게 하도록 한다.

Rosenblatt(1978) 역시 어린이는 전체적으로 의미를 이루는 덩어리인 전체 이야기와 교류(transaction)하는 경험을 해야 한다는 점을 중요시하였다. 그는 '읽기란 교류적인 것'이라고 말했다. 따라서 각 어린이는 의미를 나름대로 해석하여 받아들인다는 생각을 지지하였다. 어린이는 이미 언어 개념을 가지고 있지만 좋은 그림책을 볼 때 새롭게 터득될 수 있는 지식의 세계와 만나게 되며, 이것이 바로 책과의 교류인 것이다.

어린이는 교류 과정에서 옛날에 가지고 있던 지식을 새 지식으로 바꾸면서 새로운 것을 배우게 되는 것이다. 따라서 어린이에게는 좋은 그림책을 주는 것이 중요하다. 어린이가 그림이 독특하고 내용이 풍부한 그림책을 보는 동안, 그림책에 있는 내용에 대해 총체적으로 응답하고, 상상하고, 그리고 문자를 인식하게 된다.

Holdaway(1979)는 어린이들이 성공적으로 언어를 배우는 모델을, 어린이가 부모와의 상호관계에서 말을 배우는 방법에서 찾아내었다. 그는 이를 일컬어 습득적 학습(acquisition learning)이라고 표현하며 부모가 어린이에게 책을 읽어 주는 시간을 갖는 것에 의의를 두었다. 다시 말하면 부모가 어린이에게 책을 읽어 주는 양상은 가르치기 위해서 뿐만 아니라, 즐겁게 해 주기 위해서 읽어 주는데, 바로 이 경험이 보람있는 사회적 학습 유형이라는 것을 발견하였다. 부모와 함께 하는 독서의 경험은 어린이들에게 가장 행복하고 안정감을 느끼는 경험이라는 것이다. Holdaway는 부모가 어린이에게 책을 읽어 주는 구어 학습의 행동 순환에 기초하여 학급에서 사용될 수 있는 교수전략을 개발하였다. 소위 '함께 나누는 독서 경험(shared book experience)'의 중요성에 대해 일깨워 주었다. Holdaway는 학습의 순환 이론을 발전시키면서 학급에서 좋은 책을 사용할 것과 크기가 큰 책을 사용할 것을 제안하였다. 그가 언급한 또 다른 주제는 어린이들이 자율적인 문해 학습자가 되는 중요한 요소는 스스로 교정하고 조절하는 행위를 발전시키는 데 있어서 교사의 역할이 중요하다는 것이다.

   Routman(1988)은, 실제 교실에서 어린이를 가르치면서 독본으로부터 문학적 접근으로의 전이의 중요성, 실제 예, 추천 도서 목록을 유치원(Kindergarten)~초등학교 단계까지 소개하였다. 그녀는 어린이도 가설을 세우고, 가설에 따라 활동을 하는 중에 실수하고, 스스로 수정하는 동안 학습하게 된다고 보았다. 이런 모습은 어린이의 쓰기-긁적거리기(scribing), 거꾸로 쓰기(reversed letters), 창안하여 글자 쓰기(invented spelling), 그리고 읽기에 나타나는데, 그 과정에서 언어를 습득하게 된다고 말했다. 또한 어린이는 좋은 문학 책을 읽고 창안하고 실수하는 동안 의미가 통하지 않는다는 경험을 하고 스스로 고쳐가며 의미를 파악하게 된다고 하였다. 이와 맥락을 같이 해서 글짓기의 단계에 대해서도 언급하였다. 즉, 어린이가 한 이야기를 읽고 재구성을 할 때 보이는 단계는 네 단계로 나타나는데, ① (원문에 의거한) 반복적 양상으로 짓기, ② 부분적으로 변화시켜 짓기, ③ 대부분의 내용을 변화시켜 새 이야기 짓기, ④ 그리고 (원문의) 이야기의 요소를 유지한 채 완전히 새 이야기 짓기의 단계로 발달해 간다고 하였다.

4.10 버텨읽기와 굽혀읽기

예를 들면 영문학이 문화로서 수입되었을 때 제국주의와 밀접한 관련이 있을 수 있다. 이러한 외국문학 작품을 읽을 때는 각별히 주체적으로 읽을 필요가 있다(강내희, "영문학의 연구와 버텨읽기". 『외국문학』 1987년 봄. 제12호. pp. 135-147 참조). 영문학이 어떤 특수성으로 인하여 독서하는 우리의 판단력을 흐리게 하는 무엇을 가지고 있다면 주체적인 독서는 그 위험에 대처하는 방식으로 진행되어야 한다. 영문학이 억압의 무게를 가진다면 주체적인 독서는 그 무게에 맞서야 한다. '버텨읽기'는 이러한 주체적인 독서의 모습이다. 이에 대립되는 독서방식을 우리는 '굽혀읽기'라고 부를 수 있을 것이다. 즉 어떠한 비판의식도 없이 순종적으로 반응하며 수용적인 태도로만 읽는 것이다.

버텨읽기는 일종의 저항적 독서로서 이러한 독서법은 대상의 수용에만 몰두하는 '공부'의 방식과는 거리가 멀다. '공부'의 태도는 공부하는 사람으로 하여금 자세를 낮추고 몸을 굽히게 하는 것이므로 '굽혀읽기'의 독서방식을 택하게 한다. 반면에 버텨읽기는 독서자의 태도를 당당하게 만들고 주체적인 학문을 하게 하는 '연구'의 방식이다. 이것은 읽는 대상이 그 나타난 모습과는 다른 면을 가지고 있음을 간파하고자 하므로 깊이 읽는 것이기도 하다. 이런 점에서 버텨읽기는 문학 작품 속에 여간해서는 가려내어 보기가 힘든 모습으로 잠복해 있는 전략을 간파해내며, 그 문학이 강요하는 가치체계나 세계관의 수용에만 급급하는 굽혀읽기가 얼마나 무의미한가를 일깨우는 역할을 한다.

버텨읽기는 문학에 있어서 '재현'의 문제에 각별한 관심을 가진다. 독자의 판단력을 흐리게 하는 일이 바로 재현에서 비롯되기 때문이다. 재현은 현실속의 대상을 형상화함으로써 그 형상화된 대상을 현실과 유리시켜 어떤 '독자적인 세계'를 갖게 한다. 이 '독자적인 세계'는 현실과 완전히 유리될 수는 없지만 재현의 주체에 의해 현실세계의 실재성과 진정성을 왜곡시켜 놓을 수 있다. 영문학에 있어서 재현의 주체는 영문학의 작품세계와 이론을 구축하는 영미인이고, 우리는 재현의 객체(대상)이다. 여기서 '우리'는 한국인을 포함한 우리와 비슷한 처지에 있는 사람들, 예컨대 제3세계인 아일랜드, 아랍, 북미대륙, 카리브해, 남아프리카, 인도 등과 같은 나라의 사람들로서 강대국의 피식민지인, 피압박 국민들을 일컬을 수 있다. 이러한 나라의 사람들이 영문학에서는 중요한 재현의 대상이 되기 때문에 '우리'는 영문학에서 '타자화' 되어 있다. 영미인이 주체가 되는 영문학에서 '우리'가 타자로 형상화되어 있는 것은 당연한지 모른다. 그러나 재현을 통해 '우리'를 형상화했다는 사실에는 영미인이 '경험한' '우리'가 주체로서가 아닌 대상으로서 자리 잡고 있다는 점이 문제가 될 수 있다. 제국주의적 주체의 '경험'이 어떤 것이었느냐에 따라 '우리'의 모습도 자의적으로 바꿔지는 것이다. 제국의 변방에 있는 사람인 '우리'는 타자로 파악되면서 중심부의 주체와 '다른' 존재로 정의되며, 이처럼 타자화된 인간은 중심부의 제국주의적 주체와는 달리 주체가 되지 못하는 열등한 신분으로 인식된다. 버텨읽기가 주체적인 독서행위인 것은 바로 이러한 타자화의 과정을 재현 속에서 들추어내어 변방인/주변인으로서의 열등하고 무능한 위상을 본래의 당당한 주체로 회복시키는 일에 기여하기 때문이다.

영문학 중에서 『로빈슨 크루소』는 버텨읽기의 대상으로 좋은 자료가 될 수 있다. '크루소' 하면 우리는 무인도를 연상하고 무인도에서 혼자 수십년을 살았다는 놀라운 사실을 생각한다. 또한 그가 앵무새를 길러 말을 가르치고 프라이데이란 '식인종'을 구원한 것을 기억한다. 이런 생각들을 거의 자동적으로 한다면 우리는 하나의 버릇이 고착되어 있는 셈이다. 크루소의 '신화'가 구축한 세계를 아주 자연스럽고 당연한 것으로 받아들인다. 이것은 생경한 하나의 문화체제가 수없이 반복하여 들려짐으로써 일상경험의 한 부분이 되고 친밀하게 된 것이다. 작품 안에서 크루소는 프라이데이의 육체적, 정신적 구원자로 나온다. 그런데 깊게 살펴보면 크루소의 구원행위는 서구 중심적 태도임을 알 수 있다. 식인종에게 끌려온 프라이데이의 목숨을 구한 다음 그를 기독교인으로 만들어 영혼을 '구원'하는 데서도 이런 태도는 계속된다. 그는 "불쌍한 야만인의 영혼을 구하여 진정한 종교, 기독교의 교리를 참으로 알게 하는 신의 도구"가 되었다고 믿는다. 크루소는 무인도로 오기 전에 무어인들에게 잡힌 적이 있는데 그때 쥬리라는 아랍소년을 어떤 스페인 선장에게 팔아버리는데 쥬리가 성인이 되고 기독교로 개종하면 해방시켜 줄 것이라는 선장의 약속을 듣고서이다. 이때 쥬리는 자기를 노예로 부리려는 선장에게 "기꺼이 가겠다"고 말한다. 프라이데이도 쥬리와 비슷하게 말한다. 프라이데이는 더듬거리며 되지도 않는 영어로 "당신 좋은 일 많이 해....당신 야만사람들 좋고 점잖고 온순한 사람들 되게 가르쳐" 라고 하는 것이다. 이것은 크루소 자신이 듣고 싶어하는 말이다. 크루소는 프라이데이의 목숨을 구할 때건 영혼을 구할 때건 자기중심적으로만 생각한다고 볼 수 있다. 크루소는 문명에서 자연으로 완전히 복귀하여 서구문학에 자주 등장하는 '야생인'(Wild Man)과 같다. 그러나 그에게 자연은 어떤 특징을 실현시킬 수 있는 환경이며, 자연에 복귀한다는 것은 자연 속에 묻혀 동화된다는 것이 아니라 자연을 자기방식으로 장악한다는 것이다. 즉 자연은 인간중심적 이용의 대상일 뿐이다. 식인종이 개종, 개화되면 유럽인이 세계를 누비는 데 중요한 자산이 된다. 왜냐하면 프라이데이처럼 개화된 식인종은 그들의 세계가 문명세계에 편입되는 과정에서 도구로 이용될 수 있기 때문이다. 우리는 이 작품의 재현세계를 통해서 '크루소'의 이름과 관련된 하나의 신화가 유럽인이 비유럽인을 보는 관점, 영국인이 카리브해의 한 원주민과 그가 대변하는 사회를 보는 관점에 의하여 영향 받고 있는 제국주의적 신화임을 알 수 있다. 독서에서 우리가 주의 깊게 살펴야 할 것은 재현이 어떤 방식으로 현실에 관계를 맺는지 알아보는 것이다. 우리는 이 작품의 재현방식을 읽는 독서방식을 스스로 자기 점검할 필요가 있다. 버텨읽기와 굽혀읽기는 이를 위해 필요한 개념이다.

아래에서 이와 같은 버텨읽기 방식의 입장에 서 있는 미국 인디아나대학교 교수인 패트릭 브랜틀링거(Patrick Brantlinger)의 『로빈슨 크루소』에 대한 문화비평론적 관점을 소개한다(Patrick Brantlinger, *Crusoe's Footprints: Cultural Studies in Britain and America*, 1990. 김용규·전봉철·정병언 옮김, 『영미문화 연구-로빈슨크루소의 발자국』. 서울: 문화과학사, 2000. pp. 13-16 참조)

▌"로빈슨크루소의 발자국-악몽의 섬"

애덤 스미스(Adam Smith)에서 맑스(Karl Marx)를 거쳐 그 이후의 경제학자들에게 종종 부르주아의 합리성과 생산성의 모델이 되어 왔던 크루소는 어쩌면 그 못지않게 부르주아의 비합리성과 억압의 모델이 될 수도 있다. "식인종"들이 결국 그의 고립 속에 실제로 침입하고 있다는 사실에도 불구하고, 크루소는 2년간 자신의 발자국에 시달린다. 물론 글자 그대로 그의 진짜 발자국에 시달리는 것이 아니라, 모래 속에 찍힌 실제의 발자국처럼 그의 뇌리에 굳게 박혀 있는 정신적 이미지로서의 발자국에 시달린다. 그는 발자국에 사로잡혀 있다. 아니, 발자국이 그를 사로잡고 있다. 발자국은 고립된 크루소가 혼자서도 잘 살아갈 수 있다는 강한 자신감을 발견하면서 깜박 잊고 있었던 피할 수 없는 타자(the Other)-모든 타자들-의 이미지가 된다.

 물론, 이 모든 것은 "타자"가 나타나면서 변한다. 처음에는 "식인종들"이 나타나며, 그들로부터 크루소는 "프라이데이"를 구출한다. 총기와 기습하기에 적절한 천혜의 환경에다 이제는 프라이데이까지 조수로 거느리고 있기 때문에 크루소는 "타자"인 식인종들을 물리칠 수가 있다. 나중에 그는 유럽인 "구조대"를 만나게 된다. 그리하여 크루소는 발자국을 본 수 그가 가장 두려워했던 운명, 즉 야만인들에게 잡아먹히게 될 운명에서 벗어난다. 그러나 그는 또한 프라이데이라고 하는 한 야만인에게서 야만과는 정반대되는 것을 발견한다. 프라이데이는 식인종적 기질-크루소는 프라이데이에게서 이러한 기질을 반드시 제거해야 한다-을 지니고 있음에도 불구하고, 믿을 수 없을 정도로 유순하고 사근사근하다는 것이 밝혀진다. "왜냐하면 프라이데이가 나에게 하는 것보다 더 충직하고 사랑스럽고 성실하게 구는 하인을 둔 사람은 결코 없었기 때문이다. 그는 흥분하거나 골을 내거나 딴마음을 품지 않고 더없이 감사하는 마음으로 일에 열중했다. 그의 애정 그 자체는 마치 자식의 애정이 아버지에게 매여 있는 것처럼 나에게 매여 있었다"(211)

 크루소는 자신이 지배할(master) 수 없는 것-또는 자신을 "주인"(master)이라 부를 수 없는 것-을 그저 야만과 무인도로 간주한다. 반면에, 프라이데이는 크루소의 어두운 복제본, 즉 그림자-자아(shadow-self)에 지나지 않으며, 언제든지 크루소의 분부를 받들 준비가 되어 있다. 결국 크루소의 최초의 직관은 옳았다. 프라이데이의 발자국-즉, 진짜 발자국-은 크루소 자신의 것이었으며 2년 동안 크루소를 그토록 겁에 지리게 했던 것은 그의 그림자였던 것이다. 크루소는 프라이데이의 이름을 지어 주고, 그에게 영어를 가르치고, 그에게 주로 명령조, 제국주의의 명령법으로 말한다. 따라서 크루소는 프라이데이를 구해

준 후에도 이전과 마찬가지로 여전히 크게 고립되어 있다. 이러한 고립은 타자들의 목소리와 몸짓을 통한 자기인식, 평등, 연대 등과 반대되는 지배에 함축되어 있다. 어쩌면 발자국은 결국 환각이나 신기루, 또는 지나치게 햇빛을 많이 쬐었거나 너무 오래 고립된 데서 생겨난 산물에 지나지 않을 것이다. 그리고 어쩌면 식인종과 프라이데이 역시 대상없는 공포와 크루소 자신이 이해하지 못하는 지배욕의 그림자, 즉 환영에 지나지 않을 것이다. 식인종과 프라이데이가 발자국이 "실재"하는 것과 똑같은 의미로 "실재"하는 것은 틀림없는 사실이다. 그러나 그들은 차라리 크루소의 공포와 욕망에 의해 모래와 하늘과 물에 투사된 이미지에 불과하다고 하는 편이 더 나을지도 모른다. 궁극적으로 어떤 의미에서는 크루소가 발자국이라는 단서를 살아 있는 현실, 즉 살아 있는 사람에게 적용해도 단서를 해독할 수 없는 것과 꼭 마찬가지로 그는 "식인종"에 대해 아무 말고 할 수 없고 아무 것도 알 수 없다.

심지어는 프라이데이조차도 크루소의 창조물이다. 왜냐하면 프라이데이는 크루소가 가르쳐 준 "주인님"이라는 말밖에 하지 못하기 때문이다. 그는 사람이라기 보다는 앵무새나 다름없다. 크루소는 프라이데이의 언어를 구사하는 법을 결코 배우지 않는다. 크루소의 언어는 두 사람의 공용어이다.

아마 크루소가 발견한 발자국에 상응하는 진짜 발이 있었을 것이다. 아마 크루소가 두려워하고 싸우고 죽이거나 몰아내는 이미지와 그림자들에 상응하는 진짜 식인종들이 있었을 것이다. 그러나 크루소가 알고 있는 것은 단지 이미지들뿐이다. 이 섬과 그 자신의 경험에서 그는 오로지 자신이 원하는 것이나 발견하고 싶지 않은 것만 발견한다. 발자국의 발견은 그의 고립을 끝내지 못한다. 그것은 그의 고립을 부각시킬 뿐이다. 심지어는 프라이데이의 구출도 그의 고립을 끝내는 것이 아니라 단지 그의 고립을 다른 형태로 심화시킬 뿐이다—이제 그는 이

기심 없는/사심 없는 하인의 "주인「지배자」"일 뿐이다-크루소의 유아론은 역사를 통해서 사람들을 주인과 하인으로 갈라놓은 온갖 형태의 제국주의와 정치적 구분에 대한 우화로 읽을 수 있다. 데포(Daniel Defoe)가 의도했던 교훈이 지배-자기지배(자제)를 포함해서-가 곧 제1의 가치임을 강조하는 것임은 의심의 여지가 없다. 그러나 크루소의 지배-섬, 식인종, 프라이데이, 운명 등에 대한 지배-에서 자기지배(자제)의 정반대인 일종의 광기를 엿볼 수도 있을 것 같다.

4.11 비판적 독서

다음은 '비판적 독서'(critical reading)에 관해 살펴본다(양재한 외, 같은 책. pp. 88-89 참조). 비판적 사고란 어떠한 사실이나 상황에 대한 판단이나 평가활동을 하는 뇌의 기능이다. 비판적 사고는 객관성, 정직성, 융통성, 체계성 등을 필요로 한다. 인간에게 비판적 사고력이 부족하면 남의 말에 무조건 따르기만 하는 주관이 없는 사람이 되던가, 아니면 남의 말에 무조건 반대만 하는 편협한 사람이 되어 다른 사람들에게 무시당하거나 따돌림을 당하게 된다.

책을 읽는다는 것은 저자와 독자와의 대화이다. 비판적 읽기란 글에 대하여 독자가 개성적으로 반응하는 것을 말한다. 글을 비판적으로 읽는다는 것은 단순히 이해하며 읽기와는 달리, 그 글의 값어치, 질에 대하여 판단하는 것이므로 특히 비문학적 글인 선전문, 설명문, 광고문 등을 읽을 때 필요하다.

비판적 독서를 위해서는 다음과 같은 사항에 주안점을 둔다.

- 글의 사실성, 진실성을 비판해 본다. (설명문)
- 사상이나 논리의 타당성과 공정성, 자료의 정확성과 적절성 등을

판단한다. (논설문)
- 과장된 표현은 없는지 판단해 본다. (선전문)
- 잘못된 표현이 없나 생각해 본다. (시)
- 각 문단의 놓일 자리가 적당한지 전개의 자연성을 비판해 본다. (산문)
- 결말은 이래야만 했을까? 결말의 타당성을 비판해본다. (산문)
- 글쓴이의 태도가 주관적인가, 객관적인가를 생각해 보고, 비판해 본다. (모든 글)
- 저자의 주장은 타당한가를 비판해 본다.
- 글감이나 주제가 같은 글을 읽고, 관점이나 논조, 문체 등의 차이에 대해 토의한다.
- 글을 읽고, 인물의 성격, 행동, 의도 등을 판단한다.
- 글에 드러나 있거나 숨어 있는 필자의 의도나 목적에 대해 토의하고, 주장의 신뢰성과 수용 가능성을 판단한다.

독해력의 단계에 따른 읽기방법

양재한·김수경·김석임은 그들이 공저한 『어린이 독서지도론』에서 독해력의 단계에 따라 읽기방법을 몇 갈래로 구분하여 제시하였다(pp. 81-86).

독해는 훈련을 받으면 향상되는 일종의 기능이다. 일반적으로 학력이 높은 사람이 낮은 사람보다 독해력이 높다. 그러나 실험에 의하면 학력이 낮은 사람이라도 독해력 훈련을 받을 경우 학력이 높은 사람을 앞지를 수 있다. 이 독해력은 독서 생활만을 좌우하는 것이 아니라 학교 교육의 전반에 영향을 미친다. 독해력의 높고 낮음은 학교성적과 비례한다.

독해력은 몇 단계로 나눌 수 있으며, 각 단계마다 읽는 방법이 다르다. 만화책을 읽을 때, 신문을 읽을 때, 참고서를 읽을 때, 시를 읽을 때, 동화책을 읽을 때마다 각각 읽는 방법이 다르다. 모든 독자는 의식적으로 혹은 무의식적으로, 독서 자료와 목적에 따라 읽는 방법을 달리한다.

5.1 줄거리 읽기

초등학교 1학년에게 『토끼와 거북이』란 동화책을 읽게 한 후 대강의 줄거리를 물으면 대체로 줄거리를 잘 이해하고 있다. 이것은 이야기의 전개 과정이 시간 단위로 명확한 줄거리를 가지고 있기 때문이다.

줄거리 읽기란 긴 글을 줄거리의 형태로 간편하게 이해하고 기억하는 독해 방법이다. 줄거리 읽기는 책의 내용을 시간적 순서에 따라 재배치하는 것(대과거-중과거-과거-현재)이다. 즉 책의 내용을 시간적 순서에 따라 재배치하는 읽기의 독특한 방법이다. 줄거리 읽기는 주의 집중력이 약한 어린이와 독해력이 낮은 일반 대중에게 필수적인 기능이다.

　그림책이나, 전래동화, 생활동화 등은 줄거리가 뚜렷한 책이므로 줄거리 읽기 훈련을 쉽게 할 수 있다. 줄거리가 없거나 미숙한 책들은 언제, 어디서, 누가 무엇을 어떻게, 왜 했다는 내용으로 줄거리를 재구성하여 읽으며 독해에 도움이 된다.

5.2 요점 읽기

　줄거리 읽기가 있는 그대로의 줄거리를 순서대로 재배치하는 방법이라면, 요점 읽기는 독자 스스로 중요한 부분을 골라 읽는 방법이다. 이는 초등학교 저학년에서 길러져야 한다. 요점 읽기는 긴 글을 보다 정확하게 읽기 위한 독해의 한 방법이다. 줄거리가 눈에 보이는 사건의 나열이라면, 요점은 눈에 안 보이는 얼마쯤은 숨어 있는 어떤 생각이나 의도일 수도 있다. 요점에는 줄거리, 주제, 인물의 성격도 포함된다.

　요점 읽기 능력이 부족하면 오랜 시간 글을 읽어도 글 속에 있는 내용이 머리 속에 정리되지 않는다. 요점 고르는 능력이 부족한 사람은 읽은 글을 이야기해 보라고 하면 중언부언하거나 중요하지 않은 부분을 중요한 부분과 동등하게 말하고, 중요하지 않은 부분을 장황하게 이야기하기도 한다.

　글의 요점은 독서 자료와 목적에 따라 다를 수도 있다. 즉 교과서와 같은 설명문은 정의나 규칙이 요점이 될 수 있고, 문학 책을 읽을 때는 주제가 요점이 되고, 위인전을 읽을 때는 성장의 동기가 요점이 된다.

  요점 읽기는 초등학교 저학년에 길러져야 할 독해의 기본능력이다. 어릴 때부터 짧은 글 속에서 중요하지 않은 낱말과 문장을 찾아내는 훈련이나, 중요한 낱말이나 문장을 찾아 밑줄을 긋기, 이를 다른 사람들에게 이야기하기 훈련을 통해 요점 읽기 능력을 향상시킬 수 있다.

5.3 훑어 읽기

  뉴미디어의 발달로 정보 수집 능력은 현대인에게 무엇보다 필요한 능력이다. 따라서 정보의 홍수 속에서 현대인들은 짧은 시간 안에 필요한 정보를 많이 얻을 수 있는 능력이 필요하게 되었다. 이러한 능력을 기르는 가장 확실한 방법은 훑어 읽기이다. 정보를 얻는 것은 이미 있는 정보에 새로운 정보를 추가하여 새로운 지식 체계를 만드는 것이므로 훑어 읽기는 독자의 지식체계를 넓혀준다. 이 방법에는 목적에 따라 두 가지로 나눌 수 있다.

① 단순 훑어 읽기 : 전체적으로 무엇이 씌어져 있나 살필 경우(신문, 잡지 등을 살필 때)
② 목표 훑어 읽기 : 찾고자 하는 특정한 정보를 얻고자 자료를 읽을 경우(조사하는 숙제, 보고서 쓸 때, 참고서나 백과사전 등을 읽을 때)

  훑어 읽기는 초등학교 1학년에서 성인에 이르기까지 누구나 가지고 있어야 할 독해능력이다.

앞에서 언급한 독서기술과 독서방법에 따른 분류에서는 여기서 말하는 훑어 읽기는 '훑어 읽기'(skimming)와 '찾아 읽기'(scanning)로 분리하였다. 전자는 단순 훑어 읽기에 해당되며, 후자는 목표 훑어 읽기에 해당된다.

5.4 뭉뚱그리며 읽기

글을 이해한다는 것은 글의 내용을 한마디나 몇 개의 문장으로 뭉뚱그릴 수 있다는 말과 같다. 독서란 긴 글을 읽고 한 마디로 뭉뚱그리거나 요약하는 과정이다. 특히 문학 책을 읽거나 교과서를 공부할 때 필요한 기술이라고 할 수 있다. 뭉뚱그리기는 종합적 사고력(나열되거나 대립되어 있는 사물의 개념을 통일시켜 하나의 의미로 정립시키는 능력)을 요구한다.

또한 글의 내용을 핵심 단어나 핵심 문장으로 바꾸어 내는 요약 작업이다. 요약은 내용을 유지하면서 길이만 짧게 하는 것으로 글 속의 중요한 요소를 뽑을 수 있어야 한다. 요약이나 뭉뚱그리기 속에는 글을 비판하는 자신의 의견을 넣어서는 안 된다. 뭉뚱그리기는 초등학교 3학년부터 성인에 이르기까지 누구에게나 필요한 능력이다.

5.5 분석하며 읽기

독자가 책을 읽을 때 내부에 숨어 있는 골격을 찾아야만 완벽한 독서가 될 수 있다. 이 때 필요한 것이 분석적 독서이다. 우리가 글을 읽는 것은 그 속에 쓰여 있는 주제를 알기 위한 것이다. 주제를 알기 위해서는 글의 부분 부분을 나누어서 알아보아야 한다. 이러한 읽기를 분석적 읽기라고 한다. 분석적으로 읽기 위해서는 다음과 같은 방법들이 있다.

첫째, 글의 아웃 라인(outline)을 알아본다. 이 글은 무엇에 대한 글인가를 알기 위해 제목, 서문 등을 참조한다.

둘째, 글의 짜임을 알아본다. 글의 종류에 따라 서론, 본론, 결론 혹은 기승전결, 혹은 두괄식, 미괄식으로 분석해 볼 수 있다.

셋째, 글의 구성(plot)을 알아본다. 사건의 인과관계나 원인과 결과를 알아내는 것이다.

넷째, 저자의 의도를 알아낸다. 저자가 어떤 말을 자주 사용하며, 어떤 말에 의미를 두는지 살핀다. 핵심 단어나 핵심 문장을 파악한다.

5.6 관계 읽기

관계 읽기란 글 속의 아이디어나 중요한 개념들의 의미 관계를 따져가며 읽는 독해 방법이다. 이 읽기 방법은 예시, 분류, 특성, 정의, 유사, 비교, 순서, 인과관계, 이음말 읽기 등을 따져 보며 읽는 것이다.

5.7 구조화하며 읽기

사람의 생각에는 구조가 있다. 글의 의미를 아는 일은 이 생각의 구조를 이해하는 일이다. 줄거리 읽기가 글의 내용을 시각화하는 것이라면 구조화하기는 내용을 공간화 시키는 일이다.

첫째, 문학책은 구조화를 통해 복잡한 주제가 선명하게 드러난다. 문학책은 일반적으로 2항 대립구조(옛이야기, 선과 악, 예 : 흥부와 놀부 등)와 3항 대립구조(예 : 장발장)가 널리 사용된다.

둘째, 지식의 책은 구조화 작업을 통해서 더 잘 이해할 수 있다. 교과서용 도서의 지식체계는 크게 망구조(그물구조, 예 : 개의 특성), 연계구조(사슬구조, 예 : 개구리의 성장과정), 위계구조(나뭇가지 구조, 예 : 정부조직)의 세 가지 체계로 되어 있다. 책을 읽으면서 이런 구조를 공간화 시켜 이해할 수 있으면 아무리 복잡하고 어려운 글이라도 총체적으로 쉽게 파악할 수 있다.

5.8 문맥 읽기

글을 구성하고 있는 어휘의 이미지에는 사전적 이미지와 문맥상의 이미지가 있다. 대개 설명문, 논설문 등의 글에는 사전적 이미지가 많이 사용되나 동화나 시 같은 문학적인 글에는 문맥적인 이미지가 많이 쓰인다. 옛글에 "언간(言間)을 읽어라"는 말은 바로 문맥 읽기를 강조한 말이다.

문맥 읽기에 서툰 어린이들은 대개 감지력과 상상력이 부족한 아이들이 많으며, 동문서답을 자주하고, 시 읽기를 고통스러워한다.

감상의 단계에 따른 읽기방법

양재한·김수경·김석임은 『어린이 독서지도론』에서(pp. 86-90), 독자가 책의 내용을 있는 그대로 받아들이기보다는 스스로 생각하면서 능동적으로 의미를 창조하려는 단계를 '감상의 단계'라고 규정하고 그러한 감상의 단계에 따라 읽기 방법을 몇 갈래로 구분하였다.

첫째로 감상력은 작품에 따라 다르게 나타난다. 감동적인 작품일수록 감상력이 높게 나타난다. 그러므로 어린이의 감상력을 높이기 위해서는 감동적인 작품을 선택해야 한다.

둘째로 감상력은 언어로 표현할 때 더욱 높아진다. 작품을 읽고 말로 표현하든지 글로 표현하는 일은 감상력을 높이는 결과가 된다.

셋째로 감상은 개성적인 활동이어서 누가 가르쳐 줄 수도, 배울 수도 없다. 그러므로 교사나 부모는 감상을 말하는 어린이 앞에서 독자를 존중하는 발언을 해야 한다.

6.1 느끼며 읽기

독서를 지루하게 생각하는 대부분의 사람들의 특징 중 하나는 책의 내용에 몰입하지 못하는 현상이다. 이렇게 몰입하지 못하는 현상은 집중력이 약한 사람에게 자주 일어난다.

존 듀이가 "지식은 느낌의 중개를 거쳐 발생한다"고 한 것처럼, 책이란 느낌의 중개 없이 감상할 수 없는 독특한 세계이다. 책 속에 몰입하기 위해서는 다음과 같은 느낌의 훈련이 필요하다. 느끼며 읽는 방법에는 다음과 같은 것이 필요하다.

- 인물의 심정을 느끼며 읽는다.
- 인물의 행동을 자기의 경험과 결부시켜 읽는다.
- 배경과 장면을 상상하며 읽는다.
- 책 속에 표현된 냄새나 향기를 느끼며 읽는다.

6.2 상상하며 읽기

우리가 책을 읽으며 울고불고 하는 것은 상상력에 의한 반응이다. 이는 곧 책 속의 인물과 동일시를 맛보는 과정이기도 하다. 상상하며 읽는 것은 머리 속에 혹은 가슴 속에 어떤 이미지를 떠올리며 읽는 것이다. 이 이미지는 읽는 내용과 관계된 것이지만, 독자의 과거의 경험과 관련되어 나타난다. 즉, 책 속의 이미지를 자신의 이미지로 바꾸는 것이다. 이러한 상상하며 읽기는 문학작품을 읽는 데 없어서는 안 될 필수적인 능력이다. 상상하며 읽는 훈련에서는 다음과 같은 사항에 주의할 필요가 있다.

- 작품 속의 장면, 정경, 분위기를 상상하며 읽는다.
- 인물의 기분, 성격, 얼굴 모양을 상상하며 읽는다.
- 인물의 말투, 표정, 태도 행동, 옷차림 등을 상상하며 읽는다.
- 빛깔, 모양, 크기, 촉감, 소리, 무게 등을 상상하며 읽는다.
- 장소, 날씨, 거리, 넓이 등을 상상하며 읽는다.
- 그림을 보고 글 속에 없는 것을 상상하며 말한다.
- 이야기가 벌어지기 이전을 상상해 본다.
- 읽으면서 연상되는 것을 말해본다.

- 상상한 것을 그림으로 그려본다.

6.3 추리하며 읽기

우리가 살아가면서 누구에게나 끊임없이 필요한 것이 추리력이다. 똑같은 사실을 보고 더 많이 추리할 수 있는 사람은 좋은 생각, 풍부한 생각을 많이 할 수 있는 사람이다. 추리적 사고는 책을 읽는 과정에서 끊임없이 사고할 때 길러지며, 문자화되어 있지 않는 행간의 뜻을 알 수 있게 한다. 추리하며 읽는 훈련에 필요한 사항은 다음과 같은 것이다.

- 글을 읽으며 왜? 라고 의문을 품어 본다.
- 그래서?, 그 다음에는? 하고 생각하며 읽는다.
- 무엇 때문에? 를 생각하며 읽는다.
- 만약에 나라면? 을 생각하며 읽는다.
- 그와 반대로? 라고 생각하면서 반대 입장을 생각해 본다.
- 거론되어야 할 일이면서 생략되어 있는 것이 무엇인지 알아본다.

6.4 문제 해결하며 읽기

독서를 하는 것은 결국 세상을 살아가는 데 필요한 능력인 문제 해결력을 기르기 위한 것이다. 책을 읽고 나서 깊이 생각하면서 거기서 자신의 삶의 길을 찾고 열쇠를 찾게 된다면, 가장 훌륭한 감상력을 가지고 있는 셈이다. 문제 해결력을 기르기 위한 훈련에서 주목할 사항은 다음과 같은 것이다.

- 책을 읽으면서 주인공이나 주변 인물을 자신이라고 생각해 본다.
- 나와 주인공과의 공통점과 차이점은 무엇인가?
- 작품 속의 인물은 왜 실패했을까? 실패하게 된 원인을 알아본다. 실패하지 않기 위해서는 어떻게 해야 할까?
- 작품 속의 주인공이 성공한 이유는 무엇일까?
- 성공자와 실패자의 차이는 무엇인지 찾아본다.

영어문학 텍스트의 언어학적 이해와 독서감상 표현

이 글은 김태옥(1984)이 쓴 '문학 작품 지도법' 중에서 일부를 발췌하여 재정리한 것이다. 게재된 원전은 황적륜 외 공저, 『영어교수법』(서울: 신아사, 1984)이며 제8장에 실려 있다(pp.349-351, 366-374, 381-383 참조).

7.1 영어문학 텍스트의 언어학적 이해

하나의 문학 작품은 화법의 연속체(a connected discourse)로서 추상적인 언어학적 단위인 '텍스트'라는 개념으로 포착될 수 있다. 이 '텍스트'는 단순히 여러 개의 문법적 문장들의 집합이나 배열이 아니라, 통일성(Coherence)과 이를 실현시키는 언어의 부각작용(fore-grounding), 그리고 본질적 내부 구조(macro-structure)를 갖는 언어학적 단위다.

그러나 모든 언어 행위는 구체적인 어사 선택에서 비롯되며 어사선택은 언어 범주(linguistic categories)를 통해서만 기술될 수 있다. 따라서 텍스트의 통일성과 언어의 부각 작용, 그리고 작품의 내부 구조는 모두 그 구성 요소들에 대한 언어학적 고찰이 요청된다.

(1) 텍스트의 통일성(coherence)과 텍스트 구사 능력(textual competence)

의사 전달의 실제 단위는 문장이 아니라 발화(utterance)이다. 그리고 문학적 의사소통의 중심 요소는 하나의 작품을 '텍스트'라는 유기체로 파악하여 구사할 수 있는 작가나 독자의 텍스트 구사력이다. 작품이 지니는 통일성은 바로 이 텍스트 구사력의 발로이자 그 전제라 할 수 있다.

텍스트는 일선상에 배열된 문법적인 문장들의 단순한 집합이 아니라 하나의 독자적 체계(system)며 그 구조와 구성 요소 사이에 텍스트로서의 표현의 적절성(textual well-formedness)이 성취되어 있어야 한다. 문법적 문장들을 하나의 텍스트로 구축해 가는 힘이나 작품의 요약을 꾀할 수 있는 능력은 다 같이 이러한 텍스트 구사 능력에 의존한다.

텍스트에 있어 표층에서는 일견 일관성 없는 사상(事象)들의 나열 같지만, 사실은 텍스트로서의 통일성을 내적으로 강력히 지니면서 하나의 새로운 시적 현실을 구축해 간다. T. Todorov가 주장하는 "reading"(systematized commentary)도 (Scholes 1974: 143)한 작품을 살필 때 언어학적 범주를 그대로 문학 기준에 적용하는 것이 아니라, 작품인 하나의 유기체와 그 구성 요소간의 관계를 새로이 규명해 간다는 것이며, 한 작품은 기존의 문학적 범주들의 산물일 뿐 아니라 그 총체적인 변용(transformation)으로 보고 문법적 요소들(grammatical elements)과 주제적 요소들(thematic elements)을 독특한 방법으로 관련시켜 나간 작자의 기법을 주제, 구조, 배열의 관점에서 규명해 가야 하는 것이다.

(2) 언어의 부각 작용(fore-grounding)

일반적 표준적 표현이 아닌 특이한 어사 선택에 의한 표현의 부각 작용은 심미적 의사소통의 기본이 되는데, 이 때 표준적인 용법은 그 배경을 이루며 규범(norm)을 초월한 특수한 용법으로 표현의 정체가 발휘되는 언어 자질이 초점을 이룬다.

언어의 부각 작용은 은유, 특히 문학적 은유에서 가장 잘 살펴볼 수 있는데, 언어의 음운, 통사, 의미, 형태적 스펙트럼 전반에서 모두 다 표출될 수 있다. 이 문제에 대해서는 뒤에 가서 상세히 다뤄질 것이다.

(3) 작품의 내부 구조(macro-structure)

작품에는 주제가 있고 각 언어 요소들의 부각의 방향은 모두 그 주제가 지시하고 결정짓는다. 이 때 직접적으로 언급되는 사상(事象)들은 표층에서 비교적 산만한 관계를 가진 듯하나 심층에서는 그 주제를 실현하기 위해 강한 내적 조직을 이루고 있다. 면밀한 어사 선택, 일관성 있는 부각 작용을 통해서 텍스트에는 거시적 상관소(macro-sets)들이 엮어지고 이로써 하나의 통합적 유기체를 이루어, 일반 화법과는 판이한 또 하나의 현실을 내적으로 구축해 낸다.

이러한 뜻에서 작품의 내부 구조는 엄격한 의미의 언어학적 영역을 넘는다고 하겠다. 그것은 텍스트 구사 능력(textual competence)의 소산이며, 구체적으로 작품 안에 있는 기승전결의 틀, 또는 introduction, narration(또는 exposition), reasoning(또는 comment, demonstration) 그리고 conclusion의 맥락이거나 이야기(narrative text) 속의 사건, 인물을 중심으로 한 제기능들, 즉 유도부(orientation), 사건의 분규(complication), 감정(evaluation), 주인공의 결단(resolution), 종결부(coda)들로 볼 수도 있는데, 이는 문학 작품이 아니더라도 보편적으로 가지고 있는 이야기 텍스트의 골격이거나 보편소(narrative universals)로 보아야 할 것이다.

이상에서 말한 텍스트의 통일성, 언어의 부각 작용 그리고 작품의 내부 구조는 모두 구체적인 문법적 범주와 그들의 상호 작용을 통해서만 성취되고 기술 될 수 있다.

7.2 영어문학 텍스트의 기능 문체론적 접근

외국 문학작품을 지도하는 목적을 다음 세 가지로 설정할 수 있다. 즉 목표어의 일반적 전달 능력(communicative competence)을 배양하고, 문학적 전달 능력(literary competence)을 배양하며, 문학의 보편적 특질(literary universals)에 대한 인식을 넓혀 주는 일이다. 그러한 목표를 달성하기 위해서는 무엇보다도 목표어의 일반적인 기능적 문체(functional style)를 습득해야 하며 더욱 문학적 문체의 감식력을 길러야 한다. 그러나 종래와 같이 문체의 분석이나 감상만을 일삼을 것이 아니라 적어도 기능적 문체에 대해서는 구체적으로 이들을 생산(produce) 구사할 수 있는 훈련이 필요하다는 점이 강조된다. 그러한 노력은 작품에 대한 언어학적 이해, 언어학적 물음, 그리고 문체적 작업을 위한 학생 각자에게 주는 과제를 통해서 어느 정도 과학적인 접근이 가능할 수 있다.

기능적 문체의 개념은 Prague 학파에서 활발히 연구되어 왔으며 구체적으로 다음 세 가지 관점에서 논의될 수 있다. 즉,

① 언어의 제기능(감정 표시적, 지시적, 친교적, 시적, 매타 언어적, 능동적 기능)이란 문제를 놓고 언어 체계와 구체적인 언어 행위(제기능의 실현)의 상관성에서
② 구체적인 발화 행위의 분석과 그 구성 요소들의 선택, 활용의 문제, 표현의 적정성, 즉 발화 기능에 적절한 표현인가의 여부를 규명하는 작업에서
③ 문체적 요소는 발언의 내용, 상황, 화자의 현실에 대한 태도, 화자와 청자와의 관계와 같은 요인 등에 의해서 결정된다.

좀더 구체적으로 열거해 보면 다음과 같다.

(1) 의미와 관련된 객관적 요인

① Communication의 기능
- 일상적 communication
- 기술적, 실용적 communication
- 이론적, 과학적 communication
- 신문 잡지 등의 mass communication
- 시적, 심미적 communication

② 언어 행위의 목적
- 객관적 진술
- 호소적 진술

③ 주제에 대한 화자의 태도
- 진지한
- 유머러스한
- 냉소적인

④ 주제의 양식
- 동적 서술
- 정적 묘사

⑤ 자연발생적 요소
- 전적으로 자연발생적인 요소
- 사전 준비된 요소

(2) 발화 상황과 관련된 객관적 요인

- 사적 대 공적 배경
- 대화 대 독법
- 화자와 대상의 관계 (social role)

- 화자와 대상의 접촉 (대화)
- 대상이 자리를 같이 하지 않는 경우 (방송체)

(3) 사용된 언어 재료

- 음성
- 문자

 이상의 각 요인들은 결합 또는 중첩되며 때로는 한 요인에서 다른 요인으로 옮겨 가는 단계에서 문체적으로 복잡한 특징을 보인다(cf. Dubsky 1972).
 결국 외국인 학생에게 가장 필요한 것은 텍스트 자체에서 일차적으로 자명하게 드러나지 않는 표층적 의미 작용에 대한 지도이며, 한 표현의 사회·문화적 의미와 이에 대해 모국인들이 가지는 느낌들에 대한 해설이다. 이에 대해 Bolinger는 모든 외국 문학 교과서에 해설 책자를 첨부해서 영어를 모국어로 사용하는 사람들이 갖는 각 표현에 대한 느낌과 표층적 의미 변화를 제시해야 한다고 강조한다(1972: 119). 이것이야말로 작가의 의도와 개성이 작용하는 핵심적인 측면이기 때문이다.
 끝으로 강조되어야 할 것은 외국 문학 교육에 있어 교사의 언어학적 지식은 거의 필수적이라는 점이다. 작품에 대한 언어학적 접근 방법은 개개의 외국 문학작품의 이해뿐만 아니라 문체적 보편소(literary universals)에 대한 확인이 가능하며, 이를 통해 모국어 작품을 평가할 수 있는 힘도 아울러 길러진다. 또한 변형 규칙(Chomsky의 인지적 접근)을 이용한 문체적 요소의 과학적 포착이나 은유 작용의 언어학적 이해는 외국어의 일반적 능력은 물론 문학적 전달 능력(literary competence)을 구축하는 데도 결정적인 기능을 가질 것이다.

7.3 영어문학 텍스트의 언어학적 방법의 작품지도법

다음은 외국 문학 교실에서의 구체적인 지도 요령으로서 일반적인 문학 범주의 해설과 상세한 언어학적 물음을 통한 작품의 해설 및 이해, 그리고 문체적 작업과 변형 규칙 활용에 의한 문학 텍스트의 형식과 의미의 규명에 대해 알아보고자 한다.

(1) 배제되어야 할 접근방법들

우선 종래 문학 교실에서 답습되어 오던 몇 가지 배제되어야 할 접근방법 즉 번역, 석의(釋義 paraphrase), 요약(summary) 등에 대해 언급하겠다.

언어학적 해설은 세밀한 관찰을 통해 작품의 텍스트 자체가 제시하는 바를 해설 규명하려는 노력이므로, 이상의 접근방법들이 아무리 그 자체로서 훌륭한 의미를 지니는 학습활동이라 해도 문학작품 해설 과정에서는 될수록 배제되어야 한다.

① 번역의 배제 : 번역은 그 자체가 귀중한 연습이요, 작업이 될 수 있으나 번역 과정에서 영문 텍스트 자체보다는 번역어의 표현 기술에 더욱 많은 노력과 시간을 빼앗기기 때문에 작가가 제시하고자 하는 바의 파악이 우선되기 위해서는 이 과정에서 불필요한 노력은 배제되어야 한다. 번역 과정에서 학생들은 모국어의 등가어(等價語)를 탐색할 뿐 아니라 등가적 문체마저 찾아야 하는 힘에 겨운 작업을 하게 되기 때문이다.
② 석의(釋義 paraphrase)의 배제 : 작가가 제시한 텍스트를 또 하나의 다른 텍스트로 바꾸어 말하는 작업은 원본 텍스트를 이해·감상하는 데 오히려 해롭다. 될수록 작가의 표현에서 떠나지 말고 작

품을 해득하고 감상해야 한다.
③ 요약(summary)의 배제 : 요약은 또 다른 텍스트의 대치가 되며 많은 경우 작가가 말하고자 하는 바를 지나치게 요약함으로써 작가의 의도를 왜소하게 한다. 작가의 구상, 기획은 텍스트를 하나의 전체로 보아 줄 것을 요청하며 어떤 부분도 생략될 수 없는 것이다.
④ 기타 배제되어야 할 과정은 기성 비평가의 글을 지나치게 인용하거나 작품에 대한 객관성 없는 과찬이다. 비평가 개인의 오류를 그대로 받아들이는 위험뿐만 아니라 학생들이 스스로 생각하는 작업을 막게 될 우려가 있기 때문이다.

(2) 주제

작품의 대의, 논지, 그리고 보조적 개념과 주체와의 상관성을 학생들이 쉽게 포착하기는 어렵다. 단락별로 분석해서 주제로 통합시켜 나가는 과정이 제시되어야 한다.

이야기(narrative) 텍스트는 대체로 다음과 같은 기능으로 엮어졌으므로 사건이나 인물의 동작에 따라 주제를 파악해 나간다.

① 유도부 orientation (첫 장면 : 방향 제시)
② 사건의 분규 complication (상황의 파열)
③ 주인공의 판단 evaluation (주인공의 도래, 시련)
④ 주인공의 결단 resolution (주인공의 선행, 영향)
⑤ 종결부 coda (첫 장면의 再構成) (Van Dijk 1972: 293)

묘사적(descriptive) 텍스트에 대해서는 때로 묘사 내용과 그 뒤에 숨겨진 작가의 의도를 혼동하는 수가 있다. 이러한 텍스트는 일정한 주제 실현이라는 목적을 가지고 있으며 흔히 소설의 경우 묘사는 '분위기 조성'을 위한 기능을 뜻하는 수가 많다. 시에 있어서는 묘사 자체가 전부일 수 있으나 이때도 역시 시인이 구현하고자 하는 주제를 위해 동원된 묘사들이므로 작품에 담긴 이중적 상징 작용을 분석해서 파악해야 한다.

시에서 언어로 표현된 일련의 상황, 사상, 사건, 과정, 사물의 본질 등이 다시금 하나의 상념이나 복합적인 상념을 표현·상징하는 데 사용된다. 즉 작품의 이중적 상징 작용이 일어난다. 주제와 직접 언급되는 사상이나 명제들은 문학의 이중적 의미를 이루는 요소로서 서로가 서로를 상징한다.

그러므로 작품의 해설은 텍스트의 묘사된 사건과 사상(事象)을 면밀히 검토하고 그들이 불러일으키는 효과를 논해야 하며 모든 빛과 색채와 형태와 동작들의 상호작용에 대한 분석도 요청된다.

(3) 물음을 통한 작품 지도

작품을 다루며 교사가 어떤 물음을 던지느냐에 따라 학생들이 작품 속에서 무엇을 찾을 수 있는가가 결정된다. 인물, 주제에 대한 물음뿐만 아니라, 심미적 자질, 문체적 의미, 사회 문화적 의미 등을 물음을 통해 포착할 수 있다.

① 인물(characters)
 i) Are the characters like real people in the way they act and talk?
 ii) Are there any "stereotypes" – such as the "typical" college boy who isn't really like most college boys at all?
 iii) Are any of the characters in line with the kind of people

they seem to be?
ⅳ) Are the actions of the characters like real people you know or have known?
ⅴ) How does the author let you know what kind of person a character is, what his traits are, etc.? Does the author tell you directly? Or, does he show you what a character is like by what the character does, what he says, what others say about him?

② 구성(the plot)
ⅰ) Is there suspense in the story?; Does it keep you on edge? If so, how does the author do this?
ⅱ) Can you find a definite "turning point" in the story?
ⅲ) How does the main character solve his problem, overcome obstacles?
ⅳ) Does the plot have a logical series of happenings? Or do many things happen just by chance or coincidence?
ⅴ) Does the ending satisfy you? Or do you feel cheated by it?
ⅵ) Which is more important in the story... physical action (what the characters do) or mental action (what the characters think or feel)?
ⅶ) Do any of the characters change in the way they think or feel during the story? If so, do you think there is a good reason for the change?

③ 주제(the theme)
ⅰ) What is the "moral" or idea of the story?

ⅱ) Does the story make you think?
ⅲ) Does the ending puzzle you? If so, try to figure out why the author ended the story that way?
ⅳ) Does the author make this idea pretty obvious? Or do you have to "read between the lines"?

④ 언어적 물음(linguistic questions) : 외국어 교육과 문화 감상을 일치시키려는 노력은 문학작품에 대한 언어적 물음(linguistic questions)을 통해 효과적으로 성취될 수 있으며, 따라서 외국어 습득 과정에서의 문학작품의 감상 및 그 여러 형태의 언어학적 물음과 훈련이 그 핵심 부분을 이루어야 한다.

Jean Malmstron과 Janice Lee 공저 *Teaching English Linguistically*(1971)에 제시된 바를 중심으로 언어학적 물음들을 해설·열거해 본다. 시, 희곡, 산문에 공통된 물음으로서 작가의 구체적 어사(語辭) 선택을 파악하고 규명하기 위해 다음과 같은 물음을 던진다.

ⅰ) What is the meaning of this word in this context? What other meanings for it do you know?
   - 문제성을 지닌 낱말들 (고어, 연관술어 또는 의미 변화를 겪는 낱말들)의 풀이.
ⅱ) What part of speech is this word in this context? What other parts of speech could it be in other context? In what ways is its usage here unusual?
   - 문학어는 고의적인 다의성을 지닐 때가 많으므로 특히 시에서 가지는 한 낱말의 여러 가지 품사 기능을 밝혀야 한다.
ⅲ) What is the proportion of long to short words? What effect

  does it produce?
  - 대체로 긴 형태의 낱말들이 현학적인 경우가 많다.
ⅳ) What is the author's policy about repeating words as opposed to using a variety of synonyms?
  - 문학어에 있어 어휘의 반복 작용과 변양(變樣) 작용은 어의적 통합력을 가져오는 요인이다.
ⅴ) How frequent is the definite article *the* as opposed to the indefinite article *a (an)*? What effect does this frequency have?
ⅵ) What peculiarities in spelling or punctuation are present? How can you account for them?
  - 시대적, 방언적 요소로서 또는 작가의 특성으로서 철자법 혹은 구두법의 특수성을 지닐 수 있으므로 이를 밝혀야 한다.
ⅶ) Where can unnecessary words be cut or condensed by transformation or rewriting? What effect is produced by these changes?
  - 표현의 형식과 의미가 일치됐을 때 비로소 위대한 작품이 될 수 있다. 삭제나 변형의 연습을 통해 작품의 형식과 의미의 일치성을 경험하고 학생 자신들의 문체적 인식을 넓힐 수 있다.
ⅷ) How frequent are nonce noun modifiers? What effect do they have?
  - 흔히 사용되는 복합명사들과 작가가 임시로 만들어 낸 복합명사들을 가려내어 새로운 것의 의미 전달이 확실한가를 살핀다.
ⅸ) What is the proportion of evaluative adjectives? What effect does it have?

- 사실을 묘사하는 형용사(green, cold, hard)와 가치 판단을 말하는 형용사(good, charming, lovely)의 빈도를 밝혀 작가의 목적이 사실 묘사에 있는지, 자기 의견 제시에 있는지 공부하고, 그 글이 목적에 부합하는지 여부를 밝힌다.

x) How frequent are intensifiers? What effect do they have?
- 강조를 하기 위한 intensifiers (very, rather, quite)가 지나치게 많으면 오히려 표현을 약화시킨다.

xi) If the word order is inverted, how can it be rearranged to produce normal, modern American or British English? Why is it inverted?
- 산문에서는 강조법으로, 시에서는 운을 맞추기 위해 어순이 도치된다. 또한 고대영어에서 도치법이 더 자유롭게 사용되었다.

xii) How frequent are sentence modifiers? In what positions do they stand in the sentences... beginning, middle, or end?
- 문장 전체를 수식하는 문장 부사의 능란한 구사력이 작가의 우수성을 보이는 수가 많다.

xiii) What is the central sentence of this long sentence? What are the basic forms of its inserts? What are the relationships of the transforms to the central sentence?
- 작가의 문체를 비교할 수 있는 계기가 되며 학생들 자신의 변형을 시도해 볼 수 있다.

xiv) What types of insertion transformations characterize this author's style?
- 명사구문화(nominalization), 관계구문화(relativization), 부사구문화(adverbialization)들을 식별하고 작가의 기호, 경향을 알아보며 이를 모방해 본다.

xv) How frequent are passives? What effect do they have?
  - 문장이 be와 by의 첨가로 길어지나, 동작주를 생략할 수 있거나, 숨길 수도 있다.
xvi) How frequent are imperatives, without *you*? What effect do they have?
  - 명령법은 작가와 독자 간의 직접적 관계를 강조한다.
xvii) How often do abstract nouns appear as subjects of active verbs? What effect do they have?
  - "Research shows...", "History proves...", 추상명사가 [+animate] 주어를 대신할 때 그 진술에 대한 작가의 책임을 면하게 해 준다.
xviii) How frequent are cliches? How do they strengthen or weaken the author's purpose?
  - 상투어의 사용은 흔히 문장을 약화하거나 작가의 목적에 따라 반어적으로 쓰이고 상투적인 인물의 사고방식을 표현하기 위해 적절히 쓰일 수 있다.
xix) How frequent are regional dialect markers? Why does the author use dialect? How valid are his reasons?
  - 작중인물들의 생생한 묘사를 위해 발음, 어휘, 구문의 각 층에서 방언형을 쓸 수 있다. 인물의 무식함을 강조하기 위해서도 사용된다.
xx) What linguistic problems are caused by the historical dimension? How many archaic words appear? Can the meaning of these words be guessed from the context?
  - 언어는 항시 변하므로 고전적 어휘들은 현대어로 바꾸어 읽거나 학생들 스스로가 문맥에서 그 의미를 깨닫게 하고, 고어가 일부러 쓰인 현대적 작품은 고풍조를 위한 변양으로 보아

야 한다.

xxi) How powerfully do verbs carry the meaning without manner adverbs? How frequent are sentences of the BE+ADJECTIVE type?
- To go swiftly 대신에 to run, to be obedient 대신에 to obey, to be doubtful 대신에 to doubt를 사용하여 의미의 응축을 꾀하는 것이 흔히 쓰이는 강력한 표현법이다.

xxii) What types of comparisons appear? What are their effects?
- 직유, 은유, 유추 등의 구사력과 창조력이 작가의 문체적 우수성을 가름한다.

xxiii) How does the author use verb tenses and auxiliaries? What is the effect of his choices?
- 시간과 시제는 일치하지 않는다. 영어의 시제는 현재와 과거 둘 뿐이며 작가는 조동사(modals 포함)를 사용해서 기타 시간관계를 나타낸다. 시제의 구사에서 작가의 문체적 특성을 엿볼 수 있다.

xxiv) What is the distribution of sentence types? basic sentences (untransformed or transformed by simple transformations), fragments, sentences with conjunction transforms, with insertion transforms.
- 어떤 문형에 대한 작가의 기호나 그 양상에서 그 작가의 문체적 개성을 엿볼 수 있다.

⑤ 산문 학습을 위한 일반적 물음 : 언어학적 물음(앞의 내용 부분 참조) 이외에 다음과 같은 내용을 참고로 문학작품으로서의 산문을 교실에서 다루어 나갈 수 있고 더욱 작문과 class report의 기회로 이용할 수 있다.

ⅰ) What is the general nature of the subject-matter? Is it a person, a place, a book, an adventure, an occasion, an experience or personal whim?
ⅱ) What is the author's purpose in the essay? Is it to inform, to describe, to convince, to amuse, or to entertain?
ⅲ) What occasion and what readers did he have in mind?
ⅳ) What methods did he use in developing his essay? Definition, classification, comparison, contrast, or argument?
ⅴ) What kind of illustration, anecdotes, literary and historical allusions did he introduce? Why?
ⅵ) To what type does the essay belong? A letter, a character portrait, narrative, descriptive, historical, biographical, or critical?
ⅶ) What is the form of the essay? Compact, formal, logical, impersonal, rambling or familiar?
ⅷ) What is the tone of the essay? Serious, light, fanciful, satirical, humorous, reflective, intense, lofty, or poetic?
ⅸ) What impressions of the author's personality do you gain from his essay? How does it affect you? What makes it worth reading?
ⅹ) Have you acquired any new words, any meanings of words, any new ideas, information or impressions?

(4) 과제 : 다독과 문체적 작업

교실에서 다 같이 읽는 작품 외에 학생 각자가 자기의 영어 수준과 읽기 속도에 맞추어 작품을 소화하고 이를 교실에서 보고하는 숙제를 주는 것이 효과적이다.

　말의 용도(use)에 따라 어역(語譯 register)이 변하고, 사용자(user)에 따라 말씨(dialect)가 판이한 문체(speech style)를 택할 수 있으므로 이에 대한 훈련을 겸하기 위해 다음과 같은 과제를 줄 수 있다.

　ⅰ) Retell part of the story in the language of another character.
　　- 다른 인물의 입장에서 바꾸어 이야기해 보면 다양한 언어 훈련이 될 수 있다.
　ⅱ) Retell part of the story as it might have been written by another author.
　　- 가령 Dickens 혹은 Hemingway가 이 작품을 썼을 경우 달라질 수 있는 문체를 시도한다.
　ⅲ) Change the setting or the time of a story, and then change the language to match the new situation.
　　- 예를 들어 Shakespeare의 *Julius Caeser*를 현대판 암살 사건으로 옮겨 써보는 연습 등은 흥미있는 작업이 될 수 있다.
　ⅳ) Pretend you are a book reviewer for *Korea Times* or *Korea Journal* and review your book in the customary style of your chosen magazine or journal.
　　- 우선 한 신문이나 잡지를 택해서 거기에 실린 서평의 언어를 검토하고 이를 모방해서 써 보는 연습을 한다.
　ⅴ) Pretend to be a reporter at a scene in your book and interview a character in language appropriate to newspaper, radio, or television.
　　- 신문을 위해서는 읽을 수 있고, radio는 들을 수 있고 TV로는 시청할 수 있는 언어를 구사해야 한다. 담화의 분야(field of discourse)와 담화의 양식(mode of discourse)에 따라 상이

한 문체에 대해서 배운다.

ⅵ) Pretend you are directing a play... either an actual drama or a dramatic version of a novel or short story... and write out instructions to your actors about its language: intonation, the relationships between the language and the action.
- 연출자의 입장에서 작품의 언어를 검토하고 이를 무대에서 재현시키는 경험을 갖는다.

ⅶ) Pretending you are the author of your chosen book, write a letter to the editor of a magazine on one of its interesting aspects, using the language of the author.
- 우선 저자의 문체를 습득하고 이를 모방해서 편지를 쓴다.

ⅷ) Contrast the language of two characters who differ distinctively in age, education, sex, or cultural background.
- 사회적 계급(social dialect)이나 말씨의 변화(speech variety)를 검토해서 그 말의 사용자에 따라 言譯(register)이 어떻게 달라질 수 있는가를 알 수 있다.

ⅸ) Report the linguistic changes that are necessary to adapt the book for dramatization on television or in the movies.
- 글과 말의 대조, 그리고 영상과 말의 대조를 배운다.

ⅹ) Write a new ending for the story in language consistent with the original.
- 저자의 문체를 익힌 다음에 이를 모방해서 이야기의 새로운 끝맺음을 시도한다.

| 제 3 부 |

읽기 자료: 영어 문학텍스트

1. 영미 중단편 소설
   〈영국 편〉
   - Youth
   - The Horse Dealer's Daughter
   - To Please His Wife
   - The Gioconda Smile
   - Kew Gardens

   〈미국 편〉
   - A Rose for Emily
   - The Snow of Kilimanjaro
   - Red
   - The Black Cat
   - The Real Thing
   - The Lightening-Rod Man

2. 현대 영미 에세이
   - What Statesmen Must Know
   - The social Responsibilities of Scientists
   - Six Typical Americans
   - The Present Human Condition
   - My View of History

여기에 수록된 영국과 미국의 중단편 소설들은 모두 11편인데, 영국과 미국의 대학과 한국의 대학에서 추천도서로서 즐겨 읽는 작품들이다. 제시하면 아래와 같다.

영국편

① Joseph Conrad
② D.H. Lawrence
③ Thomas Hardy
④ Aldous Huxley
⑤ Virginia Woolf

미국편

① William Faulkner
② Earnest Hemingway
③ Somerset Maugham
④ Edgar Allan Poe
⑤ Henry James
⑥ Herman Melville

이러한 작품들을 학생들은 어떻게 읽을 것인가? 무엇보다도 우선은 이미 앞의 제1부와 제2부를 통해 학습한 독서이론과 읽기방법을 상기하고 유념하기를 권한다. 물론 작품을 읽는 목적을 어떻게 설정하느냐에 따라 읽기 방법과 읽기 전, 중, 후 활동들을 달리 할 수 있다. 이러한 학생의 여러 가지 다양한 활동은 개인별로 하거나 또는 그룹을 구성하여 협동형태(모둠활동)로 할 수도 있을 것이다.

그런데 우리 한국 학도들에게 있어 모국어가 아닌 외국어로서의 영어(EFL: English as a Foreign Language)로 쓰인 문학작품을 읽는 데에는 직면하게 될 어려움이 한두 가지가 아니다. 학생들 자신의 언어 능력과 지적 수준에 따라 다르겠지만, 어휘력 부족, 문장의 구문이나 문법적 형태에의 친숙도 결여, 사고방식과 사회적·문화적 배경의 차이 등을 비롯하여 학생들의 사기를 꺾는 장애가 많은 것은 새삼 말할 필요가 없을 것이다.

학생들은 앞에서 익힌 독서방법과 읽기기술을 기반으로 하여 접목하기를 제안한 다양한 활동들을 적극적으로 잘 활용해본다면 지구촌화된 21세기에서 필수적인 표현도구가 되어버린 영어의 사용 및 표현 능력, 의사소통 능력을 획기적으로 증대할 수 있을 것이다. 나아가 오늘날 국가 발전에 절실히 필요로 하는 '창의성'을 개발하는 데 있어 매우 큰 이득을 얻을 수 있을 것이다. 학생들에게 어릴 때부터 문학작품을 읽게 하고 그것을 창조적으로 활용하는 창조적인 독서지도는 상상력을 개발하고 문제의식을 가지도록 하며 적응능력과 대안제시 능력을 배양하게 해준다는 점에서 국가 영재교육을 위한 문학적 독서지도 접근법으로서 추진되고 있는 것이 금일의 세계적 추세이다. 따라서 이 책은 영어능력 제고와 창의성 개발이라는 "두 마리 토끼 잡기"와 "꿩 먹고 알 먹기" 식의 효과를 올릴 수 있기를 의도하는 것이다.

여기에 실린 중단편 작품을 읽을 때 다른 여타의 활동들을 하기에 앞서서 우리나라의 학생들이 EFL로서의 영어를 학습한다는 점을 가만하여, 필자는 학생들에게 다음과 같은 읽기활동을 먼저 반드시 행하기를 권하고 싶다. ① 사전을 찾지 말고 처음부터 끝까지 훑어 읽기를 하라(안정효 참조) ② 한 번 읽는 것에 머무르지 말고 여러 번(최소 10회 이상) 반복하여 소리를 내어서 읽어라(NR Theory 참조) ③ 읽기가 진전됨에 따라서 최대의 속도로 속독을 해보고 소요시간을 기록하라 ④ 이러한 읽기과정을 마친 후에는 문학작품 읽기지도에서 가장 기초가 되는 요소들, 예컨대 주제, 등장인물, 그들이 벌이는 주요 사건, 플롯, 전체 스토리 등에 관해 스스로 말과 글로 그 내용의 요지를 정리해보라는 것이다. 이와 같은 읽기 활동을 한번 이행한 후에 앞에서 배운 여러 가지의 독서 전, 중, 후의 활동을 다시 적용해보기를 권한다.

영미 중단편 소설

Youth
—by Joseph Conrad

This could have occurred nowhere but in England, where men and sea interpenetrate, so to speak—the sea entering into the life of most men, and the men knowing something or everything about the sea, in the way of amusement, of travel, or of breadwinning.

We were sitting round a mahogany table that reflected the bottle, the claret glasses, and our faces as we leaned on our elbows. There was a director of companies, an accountant, a lawyer, Marlow, and myself. The director had been a *Conway* boy, the accountant had served four years at sea, the lawyer—a fine crusted Tory, High Churchman, the best of old fellows, the soul of honor—had been chief officer in the P. & O. service in the good old days when mailboats were square-rigged at least on two masts, and used to come down the China Sea before a fair monsoon with stun'sails set alow and aloft. We all began life in the merchant service. Between the five of us there was the strong bond of the sea, and also the fellowship of the craft, which no amount of enthusiasm for yachting, cruising, and so on can give, since one is only the amusement of life and the other is life itself.

Marlow (at least I think that is how he spelt his name) told the story, or rather the chronicle, of a voyage :

"Yes, I have seen a little of the Eastern seas; but what I remember best is my first voyage there. You fellows know there are those voyages that seem ordered for the illustration of life, that might stand for a symbol of existence. You fight, work, sweat, nearly kill yourself, sometimes do kill yourself, trying to accomplish something-and you can't. Not form any fault of yours. You simply can do nothing, neither great nor little-not a thing in the world-not even marry an old maid, or get a wretched 600-ton cargo of coal to its port of destination.

"It was altogether a memorable affair. It was my first voyage to the East, and my first voyage as second mate; it was also my skipper's first command. You'll admit it was time, He was sixty if a day; a little man, with a broad, not very straight back, with bowed shoulders and one leg more bandy than the other, he had that queer twisted-about appearance you see so often in men who work in the fields. He had a nutcracker face-chin and nose trying to come together over a sunken mouth-and it was framed in iron-gray fluffy hair, that looked like a chinstrap of cotton-wool sprinkled with coaldust. And he had blue eyes in that old face of his, which were amazingly like a boy's, with that candid expression some quite common men preserve to the end of their days by a rare internal gift of simplicity of heart and rectitude of soul. What induced him to accept me was a wonder. I had come out of a crack Australian clipper, where I had been third officer, and he seemed to have a prejudice against crack clippers as aristocratic and high-toned. He said to me, 'You know, in this ship you will have to work.' I said I had to work in every ship I had ever been in. 'Ah, but this is different, and you gentlemen out of them big ships; . . . but there! I dare say you will do. Join tomorrow.'

"I joined tomorrow. It was twenty-two years ago; and I was just twenty. How time passes! It was one of the happiest days of my life. Fancy! Second mate for the first rime – a really responsible officer! I wouldn't have thrown up my new billet for a fortune. The mate looked me over carefully. He was also an old chap, but of another stamp. He had a Roman nose, a snow-white, long beard, and his name was Mahon, but he insisted that it should he pronounced Mann. He was well connected; yet there was something wrong with his luck, and he had never got on.

"As to the captain, he had been for years in coasters, then in the Mediterranean, and last in the West Indian trade. He had never been round the. Capes. He could just write a kind of sketchy hand, and didn't care for writing at all. Both were thorough good seamen of course, and between two old chaps I felt like a small boy between two grandfathers.

"The ship also was old. Her mane was the *Judea*. Queer name, isn't it? She belonged to a man Wilmer, Wilcox – some name like that; but he has been bankrupt and dead these twenty years or more, and his name don't matter. She had been laid up in Shadwell basin for ever so long. You may imagine her state. She was all rust, dust, grime—soot aloft, dirt on deck. To me it was like coming out of a palace into a ruined cottage. She was about 400 tons, had a primitive windlass, wooden latches to the doors, not a bit of brass about her, and a big square stern. There was on it, below her name in big letters, a lot of scrollwork, with the gilt off, and some sort of a coat of arms, with the motto 'Do or Die' underneath. I remember it took my fancy immensely. There was a touch of romance in it, something that made me love the old thing—something that appealed to my youth!

"We left London in ballast—sand ballast—to load a cargo of coal in a northern port for Bangkok. Bangkok! I thrilled. I had been six years at sea, but had only seen Melbourne and Sydney, very good places, charming places in their way—but Bangkok!

"We worked out of the Thames under canvas, with a North Sea pilot on board. His name was Jermyn, and he dodged all day long about the galley drying his handkerchief before the stove. Apparently he never slept. He was a dismal man, with a perpetual tear sparkling at the end of his nose, who either had been in trouble, or was in trouble, or expected 세 be in trouble—couldn't be happy unless something went wrong. He mistrusted my youth, my common sense, and my seamanship, and made a point of showing it in a hundred little ways. I dare say he was right. It seems to me I knew very little then, and I know not much more now; but I cherish a hate for that Jermyn to this day.

"We were a week working up as far as Yarmouth Roads, and then we got into a gale – the famous October gale of twenty-two years ago. It was wind, lightning, sleet, snow, and a terrific sea. We were flying light, and you may imagine how bad it was when I tell you we had smashed bulwarks and a flooded deck. On the second night she shifted her ballast into the lee bow, and by that time we had been blown off somewhere on the Dogger Bank. There was nothing for it but go below with shovels and try to right her, and there we were in that vast hold, gloomy like a cavern, the tallow dips stuck and flickering on the beams, the gale howling above, the ship tossing about like mad on her side; there we all were, Jermyn, the captain, everyone, hardly able to keep our feet, engaged on that gravedigger's work, and trying to toss shovelfuls of wet sand up to windward. At every tumble of the ship you could see vaguely in the dim light men falling down with a great flourish of shovels. One of the ship's boys (we had two), impressed by the weirdness of the scene, wept as if his heart would break. We could hear him blubbering somewhere in th shadows.

"On the third day the gale died out, and by and by a north-country tug picked us up. We took sixteen days in all to get from London to the Tyne! When we got into dock we had lost our turn for loading, and they hauled us off to a pier where we remained for a month. Mrs. Beard (the captain's name was Beard) came from Colchester to see the old man. She lived on board. The crew of runners had left, and there remained only the officers, one boy and the steward, a mulatto who answered to the name of Abraham. Mrs. Beard was an old woman, with a face all wrinkled and ruddy like a winter apple, and the figure of a young girl. She caught sight of me once, sewing on a button, and insisted on having my shirts to repair. This was something different from the captains' wives I had known on board crack clippers. When I brought her the shirts, she said ; 'And the socks? They want mending, I am sure, and John's - Captain Beard's - things are all in order now. I would be glad of something to do.' Bless the old woman. She overhauled my outfit for me, and meantime I read for the first time *Sartor Resartus* and Burnaby's *Ride to Khiva*. I didn't understand much of the first then; but I remember I preferred the soldier to the philosopher at the time; a preference which life has only confirmed. One was a man, and the other was either more - of less. However, they are both dead and Mrs. Beard is dead, and youth, strength, genius, thoughts, achievements, simple hearts - all dies. . . . No matter.

"They loaded us at last. We shipped a crew. Eight able seamen and two boys. We hauled off one evening to the buoys at the dock gates, ready to go out, and with a fair prospect of beginning the voyage next day. Mrs. Beard was to start for home by a late train. When the ship was fast we went to tea. We sat rather silent through the meal - Mahon, the old couple, and I. I finished first, and slipped away for a smoke, my cabin being in a deckhouse just against the poop. It was high water, blowing fresh with a drizzle; the double dock gates were opened, and the steam colliers were going in and out in the darkness with their lights burning bright, a great plashing of propellers, rattling of winches, and a lot of hailing on the pier-heads. I watched the procession of headlights gliding high and of green lights gliding low in the night, when suddenly a red gleam flashed at me, vanished, came into view again, and remained, The fore end of a steamer loomed up close. I shouted down the cabin, 'Come up, quick!' and then heard a startled voice saying afar in the dark, 'Stop her, sir.' A bell jingled. Another voice cried warningly, 'We are going right into that bark, sir.' The answer to this was a gruff 'All right.' and the next thing was a heavy crash as the steamer struck a glancing blow with the bluff of her bow about our forerigging. There was a moment of confusion, yelling, and running about. Steam roared. Then somebody was heard saying, 'All clear, sir.' . . . 'Are you all right?' asked the gruff voice. I had jumped forward to see the damage, and hailed back, 'I think so.' Easy astern,' said the gruff voice. A bell jingled. 'What steamer is that?' screamed Mahon. By that time she was no more to us than a bulky shadow maneuvering a little way off. They shouted at us some name — a woman's name, Miranda or Melissa — or some such thing. "This means another month in this beastly hole," said Mahon to me, as we peered with lamps about the splintered bulwarks and broken braces. 'But where's the captain?'

"We had not heard or seen anything of him all that time. We went aft to look. A doleful voice arose hailing somewhere in the middle of the dock, '*Judea* ahoy!' . . . How the devil did he get there? . . . 'Hallo!' we shouted. 'I am adrift in our boat without oars,' he cried. A belated water-man offered his services, and

Mahon struck a bargain with him for a half crown to tow our skipper alongside; but it was Mrs. Beard that came up the ladder first. They had been floating about the dock in that mizzly cold rain for nearly an hour. I was never so surprised in my life.

"It appears that when he heard my shout 'Come up' he understood at once what was thE matter, caught up his wife, ran on deck, and across, and down into our boat, which was fast to the ladder. Not bad for a sixty-year-old. Just imagine that old fellow saving heroically in his arms that old woman – the woman of his life. He set her down on a thwart, and was ready to climb back on board when the painter came adrift somehow, and away they went together. Of course in the confusion we did not hear him shouting. He looked abashed. She said cheerfully, 'I suppose it does not matter my losing the train now?' 'No, Jenny – you go below and get warm,' he growled. Then to us ; 'A sailor has no business with a wife – I say. There I was, out of the ship. Well, no harm done this time. Let's go and look at what that fool of a steamer smashed.'

"It wasn't much, but it delayed us three weeks. At the end of that time, the captain being engaged with his agents, I carried Mrs. Beard's bag to the railway station and put her all comfy into a third-class carriage. She lowered the window to say, 'You are a good young man. If you see John – Captain Beard – without his muffler at night, just remind him from me to keep his throat well wrapped up.' 'Certainly, Mrs. Beard,' I said. 'You are a good young man; I noticed how attentive you are to John – to Captain –' The train pulled out suddenly; I took my cap off to the old woman: I never saw her again . . . Pass the bottle.

"We went to sea next day. When we made that start for Bangkok we had been already three months out of London. We had expected to be a fortnight or so — at the outside.

"It was January and the weather was beautiful — the beautiful sunny winter weather that has more charm than in the summertime, because it is unexpected, and crisp, and you know it won't, it can't, last long, It's like a windfall, like a godsend, like an unexpected piece of luck.

"It lasted all down the North Sea, all down Channel; and it lasted till we were three hundred miles or so to the westward of the Lizards; then the wind went round to the sou'west and began to pipe up. In t재 days it blew a gale. The *Judea*, hove to, wallowed on the Atlantic like an old candle-box. It blew day after day : it blew with spite, without interval, without mercy, without rest. The world was nothing but an immensity of great foaming waves rushing at us, under a sky low enough to touch with the hand and dirty like a smoked ceiling. In the stormy space surrounding us there was as much flying spray as air. Day after day and night after night there was nothing round the ship but the howl of the wind, the tumult of the sea, the noise of water pouring over her deck. There was no rest for her and no rest for us. She tossed, she pitched, she stood on her head, she sat on her tail, she rolled, she groaned, and we had to hold on while on deck and cling to our bunks when below, in a constant effort of body and worry of mind.

"One night Mahon spoke through the small window of my

berth. It opened right into my very bed, and I was lying there sleepless, in my boots, feeling as though I had not slept for years, and could not if I tried. He said excitedly:

"You got the sounding rod in here, Marlow? I can't get the pumps to suck. By God! It's no child's play.'

"I gave him the sounding rod and lay down again, trying to think of various things—but I thought only of the pumps. When I came on deck they were still at it, and my watch relieved at the pumps. By the light of the lantern brought on deck to examine the sounding rod I caught a glimpse of their weary, serious faces. We pumped all the four hours. We pumped all night, all day, all the week—watch and watch. She was working herself loose, and leaked badly—not enough to drown us at once, but enough to kill us with the work at the pumps. And while we pumped the ship was going from us piecemeal: the bulwarks went, the stanchions were torn out, the ventilators smashed, the cabin door burst in. There was not a dry spot in the ship. She was being gutted bit by bit. The longboat changed, as if by magic, into matchwood where she stood in her gripes, I had lashed her myself, and was rather proud of my handiwork, which had withstood so long the malice of the sea. And we pumped. And there was no break in the weather. The sea was white like a sheet of foam, like a caldron of boiling milk ; there was not a break in the clouds, no —not the size of a man's hand—no, not for so much as ten seconds. There was for us no sky, there were for us no stars, no sun, no universe—nothing but angry clouds and an infuriated sea. We pumped watch and watch, for dear life; and it seemed to last for months, for years, for all eternity, as though we had been dead and gone to a hell for sailors. We forgot the day of the week, the name of the month, what year it was, and whether we had ever been ashore. The sails blew away, she lay broadside on under a weather cloth, the ocean poured over her, and we did not care. We turned those handles, and had the eyes of idiots. As soon as we had crawled on deck I used to take a round turn with a rope about the men, the pumps, and the mainmast, and we turned, we turned incessantly, with the water to our waists, to our necks, over our heads. It was all one. We had forgotten how it felt to be dry.

"And there was somewhere in me the thought: By Jove! This is the deuce of an adventure – something you read about; and it is my first voyage as second mate – and I am only twenty – and here I am lasting it out as well as any of these men, and keeping my chaps up to the mark. I was pleased. I would not have given up the experience for worlds. I had moments of exultation. Whenever the old dismantled craft pitched heavily with her counter high in the air, she seemed to me to throw up, like an appeal, like a defiance, like a cry to the clouds without mercy, the words written on her stern: '*Judea*, London. Do or Die.'

"O youth! The strength of it, the faith of it, the imagination of it! To me she was not an old rattletrap carting about the world a lot of coal for a freight – to me she was the endeavor, the test, the trial of life. I think of her with pleasure, with affection, with regret – as you would think of someone dead you have loved. I shall never forget her . . . Pass the bottle.

"One night when tied to the mast, as I explained, we were pumping on, deafened with the wind, and without spirit enough in us to wish ourselves dead, a heavy sea crashed aboard and swept clean over us. As soon as I got my breath I shouted, as in duty bound, 'Keep on, boys!' when suddenly I felt something hard floating on deck strike the calf of my leg. I made a grab at it and missed. It was so dark we could not see each other's faces within a foot-you understand.

"After that thump the ship kept quiet for a while, and the thing, whatever it was struck my leg again. This time I caught it -and it was a saucepan. At first, being stupid with fatigue and thinking of nothing but the pumps, I did not understand what I had in my hand. Suddenly it dawned upon me, and I shouted, 'Boys, the house on deck is gone. Leave this, and let's look for the cook.'

"There was a deckhouse forward, which contained the galley, the cook's berth, and the quaters of the crew. As we had expected for days to see it swept away, the hands had been ordered to sleep in the cabin-the only safe place in the ship. The steward, Abraham, however, persisted in clinging to his berth, stupidly, like a mule-from sheer fright I believe, like an animal that won't leave a stable falling in an earthquake. So we went to look for him. It was changing death, since once out of our lashings we were as exposed as if on a raft. But we went. The house was shattered as if a shell had exploded inside. Most of it had gone overboard-stove, men's quaters, and their property, all was gone ; but two posts, holding a portion of the bulkhead to which

Abraham's bunk was attached, remained as if by a miracle. We groped in the ruins and came upon this, and there he was, sitting in his bunk, surrounded by foam and wreckage, jabbering cheerfully to himself. He was out of his mind; completely and forever mad, with this sudden shock coming upon the fag-end of his endurance. We snatched him up, lugged him aft, and pitched him headfirst down the cabin companion. you understand there was no time to carry him down with infinite precautions and wait to see how he got on. Those below would pick him up at the bottom of the stairs all right. We were in a hurry to go back to the pumps. That business could not wait. A bad leak is an inhuman thing.

"One would think that the sole purpose of that fiendish gale had been to make a lunatic of that poor devil of a mulatto. It eased before morning, and next day the sky cleared, and as the sea went down the leak took up. When it came to bending a fresh set of sails the crew demanded to put back – and really there was nothing else to do. Boats gone, decks swept clean, cabin gutted, men without a stitch but what they stood in, stores spoiled, ship strained. We put her head for home, and – would you believe it? The wind came east right in our teeth. It blew fresh, it blew continuously. We had to beat up every inch of the way, but she did not leak so badly, the water keeping comparatively smooth. Two hours' pumping in every four is no joke – but it kept her afloat as far as Falmouth.

"The good people there live on casualties of the sea, and no doubt were glad to see us. A hungry crowd of shipwrights sharpened their chisels at the sight of that carcass of a ship. And, by Jove! they had pretty pickings off us before they were done. I fancy the owner was already in a tight place. There were delays. Then it was decided to take part of the cargo out and calk her topsides. This was done, the repairs finished, cargo reshipped; a new crew came on board, and we went out-for Bangkok. At the end of a week we were back again. The crew said they weren't going to Bangkok-a hundred and fifty days' passage-in a something hooker that wanted pumping eight hours out of the twenty-four; and the nautical papers inserted again the little paragraph: '*Judea*, Bark. Tyne to Bangkok; coals; put back to Falmouth leaky and with crew refusing duty.'

"There were more delays-more tinkering. The owner came down for a day, and said she was as right as a little fiddle. Poor old Captain Beard looked like the ghost of a Geordie skipper - through the worry and humiliation of it. Remember he was sixty, and is was his first command. Mahon said it was a foolish business, and would end badly. I loved the ship more than ever, and wanted awfully to get to Bangkok. To Bangkok! Magic name, blessed name. Mesopotamia wasn't a patch on it. Remember I was twenty, and it was my first second-mate's billet, and the East was waiting for me.

"We went out and anchored in the outer roads with a fresh crew-the third. She leaked worse than ever. It was as if those confounded shipwrights had actually made a hole in her. This time we did not even go outside. The crew simply refused to man the windlass.

"They towed us back to the inner harbor, and we became a fixture, a feature, an institution of the place. People pointed us out to visitors as 'That 'ere bark that's going to Bangkok — has been here six months — put back three times.' On holidays the small boys pulling about in boats would hail, '*Judea*, ahoy!' and if a head showed above the rail shouted, 'Where you bound to ? — Bangkok?' and jeered. We were only three on board. The poor old skipper mooned in the cabin. Mahon undertook the cooking, and unexpectedly developed all a Frenchman's genius for preparing nice little messes. I looked languidly after the rigging. We became citizens of Falmouth. Every shopkeeper knew us. At the barber's or tobacconist's they asked familiarly, 'Do you think you will ever get to Bangkok?' Meantime the owner, the underwriters, and the charterers squabbled amongst themselves in London, and our pay went on . . . Pass the bottle.

"It was horrid. Morally it was worse than pumping for life. It seemed as though we had been forgotten by the world, belonged to nobody, would get nowhere; it seemed that, as if bewitched, we would have to live for ever and ever in that inner harbor, a derision and a by-word to generations of long-shore loafers and dishonest boatmen. I obtained three months' pay and a five days' leave, and made a rush for London. It took me a day to get there and pretty well another to come back — but three months' pay went all the same. I don't know what I did with it. I went to a music hall, I believe, lunched, dined, and supped in a swell place in Regent Street, and was back on time, with nothing but a complete set of Byron's works and a new railway rug to show for three months' work. The boatman who pulled me off to the ship said: 'Hall! I thought you had left the old thing. She will never get to Bangkok.' 'That's all you know about it,' I said, scornfully – but I didn't like that prophecy at all.

"Suddenly a man, some kind of agent to somebody, appeared with full powers. He had grog-blossoms all over his face, an indomitable energy, and was a jolly soul. We leaped into life again. A hulk came alongside, took our cargo, and then we went into dry dock to get our copper stripped. No wonder she leaked. The poor thing, strained beyond endurance by the gale, had, as if in disgust, spat out all the oakum of her lower seams. She was recalked, new-coppered, and made as tight as a bottle. We went back to the hulk and reshipped our cargo.

"hen, on a fine moonlight night, all the rats left the ship.

"We had been infested with them. They had destroyed our sails, consumed more stores than the crew, affably shared our beds and our dangers, and now, when the ship was made seaworthy, concluded to clear out. I called Mahon to enjoy the spectacle. Rat after rat appeared on our rail, took a last look ver his shoulder, and leaped with a hollow thud into the empty hulk. We tried to count them, but soon lost the tale. Mahon said : 'Well, well! don't talk to me about the intelligence of rats. They ought to have left before, when we had that narrow squeak from foundering. There you have the proof how silly is the superstition about them. They leave a good ship for an old rotten hulk, where there is nothing to eat, too, the fools! . . . I don't believe they know what is safe or what is good for them, any more than you or I.'

"And after some more talk we agreed that the wisdom of rats had been grossly overrated, being in fact no greater than that of me.

"The story of the ship was known, by this all, up the Channel from Land's End to the Forelands, and we could get no crew on th south coast. They sent us one all complete from Liverpool, and we left once more – for Bangkok.

"We had fair breezes, smooth water right into the tropics, and the old *Judea* lumbered along in the sunshine. When she went eight knots everything cracked aloft, and we tied our caps to our heads; but mostly she strolled on at the rate of three miles an hour. What could you expect? She was tired – that old ship. Her youth was where mine is – where your is – you fellows who listen to this yarn; and what friend would throw your years and your weariness in your face? We didn't grumble at her. To us aft, at least, it seemed as though we had been born in her, reared in her, had lived in her for ages, had never known any other ship. I would just as soon have abused the old village church at home for not being a cathedral.

"And for me there was also my youth to make me patient. There was all the East before me, and all life, and the thought that I had been tried in that ship and had come out pretty well. And I thought of men of old who, centuries ago, went that road in ships that sailed no better, to the land of palms, and spices, and yellow sands, and of brown nations ruled by kings more cruel than Nero the Roman, and more splendid than Solomon the

Jew. The old bark lumbered on, heavy with her age and the burden of her cargo, while I lived the life of youth in ignorance and hope. She lumbered on through an interminable procession of days; and the fresh gliding flashed back at the setting sun, seemed to cry out over the darkening sea the words painted on her stern, '*Judea*, London. Do or Die.'

"Then we entered the Indian Ocean and steered northerly for Java Head. The winds were light. Weeks slipped by. She crawled on, do or die, and people at home began to think of posting us as overdue.

"One Saturday evening, I being off duty, the men asked me to give them an extra bucket of water or so-for washing clothes. As I did not wish to screw on the fresh-water pump so late, I went forward whistling, and with a key in my hand to unlock the forepeak scuttle, intending to serve the water out of a spare tank we kept there.

"The smell down below was as unexpected as it was frightful. One would have thought hundreds of paraffin lamps had been flaring and smoking in that hole for days. I was glad to get out. The man with me coughed and said, 'Funny smell, sir.' I answered negligently, 'It's good for the health, they say,' and walked aft.

"The first thing I did was to put my head down the square of the midship ventilator. As I lifted the lid a visible breath, something like a thin fog, a puff of faint haze, rose from the opening. The ascending air was hot, and had a heavy, sooty, paraffiny smell. I gave one sniff, and put down the lid gently. It was no use choking myself. The cargo was on fire.

"Next day she began to smoke in earnest. You see it was to be expected, for though the coal was of a safe kind, that cargo had been so handled, so broken up with handling, that it looked more like smithy coal than anything else. Then it had been wetted— more than once. It rained all the time we were taking it back from the hulk, and now with this long passage it got heated, and there was another case of spontaneous combustion.

"The captain called us into the cabin. He had a chart spread on the table, and looked unhappy. He said, 'The coast of West Australia is near, but I mean to proceed to our destination. It is the hurricane month, too; but we will just kiip her head for Bangkok, and fight the fire. No more putting back anywhere, if we all get roasted. We will try first to stifle this 'ere damned combustion by want of air.'

"We tried. We battened down everything, and still she smoked. The smoke kept coming out through imperceptible crevices; it forced itself through bulkheads and covers; it oozed here and there and everywhere in slender threads, in an invisible film, in an incomprehensible manner. It made its way into the cabin, into the forecastle; it poisoned the sheltered places on the deck; it could be sniffed as high as the mainyard. It was clear that if the smoke came out the air came in. This was disheartening. This combustion refused to be stifled.

"We resolved to try water, and took the hatches off. Enormous volumes of smoke, whitish, yellowish, thick, greasy, misty, choking, ascended as high as the trucks. All hands cleared out aft. Then the poisonous cloud blew away, and we went back to work in a smoke that was no thicker now than that of an ordinary factory chimney.

"We rigged the force pump, got the hose along, and by and by it burst. Well, it was as old as the ship-a prehistoric hose, and past repair. Then we pumped with the feeble head pump, drew water with buckets, and in this way managed in time to pour lots of Indian Ocean into the main hatch. The bright stream flashed in sunshine, fell into a layer of white crawling smoke, and vanished on the black surface of coal. Steam ascended mingling with the smoke. We pured salt water as into a barrel without a bottom. It was our fate to pump in that ship, to pump out of her, to pump into her; and after keeping water out of her to save ourselves from being drowned, we frantically poured water into her to save ourselves from being burnt.

"And she crawled on, do or die, in the serene weather. The sky was a miracle of purity, a miracle of azure. The sea was polished, was blue, was pellucid, was sparkling like a precious stone, extending on all sides, all round to the horizon-as if the whole terrestrial globe had been on jewel, on colossal sapphire, a single gem fashioned into a planet. And on the luster of the great calm waters the *Judea* glided imperceptibly, enveloped in languid and unclean vapors, in a lazy cloud that drifted to leeward, light and slow, a pestiferous cloud defiling the splendor of sea and sky.

"All this time of course we saw no fire. The cargo smoldered at the bottom somewhere. Once Mahon, as we were working side by side, said to me with a queer smile: 'Now, if she only would spring a tidy leak—like that time when we first left the Channel —it would put a stopper on this fire. Wouldn't it?' I remarked irrelevantly, 'Do you remember the rats?'

"We fought the fire and sailed the ship too as carefully as though nothing had been the matter. The steward cooked and attended on us. Of the other twelve men, eight worked while four rested. Everyone took his turn, captain included. There was equality, and if not exactly fraternity, then a deal of good feeling. Sometimes a man, as he dashed a bucketful of water down the hatchway, would yell out, 'Hurrah for Bangkok!' and the rest laughed, But generally we were taciturn and serious—and thirsty. Oh! how thirsty! And we had to be careful with the water. Strict allowance. The ship smoked, the sun blazed . . . Pass the bottle.

"We tried everything. We even made an attempt to dig down to the fire. No good, of course. No man could remain more than a minute below. Mahon, who went first, fainted there, and the man who went to fetch him out did likewise. We lugged them out on deck. Then I leaped down to show how easily it could be done. They had learned wisdom by that time, and contented themselves by fishing for me with a chain-hook tied to a broom handle, I believe. I did not offer to go and fetch up my shovel, which was left down below.

"Things began to look bad. We put the longboat into the water. The second boat was ready to swing out. We had also another, a fourteen-foot thing, on davits aft, where it was quite safe.

"Then, behold, the smoke suddenly decreased. We redoubled our efforts to flood the bottom of the ship. In two days there was no smoke at all. Everybody was on the broad grin. This was on a Friday. On Saturday no work, but sailing the ship of course, was done. The men washed their clothes and their faces for the first time in a fortnight, and had a special dinner given them. They spoke of spontaneous combustion with contempt, and implied they were the boys to put out combustions. Somehow we all felt as though we each had inherited a large fortune. But a beastly smell of burning hung about the ship. Captain Beard had hollow eyes and sunken cheeks. I had never noticed so much before how twisted and bowed he was. He and Mahon prowled soberly about hatches and ventilators, sniffing. It struck me suddenly poor Mahon was a very, very old chap. As to me, I was pleased and proud as though I had helped to win a great naval battle. O youth!

"The night was fine. In the morning a homeward-bound ship passed us hull down-the first we had seen for months; but we were nearing the land at last, Java Head being about 190 miles off, and nearly due north.

"Next day it was my watch on deck from eight to twelve. At breakfast the captain observed, 'It's wonderful how that smell hang about the cabin.' About ten, the mate being on the poop, I stepped down on the main deck for a moment. The carpenter's bench stood abaft the mainmast: I leaned against it sucking at my pipe, and the carpenter, a young chap, came to talk to me. He remarked. 'I think we have done very well, haven't we?' and then I perceived with annoyance the fool was trying to tilt the bench. I said curtly, 'Don't, Chips,' and immediately became aware of a queer sensation, of an absurd delusion–I seemed somehow to be in the air. I heard all round me like a pent-up breath released – as if a thousand giants simultaneously had said Phoo! – and felt a dull concussion which made my ribs ache suddenly. No doubt about it – I was in the air, and my body was describing a short parabola. But short as it was, I had the time to think several thoughts in, as far as I can remember, the following order : 'This can't be the carpenter – What is it? – Some accident – Submarine volcano? – Coals, gas! – By Jove! We are being blown up – Everybody's dead – I am falling into the afterhatch – I see fire in it.'

"The coal dust suspended in the air of the hold had glowed dull –red at the moment of the explosion. In the twinkling of an eye, in an infinitesimal fraction of a second since the first tilt of the bench, I was sprawling full length on the cargo. I picked myself up and scrambled out. It was quick like a rebound. The deck was a wilderness of smashed timber, lying crosswise like trees in a wood after a hurricane; an immense curtain of solid rags waved gently before me – it was the mainsail blown to strips. I thought : the masts will be toppling over directly; and to get out of the way bolted on all fours towards the poop ladder. The first person I saw was Mahon, with eyes like saucers, his mouth open, and the long white hair standing straight on end round his head like a silver halo. He was just about to go down when the sight of the main deck stirring, heaving up, and changing into splinters before his eyes, petrified him on the top step. I stared at him in unbelief, and he stared at me with a queer kind of shocked curiosity. I did not know that I had no hair, no eyebrows, no eyelashes, that my young mustache was burnt off, that my face was black, one cheek laid open, my nose cut, and my chin bleeding. I had lost my cap, one of my slippers, and my shirt was torn to rags. Of all this I was not aware. I was amazed to see the ship still afloat, the poop deck whole – and, most of all, to see anybody alive. Also the peace of the sky and the serenity of the sea were distinctly surprising. I suppose I expected to see them convulsed with horror . . . Pass the bottle.

"There was a voice hailing the ship from somewhere – in the air, in the sky – I couldn't tell. Presently I saw the captain – and he was mad. He asked me eagerly, 'Where's the cabin table?' and to hear such a question was a frightful shock. I had just been blown up, you understand, and vibrated with that experience – I wasn't quite sure whether I was alive. Mahon began to stamp with both feet and yelled at him, 'Good God! don't you see the deck's blown out of her?' I found my voice, and stammered out as if conscious of some gross neglect of duty, 'I don't know where the cabin table is.' It was like an absurd dream.

"Do you know what he wanted next? Well, he wanted to trim the yards. Very placidly, and as if lost in thought, he insisted on having the foreyard squared. 'I don't know if there's anybody alive,' said Mahon, alomost tearfully. 'Surely,' he said, gently, 'there will be enough left to square the foreyard.'

"The old chap, it seems, was in his own berth winding up the chronometers, when the shock sent him spinning. Immediately it occurred to him – as he said afterwards – that the ship had struck something, and ran out into the cabin. There, he saw, the cabin table had vanished somewhere. The deck being blown up, it had fallen down into the lazarette of course. Where we had our breakfast that morning he saw only a great hole in the floor. This appeared to him so awfully mysterious, and impressed him so immensely, that what he saw and heard after he got on deck were mere trifles in comparison. And, mark, he noticed directly the wheel deserted and his bark off her course – and his only thought was to get that miserable, stripped, undecked, smoldering shell of a ship back again with her head pointing at her port of destination. Bangkok! That's what he was after. I tell you this quiet, bowed, bandy-legged, almost deformed little man was immense in th singleness of his idea and in his placid ignorance of our agitation. He motioned us forward with a commanding gesture, and went to take the wheel himself.

"Yes; that was the first thing we did – trim the yards of that wreck! No one was killed, or even disabled, but everyone was more or less hurt. You should have seen them! Some were in rags, with black faces, like coal heavers, like sweeps, and had bullet heads that seemed closely cropped, but were in fact singed to the skin. Others, of the watch below, awakened by being shot out from their collapsing bunks, shivered incessantly, and kept on groaning even as we went about our work. But they all worked. That crew of Liverpool hard cases had in them the right stuff. It's my experience they always have. It is the sea that gives it – the vastness, the loneliness surrounding their dark stolid souls. Ah! Well! We stumbled, we crept, we fell, we barked our shins on the wreckage, we hauled. The masts stood, but we did not know how much they might be charred down below. It was nearly calm, but a long swell ran from the west and made her roll. They might go at any moment. We looked at them with apprehension. One could not foresee which way they would fall.

"Then we retreated aft and looked about us. The deck was a tangle of planks on edge, of planks on end, of splinter, of a ruined woodwork. The masts rose from that chaos like big trees above a matted undergrowth. The interstices of that mass of wreckage were full of something whitish, sluggish, stirring-of something that was like a greasy fog. The smoke of the invisible fire was coming up again, was trailing, like a poisonous thick mist in some valley choked with dead wood. Already lazy wisps were beginning to curl upwards amongst the mass of splinters. Here and there a piece of timber, stuck upright, resembled a post. Half of a fife rail had been shot through the foresail, and the sky make a patch of glorious blue in the ignobly soiled canvas. A portion of several boards holding together had fallen across the rail, and one end protruded over-board, like a gangway leading upon nothing, like a gangway leading over the deep sea, leading to death-as if inviting us to walk the plank at once and be done with our ridiculous troubles. And still the air, the sky-a ghost, something invisible was hailing the ship.

"Someone had the sense to look over, and there was the helmsman, who had impulsively jumped overboard, anxious to come back. He yelled and swam lustily like a merman, keeping up with the ship. We threw him a rope, and presently he stood amongst us streaming with water and very crestfallen. The captain had surrendered the wheel, and apart, elbow on rail and chin in hand, gazed at the sea wistfully. We asked ourselves, What next? I thought, Now, this is something like. This is great. I wonder what will happen. O youth!

"Suddenly Mahon sighted a steamer far astern. Captain Beard said, 'We may do something with her yet.' We hoisted two flags, which said in the international language of the sea, 'On fire, Want immediate assistance.' The steamer grew bigger rapidly, and by and by spoke with two flags on her foremast, 'I am coming to your assistance.'

"In half an hour she was abreast, to windward, within hall, and rolling slightly, with her engines stopped. We lost our composure, and yelled all together with excitement, 'We've been blown up.' A man in a white helmet, on the bridge, cried, 'Yes! All right! all right!' and he nodded his head, and smiled, and made soothing motions with his hand as though at a lot of frightened children. One of the boats dropped in the water, and walked towards us upon the sea with her long oars. Four Calashes pulled a swinging stroke. This was my first sight of Malay seamen. I've known them since, but what struck me then was their unconcern : they came alongside, and even the bowman standing up and holding to our main chains with the boathook did not deign to lift his head for a glance. I thought people who had been blown up deserved more attention.

"A little man, dry like a chip and agile like a monkey, clambered up. It was the mate of the steamer. He gave one look, and cried, 'O boys-you had better quit!'

"We were silent. He talked apart with the captain for a time - seemed to argue with him. Then they went away together to the steamer.

"When our skipper came back we learned that the steamer was the *Somerville*, Captain Nash, from West Australia to Singapore via Batavia with mails, and that the agreement was she would tow us to Anjer or Batavia, if possible, where we could extinguish the fire by scuttling, and then proceed on our voyage-to Bangkok! The old man seemed excited. 'We will do it yet,' he said to Mahon, fiercely. He shook his fist at the sky. Nobody else said a word.

"At noon the steamer began to tow. She went ahead slim and high, and what was left of the *Judea* followed at the end of seventy fathom of towrope-followed her swiftly like a cloud of smoke with mastheads protruding above. We went aloft to furl the sails. We coughed on the yards, and were careful about the bunts. Do you see the lot of us there, putting a neat furl on the sail of that ship doomed to arrive nowhere? There was not a man who didn't think that at any moment the masts would topple over. From aloft we could not see the ship for smoke, and they worked carefully, passing the gaskets with even turns. 'Harbor furl-aloft there!' cried Mahon from below.

"You understand this? I don's think one of those chaps expected to get down in the usual way. When we did I heard them saying to each other, 'Well, I thought we would come down overboard, in a lump-sticks and all-blame me if I didn't.' 'That's what I was thinking to myself,' would answer wearily another battered and bandaged scarecrow. And, mind, these were men without the drilled-in habit of obedience. To an onlooker they would be a lot of profane scallywags without a redeeming point. What made them do it—what made them obey me when I, thinking consciously how fine it was, made them drop the bunt of the foresail twice to try and do it better? What? They had no professional reputation—no examples, no praise. It wasn't a sense of duty; they all knew well enough how to shirk, and laze, and dodge—when they had a mind to it—and mostly they had. Was it the two pounds ten a month that sent them there? They didn't think their pay half good enough. No; it was something in them, something inborn and subtle and everlasting. I don't say positively that the crew of a French or German merchantman wouldn't have done it, but I doubt whether it would have been done in the same way. There was a completeness in it, something solid like a principle, and masterful like an instinct—a disclosure of something secret—of that hidden something, that gift of good or evil that makes racial difference, that shapes the fate of nations.

"It was that night at ten that, for the first time since we had been fighting it, we saw the fire. The speed of the towing had fanned the smoldering destruction. A blue gleam appeared forward, shining below the wreck of the deck. It wavered in patches, it seemed to stir and creep like the light of a glow-worm. I saw it first, and told Mahon. 'Then the game's up,' he said. 'We had better stop this towing, or she will burst out suddenly fore and aft before we can clear out.' We set up a yell;

rang bells to attract their attention; they towed on. At last Mahon and I had to crawl forward and cut the rope with an axe. There was no time to cast off the lashings. Red tongues could be seen licking the wilderness of splinters under our feet as we made our way back to the poop.

"Of course they very soon found out in the steamer that the rope was gone. She gave a loud blast of her whistle, her lights were seen sweeping in a wide circle, she came up ranging close alongside, and stopped. We were all in a tight group on the poop looking at her. Every man had saved a litter bundle or a bag. Suddenly a conical flame with a twisted top shot up forward and threw upon the black sea a circle of light, with the two vessels side by side and heaving gently in its center. Captain Beard had been sitting on the gratings still and mute for hours, but now he rose slowly and advanced in front of us, to mizzen-shrouds. Captain Nash hailed : 'Come along! Look sharp. I have mailbags on board. I will take you and your boats to Singapore.'

"Thank you! said our skipper. 'We must see the last of the ship.'

"'I can't stand by any longer,' shouted the other. 'Mails—you know.'

"'Ay! ay! We are all right.'

"Very well! I'll report you in Singapore. . . . Good-by!'

"He waved his hand. Our men dropped their bundles quietly. The steamer moved ahead, and passing out of the circle of light, vanished at once from our sight, dazzled by the fire which burned fiercely. And then I knew that I would see the East first as commander of a small boat. I thought it fine; and the fidelity to the old ship was fine. We should see the last of her. Oh, the glamor of youth! Oh, the fire of it, more dazzling than the flames of the burning ship, throwing a magic light on the wide earth, leaping audaciously to the sky, presently to be quenched by time, more cruel, more pitiless, more bitter than the sea－and like the flames of the burning ship surrounded by an impenetrable night.

"The old man warned us in his gentle and inflexible way that it was part of our duty to save for the underwriters as much as we could of the ship's gear. Accordingly we went to work aft, while she blazed forward to give us plenty of light. We lugged out a lot of rubbish. What didn't we save? An old barometer fixed with an absurd quantity of screws nearly cost me my life : a sudden rush of smoke came upon me, and I just got away in time. There were various stores, bolts of canvas, coils of rope; the poop looked like a marine bazaar, and the boats were lumbered to the gunwales. One would have thought the old man wanted to take as much as he could of his first command with him. He was very, very quiet, but off his balance evidently. Would you believe it? He wanted to take a length of old stream-cable and a kedge anchor with him in the longboat. We said, 'Ay, ay, sir,' deferentially, and on the quiet let the things slip overboard. The heavy medicine chest went that way, two bags of green coffee, tins of paint－fancy, paint!－a whole lot of things. Then I was ordered with two hands into the boats to make a stowage and get them ready against the time it would be proper for us to leave the ship.

"We put everything straight, stepped the longboat's mast for our skipper, who was to take charge of her, and I was not sorry to sit down for a moment. My face felt raw, every limb ached as if broken, I was aware of all my ribs, and would have sworn to a twist in the backbone. The boats, fast astern, lay in a deep shadow, and all around I could see the circle of the sea lighted by the fire. A gigantic flame arose forward straight and clear. It flared fierce, with noises like a whirr of wings, with rumbles as of thunder. There were cracks, detonations, and from the cone of flame the sparks flew upwards, as man is born to trouble, to leaky ships, and to ships that burn.

"What bothered me was that the ship, lying broadside to the swell and to such wind as there was – a mere breath – the boats would not keep astern where there were safe, but persisted, in a pigheaded way boats have, in getting under the counter and then swinging alongside. They were knocking about dangerously and coming near the flame, while the ship rolled on them, and, of course, there was always the danger of the masts going over the side at any moment. I and my two boatkeepers kept them off as best we could, with oars and boathooks; but to be constantly at it became exasperating, since there was no reason why we should not leave at once. We could not see those on board, nor could we imagine what caused the delay. The boatkeepers were swearing feebly, and I had not only my share of the work but also to keep at it two men who showed a constant inclination to lay themselves down and let things slide.

"At last I hailed, 'On deck there,' and someone looked over. 'We're ready here,' I said. The head disappeared, and very soon popped up again. 'The captain says, All right, sir, and to keep the boats well clear of the ship.'

"Half and hour passed. Suddenly there was frightful racket, rattle, clanking of chain, hiss of water, and millions of sparks flew up into the shivering column of smoke that stood leaning slightly above the ship. The catheads had burned away, and the two red-hot anchors had gone to the bottom, tearing out after them two hundred fathom of red-hot chain. The ship trembled, the mass of flame swayed as if ready to collapse, and the fore-topgallant mast fell. It darted down like an arrow of fire, shot under, and instantly leaping up within an oar's length of the boats, floated quietly, very black on the luminous sea. I hailed the deck again. After some time a man in an unexpectedly cheerful but also muffled tone, as though he had been trying to speak with his mouth shut, informed me, 'Coming directly, sir,' and vanished. For a long time I heard nothing but the whirr and roar of the fire. There were also whistling sounds. The boats jumped, tugged at the painters, ran at each other playfully, knocked their sides together, or, do what we would, swung in a bunch against the ship's side. I couldn't stand it any longer, and swarming up a rope, clambered aboard over the stern.

"It was as bright as day. Coming up like this, the sheet of fire facing me was terrifying sight, and the heat seemed hardly bearable at first. On a settee cushion dragged out of the cabin Captain Beard, his legs drawn up and one arm under his head, slept with the light playing on him. Do you know what the rest were busy about? They were sitting on deck right aft, round an open case, eating bread and cheese and drinking bottled stout.

"On the background of flames twisting in fierce tongues above their heads they seemed at home like salamanders, and looked like a band of desperate pirates. The fire sparkled in the whites of their eyes, gleamed on patches of white skin seen through the torn shirts. Each had the marks as of a battle about him − bandaged heads, tied-up arms, a strip of dirty rag round a knee − and each man had a bottle between his legs and a chunk of cheese in his hand. Mahon got up. With his handsome and disreputable head, his hooked profile, his long white beard, and with an uncorked bottle in his hand, he resembled one of those reckless sea robbers of old making merry amidst violence and disaster. 'The last meal on board,' he explained solemnly. 'We had nothing to eat all day, and it was no use leaving all this.' He flourished the bottle and indicated the sleeping skipper. 'He said he couldn't swallow anything, so I got him to lie down,' he went on; and as I stared, 'I don't know whether you are aware, young fellow, the man had no sleep to speak of for days − and there will be dam' little sleep in the boats.' 'There will be no boats by and by if you fool about much longer,' I said, indignantly. I walked up to the skipper and shock him by the shoulder. At last he opened his eyes, but did not move. 'Time to leave her, sir,' I said quietly.

"He got up painfully, looked at the flames, at the sea sparkling round the ship, and black, black as ink farther away; he looked at the stars shinning dim through a thin veil of smoke in a sky black, black as Erebus

"Youngest first,' he said.

"And the ordinary seaman, wiping his mouth with the back of his hand, got up, clambered over the taffrail and vanished. Others followed. One, on the point of going over, stopped short to drain his bottle, and with a great swing of his arm flung in at the fire. 'Take this!' he cried.

"The skipper lingered disconsolately, and we left him to commune alone for a while with his first command. Then I went up again and brought him away at last. It was time. The ironwork on the poop was hot to the touch.

"Then the painter of the longboat was cut, and the three boats, tied together, drifted clear of the ship. It was just sixteen hours after the explosion when we abandoned her. Mahon had charge of the second boat, and I had the smallest—the fourteen-foot thing. The longboat would have taken the lot of us; but the skipper said we must save as much property as we could—for the underwriters—and so I got my first command. I had two men with me, a bag of biscuits, a few tins of meat, and a breaker of water. I was ordered to keep close to the longboat, that in case of bad weather we might be taken into her.

"And do you know what I thought? I thought I would part company as soon as I could. I wanted to have my first command all to myself. I wasn't going to sail in a squadron if there were a chance for independent cruising. I would make land by myself. I would beat the other boats. Youth! All youth! The silly, charming, beautiful youth.

"But we did not make a start at once. We must see the last of the ship. And so the boats drifted about that night, heaving and setting on the swell. The men dozed, waked, sighed, groaned. I looked at the burning ship.

"Between the darkness of earth and heaven she was burning fiercely upon a disc of purple sea shot by the blood-red play of gleams; upon a disc of water glittering and sinister. A high, clear flame, an immense and lonely flame, ascended from the ocean, and from its summit the black smoke poured continuously at the sky. She burned furiously; mournful and imposing like a funeral pile kindled in the night, surrounded by the sea, watched over by the stars. A magnificent death had come like a grace, like a gift, like a reward to that old ship at the end of her laborious day. The surrender of her weary ghost to the keeper of stars and sea was stirring like the sight of a glorious triumph. The masts fell just before daybreak, and for a moment there was a burst and turmoil of sparks that seemed to fill with flying fire the night patient and watchful, the vast night lying silent upon the sea. At daylight she was only a charred shell, floating still under a cloud of smoke and bearing a glowing mass of coal within.

"Then the oars were got out, and the boat forming in a line moved round her remains as if in procession-the longboat leading. As we pulled across her stern a slim dart of fire shot out viciously at us, and suddenly she went down, head first, in a great hiss of steam. The unconsumed stern was the last to sink; but the paint had gone, had cracked, had peeled off, and there were no letters, there was no word, no stubborn device that was like her soul, to flash at the rising sun her creed and her name.

"We made our way north. A breeze sprang up, and about noon all the boats came together for the last time. I had no mast of sail in mine, but I made a mast out of a spare oar and hoisted a boat-awning for a sail, with a boathook for a yard. She was certainly over-masted, but I had the satisfaction of knowing that with the wind aft I could beat the other two. I had to wait for them. Then we all had a look at the captain's chart, and, after a sociable meal of hard bread and water, got our last instructions. These were simple: steer north, and keep together as mush as possible. 'Be careful with that jury-rig, Marlow,' said the captain; and Mahon as I sailed proudly past his boat, wrinkled his curved nose and hailed, 'You will sail that ship of yours under water, if you don't look out, young fellow.' He was a malicious old man – and may the deep sea where he sleeps now rock him gently, rock him tenderly to the end of time!

"Before sunset a thick rain-squall passed over the two boats, which were far astern, and that was the last I saw of them for a time. Next day I sat steering my cockle-shell – my first command – with nothing but water and sky round me. I did sight in the afternoon the upper sails of a ship far away, but said nothing, and my men did not notice her. You see I was afraid she might be homeward bound, and I had no mind to turn back from the portals of the East. I was steering for Jave – another blessed name – like Bangkok, you know. I steered many days.

"I need not tell you what it is to be knocking about in an open boat. I remember nights and days of calm, when we pulled, we pulled, and the boat seemed to stand still, as if bewitched within the circle of the sea horizon. I remember the heat, the deluge of rain-squalls that kept us baling for dear life (but filled our water cask), and I remember sixteen hours on end with a mouth dry as a cinder and a steering oar over the stern to keep my first command head on to a breaking sea. I did not know how good a man I was till then. I remember the drawn faces, the dejected figures of my two men, and I remember my youth and the feeling that will never come back any more - the feeling that I could last forever, outlast the sea, the earth, and all men; the deceitful feeling that lures us on to joys, to perils, to love, to vain effort - to death; the triumphant conviction of strength, the heat of life in the handful of dust, the glow in the heart that with every year grows dim, grows cold, grows small, and expires - and expires, too soon, too soon - before life itself.

"And this is how I see the East. I have seen its secret places and have looked into its very soul ; but now I see it always from a small boat, a high outline of mountains, blue and afar in the morning; like faint mist at noon ; a jagged wall of purple at sunset. I have the feel of the oar in my hand, the vision of a scorching blue sea in my eyes. And I see a bay, a wide bay, smooth as glass and polished like ice, shimmering in the dark. A red light burns far off upon the gloom of the land, and the night is soft and warm. We drag at the oars with aching arms, and suddenly a puff of wind, a puff faint and tepid and laden with strange odors of blossoms, of aromatic wood, comes out of the still night - the first sigh of the East on my face. That I can never forget. It was impalpable and enslaving, like a charm, like a whispered promise of mysterious delight.

"We had been pulling this finishing spell for eleven hours. Two pulled, and he whose turn it was to rest sat at the tiller. We had made out the red light in that bay and steered for it, guessing it must mark some small coasting port. We passed two vessels, outlandish and high-sterned, sleeping at anchor, and approaching the light, now very dim, ran the boat's nose against the end of a jutting wharf. We were blind with fatigue. My men dropped the oars and fell off the thwarts as if dead. I made fast to a pile. A current rippled softly. The scented obscurity of the shore was grouped into vast masses, a density of colossal clumps of vegetation, probably — mute and fantastic shapes. And at their foot the semicircle of a beach gleamed faintly, like an illusion. There was not a light, not a stir, not a sound. The mysterious East faced me, perfumed like a flower, silent like death, dark like a grave.

"And I sat weary beyond expression, exulting like a conqueror, sleepless and entranced as if before a profound, a fateful enigma.

"A splashing of oars, a measured dip reverberating on the level of water, intensified by the silence of the shore into loud claps, made me jump up. A boat, a European boat, was coming in. I invoked the name of the dead; I hailed : '*Judea* ahoy!' A thin shout answered.

"It was the captain. I had beaten the flagship by three hours, and I was glad to hear the old man's voice again, tremulous and tired. 'Is it you, Marlow?' 'Mind the end of that jetty, sir,' I cried.

"He approached cautiously, and brought up with the deep-sea

lead line which we had saved - for the underwriters. I eased my painter and fell alongside. He sat, a broken figure at the stern, wet with dew, his hands clasped in his lap. His men were asleep already. 'I had a terrible time of it.' he murmured. 'Mahon is behind - not very far.' We conversed in whispers, in low whispers, as if afraid to wake up the land. Guns, thunder, earthquakes would not have awakened the men just then.

"Looking round as we talked, I saw away at sea a bright light traveling in the night. 'There's a steamer passing the bay.' I said. She was not passing, she was entering, and she even came close and anchored. 'I wish,' said the old man, 'you would find out whether she is English. Perhaps they could give us a passage somewhere.' He seemed nervously anxious. So by dint of punching and kicking I started one of my men into a state of somnambulism, and giving him an oar, took another and pulled towards the lights of the steamer.

"There was a murmur of voices in her, metallic hollow clangs of the engine room, footsteps on the deck. Her ports shone, round like dilated eyes. Shapes moved about, and there was a shadowy man high up on the bridge. He heard my oars.

"And then, before I could open my lips, the East spoke to me, but it was in a Western voice. A torrent of words was poured into the enigmatical, the fateful silence ; outlandish, angry words, mixed with words and even whole sentences of good English, less strange but even more surprising. The voice swore and cursed violently; it riddled the solemn peace of the bay by a volley of abuse. It began by calling me Pig, and from that went crescendo into unmentionable adjectives – in English. The man up there raged aloud in two languages, and with a sincerity in his fury that almost convinced me I had, in some way, sinned against the harmony of the universe. I could hardly see him, but began to think he would work himself into a fit.

"Suddenly he ceased, and I could hear him snorting and blowing like a porpoise, I said:

"What steamer is this, pray?'

"'Eh! What's this? And who are you?'

"'Castaway crew of an English bark burnt at sea. We came here tonight. I am the second mate. The captain is in the longboat, and wishes to know if you would give us a passage somewhere.'

"'Oh, my goodness! I say. . . . This is the *Celestial* from Singapore on her return trip. I'll arrange with your captain in the morning. . . . and, . . . I say, . . . did you hear me just now?'

"'I should think the whole bay heard you.'

"'I thought you were a shoreboat. Now, look here – this infernal lazy scoundrel of a caretaker has gone to sleep again – curse him. The light is out, and I nearly ran foul of the end of this damned jetty. This is the third time he plays me this trick. Now, I ask you, can anybody stand this kind of thing? It's enough to drive a man out of his mind. I'll report him . . . I'll get the Assistant Resident to give him the sack, by – I See – there's no light. It's out, isn't it? I take you to witness the light's out. There should be a light, you know. A red light on the –'

"'There was a light,' I said mildly.

"'But it's out, man! What's the use of talking like this? You can see for yourself it's out-don't you? If you had to take a valuable steamer along this Godforsaken coast you would want a light, too. I'll kick him from end to end of his miserable wharf. You'll see if I don't. I will-'

"'So I may tell my captain you'll take us?' I broke in.

"'Yes, I'll take you. Good night,' he said, brusquely.

"I pulled back, made fast again to the jetty, and then went to sleep at last. I had faced the silence of the East. I had heard some of its language. But when I opened my eyes again the silence was as complete as though it had never been broken. I was lying in a flood of light, and the sky had never looked so far, so high, before. I opened my eyes and lay without moving.

"And then I saw the men of the East-they were looking at me. The whole length of the jetty was full of people. I saw brown, bronze, yellow faces, the black eyes, the glitter, the color of an Eastern crowd. And all these beings stared without a murmur, without a sigh, without a movement. They stared down at the boats, at the sleeping men who at night had come to them from the sea. Nothing moved. The fronds of palms stood still against the sky. Not a branch stirred along the shore, and the brown roofs of hidden houses peeped through the green foliage, through the big leaves that hung shining and still like leaves forged of heavy metal. This was the East of the ancient navigators, so old, so mysterious, resplendent and somber, living and unchanged, full of danger and promise. And these were the men. I sat up suddenly. A wave of movement passed through the crowd from end to end, passed along the heads, swayed the bodies, ran along the jetty like a ripple on the water, like a breath of wind on a field - and all was still again. I see it now - the wide sweep of the bay, the glittering sands, the wealth of green infinite and varied, the sea blue like the sea of a dream, the crowd of attentive faces, the blaze of vivid color - the water reflecting it all, the curve of the shore, the jetty, the high-sterned outlandish craft floating still. and the three boats with the tired men from the West sleeping, unconscious of the land and the people and of the violence of sunshine. They slept thrown across the thwarts, curled on bottom-boards, in the careless attitudes of death. The head of the old skipper, leaning back in the stern of the longboat, had fallen on his breast, and he looked as though he would never wake. Farther out old Mahon's face was upturned to the sky, with the long white beard spread out on his breast, as though he had been shot where he sat at the tiller; and a man, all in a heap in the bows of the boat, slept with both arms embracing the stemhead and with his cheek laid on the gunwhale. The East looked at them without a sound.

"I have known its fascination since; I have seen the mysterious shores, the still water, the lands of brown nations, where a stealthy Nemesis lies in wait, pursues, overtakes so many of the conquering race, who are proud of their wisdom, of their knowledge, of their strength. But for me all the East is contained in that vision of my youth. It is all in that moment when I opened my young eyes on it. I came upon in from a tussle with the sea - and I was young - and I saw it looking at me. And this is all that is left of it! Only a moment; a moment of strength, of romance, of glamor-of youth! . . . A flick of sunshine upon a strange shore, the time to remember, the time for a sigh, and-good-by-Night-Good-by . . . !"

He drank.

"Ah! the good old time-the good old time. Youth and the sea. Glamor and the sea! The good, strong sea, the salt, bitter sea, that could whisper to you and roar at you and knock your breath out of you."

He drank again.

"By all that's wonderful it is the sea, I believe, the sea itself-or is it youth alone? Who can tell? But you here-you all had something out of life : money, love-whatever one gets on shore-and, tell me, wasn't that the best time, that time when we were young at sea ; young and had nothing, on the sea that gives nothing, expect hard knocks-and sometimes a chance to feel you strength-that only-that you all regret?"

And we all nodded at him : the man of finance, the man of accounts, the man of law, we all nodded at him over the polished table that like a still sheet of brown water reflected our faces, lined, wrinkled; our faces marked by toil, by deceptions, by success, by love; our weary eyes looking still, looking always, looking anxiously for something out of life, that while it is expected is already gone-has passed unseen, in a sigh, in a flash-together with the youth, with the strength, with the romance of illusions.

The Horse Dealer's Daughter
—by D.H. Lawrence

"Well, Mabel, and what are you going to do with yourself?" asked Joe, with foolish flippancy. He felt quite safe himself. Without listening for an answer, he turned aside, worked a grain of tobacco to the tip of his tongue, and spat it out. He did not care about anything, since he felt safe himself.

The three brothers and the sister sat round the desolate breakfast-table, attempting some sort of desultory consultation. The morning's post had given the final tap to the family fortunes, and all was over. The dreary dining-room itself, with its heavy mahogany furniture, looked as if it were waiting to be done away with.

But the consultation amounted to nothing. There was a strange air of ineffectuality about the three men, as they sprawled at table, smoking and reflecting vaguely on their own condition. The girl was alone, a rather short, sullen-looking young woman of twenty-seven. She did not share the same life as her brothers. She would have been good-looking, save for the impressive fixity of her face, "bull-dog," as her brothers called it.

There was a confused tramping of horses' feet outside. The three men all sprawled round in their chairs to watch. Beyond the dark holly bushes that separated the strip of lawn from the high-road, they could see a cavalcade of shire horses swinging out of their own yard, being taken for exercise. This was the last time. These were the last horses that would go through their hands. The young men watched with critical, callous look. They were all frightened at the collapse of their lives, and the sense of disaster in which they were involved left them no inner freedom.

Yet they were three fine, well-set fellows enough. Joe, the eldest, was a man of thirty-three, broad and handsome in a hot, flushed way. His face was red, he twisted his black moustache over a thick finger, his eyes were shallow and restless. He had a sensual way of uncovering his teeth when he laughed, and his bearing was stupid. Now he watched the horses with a glazed look of helplessness in his eyes, a certain stupor of downfall.

The great draught-horses swung past. They were tied head to tail, four of them, and they heaved along to where a lane branched off from the high-road, planting their great hoofs floutingly in the fine black mud, swinging their great rounded haunches sumptuously, and trotting a few sudden steps as they were led into the lane, round the corner. Every movement showed a massive, slumbrous strength, and a stupidity which held them in subjection. The groom at the head looked back, jerking the leading rope. And the cavalcade moved out of sight up the lane, the tail of the last horse, bobbed up tight and stiff, held out taut from the swinging great haunches as they rocked behind the hedges in a motion-like sleep.

Joe watched with glazed hopeless eyes. The horses were almost like his own body to him. He felt he was done for now. Luckily he was engaged to a woman as old as himself, and therefore her father, who was steward of a neighbouring estate, would provide him with a job. He would marry and go into harness. His life was over, he would be a subject animal now.

He turned uneasily aside, the retreating steps of the horses echoing in his ears. Then, with foolish restlessness, he reached for the scraps of bacon-rind from the plates, and making a faint whistling sound, flung them to the terrier that lay against the fender. He watched the dog swallow them, and waited till the creature looked into his eyes. Then a faint grin came on his face, and in a high, foolish voice he said:

"You won't get much more bacon, shall you, you little b____?"

The dog faintly and dismally wagged its tail, then lowered its haunches, circled round, and lay down again.

There was another helpless silence at the table. Joe sprawled uneasily in his seat, not willing to go till the family conclave was dissolved. Fred Henry, the second brother, was erect, clean-limbed, alert. He had watched the passing of the horses with more *sang-froid*.[1] If he was an animal, like Joe, he was an animal which controls, not one which is controlled. He was master of any horse, and he carried himself with a well-tempered air of mastery. But he was not master of the situations of life. He pushed his coarse brown moustache upwards, off his lip, and glanced irritably at his sister, who sat impassive and inscrutable.

"You'll go and stop with Lucy for a bit, shan't you?" he asked. The girl did not answer.

---

1) 불어로 'Coolness'의 뜻이다.

"I don't see what else you can do," persisted Fred Henry.

"Go as a skivvy," Joe interpolated laconically.

The girl did not move a muscle.

"If I was her, I should go in for training for a nurse," said Malcolm, the youngest of them all. He was the baby of the family, a young man of twenty-two, with a fresh, jaunty *museau*.[2]

But Mabel did not take any notice of him. They had talked at her and round her for so many years, that she hardly heard them at all.

The marble clock on the mantelpiece softly chimed the half-hour, the dog rose uneasily from the hearth-rug and looked at the party at the breakfast-table. But still they sat in an ineffectual conclave.

"Oh, all right," said Joe suddenly, apropos of nothing. "I'll get a move on."

He pushed back his chair, straddled his knees with a downward jerk, to get them free, in horsey fashion, and went to the fire. Still he did not go out of the room; he was curious to know what the others would do or say. He began to charge his pipe, looking down at the dog and saying in a high, affected voice:

"Going wi' me? Going wi' me are ter? Tha'rt goin' further than tha counts on just now, dost hear?"

The dog faintly wagged his tail, the man stuck out his jaw and covered his pipe with his hands, and puffed intently, losing

---

2) 불어`로 'Face'의 뜻이다.

himself in the tobacco, looking down all the while at the dog with an absent brown eye. The dog looked up at him in mournful distrust. Joe stood with his knees stuck out, in real horsey fashion.

"Have you had a letter from Lucy?" Fred Henry asked of his sister.

"Last week," came the neutral reply.

"And what does she say?"

There was no answer.

"Does she *ask* you to go and stop there?" persisted Fred Henry.

"She says I can if I like."

"Well, then? you'd better. Tell her you'll come on Monday."

This was received in silence.

"That's what you'll do then, is it?" said Fred Henry, in some exasperation.

But she made no answer. There was a silence of futility and irritation in the room. Malcolm grinned fatuously.

"You'll have to make up your mind between now and next Wednesday," said Joe loudly, "or else find yourself lodgings on the kerbstone."

The face of the young woman darkened, but she sat on immutable.

"Here's Jack Ferguson!" exclaimed Malcolm, who was looking aimlessly out of the window.

"Where?" exclaimed Joe loudly.

"Just gone past."

"Coming in?"

Malcolm craned his neck to see the gate.

"Yes," he said.

There was a silence. Mabel sat on like one condemned, at the head of the table. Then a whistle was heard from the kitchen. The dog got up and barked sharply. Joe opened the door and shouted:

"Come on"

After a moment a young man entered. He was muffled up in over-coat and a purple woollen scarf, and his tweed cap, which he did not remove, was pulled down on his head. He was of medium height, his face was rather long and pale, his eyes looked tired.

"Hello, Jack! Well, Jack!" exclaimed Malcolm and Joe. Fred Henry merely said: "Jack."

"What's doing?" asked the newcomer, evidently addressing Fred Henry.

"Same. We've got to be out by Wednesday. Got a cold?"

"I have-got it bad, too."

"Why don't you stop in?"

"*Me* stop in? When I can't stand on my legs, perhaps I shall have a chance." The young man spoke huskily. He had a slight Scotch accent.

"It's a knock-out, isn't it," said Joe, boisterously, "if a doctor goes round croaking with a cold. Looks bad for the patients, doesn't it?"

The young doctor looked at him slowly.

"Anything the matter with *you*, then?" he asked sarcastically.

"Not as I know of. Damn your eyes, 1 hope not. Why?"

"I thought you were very concerned about the patients, wondered if you might be one yourself."

"Damn it, no, I've never been patient to no flaming doctor, and hope I never shall be," returned Joe.

At this point Mabel rose from the table, and they all seemed to become aware of her existence. She began putting the dishes together.

The young doctor looked at her, but did not address her. He had not greeted her. She went out of the room with the tray, her face impassive and unchanged

"When are you off then, all of you?" asked the doctor.

"I'm catching the eleven-forty," replied Malcolm. "Are you goin' down wi' th' trap, Joe?"

"Yes, I've told you I'm going down wi' th' trap, haven't I?"

"We'd better be getting her in then. So long Jack, if I don't see you before I go," said Malcolm, shaking hands.

He went out, followed by Joe, who seemed to have his tail between his legs .

"Well, this is the devil's own," exclaimed the doctor, when he was left alone with Fred Henry. "Going before Wednesday, are you?"

"That's the orders," replied the other.

"Where, to Northampton?"

"That's it."

"The devil!" exclaimed Ferguson, with quiet chagrin.

And there was silence between the two.

"All settled up, are you?" asked Ferguson.

"About."

There was another pause.

"Well, I shall miss yer, Freddy, boy," said the young doctor.

"And I shall miss thee, Jack," returned the other.

"Miss you like hell," mused the doctor.

Fred Henry turned aside. There was nothing to say. Mabel came in again, to finish clearing the table.

"What are *you* going to do, then, Miss Pervin?" asked Ferguson. "Going to your sister's, are you?"

Mabel looked at him with her steady, dangerous eyes, that always made him uncomfortable, unsettling his superficial ease.

"No," she said.

"Well, what in the name of fortune *are* you going to do? Say what you mean to do," cried Fred Henry, with futile intensity.

But she only averted her head, and continued her work. She folded the white table-cloth, and put on the chenille cloth.

"The sulkiest bitch that ever trod!" muttered her brother.

But she finished her task with perfectly impassive face, the young doctor watching her interestedly all the while. Then she went out.

Fred Henry stared after her, clenching his lips, his blue eyes fixing in sharp antagonism, as he made a grimace of sour exasperation.

"You could bray her into bits, and that's all you'd get out of her," he said, in a small, narrowed tone.

The doctor smiled faintly.

"What's she *going* to do, then?" he asked.

"Strike me if I know!" returned the other.

There was a pause. Then the doctor stirred.

"I'll be seeing you tonight, shall I?" he said to his friend.

"Ay—where's it to be? Are we going over to Jessdale?"

"I don't know. I've got such a cold on me. I'll come round to the 'Moon and Stars', anyway."

"Let Lizzie and May miss their night for once, eh?"

"That's it—if I feel as I do now."

"All's one —"

The two young men went through the passage and down to the back door together. The house was large, but it was servantless now, and desolate. At the back was a small brick house-yard and beyond that a big square, graveled fine and red, and having stables on two sides. Sloping, dank, winter-dark fields stretched away on the open sides.

But the stables were empty. Joseph Pervin, the father of the family, had been a man of no education, who had become a fairly large horse dealer. The stables had been full of horses, there was a great turmoil and come-and-go of horses and of dealers and grooms. Then the kitchen was full of servants. But of late things had declined. The old man had married a second time, to retrieve his fortunes. Now he was dead and everything was gone to the dogs, there was nothing but debt and threatening.

For months, Mabel had been servantless in the big house, keeping the home together in penury for her ineffectual brothers. She had kept house for ten years. But previously it was with unstinted means. Then, however brutal and coarse everything was, the sense of money had kept her proud, confident. The men might be foul-mouthed, the women in the kitchen might have bad reputations, her brothers might have illegitimate children. But so long as there was money, the girl felt herself established, and brutally proud, reserved.

No company came to the house, save dealers and coarse men. Mabel had no associates of her own sex, after her sister went away. But she did not mind. She went regularly to church, she attended to her father. And she lived in the memory of her mother, who had died when she was fourteen, and whom she had loved. She had loved her father, too, in a different way, depending upon him, and feeling secure in him, until at the age of fifty-four he married again. And then she had set hard against him. Now he had died and left them all hopelessly in debt.

She had suffered badly during the period of poverty. Nothing, however, could shake the curious, sullen, animal pride that dominated each member of the family. Now, for Mabel, the end had come. Still she would not cast about her. She would follow her own way just the same. She would always hold the keys of her own situation. Mindless and persistent, she endured from day to day. Why should she think? Why should she answer anybody? It was enough that this was the end, and there was no way out. She need not pass any more darkly along the main street of the small town, avoiding every eye. She need not demean herself any more, going into the shops and buying the cheapest food. This was at an end. She thought of nobody, not even of herself Mindless and persistent, she seemed in a sort of ecstasy to be coming nearer to her fulfillment, her own glorification, approaching her dead mother, who was glorified.

In the afternoon, she took a little bag, with shears and sponge and a small scrubbing-brush, and went out. It was a grey, wintry day, with saddened, dark green fields and an atmosphere blackened by the smoke of foundries not far off. She went quickly, darkly along the causeway, heeding nobody, through the town to the churchyard.

There she always felt secure, as if no one could see her, although as a matter of fact she was exposed to the stare of everyone who passed along under the churchyard wall. Nevertheless, once under the shadow of the great looming church, among the graves, she felt immune from the world, reserved within the thick churchyard wall as in another country.

Carefully she clipped the grass from the grave, and arranged the pinky white, small chrysanthemums in the tin cross. When this was done, she took an empty jar from a neighbouring grave, brought water, and carefully, most scrupulously sponged the marble headstone and the coping-stone.

It gave her sincere satisfaction to do this. She felt in immediate contact with the world of her mother. She took minute pains, went through the park in a state bordering on pure happiness, as if in performing this task she came into a subtle, intimate connection with her mother. For the life she followed here in the world was far less real than the world of death she inherited from her mother.

The doctor's house was just by the church. Ferguson, being a mere hired assistant, was slave to the country-side. As he hurried now to attend to the out-patients in the surgery, glancing across the graveyard with his quick eye, he saw the girl at her task at the grave. She seemed so intent and remote, it was like looking into another world. Some mystical element was touched in him. He slowed down as he walked, watching her as if spellbound.

She lifted her eyes, feeling him looking. Their eyes met. And each looked away again at once, each feeling, in some way, found out by the other. He lifted his cap and passed on down the road. There remained distinct in his consciousness, like a vision, the memory of her face, lifted from the tombstone in the churchyard, and looking at him with slow, large, portentous eyes. It *was* portentous, her face. It seemed to mesmerize him. There was a heavy power in her eyes which laid hold of his whole being, as if he had drunk some powerful drug. He had been feeling weak and done before. Now the life came back into him, he felt delivered from his own fretted, daily self.

He finished his duties at the surgery as quickly as might be, hastily filling up the bottles of the waiting people with cheap drugs. Then, in perpetual haste, he set off again to visit several cases in another part of his round, before tea-time. At all times he preferred to walk lf he could, but particularly when he was not well. He fancied the motion restored him.

The afternoon was falling. It was grey, deadened, and wintry, with a slow, moist, heavy coldness sinking in and deadening all the faculties. But why should he think or notice? He hastily climbed the hill and turned across the dark green fields, following the black cinder-track. In the distance, across a shallow dip in the country, the small town was clustered like smouldering ash, a tower, a spire, a heap of low, raw, extinct houses. And on the nearest fringe of the town, sloping into the dip, was Oldmeadow, the Pervins' house. He could see the stables and the outbuildings distinctly, as they lay towards him on the slope. Well, he would not go there many more times! Another resource would be lost to him, another place gone: the only company he cared for in the alien, ugly little town he was losing. Nothing but work, drudgery, constant hastening from dwelling to dwelling among the colliers and the iron-workers. It wore him out, but at the same time he had a craving for it. It was a stimulant to him to be in the homes of the working people, moving, as it were, through the innermost body of their life. His nerves were excited and gratified. He could come so near, into the very lives of the rough, inarticulate, powerfully emotional men and women. He grumbled, he said he hated the hellish hole. But as a matter of fact it excited him, the contact with the rough, strongly-feeling people was a stimultant applied direct to his nerves.

Below Oldmeadow, in the green, shallow, soddened hollow of fields, lay a square, deep pond. Roving across the landscape, the doctor's quick eye detected a figure in black passing through the gate of the field, down towards the pond. He looked again. It would be Mabel Pervin. His mind suddenly became alive and attentive.

Why was she going down there? He pulled up on the path on

the slope above, and stood staring. He could just make sure of the small black figure moving in the hollow of the failing day. He seemed to see her in the midst of such obscurity, that he was like a clairvoyant, seeing rather with the mind's eye than with ordinary sight. Yet he could see her positively enough, whilst he kept his eye attentive. He felt, if he looked away from her, in the thick, ugly falling dusk, he would lose her altogether.

He followed her minutely as she moved,, direct and intent, like something transmitted rather than stirring in voluntary activity, straight down the field towards the pond. There she stood on the bank for a moment. She never raised her head. Then she waded slowly into the water.

He stood motionless as the small black figure walked slowly and deliberately towards the center of the pond, very slowly, gradually moving deeper into the motionless water, and still moving forward as the water got up to her breast. Then he could see her no more in the dusk of the dead afternoon.

"There!" he exclaimed. "Would you believe it?"

And he hastened straight down, running over the wet, soddened fields, pushing through the hedges, down into the depression of callous wintry obscurity. It took him several minutes to come to the pond. He stood on the bank, breathing heavily. He could see nothing. His eyes seemed to penetrate the dead water. Yes, perhaps that was the dark shadow of her black clothing beneath the surface of the water.

He slowly ventured into the pond. The bottom was deep, soft clay, he sank in, and the water clasped dead cold round his legs.

As he stirred he could smell the cold, rotten clay that fouled up into the water. It was objectionable in his lungs. Still, repelled and yet not heeding, he moved deeper into the pond. The cold water rose over his thighs, over his loins, upon his abdomen. The lower part of his body was all sunk in the hideous cold element. And the bottom was so deeply soft and uncertain, he was afraid of pitching with his mouth underneath. He could not swim, and was afraid.

He crouched a little, spreading his hands under the water and moving them round, trying to feel for her. The dead cold pond swayed upon his chest. He moved again, a little deeper, and again, with his hands underneath, he felt all around under the water. And he touched her clothing. But it evaded his fingers. He made a desperate effort to grasp it.

And so doing he lost his balance and went under, horribly, suffocating in the foul earthy water, struggling madly for a few moments. At last, after what seemed an eternity, he got his footing, rose again into the air and looked around. He gasped, and knew he was in the world. Then he looked at the water. She had risen near him. He grasped her clothing, and drawing her nearer, turned to take his way to land again.

He went very slowly, carefully, absorbed in the slow progress. He rose higher, climbing out of the pond. The water was now only about his legs; he was thankful, full of relief to be out of the clutches of the pond. He lifted her and staggered onto the bank, out of the horror of wet, grey clay.

He laid her down on the bank. She was quite unconscious and

running with water. He made the water come from her mouth, he worked to restore her. He did not have to work very long before he could feel the breathing begin again in her; she was breathing naturally. He worked a little longer. He could feel her live beneath his hands; she was coming back. He wiped her face, wrapped her in his overcoat, looked round into the dim, dark grey world, then lifted her and staggered down the bank and across the fields.

It seemed an unthinkably long way, and his burden so heavy he felt he would never get to the house. But at last he was in the stable-yard, and then in the house-yard. He opened the door and went into the house. In the kitchen he laid her down on the hearth-rug and called. The house was empty. But the fire was burning in the grate.

Then again he kneeled to attend to her. She was breathing regularly, her eyes were wide open and as if conscious, but there seemed something missing in her look. She was conscious in herself, but unconscious of her surroundings.

He ran upstairs, took blankets from a bed, and put them before the fire to warm. Then he removed her saturated, earthy-smelling clothing, rubbed her dry with a towel, and wrapped her naked in the blankets. Then he went into the dining-room, to look for spirits. There was a little whisky. He drank a gulp himself, and put some into her mouth.

The effect was instantaneous. She looked full into his face, as if she had been seeing him for some time, and yet had only just become conscious of him.

"Dr. Ferguson?" she said.

"What?" he answered.

He was divesting himself of his coat, intending to find some dry clothing upstairs. He could not bear the smell of the dead, clayey water, and he was mortally afraid for his own health.

"What did I do?" she asked.

"Walked into the pond," he replied. He had begun to shudder like one sick, and could hardly attend to her. Her eyes remained full on him, he seemed to be going dark in his mind, looking back at her helplessly. The shuddering became quieter in him, his life came back to him, dark and unknowing, but strong again.

"Was I out of my mind?" she asked, While her eyes were fixed on him all the time.

"Maybe, for the moment," he replied. He felt quiet, because his strength had come back. The strange fretful strain had left him.

"Am I out of my mind now?" she asked.

"Are you?" he reflected a moment. "No," he answered truthfully.

"1 don't see that you are." He turned his face aside. He was afraid now, because he felt dazed, and felt dimly that her power was stronger than his, in this issue. And she continued to look at him fixedly all the time.

"Can you tell me where I shall find some dry things to put on?" he asked.

"Did you dive into the pond for me?" she asked.

"No," he answered. "I walked in. But 1 went in over head as well."

There was silence for a moment. He hesitated. He very much

wanted to go upstairs to get into dry clothing. But there was another desire in him. And she seemed to hold him. His will seemed to have gone to sleep, and left him, standing there slack before her. But he felt warm inside himself. He did not shudder at all, though his clothes were sodden on him.

"Why did you?" she asked.

"Because I didn't want you to do such a foolish thing," he said.

"It wasn't foolish," she said, still gazing at him as she lay on the floor, with a sofa cushion under her head. "It was the right thing to do. I knew best, then."

"I'll go and shift these wet things," he said. But still he had not the power to move out of her presence, until she sent him. It was as if she had the life of his body in her hands, and he could not extricate himself. Or perhaps he did not want to.

Suddenly she sat up. Then she became aware of her own immediate condition. She felt the blankets about her, she knew her own limbs. For a moment it seemed as if her reason were going. She looked round, with wild eye, as if seeking something. He stood still with fear. She saw her clothing lying scattered.

"Who undressed me?" she asked, her eyes resting full and inevitable on his face.

"I did," he replied, "to bring you round."

For some moments she sat and gazed at him awfully, her lips parted.

"Do you love me, then?" she asked.

He only stood and stared at her, fascinated. His soul seemed to melt.

She shuffled forward on her knees, and put her arms round him, round his legs, as he stood there, pressing her breasts against his knees and thighs, clutching him with strange, convulsive certainty, pressing his thighs against her, drawing him to her face, her throat, as she looked up at him with flaring, humble eyes of transfiguration, triumphant in first possession.

"You love me," she murmured, in strange transport, yearning and triumphant and confident. "You love me. I know you love me, I know."

And she was passionately kissing his knees, through the wet clothing, passionately and indiscriminately kissing his knees, his legs, as if unaware of everything.

He looked down at the tangled wet hair, the wild, bare, animal shoulders. He was amazed, bewildered, and afraid. He had never thought of loving her. He had never wanted to love her. When he rescued her and restored her, he was a doctor, and she was a patient. He had had no single personal thought of her. Nay, this introduction of the personal element was very distasteful to him, a violation of his professional honour. It was horrible to have her there embracing his knees. It was horrible. He revolted from it, violently. And yet—and yet—he had not the power to break away.

She looked at him again, With the same supplication of powerful love, and that same transcendent, frightening light of triumph. In view of the delicate flame which seemed to come from her face like a light, he was powerless. And yet he had never intended to love her. He had never intended. And something stubborn in him could not give way.

"You love me," she repeated, in a murmur of deep, rhapsodic assurance. "You love me."

Her hands were drawing him, drawing him down to her. He was afraid, even a little horrified. For he had, really, no intention of loving her. Yet her hands were drawing him towards her. He put out his hand quickly to steady himself, and grasped her bare shoulder. A flame seemed to burn the hand that grasped her soft shoulder. He had no intention of loving her: his whole will was against his yielding. It was horrible. And yet wonderful was the touch of her shoulders, beautiful the shining of her face. Was she perhaps mad? He had a horror of yielding to her. Yet something in him ached also.

He had been staring away at the door, away from her. But his hand remained on her shoulder. She had gone suddenly very still. He looked down at her. Her eyes were now wide with fear, with doubt, the light was dying from her face, a shadow of terrible greyness was returning. He could not bear the touch of her eyes' question upon him, and the look of death behind the question.

With an inward groan he gave way, and let his heart yield towards her. A sudden gentle smile came on his face. And her eyes, which never left his face, slowly, slowly filled with tears. He watched the strange water rise in her eyes, like some slow fountain coming up. And his heart seemed to burn and melt away in his breast.

He could not bear to look at her any more. He dropped on his knees and caught her head with his arms and pressed her face against his throat. She was very still. His heart, which seemed to have broken, was burning with a kind of agony in his breast. And he felt her slow, hot tears wetting his throat. But he could not move.

He felt the hot tears wet his neck and the hollows of his neck, and he remained motionless, suspended through one of man's eternities. Only now it had become indispensable to him to have her face pressed close to him; he could never let her go again. He could never let her head go away from the close clutch of his arm. He wanted to remain like that for ever, with his heart hurting him in a pain that was also life to him. Without knowing, he was looking down on her damp, soft brown hair.

Then, as it were suddenly, he smelt the horrid stagnant smell of that water. And at the same moment she drew away from him and looked at him. Her eyes were wistful and unfathomable. He was afraid of them, and he fell to kissing her, not knowing what he was doing. He wanted her eyes not to have that terrible, wistful, unfathomable look.

When she turned her face to him again, a faint delicate flush was glowing, and there was again dawning that terrible shining of joy in her eyes, which really terrified him, and yet which he now wanted to see, because he feared the look of doubt still more.

"You love me?" she said, rather faltering.

"Yes." The word cost him a painful effort. Not because it wasn't true. But because it was too newly true, the saying seemed to tear open again his newly-torn heart. And he hardly wanted it to be true, even now.

She lifted her face to him, and he bent forward and kissed her on the mouth, gently, with the one kiss that is an eternal pledge. And as he kissed her his heart strained again in his breast. He never intended to love her. But now it was over. He had crossed over the gulf to her, and all that he had left behind had shrivelled and become void.

After the kiss, her eyes again slowly filled with tears. She sat still, away from him, with her face drooped aside, and her hands folded in her lap. The tears fell very slowly. There was complete silence. He too sat there motionless and silent on the hearth-rug. The strange pain of his heart that was broken seemed to consume him. That he should love her? That this was love! That he should be ripped open in this way! Him, a doctor! How they would all jeer if they knew! It was agony to him to think they might know.

In the curious naked pain of the thought he looked again to her. She was sitting there drooped into a muse. He saw a tear fall, and his heart flared hot. He saw for the first time that one of her shoulders was quite uncovered, one arm bare, he could see one of her small breasts; dimly, because it had become almost dark in the room.

"Why are you crying?" he asked, in an altered voice.

She looked up at him. and behind her tears the consciousness of her situation for the first time brought a dark look of shame to her eyes.

"I'm not crying, really," she said, watching him, half frightened.

He reached his hand, and softly closed it on her bare arm.

"I love you! I love you!" he said in a soft, low vibrating voice, unlike himself.

She shrank, and dropped her head. The soft, penetrating grip of his hand on her arm distressed her. She looked up at him.

"I want to go," she said. "I want to go and get you some dry things."

"Why?" he said. "I'm all right."

"But I want to go," she said. "And I want you to change your things."

He released her arm, and she wrapped herself in the blanket, looking at him rather frightened. And still she did not rise.

"Kiss me," she said wistfully.

He kissed her, but briefly, half in anger.

Then, after a second, she rose nervously, all mixed up in the blanket. He watched her in her confusion as she tried to extricate herself and wrap herself up so that she could walk. He watched her relentlessly, as she knew. And as she went, the blanket trailing, and as he saw a glimpse of her feet and her white leg, he tried to remember her as she was when he had wrapped her in the blanket. But then he didn't want to remember, because she had been nothing to him then, and his nature revolted from remembering her as she was when she was nothing to him.

A tumbling, muffled noise from within the dark house startled him. Then he heard her voice: "There are clothes." He rose and went to the foot of the stairs, and gathered up the garments she had thrown down. Then he came back to the fire, to rub himself down and dress. He grinned at his own appearance when he had finished.

The fire was sinking, so he put on coal. The house was now quite dark, save for the light of a street-lamp that shone in faintly from beyond the holly trees. He lit the gas with matches he found on the mantelpiece. Then he emptied the pockets of his own clothes, and threw all his wet things in a heap into the scullery. After which he gathered up her sodden clothes, gently, and put them in a separate heap on the copper-top in the scullery.

It was six o'clock on the clock. His own watch had stopped. He ought to go back to the surgery. He waited, and still she did not come down. So he went to the foot of the stairs and called:

"I shall have to go."

Almost immediately he heard her coming down. She had on her best dress of black voile, and her hair was tidy, but still damp. She looked at him—and in spite of herself, smiled.

"I don't like you in those clothes," she said.

"Do I look a sight?" he answered.

They were shy of one another.

"I'll make you some tea," she said.

"No, I must go."

"Must you?" And she looked at him again with the wide, strained, doubtful eyes. And again, from the pain of his breast, he knew how he loved her. He went and bent to kiss her, gently, passionately, with his heart's painful kiss.

"And my hair smells so horrible," she murmured in distraction.

"And I'm so awful, I'm so awful! Oh no, I'm too awful." And she broke into bitter, heart-broken sobbing. "You can't want to love me, I'm horrible,"

"Don't be silly, don't be silly," he said, trying to comfort her, kissing her, holding her in his arms. "I want you, I want to marry you, we're going to be married, quickly, quickly-to-morrow if I can."

But she only sobbed terribly, and cried:

"I feel awful. I feel awful. I feel I'm horrible to you."

"No, I want you, I want you," was all he answered, blindly, with that terrible intonation which frightened her almost more than her horror lest he should *not* want her.

To Please His Wife

―by Thomas Hardy

The interior of St. James's Church, in Havenpool Town, was slowly darkening under the close clouds of a winter afternoon. It was Sunday : service had just ended, the face of the parson in the pulpit was buried in his hands, and the congregation, with a cheerful sigh of release, were rising from their knees to depart.

For the moment the stillness was so complete that the surging of the sea could be heard outside the harbour-bar. Then it was broken by the footsteps of the clerk going towards the west door to open it in the usual manner for the exit of the assembly. Before, however, he had reached the doorway, the latch was lifted from without, and the dark figure of a man in a sailor's garb appeared against the light.

The clerk stepped aside, the sailor closed the door gently behind him, and advanced up the nave till he stood at the chancel-step. The parson looked up from the private little prayer which, after so many for the parish, he quite fairly took for himself, rose to his feet, and stared at the intruder.

'I beg you pardon, sir,' said the sailor, addressing the minister in a voice distinctly audible to all the congregation. 'I have come here to offer thanks for my narrow escape from shipwreck. I am given to understand that it is a proper thing to do, if you have no objection?'

'I have no objection ; certainly. It is usual to mention any such wish before service, so that the proper words may be used in the General Thanksgiving. But if you wish, we can read from the form for use after a storm at sea.'

'Ay, sure ; I ain't particular,' said the sailor.

The clerk thereupon directed the sailor to the page in the prayer-book where the collect of thanksgiving would be found, and the rector began reading it, the sailor kneeling where he stood, and repeating it after him word by word in a distinct voice. The people, who had remained agape and motionless at the proceeding, mechanically knelt down likewise ; but they continued to regard the isolated form of the sailor who, in the precise middle of the chancel-step, remained fixed on his knees, facing the east, his hat beside him, his hands joined, and he quite unconscious of his appearance in their regard.

When his thanksgiving had come to an end he rose ; the people rose also ; and all went out of church together. As soon as the sailor emerged, so that the remaining daylight fell upon his face, old inhabitants began to recognize him as no other than Shadrach Jolliffe, a young man who had not been seen at Havenpool for several years. A son of the town, his parents had died when he was quite young, on which account he had early gone to sea, in the Newfoundland trade.

He talked with this and that townsman as he walked, informing them that, since leaving his native place years before, he had become captain and owner of a small coasting-ketch, which had providentially been saved from the gale as well as himself. Presently he drew near to two girls who were going out of the churchyard in front of him ; they had been sitting in the nave at his entry, and had watched his doings with deep interest, afterwards discussing him as they moved out of church together. One was a slight and gentle creature ; the other a tall, large-framed, deliberative girl. Captain Jolliffe regarded the loose curls of their hair, their backs and shoulders, down to their heels, for some time.

'Who may them two maids be?' he whispered to his neighbour.
'The little one is Emily Hanning ; The tall one Joanna Phippard.'
'Ah! I recollect 'em now, to be sure.'

He advanced to their elbow, and genially stole a gaze at them.
'Emily, you don't know me?' said the sailor, turning his beaming brown eyes on her.

'I think I do, Mr, Jolliffe,' said Emily shyly.

The other girl looked straight at him with her dark eyes.

'The face of Miss Joanna I don't call to mind so well,' he continued. 'But I know her beginnings and kindred.'

They walked and talked together, Jolliffe narrating particulars of his late narrow escape, till they reached the corner of Sloop Lane, in which Emily Hanning dwelt, when, with a nod and smile, she left them. Soon the sailor parted also from Joanna, and having no especial errand or appointment, turned back towards Emily's house. She lived with her father, who called himself an accountant, the daughter, however, keeping a little stationery-shop as a supplemental provision for the gaps of his somewhat uncertain business. On entering Jolliffe found father and daughter about to begin tea.

'O, I didn't know it was tea-time,' he said. 'Ah, I'll have a cup with much pleasure.'

He remained to tea and long afterwards, telling more tales of his seafaring life. Several neighbours called to listen, and were asked to come in. Somehow Emily Hanning lost her heart to the sailor that Sunday night, and in the course of a week or two there was a tender understanding between them.

One moonlight evening in the next month Shadrach was ascending out of the town by the long straight road eastward, to an elevated suburb where the more fashionable houses stood – if anything near this ancient port could be called fashionable – when he saw a figure before him whom, from her manner of glancing back, he took to be Emily. But, on coming up, he found she was Joanna Phippard. He gave a gallant greeting, and walked beside her.

'Go along,' she said, or 'Emily will be jealous!'

He seemed not to like the suggestion, and remained.

What was said and what was done on that walk never could be clearly recollected by Shadrach ; but in some way or other Joanna contrived to wean him away from her gentler and younger rival. From that week onwards, Jolliffe was seen more and more in the wake of Joanna Phippard and less in the company of Emily, and it was soon rumoured about the quay that old Jolliffe's son, who had come home from sea, was going to be married to the former young woman, to the great disappointment of th latter.

Just after this report had gone about, Joanna dressed herself for a walk one morning, and started for Emily's house in the little cross-street. Intelligence of the deep sorrow of her friend on account of the loss of Shadrach had reached her ears also, and her conscience reproached her for winning him away.

Joanna was not altogether satisfied with the sailor. She liked his attentions, and she coveted the dignity of matrimony ; but she had never been deeply in love with Jolliffe. For one thing, she was ambitious, and socially his position was hardly so good as her own, and there was always the chance of an attractive woman mating considerably above her. It had long been in her mind that she would not strongly object to give him back again to Emily if her friend felt so very badly about him. To this end she had written a letter of renunciation to Shadrach, which letter she carried in her hand, intending to send it if personal observation of Emily convinced her that her fiend was suffering.

Joanna entered Sloop Lane and stepped down into the stationery-shop, which was below the pavement level. Emily's father was never at home at this hour of the day, and it seemed as though Emily were not at home either, for the visitor could make nobody hear. Customers came so seldom hither that a five minutes' absence of the proprietor counted for little. Joanna waited in the little shop, where Emily had tastefully set out-as women can-articles in themselves of slight value, so as to obscure the meagreness of the stock-in-trade ; till she saw a figure pausing without the window apparently absorbed in the contemplation of the sixpenny books, packets of paper, and prints hung on a string. It was Captain Shadrach Jolliffe, peering in to ascertain if Emily were there alone. Moved by an impulse of reluctance to meet him in a spot which breathed of Emily, Joanna slipped through the door that communicated with the parlour at the back. She had frequently done so before, for in her friendship with Emily she had the freedom of the house without ceremony.

Jolliffe entered the shop. Through the thin blind which screened the glass partition she could see that he was disappointed at not finding Emily there. He was about to go out again, when Emily's form darkened the doorway, hastening home from some errand. At sight of Jolliffe she started back as if she would have gone out again.

'Don't run away, Emily ; don't !' said he. 'What can make 'ee afraid?'

'I'm not afraid, Captain Jolliffe. Only—only I saw you all of a sudden, and—it made me jump!' Her voice showed that her heart had jumped even more than the rest of her.

'I just called as I was passing,' he said.

'For some paper?' She hastened behind the counter.

'No, no, Emily; why do you get behind there? Why not stay by me? You seem to hate me.'

'I don't hate you. How can I ?'

'Then come out, so that we can talk like Christians.'

Emily obeyed with a fitful laugh, till she stood again beside him in the open part of the shop.

'There's a dear,' he said.

'You mustn't say that, Captain Jolliffe ; because the words belong to somebody else.'

'Ah! I know what you mean. But, Emily, upon my life I didn't know till this morning that you cared one bit about me, or I should not have done as I have done. I have the best of feelings for Joanna, but I know that from the beginning she hasn't cared for me more than in a friendly way ; and I see now the one I ought to have asked to be my wife. You know, Emily, when a man comes home from sea after a long voyage he's as blind as a bat – he can't see who's who in women. They are all alike to him, beautiful creatures, and he takes the first that comes easy, without thinking if she loves him, or if he might not soon love another better than her. From the first I inclined to you most, but you were so backward and shy that I thought you didn't want me to bother 'ee, and so I went to Joanna.'

'Don't say any more, Mr. Jolliffe, don't!' said she, chocking. 'You are going to marry Joanna next month, and it is wrong to – to–'

'O Emily, my darling!' he cried, and clasped her little figure in his arms before she was aware.

Joanna, behind the curtain, turned pale, tried to withdraw her eyes, but could not.

'It is only you I love as a man ought to love the woman he is going to marry ; and I know this from what Joanna has said, that she will willingly let me off! She wants to marry higher, I know, and only said "Yes" to me out of kindness. A fine, tall girl like her isn't the sort for a plain sailor's wife ; you be the best suited for that'

He kissed her and kissed her again, her flexible form quivering in the agitation of his embrace.

'I wonder — are you sure — Joanna is going to break off with you? O, are you sure? Because — '

'I know she would not wish to make us miserable. She will release me.'

'O, I hope — I hope she will ! Don't stay any longer, Captain Jolliffe!'

He lingered, however, till a customer came for a penny stick of sealing-wax, and then he withdrew.

Green envy had overspread Joanna at the scene. She looked about for a way of escape. To get out without Emily's knowledge of her visit was indispensable. She crept from the parlour into the passage, and thence to the back door of the house, where she let herself noiselessly into the street.

The sight of that caress had reversed all her resolutions. She could not let Shadrach go. Reaching home she burnt the letter, and told her mother that if Captain Jolliffe called she was too unwell to see him.

Shadrach, however, did not call. He sent her a note expressing in simple language the state of his feelings ; and asked to be allowed to take advantage of the hints she had given him that her affection, too, was little more than friendly, by cancelling the engagement.

Looking out upon the harbour and the island beyond he waited and waited in his lodgings for and answer that did not come. The suspense grew to be so intolerable that after dark he went up the High Street. He could not resist calling at Joanna's to learn his fate.

Her mother said her daughter was too unwell to see him, and to his questioning admitted that it was in consequence of a letter received from himself, which had distressed her deeply.

'You know what it was about, perhaps, Mrs. Phippard?' he said

Mrs. Phippard owned that she did, adding that it put them in a very painful position. Thereupon Shadrach, fearing that he had been guilty of an enormity, explained that if his letter had pained Joanna it must be owing to a misunderstanding, since he had thought it would be a relief to her. If otherwise, he would hold himself bound by his word, and she was to think of the letter as never having been written.

Next morning he received an oral message from the young woman, asking him to fetch her home from a meeting that evening. This he did, and while walking from the Town Hall to her door, with her hand in his arm, she said ;

'It is all the same as before between us, isn't it, Shadrach? Your letter was sent in mistake?'

'It is all the same as before, ' he answered, 'if you say it must be.'

'I wish it to be,' she murmured, with hard lineaments, as she thought of Emily.

Shadlach was a religious and scrupulous man, who respected his word as his life. Shortly afterwards the wedding took place,

Jolliffe having conveyed to Emily as gently as possible the error he had fallen into when estimating Joanna's mood as one of indifference.

II

A month after the marriage Joanna's mother died, and the couple were obliged to turn their attention to very practical matters. Now that she was left without a parent, Joanna could not bear the notion of her husband going to sea again, but the question was, What could he do at home? They finally decided to take on a small grocer's shop in High Street, the goodwill and stock of which were waiting to be disposed of at that time. Shadrach knew nothing of shopkeeping, and Joanna very little, but they hoped to learn.

To the management of this grocery business they now devoted all their energies, and continued to conduct it for many succeeding years, without great success. Two sons were born to them, whom their mother loved to idolatry, although she had never passionately loved her husband ; and she lavished upon them all her forethought and care. But the shop did not thrive, and the large dreams she had entertained of her sons' education and career became attenuated in the face of realities. Their schooling was of the plainest, but, being by the sea, they grew alert in all such nautical arts and enterprises as were attractive to their age.

The great interest of the Jolliffes' married life, outside their own immediate household, had lain in the marriage of Emliy. By one of those odd chances which lead those that lurk in unexpected corners to be discovered, while the obvious are passed by, the gentle girl had been seen and loved by a thriving merchant of the town, a widower, some years older than herself, though still in the prime of life. At first Emily had declared that she never, never could merry anyone ; but Mr. Lester had quietly persevered, and had at last won her reluctant assent. Two children also were the fruits of this union, and, as they grew and prospered, Emily declared that she had never supposed that she could live to be so happy.

The worthy merchant's home, one of those large, substantial brick mansions frequently jammed up in old-fashioned towns, faced directly on the High Street, nearly opposite to the grocery shop of the Jolliffes, and it now became the pain of Joanna to behold the woman whose place she had usurped out of pure covetousness, looking down from her position of comparative wealth upon the humble shop-window with its dusty sugar-loaves, heaps of raisins, and canisters of tea, over which it was her own lot to preside. The business having so dwindled, Joanna was obliged to serve in the shop herself, and it galled and mortified her that Emily Lester, sitting in her large drawing-room over the way, could witness her own dancings up and down behind the counter at the beck and call of wretched twopenny customers, whose patronage she was driven to welcome gladly ; persons to whom she was compelled to be civil in the street, while Emily was bounding along with her children and her governess, and conversing with the genteelest people of the town and neighbourhood. This was what she had gained by not letting Shadrach Jolliffe, whom she had so faintly loved, carry his affection elsewhere.

Shadrach was a good and honest man, and he had been faithful to her in heart and in deed. Time had clipped the wings of his love for Emily in his devotion to the mother of his boys; he had quite lived down that impulsive earlier fancy, and Emily had become in his regard nothing more than a friend. It was the same with Emily's feeling for him. Possibly, had she found the least cause for jealousy, Joanna would almost have been better satisfied. It was in the absolute acquiescence of Emily and Shadrach in the results she herself had contrived that her discontent found nourishment.

Shadrach was not endowed with the marrow shrewdness necessary for developing a retail business in the face of many competitors. Did a customer inquire if the grocer could really recommend the wondrous substitute for eggs which a persevering bagman had forced into his stock, he would answer that 'when you did not put eggs into a pudding it was difficult to taste them there'; and when he was asked if his 'real Mocha coffee' was real Mocha, he would say grimly, 'as understood in small shops.' The way to wealth was not by this route.

One summer day, when the big brick house opposite was reflecting the oppressive sun's heat into the shop, and nobody was present but husband and wife, Joanna looked across at Emily's door, where a wealthy visitor's carriage had drawn up.

Traces of patronage had been visible in Emily's manner of late.

'Shadrach, the truth is, you are not a business-man, his wife sadly murmured. 'You were not brought up to shopkeeping, and it is impossible for a man to make a fortune at an occupation he has jumped into, as you did into this.'

Jolliffe agreed with her, in this as in everything else. 'Not that I care a rope's end about making a fortune,' he said cheerfully. 'I am happy enough, and we can rub on somehow.'

She looked again at the great house through the screen of bottled pickles.

'Rub on - yes,' she said bitterly. 'But see how well off Emmy Lester is, who used to be so poor! Her boys will go to College, no doubt ; and think of yours- obliged to go the Parish School!'

Shadrach's thoughts had flown to Emily.

'Nobody,' he said good-humouredly, 'ever did Emily a better turn than you did, Joanna, when you warned her off me and put an end to that little simpering nonsense between us, so as to leave it in her power to say "Ay" to Lester when he came along.'

This almost maddened her.

'Don't speak of bygones!' she implored, in stern sadness. 'But think, for the boys' and my sake, if not for your own, what are we to do to get richer?'

'Well,' he said, becoming serious, 'to tell the truth, I have always felt myself unfit for this business, though I've never liked to say so. I seem to want more room for sprawling ; a more open space to strike out in than here among friends and neighbours. I could get rich as well as any man, if I tried my own way.'

'I wish you would! What is your way?'

'To go to sea again.'

She had been the very one to keep him at home, hating the semi-widowed existence of sailors' wives. But her ambition checked her instincts now, and she said ; 'Do you think success really lies that way?'

'I am sure it lies in no other.'

'Do you want to go, Shadrach?'

'Not for the pleasure of it, I can tell 'ee. There's no such pleasure at sea, Joanna, as I can find in my back parlour here. To speak honest, I have no love for the brine. I never had much. But if it comes to a question of a fortune for you and the lads, it is another thing. That's the only way to it for one born and bred a seafarer as I.'

'Would it take long to earn?'

'Well, that depends ; perhaps not.'

The next morning Shadrach pulled from a chest of drawers the nautical jacket he had worn during the first months of his return, brushed out the moths, donned it, and walked down to the quay. The port still did a fair business in the Newfoundland trade, though not so much as formerly.

It was not long after this that he invested all he possessed in purchasing a part-ownership in a brig, of which he was appointed captain. A few months were passed in coast-trading, during which interval Shadrach wore off the land-rust that had accumulated upon him in his grocery phase ; and in the spring the brig sailed for Newfoundland.

Joanna lived on at home with her sons, who were now growing up into strong lads, and occupying themselves in various ways about the harbour and quay.

'Never mind, let them work a little,' their fond mother said to herself . 'Our necessities compel it now, but when Shadrach comes home they will be only seventeen and eighteen, and they shall be removed from the port, and their education throughly taken in hand by a tutor ; and with the money they'll have they will perhaps be as near to gentlemen as Emmy Lester's precious two, with their algebra and their Latin!'

The date for Shadrach's return drew near and arrived, and he did not appear. Joanna was assured that there was no cause for anxiety, sailing-ships being so uncertain in their coming ; which assurance proved to be well grounded, for late one wet evening, about a month after the calculated time, the ship was announced as at hand, and presently the slip-slop step of Shadrach as the sailor sounded in the passage, and he entered. The boys had gone out and had missed him, and Joanna was sitting alone.

As soon as the first emotion of reunion between the couple had passed, Jolliffe explained the delay as owing to a small speculative contract, which had produced good results.

'I was determined not to disappoint 'ee,' he said; 'and I think you'll own that I haven't!'

With this he pulled out an enormous canvas bag, full and rotund as the money-bag of the giant whom Jack slew, untied it, and shock the contents out into her lap as she sat in her low chair by the fire. A mass of sovereigns and guineas (there were guineas on the earth in those days) fell into her lap with a sudden thud, weighing down her gown to the floor.

'There!' said Shadrach complacently. 'I told 'ee, dear, I'd do it ; and have I done it or no?'

Somehow her face, after the first excitement of possession, did not retain its glory.

'It is a lot of gold, indeed,' she said. 'And – is this all?'

'All? Why, dear Joanna, do you know you can count to three hundred in that heap? It is a fortune!'

"Yes – yes. A fortune – judged by sea ; but judged by land –'

However, she banished considerations of the money for the nonce. Soon the boys came in, and next Sunday Shadrach returned thanks to God – this time by the more ordinary channel of the italics in the General Thanksgiving. But a few days after, when the question of investing the money arose, he remarked that she did not seem so satisfied as he had hoped.

'Well, you see, Shadrach,' she answered, 'we count by hundreds ; they count by thousands' (nodding towards the other side of the street). 'They have set up a carriage and pair since you left.'

'O, have they?'

'My dear Shadrach, you don't know how the world moves. However, we'll do the best we can with it. But they are rich, and we are poor still!'

The greater part of a year was desultorily spent. She moved sadly about the house and shop, and the boys were still occupying themselves in and around the harbour.

'Joanna,' he said, one day, 'I see by your movements that it is not enough.'

'It is not enough,' said she. 'My boys will have to live by steering the ships that the Lesters own ; and I was once above her!'

Jolliffe was not an argumentative man, and he only murmured that he thought he would make another voyage. He meditated for several days, and coming home from the quay one afternoon said suddenly;

'I could do it for 'ee, dear, in one more trip, for certain, if-if-'

'Do what, Shadrach?'

'Enable 'ee to count by thousands instead of hundreds.'

'If what?'

'If I might take the boys.'

She turned pale.

'Don't say that Shadrach,' she answered hastily.

'Why?'

'I don't like to hear it! There's danger at sea. I want them to be something genteel, and no danger to them. I couldn't let them risk their lives at sea. O, I couldn't ever, ever!'

'Very well, dear, it shan't be done.'

Next day, after a silence, she asked a question.

'If they were to go with you it would make a great deal of difference, I suppose, to the profit?'

' 'Twould treble what I should get from the venture single-handed. Under my eye they would be as good as two more of myself.'

Later on she said : 'Tell me more about this.'

'Well, the boys are almost as clever as master-mariners in handling a craft, upon my life! There isn't a more cranky place in the Northern Seas than about the sandbanks of this harbour, and they've practised here from their infancy. And they are so steady. I couldn't get their steadiness and their trustworthiness in half a dozen men twice their age.'

'And is it very dangerous at sea ; now, too, there are rumours of war? ' she asked uneasily.

'O, well, there be risks. Still . . . '

The idea grew and magnified, and the mother's heart was crushed and stifled by it. Emmy was growing too patronizing ; it could not be borne. Shadrach's wife could not help nagging him about their comparative poverty. The young men, amiable as their father, when spoken to on the subject of a voyage of enterprise, were quite willing to embark ; and though they, like their father, had no great love for the sea, they became quite enthusiastic when the proposal was detailed.

Everything now hung upon their mother's assent. She withheld it long, but at last have the word ; the young men might accompany their father. Shadrach was unusually cheerful about it ; Heaven had preserved him hitherto, and he had uttered his thanks. God would not forsake those who were faithful to him.

All that the Jolliffes possessed in the world was put into the enterprise. The grocery stock was pared down to the least that possibly could afford a bare sustenance to Joanna during the absence, which was to last through the usual 'New-f'nland spell.' How she would endure the weary time she hardly knew, for the boys had been with her formerly ; but she nerved herself for the trial.

The ship was laden with boots and shoes, ready-made clothing, fishing-tackle, butter, cheese, cordage, sailcloth, and many other commodities, and was to bring back oil, furs, skins, fish, cranberries, and what else came to hand. But much speculative trading to other ports was to be undertaken between the voyages out and homeward, and thereby much money made.

III

The brig sailed on a Monday morning in spring ; but Joanna did not witness its departure. She could not bear the sight that she had been the means of bringing about. Knowing this, her husband told her overnight that they were to sail some time before noon next day ; hence when, awakening at five the next morning, she heard them bustling about downstairs, she did not hasten to descend, but lay trying to nerve herself for the parting, imagining they would leave about nine, as her husband had done on his previous voyage. When she did descend she beheld words chalked upon the sloping face of the bureau ; but no husband or sons. In the hastily-scrawled lines Shadrach said they had gone off thus not to pain her by a leave-taking ; and the sons had chalked under his words ; 'Good-bye, mother! '

She rushed to the quay, and looked down the harbour towards the blue rim of the sea, but she could only see the masts and bulging sails of the *Joanna* ; no human figures. ' 'Tis I have sent them!' she said wildly, and burst into tears. In the house the chalked 'Good-bye' nearly broke her heart. But when she had re-entered the front room, and looked across at Emily's, a gleam of triumph lit her thin face at her anticipated release from the thraldom of subservience.

To do Emily Lester justice, her assumption of superiority was mainly a figment of Joanna's brain. That the circumstances of the merchant's wife were more luxurious than Joanna's, the former could not conceal ; though whenever the two met, which was not very often now, Emily endeavoured to subdue the difference by every means in her power.

The first summer lapsed away ; and Joanna meagrely maintained herself by the shop, which now consisted of little more than a window and a counter. Emily was, in truth, her only large customer ; and Mrs. Lester's kindly readiness to buy anything and everything without questioning the quality had a sting of bitterness in it, for it was the uncritical attitude of a patron, and almost of a donor. The long dreary winter moved on ; the face of the bureau had been turned to the wall to protect the chalked words of farewell, for Joanna could never bring herself to rub them out; and she often glanced at them with wet eyes. Emily's handsome boys came home for the Christmas holidays ; the University was talked of for them ; and still Joanna subsisted as it were with held breath, like a person submerged. Only one summer more, and the 'spell' would end. Towards the close of the time Emily called on her quondam friend. She had heard that Joanna began to feel anxious ; she had received no letter from husband or sons for some months. Emily's silks rustled arrogantly when, in response to Joanna's almost dumb invitation, she squeezed through the opening of the counter and into the parlour behind the shop.

'You are all success, and I am all the other way!' said Joanna.

'But why do you think so?' said Emily. 'They are to bring back a fortune, I hear.'

'Ah! will they come? The doubt is more than a woman can bear. All three in one ship-think of that! And I have not heard of them for months! '

'But the time is not up. You should not meet misfortune half-way.'

'Nothing will repay me for the grief of their absence!'

'Then why did you let them go? You were doing fairly well.'

'I made them go!' she said, turning vehemently upon Emily. 'And I'll tell you why! I could not bear that we should be only muddling on, and you so rich and thriving! Now I have told you, and you may hate me if you will!'

'I shall never hate you, Joanna.'

And she proved the truth of her words afterwards. The end of autumn came, and the brig should have been in port ; but nothing like the Joanna appeared in the channel between the sands. It was now really time to be uneasy. Joanna Jolliffe sat by the fire, and every gust of wind caused her a cold thrill. She had always feared and detested the sea, to her it was a treacherous, restless, slimy creature, glorying in the griefs of women. 'Still,' she said, 'they must come!'

She recalled to her mind that Shadrach had said before starting that if they returned safe and sound, with success crowning their enterprise, he would go as he had gone after his shipwreck, and kneel with his sons in the church, and offer sincere thanks for their deliverance. She went to church regularly morning and afternoon, and sat in the most forward pew, nearest the chancel-step. Her eyes were mostly fixed on that step, where Shadrach had knelt in the bloom of his young manhood ; she knew to an inch the spot which his knees had pressed twenty winters before, his outline as he had knelt, his hat on the step beside him. God was good. Surely her husband must kneel there again : a son on each side as he had said, George just here, Jim just there. By long watching the spot as she worshipped became as if she saw the three returned ones there kneeling ; the two slim outlines of her boys, the more bulky form between them ; their hands clasped, their heads shaped against the eastern wall. The fancy grew almost to an hallucination ; she could never turn her worn eyes to the step without seeing them there.

Nevertheless they did not come. Heaven was merciful, but it was not yet pleased to relieve her soul. This was her purgation for the sin of making them the slaves of her ambition. But it became more than purgation soon, and her mood approached despair. Months had passed since the brig had been due, but it had not returned.

Joanna was always hearing or seeing evidences of their arrival. When on the hill behind the port, whence a view of the open Channel could be obtained, she felt sure that a little speck on the horizon, breaking the eternally level waste of waters southward, was the truck of the *Joanna*'s mainmast. Or when indoors, a shout or excitement of any kind at the corner of the Town Cellar, where the High Street joined the Quay, caused her to spring to her feet and cry : 'Tis they!'

But it was not. The visionary forms knelt every Sunday afternoon on the chancel-step, but not the real. Her shop had, as it were, eaten itself hollow. In the apathy which had resulted from her loneliness and grief she had ceased to take in the smallest supplies, and thus had sent away her last customer.

In this strait Emliy Lester tried by every means in her power to aid the afflicted woman ; but she met with constant repulses.

'I don't like you! I can't bear to see you!' Joanna would whisper hoarsely when Emily came to her and made advances.

'But I want to help and soothe you, Joanna,' Emily would say.

'You are a lady, with a rich husband and fine sons! What can you want with a bereaved crone like me!'

'Joanna, I want this ; I want you to come and live in my house, and not stay alone in this dismal place any longer.'

'And suppose they come and don't find me at home? You wish to separate me and mine! No, I'll stay here. I don't like you, and I can't thank you, whatever kindness you do me!'

However, as time went on Joanna could not afford to pay the rent of the shop and house without an income. She was assured that all hope of the return of Shadrach and his sons was vain, and she reluctantly consented to accept the asylum of the Lester' house. Here she was allotted a room of her own on the second floor, and went and came as she chose, without contact with the family. Her hair greyed and whitened, deep lines channelled her forehead, and her form grew gaunt and stooping. But she still expected the lost ones, and when she met Emily on the staircase she would say morosely : 'I know why you've got me here! They'll come, and be disappointed at not finding me at home, and perhaps go away again, and then you'll be revenged for my taking Shadrach away from 'ee!'

Emily Lester bore these reproaches from the grief-stricken soul. She was sure – all the people of Havenpool were sure – that Shadrach and his sons had gone to the bottom. For years the vessel had been given up as lost. Nevertheless, when awakened at night by any noise, Joanna would rise from bed and glance at the shop opposite by the light from the flickering lamp, to make sure it was not they.

It was a damp and dark December night, six years after the departure of the brig *Joanna*. The wind was from the sea, and brought up a fishy mist which mopped the face like moist flannel. Joanna had prayed her usual prayer for the absent ones with more fervour and confidence than she had felt for months, and had fallen asleep about eleven. It must have been between one and two when she suddenly started up. She had certainly heard steps in the street, and the voices of Shadrach and her sons calling at the door of the grocery shop. She sprang out of bed, and, hardly knowing what clothing she dragged on herself, hastened down Emily's large and carpeted staircase, put the candle on the hall-table, unfastened the bolts and chain, and stepped into the street. The mist, blowing up the street from the Quay, hindered her seeing the shop, although it was so near ; but she had crossed to it in a moment. How was it? Nobody stood there. The wretched woman walked wildly up and down with her bare feet-there was not a soul. She returned and knocked with all her might at the door which had once been her own-they might have been admitted for the night, unwilling to disturb her till the morning. It was not till several minutes had elapse that the young man who now kept the shop looked out of an upper window, and saw the skeleton of something human standing below half-dressed.

'Has anybody come?' asked the form.

'O, Mrs. Jolliffe, I didn't know it was you,' said the young man kindly, for he was aware how her baseless expectations moved her. 'No; nobody has come.'

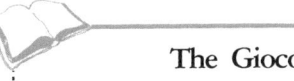

The Gioconda Smile
—by Aldous Huxley

I

"Miss Spence will be down directly, sir."

"Thank you," said Mr. Hutton, without turning round. Janet Spence's parlourmaid was so ugly—ugly on purpose, it always seemed to him, malignantly, criminally ugly—that he could not bear to look at her more than was necessary. The door closed. Left to himself, Mr. Hutton got up and began to wander round the room, looking with meditative eyes at the familiar objects it contained.

Photographs of Greek statuary, photographs of the Roman Forum, coloured prints of Italian masterpieces, all very safe and well known. Poor, dear Janet, what a prig—what an intellectual snob! Her real taste was illustrated in that water-colour by the pavement artist, the one she had paid half a crown for (and thirty-five shillings for the frame). How often he had heard her tell the story, how often expatiate on the beauties of that skilful imitation of an oleograph! "A real Artist in the streets," and you could hear the capital A in Artist as she spoke the words. She made you feel that part of his glory had entered into Janet Spence when she tendered him that half-crown for the copy of the oleograph. She was implying a compliment to her own taste and penetration. A genuine Old Master for half a crown. Poor, dear Janet!

Mr. Hutton came to a pause in front of a small oblong mirror. Stooping a little to get a full view of his face, he passed a white, well-manicured finger over his moustache. It was as curly, as freshly auburn as it had been twenty years ago. His hair still retained its colour, and there was no sign of baldness yet—only a certain elevation of the brow. "Shakespearean," thought Mr. Hutton with a smile, as he surveyed the smooth and polished expanse of his forehead.

Others abide our question, thou art free.... Footsteps in the sea....Majesty....Shakespeare, thou shouldst be living at this hour. No, that was Milton, wasn't it? Milton, the Lady of Christ's. There was no lady about him. He was what the women would call a manly man. That was why they liked him—for the curly auburn moustache and the discreet redolence of tobacco. Mr. Hutton smiled again; he enjoyed making fun of himself. Lady of Christ's? No, no. He was the Christ of Ladies. Very pretty, very pretty. The Christ of Ladies. Mr. Hutton wished there were somebody he could tell the joke to. Poor, dear Janet wouldn't appreciate it, alas!

He straightened himself up, patted his hair, and resumed his peregrination. Damn the Roman Forum; he hated those dreary photographs.

Suddenly he became aware that Janet Spence was in the room, standing near the door. Mr. Hutton started, as though he had been taken in some felonious act. To make these silent and spectral appearances was one of Janet Spence's peculiar talents. Perhaps she had been there all the time, had seen him looking at himself in the mirror. Impossible! But, still, it was disquieting.

"Oh, you gave me such a surprise," said Mr. Hutton, recovering his smile and advancing with outstretched hand to meet her.

Miss Spence was smiling too: her Gioconda smile, he had once called it in a moment of half-ironical flattery. Miss Spence had taken the compliment seriously, and always tried to live up to the Leonardo standard. She smiled on in silence while Mr. Hutton shook hands; that was part of the Gioconda business.

"I hope you're well," said Mr. Hutton. "You look it."

What a queer face she had! That small mouth pursed forward by the Gioconda expression into a little snout with a round hole in the middle as though for whistling—it was like a penholder seen from the front. Above the mouth a well-shaped nose, finely aquiline. Eyes large, lustrous, and dark, with the largeness, lustre, and darkness that seems to invite sties and an occasional bloodshot suffusion.

They were fine eyes, but unchangingly grave. The penholder might do its Gioconda trick, but the eyes never altered in their earnestness. Above them, a pair of boldly arched, heavily pencilled black eyebrows lent a surprising air of power, as of a Roman matron, to the upper portion of the face. Her hair was dark and equally Roman; Agrippina from the brows upward.

"I thought I'd just look in on my way home," Mr. Hutton went on. "Ah, it's good to be back here"—he indicated with a wave of his hand the flowers in the vases, the sunshine and greenery beyond the windows-"it's good to be back in the country after a stuffy day of business in town."

Miss Spence, who had sat down, pointed to a chair at her side.

"No, really, I can't sit down," Mr. Hutton protested. "I must get back to see how poor Emily is. She was rather seedy this morning." He sat down, nevertheless. "It's these wretched liver chills. She's always getting them. Women-" He broke off and coughed, so as to hide the fact that he had uttered. He was about to say that women with weak digestions ought not to marry; but the remark was too cruel, and he didn't really believe it. Janet Spence, moreover, was a believer in eternal flames and spiritual attachments. "She hopes to be well enough," he added, "to see you at luncheon tomorrow. Can you come? Do!" He smiled persuasively. "It's my invitation, too, you know."

She dropped her eyes, and Mr. Hutton almost thought that he detected a certain reddening of the cheek. It was a tribute; he stroked his moustache.

"I should like to come if you think Emily's really well enough to have a visitor."

"Of course. You'll do her good. You'll do us both good. In married life three is often better company than two."

"Oh, you're cynical."

Mr. Hutton always had a desire to say "Bow-wow-wow" whenever that last word was spoken. It irritated him more than any other word in the language. But instead of barking he made haste to protest.

"No, no. I'm only speaking a melancholy truth. Reality doesn't always come up to the ideal, you know. But that doesn't make me believe any the less in the ideal. Indeed, I believe in it passionately—the ideal of a matrimony between two people in perfect accord. I think it's realizable. I'm sure it is."

He paused significantly, and looked at her with an arch expression. A virgin of thirty-six, but still unwithered; she had her charms. And there was something really rather enigmatic about her. Miss Spence made no reply, but continued to smile. There were times when Mr. Hutton got rather bored with the Gioconda. He stood up.

"I must really be going now. Farewell, mysterious Gioconda." The smile grew intenser, focused itself, as it were, in a narrower snout. Mr. Hutton made a Cinquecento gesture, and kissed her extended hand. It was the first time he had done such a thing; the action seemed not to be resented. "I look forward to tomorrow."

"Do you?"

For answer, Mr. Hutton once more kissed her hand, then turned to go. Miss Spence accompanied him to the porch.

"Where's your car?" she asked.

"I left it at the gate of the drive."

"I'll come and see you off."

"No, no." Mr. Hutton was playful, but determined. "You must do no such thing. I simply forbid you."

"But I should like to come," Miss Spence protested, throwing a rapid Gioconda at him.

Mr. Hutton held up his hand. "No," he repeated, and then, with a gesture that was almost the blowing of a kiss, he started to run down the drive, lightly, on his toes, with long, bounding strides like a boy's. He was proud of that run; it was quite marvellously youthful. Still, he was glad the drive was no longer. At the last bend, before passing out of sight of the house, he halted and turned round. Miss Spence was still standing on the steps smiling her smile. He waved his hand, and this time quite definitely and overtly wafted a kiss in her direction. Then, breaking once more into his magnificent canter, he rounded the last dark promontory of trees. Once out of sight of the house he let his high paces decline to a trot, and finally to a walk. He took out his handkerchief and began wiping his neck inside his collar. What fools, what fools! Had there ever been such an ass as poor, dear Janet Spence? Never, unless it was himself. Decidedly he was the more malignant fool, since he, at least, was aware of his folly and still persisted in it. Why did he persist? Ah, the problem that was himself, the problem that was other people....

He had reached the gate. A large, prosperous looking motor was standing at the side of the road.

"Home, M'Nab." The chauffeur touched his cap. "And stop at the cross-roads on the way, as usual," Mr. Hutton added, as he opened the door of the car. "Well?" he said, speaking into the obscurity that lurked within.

"Oh, Teddy Bear, what an age you've been!" It was a fresh and childish voice that spoke the words. There was the faintest hint of Cockney impurity about the vowel sounds.

Mr. Hutton bent his large form and darted into the car with

the agility of an animal regaining its burrow.

"Have I?" he said, as he shut the door. The machine began to move. "You must have missed me a lot if you found the time so long." He sat back in the low seat; a cherishing warmth enveloped him.

'Teddy Bear...." and with a sign of contentment a charming little head declined on to Mr. Hutton's shoulder. Ravished, he looked down sideways at the round, babyish face.

"Do you know, Doris, you look like the pictures of Louise de Kerouaille." He passed his fingers through a mass of curly hair.

"Who's Louise de Kera-whatever-it-is?" Doris spoke from remote distances.

"She was, alas! *Fuit.* We shall all be "was" one of these days. Meanwhile...."

Mr Hutton covered the babyish face with kisses. The car rushed smoothly along. M'Nab's back, through the front window, was stonily impassive, the back of a statue.

"Your hands," Doris whispered. "Oh, you mustn't touch me. They give me electric shocks."

Mr. Hutton adored her for the virgin imbecility of the words. How late in one's existence one makes the discovery of one's body!

"The electricity isn't in me, it's in you." He kissed her again, whispering her name several times: Doris, Doris, Doris. The scientific appellation of the sea-mouse, he was thinking as he kissed the throat she offered him, white and extended like the throat of a victim awaiting the sacrificial knife. The sea-mouse was a sausage with iridescent fur: very peculiar. Or was Doris the sea-cucumber, which turns itself inside out in moments of alarm? He would really have to go to Naples again, just to see the aquarium. These sea creatures were fabulous, unbelievably fantastic.

"Oh, Teddy Bear!" (More zoology; but he was only a land animal. His poor little jokes!) "Teddy Bear, I'm so happy."

"So am I," said Mr. Hutton. Was it true?

"But I wish I knew if it were right. Tell me, Teddy Bear, is it right or wrong?"

"Ah, my dear, that's just what I've been wondering for the last thirty years."

"Be serious, Teddy Bear. I want to know if this is right; if it's right that I should be here with you and that we should love one another, and that it should give me electric shocks when you touch me."

"Right? Well, it's certainly good that you should have electric shocks rather than sexual repressions. Read Freud; repressions are the devil."

"Oh, you don't help me. Why aren't you ever serious? If only you knew how miserable I am sometimes, thinking it's not right. Perhaps, you know, there is a hell, and all that. I don't know what to do. Sometimes I think I ought to stop loving you."

"But could you?" asked Mr. Hutton, confident in the powers of his seduction and his moustache.

"No, Teddy Bear, you know I couldn't. But I could run away, I could hide from you, I could lock myself up and force myself not to come to you."

"Silly little thing!" He tightened his embrace.

"Oh, dear, I hope it isn't wrong. And there are times when I don't care if it is."

Mr. Hutton was touched. He had a certain protective affection for this little creature. He laid his cheek against her hair and so, interlaced, they sat in silence, while the car, swaying and pitching a little as it hastened along, seemed to draw in the white road and the dusty hedges towards it devouringly.

"Good-bye, good-bye."

The car moved on, gathered speed, vanished round a curve, and Doris was left standing by the sign-post at the cross-roads, still dizzy and weak with the languor born of those kisses and the electrical touch of those gentle hands. She had to take a deep breath, to draw herself up deliberately, before she was strong enough to start her homeward walk. She had half a mile in which to invent the necessary lies.

Alone, Mr. Hutton suddenly found himself the prey of an appalling boredom.

II

Mrs. Hutton was lying on the sofa in her boudoir, playing Patience. In spite of the warmth of the July evening a wood fire was burning on the hearth. A black Pomeranian, extenuated by the heat and the fatigues of digestion, slept before the blaze.

"Phew! Isn't it rather hot in here?" Mr. Hutton asked as he

entered the room.

"You know I have to keep warm, dear." The voice seemed breaking on the verge of tears. "I get so shivery."

"I hope you're better this evening."

"Not much, I'm afraid."

The conversation stagnated. Mr. Hutton stood leaning his back against the mantelpiece. He looked down at the Pomeranian lying at his feet, and with the toe of his right boot he rolled the little dog over and rubbed its white-flecked chest and belly. The creature lay in an inert ecstasy. Mrs. Hutton continued to play Patience. Arrived at an *impasse*, she altered the position of one card, took back another, and went on playing. Her Patiences always came out.

"Dr. Libbard thinks I ought to go to Llandrindod Wells this summer."

"Well, go, my dear – go, most certainly."

Mr. Hutton was thinking of the events of the afternoon: how they had driven, Doris and he, up to the hanging wood, had left the car to wait for them under the shade of the trees, and walked together out into the windless sunshine of the chalk down.

"I'm to drink the waters for my liver, and he thinks I ought to have massage and electric treatment, too."

Hat in hand, Doris had stalked four blue butterflies that were dancing together round a scabious flower with a motion that was like the flickering of blue fire. The blue fire burst and scattered into whirling sparks; she had given chase, laughing and shouting like a child.

"I'm sure it will do you good, my dear."

"I was wondering if you'd come with me, dear."

"But you know I'm going to Scotland at the end of the month."

Mrs. Hutton looked up at him entreatingly. "It's the journey," she said. "The thought of it is such a nightmare. I don't know if I can manage it. And you know I can't sleep in hotels. And then there's the luggage and all the worries. I can't go alone."

"But you won't be alone. You'll have your maid with you." He spoke impatiently. The sick woman was usurping the place of the healthy one. He was being dragged back from the memory of the sunlit down and the quick, laughing girl, back to this unhealthy, overheated room and its complaining occupant.

"I don't think I shall be able to go."

"But you must, my dear, if the doctor tells you to. And, besides, a change will do you good."

"I don't think so."

"But Libbard thinks so, and he knows what he's talking about."

"No, I can't face it. I'm too weak. I can't go alone." Mrs. Hutton pulled a handkerchief out of her black silk bag, and put it to her eyes.

"Nonsense, my dear, you must make the effort."

"I had rather be left in peace to die here." She was crying in earnest now.

"O Lord! Now do be reasonable. Listen now, please." Mrs. Hutton only sobbed more violently. "Oh, what is one to do?" He shrugged his shoulders and walked out of the room.

Mr. Hutton was aware that he had not behaved with proper

patience; but he could not help it. Very early in his manhood he had discovered that not only did he not feel sympathy for the poor, the weak, the diseased, and deformed, he actually hated them. Once, as an undergraduate, he spent three days at a mission in the East End. He had returned, filled with a profound and ineradicable disgust. Instead of pitying, he loathed the unfortunate. It was not, he knew, a very comely emotion, and he had been ashamed of it at first. In the end he had decided that it was temperamental, inevitable, and had felt no further qualms. Emily had been healthy and beautiful when he married her. He had loved her then. But now-was it his fault that she was like this?

Mr. Hutton dined alone. Food and drink left him more benevolent than he had been before dinner. To make amends for his show of exasperation he went up to his wife's room and offered to read to her. She was touched, gratefully accepted the offer, and Mr. Hutton, who was particularly proud of his accent, suggested a little light reading in French.

"French? I am so fond of French." Mrs. Hutton spoke of the language of Racine as though it were a dish of green peas.

Mr. Hutton ran down to the library and returned with a yellow volume. He began reading. The effort of pronouncing perfectly absorbed his whole attention. But how good his accent was! The fact of its goodness seemed to improve the quality of the novel he was reading.

At the end of fifteen pages an unmistakable sound aroused him. He looked up; Mrs. Hutton had gone to sleep. He sat still for a little while, looking with a dispassionate curiosity at the sleeping face. Once it had been beautiful; once, long ago, the sight of it, the recollection of it, had moved him with an emotion profounder, perhaps, than any he had felt before or since. Now it was lined and cadaverous. The skin was stretched tightly over the cheekbones, across the bridge of the sharp, bird-like nose. The closed eyes were set in profound bone-rimmed sockets. The lamplight striking on the face from the side emphasized with light and shade its cavities and projections. It was the face of a dead Christ by Morales.

> *Le squelette etait invisible*
> *Au temps heureux de l'art paien.*

He shivered a little, and tiptoed out of the room.

On the following day Mrs. Hutton came down to luncheon. She had had some unpleasant palpitations during the night, but she was feeling better now. Besides, she wanted to do honour to her guest. Miss Spence listened to her complaints about Llandrindod Wells, and was loud in sympathy, lavish with advice. Whatever she said was always said with intensity. She leaned forward, aimed, so to speak, like a gun, and fired her words. Bang! the charge in her soul was ignited, the words whizzed forth at the narrow barrel of her mouth. She was a machine-gun riddling her hostess with sympathy. Mr. Hutton had undergone similar bombardments, mostly of a literary or philosophic character — bombardments of Maeterlinck, of Mrs. Besant, of Bergson, of

William James. Today, the missiles were medical. She talked about insomnia, she expatiated on the virtues of harmless drugs and beneficent specialists. Under the bombardment Mrs. Hutton opened out, like a flower in the sun.

Mr. Hutton looked on in silence. The spectacle of Janet Spence evoked in him an unfailing curiosity. He was not romantic enough to imagine that every face masked an interior physiognomy of beauty or strangeness, that every woman's small talk was like a vapour hanging over mysterious gulfs. His wife, for example, and Doris; they were nothing more than what they seemed to be. But with Janet Spence it was somehow different. Here one could be sure that there was some kind of a queer face behind the Gioconda smile and the Roman eyebrows. The only question was: What exactly was there? Mr. Hutton could never quite make out.

"But perhaps you won't have to go to Llandrindod after all," Miss Spence was saying. "If you get well quickly, Dr. Libbard will let you off."

"I only hope so. Indeed, I do really feel rather better today."

Mr. Hutton felt ashamed. How much was it his own lack of sympathy that prevented her from feeling well every day? But he comforted himself by reflecting that it was only a case of feeling, not of being better. Sympathy does not mend a diseased liver or a weak heart.

"My dear, I wouldn't eat those red currants if I were you," he said, suddenly solicitous. "You know that Libbard has banned everything with skins and pips."

"But I am so fond of them," Mrs. Hutton protested, "and I feel so well today."

"Don't be a tyrant," said Miss Spence, looking first at him and then at his wife. "Let the poor invalid have what she fancies; it will do her good." She laid her hand on Mrs. Hutton's arm and patted it affectionately two or three times.

"Thank you, my dear." Mrs. Hutton helped herself to the stewed currants.

"Well, don't blame me if they make you ill again."

"Do I ever blame you, dear?"

"You have nothing to blame me for," Mr. Hutton answered playfully. "I am the perfect husband."

They sat in the garden after luncheon. From the island of shade under the old cypress tree they looked out across a flat expanse of lawn, in which the parterres of flowers shone with a metallic brilliance.

Mr. Hutton took a deep breath of the warm and fragrant air. "It's good to be alive," he said.

"Just to be alive," his wife echoed, stretching one pale, knot-jointed hand into the sunlight.

A maid brought the coffee; the silver pots and the little blue cups were set on a folding table near the group of chairs.

"Oh, my medicine!" exclaimed Mrs. Hutton. "Run in and fetch it, Clara, will you? The white bottle on the sideboard."

"I'll go," said Mr. Hutton. "I've got to go and fetch a cigar in any case."

He ran in towards the house. On the threshold he turned round for an instant. The maid was walking back across the lawn. His wife was sitting up in her deck-chair, engaged in opening her white parasol. Miss Spence was bending over the table, pouring out the coffee. He passed into the cool obscurity of the house.

"Do you like sugar in your coffee?" Miss Spence inquired.

"Yes, please. Give me rather a lot. I'll drink it after my medicine to take the taste away."

Mrs. Hutton leaned back in her chair, lowering the sunshade over her eyes, so as to shut out from her vision the burning sky.

Behind her, Miss Spence was making a delicate clinking among the coffee cups.

"I've given you three large spoonfuls. That ought to take the taste away. And here comes the medicine."

Mr. Hutton had reappeared, carrying a wine-glass, half full of a pale liquid.

"It smells delicious," he said, as he handed it to his wife.

"That's only the flavouring." She drank it off at a gulp, shuddered, and made a grimace. "Ugh, it's so nasty. Give me my coffee."

Miss Spence gave her the cup; she sipped at it. "You've made it like syrup. But it's very nice, after that atrocious medicine."

At half-past three Mrs. Hutton complained that she did not feel as well as she had done, and went indoors to lie down. Her husband would have said something about the red currants, but checked himself; the triumph of an "I told you so" was too cheaply won. Instead, he was sympathetic, and gave her his arm to the house.

"A rest will do you good," he said. "By the way, I shan't be back till after dinner."

"But why? Where are you going?"

"I promised to go to Johnson's this evening. We have to discuss the war memorial, you know."

"Oh, I wish you weren't going." Mrs. Hutton was almost in tears. "Can't you stay? I don't like being alone in the house."

"But, my dear, I promised – weeks ago." It was a bother having to lie like this. "And now I must get back and look after Miss Spence."

He kissed her on the forehead and went out again into the garden. Miss Spence received him aimed and intense.

"Your wife is dreadfully ill," she fired off at him.

"I thought she cheered up so much when you came."

"That was purely nervous, purely nervous. I was watching her closely. With a heart in that condition and her digestion wrecked –yes, wrecked–anything might happen."

"Libbard doesn't take so gloomy a view of poor Emily's health." Mr. Hutton held open the gate that led from the garden into the drive; Miss Spence's car was standing by the front door.

"Libbard is only a country doctor. You ought to see a specialist."

He could not refrain from laughing. "You have a macabre passion for specialists."

Miss Spence held up her hand in protest. "I am serious. I think poor Emily is in a very bad state. Anything might happen – at any moment."

He handed her into the car and shut the door. The chauffeur started the engine and climbed into his place, ready to drive off.

"Shall I tell him to start?" He had no desire to continue the conversation.

Miss Spence leaned forward and shot a Gioconda in his direction. "Remember, I expect you to come and see me again soon."

Mechanically he grinned, made a polite noise, and, as the car moved forward, waved his hand. He was happy to be alone.

A few minutes afterwards Mr. Hutton himself drove away. Doris was waiting at the cross-roads. They dined together twenty miles from home, at a roadside hotel. It was one of those bad, expensive meals which are only cooked in country hotels, frequented by motorists. It revolted Mr. Hutton, but Doris enjoyed it. She always enjoyed things. Mr. Hutton ordered a not very good brand of champagne. He was wishing he had spent the evening in his library.

When they started homewards Doris was a little tipsy and extremely affectionate. It was very dark inside the car, but looking forward, past the motionless form of M'Nab, they could see a bright and narrow universe of forms and colours scooped out of the night by the electric head-lamps.

It was after eleven when Mr. Hutton reached home. Dr. Libbard met him in the hall. He was a small man with delicate hands and well-formed features that were almost feminine. His brown eyes were large and melancholy. He used to waste a great deal of time sitting at the bedside of his patients, looking sadness through those eyes and talking in a sad, low voice about nothing in particular. His person exhaled a pleasing odour, decidedly antiseptic but at the same time suave and discreetly delicious.

"Libbard?" said Mr. Hutton in surprise. "You here? Is my wife ill?"

"We tried to fetch you earlier," the soft, melancholy voice replied. "It was thought you were at Mr. Johnson's, but they had no news of you there."

"No, I was detained. I had a breakdown." Mr. Hutton answered irritably. It was tiresome to be caught out in a lie.

"Your wife wanted to see you urgently."

"Well, I can go now," Mr. Hutton moved towards the stairs.

Dr. Libbard laid a hand on his arm. "I am afraid it's too late."

"Too late?" He began fumbling with his watch; it wouldn't come out of the pocket.

"Mrs. Hutton passed away half an hour ago."

The voice remained even in its softness, the melancholy of the eyes did not deepen. Dr. Libbard spoke of death as he would speak of a local cricket match. All things were equally vain and equally deplorable.

Mr. Hutton found himself thinking of Janet Spence's words. At any moment – at any moment. She had been extraordinarily right.

"What happened?" he asked. "What was the cause?"

Dr. Libbard explained. It was heart failure brought on by a violent attack of nausea, caused in its turn by the eating of something of an irritant nature. Red currants? Mr. Hutton suggested. Very likely. It had been too much for the heart. There was chronic valvular disease: something had collapsed under the strain. It was all over; she could not have suffered much.

III

"It's a pity they should have chosen the day of the Eton and Harrow match for the funeral," old General Grego was saying as he stood, his top hat in his hand, under the shadow of the lych gate, wiping his face with his handkerchief.

Mr Hutton overheard the remark and with difficulty restrained a desire to inflict grievous bodily pain on the General. He would have liked to hit the old brute in the middle of his big red face. Monstrous great mulberry, spotted with meal! Was there no respect for the dead? Did nobody care? In theory he didn't much care; let the dead bury their dead. But here, at the graveside, he had found himself actually sobbing. Poor Emily, they had been pretty happy once. Now she was lying at the bottom of a seven foot hole. And here was Grego complaining that he couldn't go to the Eton and Harrow match.

Mr. Hutton looked round at the groups of black figures that were drifting slowly out of the churchyard towards the fleet of cabs and motors assembled in the road outside. Against the brilliant background of the July grass and flowers and foliage, they had a horribly alien and unnatural appearance. It pleased him to think that all these people would soon be dead, too.

That evening Mr. Hutton sat up late in his library reading the life of Milton. There was no particular reason why he should have chosen Milton; it was the book that first came to hand, that was all. It was after midnight when he had finished. He got up from his armchair, unbolted the French windows, and stepped out on to the little paved terrace. The night was quiet and clear. Mr. Hutton looked at the stars and at the holes between them, dropped his eyes to the dim lawns and hueless flowers of the garden, and let them wander over the farther landscape, black and grey under the moon.

He began to think with a kind of confused violence. There were the stars, there was Milton. A man can be somehow the peer of stars and night. Greatness, nobility. But is there seriously a difference between the noble and the ignoble? Milton, the stars, death, and himself—himself. The soul, the body; the higher and the lower nature. Perhaps there was something in it, after all. Milton had a god on his side and righteousness. What had he? Nothing, nothing whatever. There were only Doris's little breasts. What was the point of it all? Milton, the stars, death, and Emily in her grave, Doris and himself—always himself...

Oh, he was a futile and disgusting being. Everything convinced him of it. It was a solemn moment. He spoke aloud: "I will, I will." The sound of his own voice in the darkness was appalling; it seemed to him that he had sworn that infernal oath which binds even the gods. "I will, I will." There had been New Year's days and solemn anniversaries in the past, when he had felt the same contritions and recorded similar resolutions. They had all thinned away, these resolutions, like smoke, into nothingness. But this was a greater moment and he had pronounced a more fearful oath. In the future it was to be different. Yes, he would live by reason, he would be industrious, he would curb his appetites, he would devote his life to some good purpose. It was resolved and it would be so.

In practice he saw himself spending his mornings in agricultural pursuits, riding round with the bailiff, seeing that his land was farmed in the best modern way-silos and artificial manures and continuous cropping, and all that. The remainder of the day should be devoted to serious study. There was that book he had been intending to write for so long? *The Effect of Diseases on Civilization.*

Mr. Hutton went to bed humble and contrite, but with a sense that grace had entered into him. He slept for seven and a half hours, and woke to find the sun brilliantly shining. The emotions of the evening before had been transformed by a good night's rest into his customary cheerfulness. It was not until a good many seconds after his return to conscious life that he remembered his resolution, his Stygian oath. Milton and death seemed somehow different in the sunlight. As for the stars, they were not there. But the resolutions were good; even in the daytime he could see that. He had his horse saddled after breakfast, and rode round the farm with the bailiff. After luncheon he read Thucydides on the plague at Athens. In the evening he made a few notes on malaria in Southern Italy. While he was undressing he remembered that there was a good anecdote in Skelton's jest-book about the Sweating Sickness. He would have made a note of it if only he could have found a pencil.

On the sixth morning of his new life Mr. Hutton found among his correspondence an envelope addressed in that peculiarly vulgar handwriting which he knew to be Doris's. He opened it, and began to read. She didn't know what to say; words were so inadequate. His wife dying like that, and so suddenly—it was too terrible. Mr. Hutton sighed, but his interest revived somewhat as he read on:

"Death is so frightening, I never think of it when I can help it. But when something like this happens, or when I am feeling ill or depressed, then I can't help remembering it is there so close, and I think about all the wicked things I have done and about you and me, and I wonder what will happen, and I am so frightened. I am so lonely, Teddy Bear, and so unhappy, and I don't know what to do. I can't get rid of the idea of dying. I am so wretched and helpless without you. I didn't mean to write to you; I meant to wait till you were out of mourning and could come and see me again, but I was so lonely and miserable, Teddy Bear, I had to write. I couldn't help it. Forgive me, I want you so much; I have nobody in the world but you. You are so good and gentle and understanding; there is nobody like you. I shall never forget how good and kind you have been to me, and you are so clever and know so much, I can't understand how you ever came to pay any attention to me, I am so dull and stupid, much less like me and love me, because you do love me a little, don't you, Teddy Bear?"

Mr. Hutton was touched with shame and remorse. To be thanked like this, worshipped for having seduced the girl—it was too much. It had just been a piece of imbecile wantonness. Imbecile, idiotic: there was no other way to describe it. For, when all was said, he had derived very little pleasure from it. Taking all things together, he had probably been more bored than amused. Once upon a time he had believed himself to be a hedonist. But to be a hedonist implies a certain process of reasoning, a deliberate choice of known pleasures, a rejection of known pains. This had been done without reason, against it. For he knew beforehand-so well, so well-that there was no interest or pleasure to be derived from these wretched affairs. And yet each time the vague itch came upon him he succumbed, involving himself once more in the old stupidity. There had been Maggie, his wife's maid, and Edith, the girl on the farm, and Mrs. Pringle, and the waitress in London, and others-there seemed to be dozens of them. It had all been so stale and boring. He knew it would be; he always knew. And yet, and yet....Experience doesn't teach.

Poor little Doris! He would write to her kindly, comfortingly, but he wouldn't see her again. A servant came to tell him that his horse was saddled and waiting. He mounted and rode off. That morning the old bailiff was more irritating than usual.

Five days later Doris and Mr. Hutton were sitting together on the pier at Southend; Doris, in white muslin with pink garnishings, radiated happiness; Mr. Hutton, legs outstretched and chair tilted, had pushed the panama back from his forehead and was trying to feel like a tripper. That night, when Doris was asleep, breathing and warm by his side, he recaptured, in this moment of darkness and physical fatigue, the rather cosmic emotion which had possessed him that evening, not a fortnight ago, when he had made his great resolution. And so his solemn oath had already gone the way of so many other resolutions. Unreason had triumphed; at the first itch of desire he had given way. He was hopeless, hopeless.

For a long time he lay with closed eyes, ruminating his humiliation. The girl stirred in her sleep. Mr. Hutton turned over and looked in her direction. Enough faint light crept in between the half-drawn curtains to show her bare arm and shoulder, her neck, and the dark tangle of hair on the pillow. She was beautiful, desirable. Why did he lie there moaning over his sins? What did it matter? If he were hopeless, then so be it; he would make the best of his hopelessness. A glorious sense of irresponsibility suddenly filled him. He was free, magnificently free. In a kind of exaltation he drew the girl towards him. She woke, bewildered, almost frightened under his rough kisses.

The storm of his desire subsided into a kind of serene merriment. The whole atmosphere seemed to be quivering with enormous silent laughter.

"Could anyone love you as much as I do, Teddy Bear?" The question came faintly from distant worlds of love.

"I think I know somebody who does," Mr. Hutton replied. The submarine laughter was swelling, rising, ready to break the surface of silence and resound.

"Who? Tell me. What do you mean?" The voice had come very close; charged with suspicion, anguish, indignation, it belonged to this immediate world.

"A-ah!"

"Who?"

"You'll never guess." Mr. Hutton kept up the joke until it began to grow tedious, and then pronounced the name: "Janet Spence."

Doris was incredulous. "Miss Spence of the Manor? That old woman?" It was too ridiculous. Mr. Hutton laughed, too.

"But it's quite true," he said. "She adores me." Oh, the vast joke! He would go and see her as soon as he returned – see and conquer. "I believe she wants to marry me," he added.

"But you wouldn't...you don't intend..."

The air was fairly crepitating with humour. Mr. Hutton laughed aloud. "I intend to marry you," he said. It seemed to him the best joke he had ever made in his life.

When Mr. Hutton left Southend he was once more a married man. It was agreed that, for the time being, the fact should be kept secret. In the autumn they would go abroad together, and the world should be informed. Meanwhile he was to go back to his own house and Doris to hers.

The day after his return he walked over in the afternoon to see Miss Spence. She received him with the old Gioconda.

"I was expecting you to come."

"I couldn't keep away," Mr. Hutton gallantly replied.

They sat in the summer-house. It was a pleasant place – a little old stucco temple bowered among dense bushes of evergreen. Miss Spence had left her mark on it by hanging up over the seat a blue-and-white Della Robbia plaque.

"I am thinking of going to Italy this autumn," said Mr. Hutton.

He felt like a ginger-beer bottle, ready to pop with bubbling humorous excitement.

"Italy..." Miss Spence closed her eyes ecstatically. "I feel drawn there, too."

"Why not let yourself be drawn?"

"I don't know. One somehow hasn't the energy and initiative to set out alone."

"Alone..." Ah, sound of guitars and throaty singing! "Yes, travelling alone isn't much fun."

Miss Spence lay back in her chair without speaking. Her eyes were still closed. Mr. Hutton stroked his moustache. The silence prolonged itself for what seemed a very long time.

Pressed to stay to dinner, Mr. Hutton did not refuse. The fun had hardly started. The table was laid in the loggia. Through its arches they looked out on to the sloping garden, to the valley below and the farther hills. Light ebbed away; the heat and silence were oppressive. A huge cloud was mounting up the sky, and there were distant breathings of thunder. The thunder drew nearer, a wind began to blow, and the first drops of rain fell. The table was cleared. Miss Spence and Mr. Hutton sat on in the growing darkness.

Miss Spence broke a long silence by saying meditatively:

"I think everyone has a right to a certain amount of happiness, don't you?"

"Most certainly." But what was she leading up to? Nobody makes generalizations about life unless they mean to talk about themselves. Happiness: he looked back on his own life, and saw a cheerful, placid existence disturbed by no great griefs or discomforts or alarms. He had always had money and freedom; he had been able to do very much as he wanted. Yes, he supposed he had been happy-happier than most men. And now he was not merely happy; he had discovered in irresponsibility the secret of gaiety. He was about to say something about his happiness when Miss Spence went on speaking.

"People like you and me have a right to be happy some time in our lives."

"Me?" said Mr. Hutton, surprised.

"Poor Henry! Fate hasn't treated either of us very well."

"Oh, well, it might have treated me worse."

"You're being cheerful. That's brave of you. But don't think I can't see behind the mask."

Miss Spence spoke louder and louder as the rain came down more and more heavily. Periodically the thunder cut across her utterances. She talked on, shouting against the noise.

"I have understood you so well and for so long."

A flash revealed her, aimed and intent, leaning towards him. Her eyes were two profound and menacing gun-barrels. The darkness re-engulfed her.

"You were a lonely soul seeking a companion soul. I could sympathize with you in your solitude. Your marriage...."

The thunder cut short the sentence. Miss Spence's voice became audible once more with the words:

"...could offer no companionship to a man of your stamp. You needed a soul mate."

A soul mate─he! a soul mate. It was incredibly fantastic. "Georgette Leblanc, the ex-soul mate of Maurice Maeterlinck." He had seen that in the paper a few days ago. So it was thus that Janet Spence had painted him in her imagination─as a soul-mater. And for Doris he was a picture of goodness and the cleverest man in the world. And actually, really, he was what?─ Who knows?

"My heart went out to you. I could understand; I was lonely, too." Miss Spence laid her hand on his knee. "You were so patient." Another flash. She was still aimed, dangerously. "You never complained. But I could guess─I could guess."

"How wonderful of you!" So he was an *ame incomprise*. "Only a woman's intuition..."

The thunder crashed and rumbled, died away, and only the sound of the rain was left. The thunder was his laughter, magnified, externalized. Flash and crash, there it was again, right on top of them.

"Don't you feel that you have within you something that is akin to this storm?" He could imagine her leaning forward as she uttered the words. "Passion makes one the equal of the elements."

What was his gambit now? Why, obviously, he should have said "yes," and ventured on some unequivocal gesture. But Mr. Hutton suddenly took fright. The ginger beer in him had gone flat. The woman was serious─terribly serious. He was appalled.

Passion? "No," he desperately answered. "I am without passion."

But his remark was either unheard or unheeded, for Miss Spence went on with a growing exaltation, speaking so rapidly, however, and in such a burningly intimate whisper that Mr. Hutton found it very difficult to distinguish what she was saying. She was telling him, as far as he could make out, the story of her life. The lightning was less frequent now, and there were long intervals of darkness. But at each flash he saw her still aiming towards him, still yearning forward with a terrifying intensity. Darkness, the rain, and then flash! her face was there, close at hand. A pale mask, greenish white; the large eyes, the narrow barrel of the mouth, the heavy eyebrows. Agrippina, or wasn't it rather-yes, wasn't it rather George Robey?

He began devising absurd plans for escaping. He might suddenly jump up, pretending he had seen a burglar-Stop thief! stop thief!-and dash off into the night in pursuit. Or should he say that he felt faint, a heart attack? or that he had seen a ghost -Emily's ghost-in the garden? Absorbed in his childish plotting, he had ceased to pay any attention to Miss Spence's words. The spasmodic clutching of her hand recalled his thoughts.

"I honoured you for that, Henry," she was saying.

Honoured him for what?

"Marriage is a sacred tie, and your respect for it, even when the marriage was, as it was in your case, an unhappy one, made me respect you and admire you, and-shall I dare say the word?-"

Oh, the burglar, the ghost in the garden! But it was too late.

"...yes, love you, Henry, all the more. But we're free now, Henry."

Free? There was a movement in the dark, and she was kneeling on the floor by his chair.

"Oh, Henry, Henry, I have been unhappy, too."

Her arms embraced him, and by the shaking of her body he could feel that she was sobbing. She might have been a suppliant crying for mercy.

"You mustn't, Janet," he protested. Those tears were terrible, terrible. "Not now, not now! You must be calm; you must go to bed." He patted her shoulder, then got up, disengaging himself from her embrace. He left her still crouching on the floor beside the chair on which he had been sitting.

Groping his way into the hall, and without waiting to look for his hat, he went out of the house, taking infinite pains to close the front door noiselessly behind him. The clouds had blown over, and the moon was shining from a clear sky. There were puddles all along the road, and a noise of running water rose from the gutters and ditches. Mr. Hutton splashed along, not caring if he got wet.

How heart-rendingly she had sobbed! With the emotions of pity and remorse that the recollection evoked in him there was a certain resentment: why couldn't she have played the game that he was playing — the heartless, amusing game? Yes, but he had known all the time that she wouldn't, she couldn't, play that game: he had known and persisted.

What had she said about passion and the elements? Something absurdly stale, but true, true. There she was, a cloud black-bosomed and charged with thunder, and he, like some absurd little Benjamin Franklin, had sent up a kite into the heart of the menace. Now he was complaining that his toy had drawn the lightning.

She was probably still kneeling by that chair in the loggia, crying.

But why hadn't he been able to keep up the game? Why had his irresponsibility deserted him, leaving him suddenly sober in a cold world? There were no answers to any of his questions. One idea burned steady and luminous in his mind-the idea of flight. He must get away at once.

IV

"What are you thinking about, Teddy Bear?"
"Nothing."
There was a silence. Mr. Hutton remained motionless, his elbows on the parapet of the terrace, his chin in his hands, looking down over Florence. He had taken a villa on one of the hilltops to the south of the city. From a little raised terrace at the end of the garden one looked down a long fertile valley on to the town and beyond it to the bleak mass of Monte Morello and, eastward of it, to the peopled hill of Fiesole, dotted with white houses. Everything was clear and luminous in the September sunshine.

"Are you worried about anything?"
"No, thank you."
"Tell me, Teddy Bear."
"But, my dear, there's nothing to tell." Mr. Hutton turned round, smiled and patted the girl's hand. "I think you'd better go in and have your siesta. It's too hot for you here."

"Very well, Teddy Bear. Are you coming, too?"

"When I've finished my cigar."

"All right. But do hurry up and finish it, Teddy Bear." Slowly, reluctantly, she descended the steps of the terrace and walked towards the house.

Mr. Hutton continued his contemplation of Florence. He had need to be alone. It was good sometimes to escape from Doris and the restless solicitude of her passion. He had never known the pains of loving hopelessly, but he was experiencing now the pains of being loved. These last weeks had been a period of growing discomfort. Doris was always with him, like an obsession, like a guilty conscience. Yes, it was good to be alone.

He pulled an envelope out of his pocket and opened it, not without reluctance. He hated letters; they always contained something unpleasant – nowadays, since his second marriage. This was from his sister. He began skimming through the insulting home-truths of which it was composed. The words "indecent haste," "social suicide," "scarcely cold in her grave," "person of the lower classes," all occurred. They were inevitable now in any communication from a well-meaning and right-thinking relative. Impatient, he was about to tear the stupid letter to pieces when his eye fell on a sentence at the bottom of the third page. His heart beat with uncomfortable violence as he read it. It was too monstrous! Janet Spence was going about telling everyone that he had poisoned his wife in order to marry Doris. What damnable malice! Ordinarily a man of the suavest temper, Mr. Hutton found himself trembling with rage. He took the childish satisfaction of calling names-he cursed the woman.

Then suddenly he saw the ridiculous side of the situation. The notion that he should have murdered anyone in order to marry Doris! If they only knew how miserably bored he was. Poor, dear Janet! She had tried to be malicious; she had only succeeded in being stupid.

A sound of footsteps aroused him; he looked round. In the garden below the little terrace the servant girl of the house was picking fruit. A Neapolitan, strayed somehow as far north as Florence, she was a specimen of the classical type-a little debased. Her profile might have been taken from a Sicilian coin of a bad period. Her features, carved floridly in the grand tradition, expressed an almost perfect stupidity. Her mouth was the most beautiful thing about her; the calligraphic hand of nature had richly curved it into an expression of mulish bad temper....Under her hideous black clothes, Mr. Hutton divined a powerful body, firm and massive. He had looked at her before with a vague interest and curiosity. Today the curiosity defined and focused itself into a desire. An idyll of Theocritus. Here was the woman; he, alas, was not precisely like a goatherd on the volcanic hills. He called to her.

"Armida!"

The smile with which she answered him was so provocative, attested so easy a virtue, that Mr. Hutton took fright. He was on the brink once more-on the brink. He must draw back, oh! quickly, quickly, before it was too late. The girl continued to look up at him.

"*Ha chiamato?*" she asked at last.

Stupidity or reason? Oh, there was no choice now. It was imbecility every time.

"*Scendo*," he called back to her. Twelve steps led from the garden to the terrace. Mr. Hutton counted them. Down, down, down, down ···He saw a vision of himself descending from one circle of the inferno to the next-from a darkness full of wind and hail to an abyss of stinking mud.

V

For a good many days the Hutton case had a place on the front page of every newspaper. There had been no more popular murder trial since George Smith had temporarily eclipsed the European War by drowning in a warm bath his seventh bride. The public imagination was stirred by this tale of a murder brought to light months after the date of the crime. Here, it was felt, was one of those incidents in human life, so notable because they are so rare, which do definitely justify the ways of God to man. A wicked man had been moved by an illicit passion to kill his wife. For months he had lived in sin and fancied security − only to be dashed at last more horribly into the pit he had prepared for himself. Murder will out, and here was a case of it. The readers of the newspapers were in a position to follow every movement of the hand of God. There had been vague, but persistent rumours in the neighbourhood; the police had taken action at last. Then came the exhumation order, the post-mortem examination, the inquest, the evidence of the experts, the verdict of the coroner's jury, the trial, the condemnation. For once Providence had done its duty, obviously, grossly, didactically, as in a melodrama. The newspapers were right in making of the case the staple intellectual food of a whole season.

Mr. Hutton's first emotion when he was summoned from Italy to give evidence at the inquest was one of indignation. It was a monstrous, a scandalous thing that the police should take such idle, malicious gossip seriously. When the inquest was over he would bring an action for malicious prosecution against the Chief Constable; he would sue the Spence woman for slander.

The inquest was opened; the astonishing evidence unrolled itself. The experts had examined the body, and had found traces of arsenic; they were of opinion that the late Mrs. Hutton had died of arsenic poisoning.

Arsenic poisoning....Emily had died of arsenic poisoning? After that, Mr. Hutton learned with surprise that there was enough arsenicated insecticide in his greenhouses to poison an army.

It was now, quite suddenly, that he saw it: there was a case against him. Fascinated, he watched it growing, growing, like some monstrous tropical plant. It was enveloping him, surrounding him; he was lost in a tangled forest.

When was the poison administered? The experts agreed that it must have been swallowed eight or nine hours before death. About lunch-time? Yes, about lunch-time. Clara, the parlour-maid, was called. Mrs. Hutton, she remembered, had asked her to go and fetch her medicine. Mr. Hutton had volunteered to go instead; he had gone alone. Miss Spence-ah, the memory of the storm, the white aimed face! the horror of it all!-Miss Spence confirmed Clara's statement, and added that Mr. Hutton had come back with the medicine already poured out in a wineglass, not in the bottle.

Mr. Hutton's indignation evaporated. He was dismayed, frightened. It was all too fantastic to be taken seriously, and yet this nightmare was a fact?-it was actually happening.

M'Nab had seen them kissing, often. He had taken them for a drive on the day of Mrs. Hutton's death. He could see them reflected in the windscreen, sometimes out of the tail of his eye.

The inquest was adjourned. That evening Doris went to bed with a headache. When he went to her room after dinner, Mr. Hutton found her crying.

"What's the matter?" He sat down on the edge of her bed and began to stroke her hair. For a long time she did not answer, and he went on stroking her hair mechanically, almost unconsciously; sometimes, even, he bent down and kissed her bare shoulder. He had his own affairs, however, to think about. What had happened? How was it that the stupid gossip had actually come true? Emily had died of arsenic poisoning. It was absurd, impossible. The order of things had been broken, and he was at the mercy of an irresponsibility. What had happened, what was going to happen? He was interrupted in the midst of his thoughts.

"It's my fault-it's my fault!" Doris suddenly sobbed out. "I shouldn't have loved you; I oughtn't to have let you love me. Why was I ever born?"

Mr. Hutton didn't say anything, but looked down in silence at the abject figure of misery lying on the bed.

"If they do anything to you I shall kill myself."

She sat up, held him for a moment at arm's length, and looked at him with a kind of violence, as though she were never to see him again.

"I love you, I love you, I love you." She drew him, inert and passive, towards her, clasped him, pressed herself against him. "I didn't know you loved me as much as that, Teddy Bear. But why did you do it - why did you do it?"

Mr. Hutton undid her clasping arms and got up. His face became very red. "You seem to take it for granted that I murdered my wife," he said. "It's really too grotesque. What do you all take me for? A cinema hero?" He had begun to lose his temper. All the exasperation, all the fear and bewilderment of the day, was transformed into a violent anger against her. "It's all such damned stupidity. Haven't you any conception of a civilized man's mentality? Do I look the sort of man who'd go about slaughtering people? I suppose you imagined I was so insanely in love with you that I could commit any folly. When will you women understand that one isn't insanely in love? All one asks for is a quiet life, which you won't allow one to have. I don't know what the devil ever induced me to marry you. It was all a damned stupid, practical joke. And now you go about saying I'm a murderer. I won't stand it."

Mr. Hutton stamped towards the door. He had said horrible

things, he knew — odious things that he ought speedily to unsay. But he wouldn't. He closed the door behind him.

"Teddy Bear!" He turned the handle; the latch clicked into place. "Teddy Bear!" The voice that came to him through the closed door was agonized. Should he go back? He ought to go back. He touched the handle, then withdrew his fingers and quickly walked away. When he was half-way down the stairs he halted. She might try to do something silly — throw herself out of the window or God knows what! He listened attentively; there was no sound. But he pictured her very clearly tiptoeing across the room, lifting the sash as high as it would go, leaning out into the cold night air. It was raining a little. Under the window lay the paved terrace. How far below? Twenty-five or thirty feet? Once, when he was walking along Piccadilly, a dog had jumped out of a third-storey window of the Ritz. He had seen it fall; he had heard it strike the pavement. Should he go back? He was damned if he would; he hated her.

He sat for a long time in the library. What had happened? What was happening? He turned the question over and over in his mind and could find no answer. Suppose the nightmare dreamed itself out to its horrible conclusion. Death was waiting for him. His eyes filled with tears; he wanted so passionately to live. "Just to live." Poor Emily had wished it, too, he remembered: "Just to be alive." There were still so many places in this astonishing world unvisited, so many queer delightful people still unknown, so many lovely women never so much as seen. The huge white oxen would still be dragging their wains along the

Tuscan roads, the cypresses would still go up, straight as pillars, to the blue heaven; but he would not be there to see them. And the sweet southern wines - Tear of Christ and Blood of Judas - others would drink them, not he. Others would walk down the obscure and narrow lanes between the bookshelves in the London Library, sniffing the dusty perfume of good literature, peering at strange titles, discovering unknown names, exploring the fringes of vast domains of knowledge. He would be lying in a hole in the ground. And why, why? Confusedly he felt that some extraordinary kind of justice was being done. In the past he had been wanton and imbecile and irresponsible. Now Fate was playing as wantonly, as irresponsibly, with him. It was tit for tat, and God existed after all.

He felt that he would like to pray. Forty years ago he used to kneel by his bed every evening. The nightly formula of his childhood came to him almost unsought from some long unopened chamber of the memory. "God bless Father and Mother, Tom and Cissie and the Baby, Mademoiselle and Nurse, and everyone that I love, and make me a good boy. Amen." They were all dead now - all except Cissie.

His mind seemed to soften and dissolve; a great calm descended upon his spirit. He went upstairs to ask Doris's forgiveness. He found her lying on the couch at the foot of the bed. On the floor beside her stood a blue bottle of liniment, marked "Not to be taken"; she seemed to have drunk about half of it.

"You didn't love me," was all she said when she opened her eyes to find him bending over her.

Dr. Libbard arrived in time to prevent any very serious consequences. "You mustn't do this again," he said while Mr. Hutton was out of the room.

"What's to prevent me?" she asked defiantly.

Dr. Libbard looked at her with his large, sad eyes. "There's nothing to prevent you," he said. "Only yourself and your baby. Isn't it rather bad luck on your baby, not allowing it to come into the world because you want to go out of it?"

Doris was silent for a time. "All right," she whispered. "I won't."

Mr. Hutton sat by her bedside for the rest of the night. He felt himself now to be indeed a murderer. For a time he persuaded himself that he loved this pitiable child. Dozing in his chair, he woke up, stiff and cold, to find himself drained dry, as it were, of every emotion. He had become nothing but a tired and suffering carcase. At six o'clock he undressed and went to bed for a couple of hours' sleep. In the course of the same afternoon the coroner's jury brought in a verdict of "Wilful Murder," and Mr. Hutton was committed for trial.

VI

Miss Spence was not at all well. She had found her public appearances in the witness-box very trying, and when it was all over she had something that was very nearly a breakdown. She slept badly, and suffered from nervous indigestion. Dr. Libbard used to call every other day. She talked to him a great deal—

mostly about the Hutton case...Her moral indignation was always on the boil. Wasn't it appalling to think that one had had a murderer in one's house? Wasn't it extraordinary that one could have been for so long mistaken about the man's character? (But she had had an inkling from the first.) And then the girl he had gone off with-so low class, so little better than a prostitute. The news that the second Mrs. Hutton was expecting a baby-the posthumous child of a condemned and executed criminal- revolted her; the thing was shocking-an obscenity. Dr. Libbard answered her gently and vaguely, and prescribed bromide.

One morning he interrupted her in the midst of her customary tirade. "By the way," he said in his soft, melancholy voice, "I suppose it was really you who poisoned Mrs. Hutton."

Miss Spence stared at him for two or three seconds with enormous eyes, and then quietly said, "Yes." After that she started to cry.

"In the coffee, I suppose."

She seemed to nod assent. Dr. Libbard took out his fountain-pen, and in his neat, meticulous calligraphy wrote out a prescription for a sleeping draught.

Kew Gardens[1]

—by Virginia Woolf

From the oval-shaped flower-bed there rose perhaps a hundred stalks spreading into heart-shaped or tongue-shaped leaves half-way up and unfurling at the tip red or blue or yellow petals marked with spots of colour raised upon the surface; and from the red, blue or yellow gloom of the throat emerged a straight bar, rough with gold dust and slightly clubbed at the end. The petals were voluminous enough to be stirred by the summer breeze, and when they moved, the red, blue and yellow lights passed one over the other, staining an inch of the brown earth beneath with a spot of the most intricate colour. The light fell either upon the smooth, grey back of a pebble, or the shell of a snail with its brown, circular veins, or falling into a raindrop, it expanded with such intensity of red, blue and yellow the thin walls of water that one expected them to burst and disappear. Instead, the drop was left in a second silver grey once more, and the light now settled upon the flesh of a leaf, revealing the branching thread of fibre beneath the surface, and again it moved on and spread its illumination in the vast green spaces beneath the dome of the heart-shaped and tongue-shaped leaves. Then the breeze stirred rather more

---

1) 1841년에 국가기관으로 설립되었다. 'Kew Gardens'는 왕립식물원들의 중심이다. 영국 서레이주의 'Kew'라는 런던 교외에 자리하고 있다.

briskly overhead and the colour was flashed into the air above, into the eyes of the men and women who walk in Kew Gardens in July.

The figures of these men and women straggled past the flower-bed with a curiously irregular movement not unlike that of the white and blue butterflies who crossed the turf in zig-zag flights from bed to bed. The man was about six inches in front of the woman, strolling carelessly, while she bore on with greater purpose, only turning her head now and then to see that the children were not too far behind. The man kept this distance in front of the woman purposely, though perhaps unconsciously, for he wished to go on with his thoughts.

"Fifteen years ago I came here with Lily," he thought. "We sat somewhere over there by a lake and I begged her to marry me all through the hot afternoon. How the dragonfly kept circling round us: how clearly I see the dragonfly and her shoe with the square silver buckle at the toe. All the time I spoke I saw her shoe and when it moved impatiently I knew without looking up what she was going to say: the whole of her seemed to be in her shoe. And my love, my desire, were in the dragonfly; for some reason I thought that if it settled there, on that leaf, the broad one with the red flower in the middle of it, if the dragonfly settled on the leaf she would say 'Yes' at once. But the dragonfly went round and round: it never settled anywhere - of course not, happily not, or I shouldn't be walking here with Eleanor and the children. Tell me, Eleanor. D'you ever think of the past?"

"Why do you ask, Simon?"

"Because I've been thinking of the past. I've been thinking of Lily, the woman I might have married.... Well, why are you silent? Do you mind my thinking of the past?"

"Why should I mind, Simon? Doesn't one always think of the past, in a garden with men and women lying under the trees. Aren't they one's past, all that remains of it, those men and women, those ghosts lying under the trees.... one's happiness, one's reality?"

"For me, a square silver shoe buckle and a dragonfly –"

"For me, a kiss. Imagine six little girls sitting before their easels twenty years ago, down by the side of a lake, painting the water-lilies, the first red water-lilies I'd ever seen. And suddenly a kiss, there on the back of my neck. And my hand shook all the afternoon so that I couldn't paint. I took out my watch and marked the hour when I would allow myself to think of the kiss for five minutes only – it was so precious–the kiss of an old grey-haired woman with a wart on her nose, the mother of all my kisses all my life. Come, Caroline, come, Hubert."

They walked on past the flower-bed, now walking four abreast, and soon diminished in size among the trees and looked half transparent as the sunlight and shade swam over their backs in large trembling irregular patches.

In the oval flower-bed the snail, whose shell had been stained red, blue and yellow for the space of two minutes or so, now appeared to be moving very slightly in its shell, and next began to labour over the crumbs of loose earth which broke away and rolled down as it passed over them. It appeared to have a definite goal in front of it, differing in this respect from the singular high stepping angular green insect who attempted to cross in front of it, and waited for a second with its antennae trembling as if in deliberation, and then stepped off as rapidly and strangely in the opposite direction. Brown cliffs with deep green lakes in the hollows, flat, blade-like trees that waved from root to tip, round boulders of grey stone, vast crumpled surfaces of a thin crackling texture - all these objects lay across the snail's progress between one stalk and another to his goal. Before he had decided whether to circumvent the arched tent of a dead leaf or to breast it there came past the bed the feet of other human beings.

This time they were both men. The younger of the two wore an expression of perhaps unnatural calm; he raised his eyes and fixed them very steadily in front of him while his companion spoke, and directly his companion had done speaking he looked on the ground again and sometimes opened his lips only after a long pause and sometimes did not open them at all. The elder man had a curiously uneven and shaky method of walking, jerking his hand forward and throwing up his head abruptly, rather in the manner of an impatient carriage horse tired of waiting outside a house; but in the man these gestures were irresolute and pointless. He talked almost incessantly; he smiled to himself and again began to talk, as if the smile had been an answer. He was talking about spirits - the spirits of the dead, who, according to him, were even now telling him all sorts of odd things about their experiences in Heaven.

"Heaven was known to the ancients as Thessaly, William, and now, with this war, the spirit matter[2] is rolling between the hills like thunder." He paused, seemed to listen, smiled, jerked his head and continued:

"You have a small electric battery and a piece of rubber to insulate the wire—isolate?—insulate?—well, we'll skip the details, no good going into details that wouldn't be understood—and in short the little machine stands in any convenient position by the head of the bed, we will say, on a neat mahogany stand. All arrangements being properly fixed by workmen under my direction, the widow applies her ear and summons the spirit by sign as agreed. Women! Widows! Women in black—"

Here he seemed to have caught sight of a woman's dress in the distance, which in the shade looked a purple black. He took off his hat, placed his hand upon his heart, and hurried towards her muttering and gesticulating feverishly. But William caught him by the sleeve and touched a flower with the tip of his walking-stick in order to divert the old man's attention. After looking at it for a moment in some confusion the old man bent his ear to it and seemed to answer a voice speaking from it, for he began talking about the forests of Uruguay which he had visited hundreds of years ago in company with the most beautiful young woman in Europe. He could be heard murmuring about forests of Uruguay blanketed with the wax petals of tropical roses, nightingales, sea beaches, mermaids, and women drowned at sea, as he

---

[2] 달리 말해 '심령주의'(spiritualism)를 뜻한다. 'Thessaly'는 그리스의 한 지역이다. 'This war'는 'World War I'를 뜻한다.

suffered himself to be moved on by William, upon whose face the look of stoical patience grew slowly deeper and deeper.

Following his steps so closely as to be slightly puzzled by his gestures came two elderly women of the lower middle class, one stout and ponderous, the other rosy cheeked and nimble. Like most people of their station they were frankly fascinated by other signs of eccentricity betokening a disordered brain, especially in the well-to-do; but they were too far off to be certain whether the gestures were merely eccentric or genuinely mad. After they had scrutinized the old man's back in silence for a moment and given each other a queer, sly look, they went on energetically piecing together their very complicated dialogue:

"Nell, Bert, Lot, Cess, Phil, Pa, he says, I says, she says, I says, I says –"

"My Bert, Sis, Bill, Grandad, the old man, sugar,

Sugar, flour, kippers, greens,

Sugar, sugar, sugar."

The ponderous woman looked through the pattern of falling words at the flowers standing cool, firm, and upright in the earth, with a curious expression. She saw them as a sleeper waking from a heavy sleep sees a brass candlestick reflecting the light in an unfamiliar way, and closes his eyes and opens them, and seeing the brass candlestick again, finally starts broad awake and stares at the candlestick with all his powers. So the heavy woman came to a standstill opposite the oval-shaped flower-bed, and ceased even to pretend to listen to what the other woman was saying. She stood there letting the words fall over her, swaying the top part of her body slowly backwards and forwards, looking at the flowers. Then she suggested that they should find a seat and have their tea.

The snail had now considered every possible method of reaching his goal without going round the dead leaf or climbing over it. Let alone the effort needed for climbing a leaf, he was doubtful whether the thin texture which vibrated with such an alarming crackle when touched even by the tips of his horns would bear his weight; and this determined him finally to creep beneath it, for there was a point where the leaf curved high enough from the ground to admit him. He had just inserted his head in the opening and was taking stock of the high brown roof and was getting used to the cool brown light when two other people came past outside on the turf. This time they were both young, a young man and a young woman. They were both in the prime of youth, the season before the smooth pink folds of the flower have burst their gummy case, when the wings of the butterfly, though fully grown, are motionless in the sun.

"Lucky it isn't Friday," he observed.

"Why? D'you believe in luck?"

"They make you pay sixpence on Friday."

"What's a sixpence anyway? Isn't it worth sixpence?"

"What's 'it' – what do you mean by 'it'?"

"O, anything – I mean – you know what I mean."

Long pauses came between each of these remarks; they were uttered in toneless and monotonous voices. The couple stood still on the edge of the flower-bed, and together pressed the end of her parasol deep down into the soft earth. The action and the fact that his hand rested on the top of hers expressed their feelings in a strange way, as these short insignificant words also expressed something, words with short wings for their heavy body of meaning, inadequate to carry them far and thus alighting awkwardly upon the very common objects that surrounded them, and were to their inexperienced touch so massive; but who knows (so they thought as they pressed the parasol into the earth) what precipices aren't concealed in them, or what slopes of ice don't shine in the sun on the other side? Who knows? Who has ever seen this before? Even when she wondered what sort of tea they gave you at Kew, he felt that something loomed up behind her words, and stood vast and solid behind them; and the mist very slowly rose and uncovered – O, Heavens, what were those shapes? – little white tables, and waitresses who looked first at her and then at him; and there was a bill that he would pay with a real two-shilling piece, and it was real, all real, he assured himself, fingering the coin in his pocket, real to everyone except to him and to her; even to him it began to seem real; and then – but it was too exciting to stand and think any longer, and he pulled the parasol out of the earth with a jerk and was impatient to find the place where one had tea with other people, like other people.

"Come along? Trissie; it's time we had our tea."

"Wherever *does* one have one's tea?" she asked with the oddest thrill of excitement in her voice, looking vaguely round and letting herself be drawn down the grass path, trailing her parasol; turning her head this way and that way forgetting her tea, wishing to go down there and then down there, remembering orchids and cranes among wild flowers, a Chinese pagoda and a crimson crested bird; but he bore her on.

    Thus one couple after another with much the same irregular and aimless movement passed the flower-bed and were enveloped in layer after layer of green-blue vapour, in which at first their bodies had substance and a dash of colour but later both substance and colour dissolved in the green-blue atmosphere. How hot it was! So hot that even the thrush chose to hop, like a mechanical bird, in the shadow of the flowers, with long pauses between one movement and the next; instead of rambling vaguely the white butterflies dance one above another, making with their white shifting flakes the outline of a shattered, marble column above the tallest flowers; the glass roofs of the palm house shone as if a whole market full of shiny green umbrellas had opened in the sun; and in the drone of the aeroplane the voice of the summer sky murmured its fierce soul. Yellow and black, pink and snow white, shapes of all these colours, men, women, and children were spotted for a second upon the horizon, and then, seeing the breadth of yellow that lay upon the grass, they wavered and sought shade beneath the trees, dissolving like drops of water in the yellow and green atmosphere, staining it faintly with red and blue. It seemed as if all gross and heavy bodies had sunk down in the heat motionless and lay huddled upon the ground, but their voices went wavering from them as if they were flames lolling from the thick waxen bodies of candles. Voices. Yes, voices. Wordless voices, breaking the silence suddenly with such depth of contentment, such passion of desire, or, in the voices of children, such freshness of surprise; breaking the silence? But there was no silence; all the time the motor omnibuses were turning their wheels and changing their gear; like a vast nest of Chinese boxes all of wrought steel turning ceaselessly one within another the city murmured; on the top of which the voices cried aloud and the petals of myriads of flowers flashed their colours into the air.

미국 편

A Rose for Emily
— by William Faulkner

When Miss Emily Grierson died, our whole town went to her funeral: the men through a sort of respectful affection for a fallen monument, the women mostly out of curiosity to see the inside of her house, which no one save an old manservant—a combined gardener and cook—had seen in at least ten years.

It was a big, squarish frame house that had once been white, decorated with cupolas and spires and scrolled balconies in the heavily lightsome style of the seventies, set on what had once been our most select street. But garages and cotton gins had encroached and obliterated even the august names of that neighborhood; only Miss Emily's house was left, lifting its stubborn and coquettish decay above the cotton wagons and the gasoline pumps—an eyesore among eyesores. And now Miss Emily had gone to join the representatives of those august names where they lay in the cedar-bemused cemetery among the ranked and anonymous graves of Union and Confederate soldiers who fell at the battle of Jefferson.

Alive, Miss Emily had been a tradition, a duty, and a care; a sort of hereditary obligation upon the town, dating from that day in 1894 when Colonel Sartoris, the mayor-he who fathered the edict that no Negro woman should appear on the streets without an apron-remitted her taxes, the dispensation dating from the death of her father on into perpetuity. Not that Miss Emily would have accepted charity. Colonel Sartoris invented an involved tale to the effect that Miss Emily's father had loaned money to the town, which the town, as a matter of business, preferred this way of repaying. Only a man of Colonel Sartoris' generation and thought could have invented it, and only a woman could have believed it.

When the next generation, with its more modern ideas, became mayors and aldermen, this arrangement created some little dissatisfaction. On the first of the year they mailed her a tax notice. February came, and there was no reply. They wrote her a formal letter, asking her to call at the sheriff's office at her convenience. A week later the mayor wrote her himself, offering to call or to send his car for her, and received in reply a note on paper of an archaic shape, in a thin, flowing calligraphy in faded ink, to the effect that she no longer went out at all. The tax notice was also enclosed, without comment.

They called a special meeting of the Board of Aldermen. A deputation waited upon her, knocked at the door through which no visitor had passed since she ceased giving china-painting lessons eight or ten years earlier. They were admitted by the old Negro into a dim hall from which a stairway mounted into still more shadow. It smelled of dust and disuse-a close, dank smell. The Negro led them into the parlor. It was furnished in heavy, leather-covered furniture. When the Negro opened the blinds of one window, they could see that the leather was cracked; and when they sat down, a faint dust rose sluggishly about their thighs, spinning with slow motes in the single sun-ray. On a tarnished gilt easel before the fireplace stood a crayon portrait of Miss Emily's father.

They rose when she entered-a small, fat woman in black, with a thin gold chain descending to her waist and vanishing into her belt, leaning on an ebony cane with a tarnished gold head. Her skeleton was small and spare; perhaps that was why what would have been merely plumpness in another was obesity in her. She looked bloated, like a body long submerged in motionless water, and of that pallied hue. Her eyes, lost in the fatty ridges of her face, looked like two small pieces of coal pressed into a lump of dough as they moved from one face to another while the visitors stated their errand.

She did not ask them to sit. She just stood in the door and listened quietly until the spokesman came to a stumbling halt. Then they could hear the invisible watch ticking at the end of the gold chain.

Her voice was dry and cold. "I have no taxes in Jefferson. Colonel Sartoris explained it to me. Perhaps one of you can gain access to the city records and satisfy yourselves."

"But we have. We are the city authorities, Miss Emily. Didn't you get a notice from the sheriff, signed by him?"

"I received a paper, yes," Miss Emily said. "Perhaps he considers himself the sheriff....I have no taxes in Jefferson."

"But there is nothing on the books to show that, you see. We must go by the —"

"See Colonel Sartoris. I have no taxes in Jefferson."

"But, Miss Emily—"

"See Colonel Sartoris."(Colonel Sartoris had been dead almost ten years.) "I have no taxes in Jefferson. Tobe!" The Negro appeared. "Show these gentlemen out."

II

So she vanquished them, horse and foot, just as she had vanquished their fathers thirty years before about the smell. That was two years after her father's death and a short time after sweetheart—the one we believed would marry her—had deserted her. After her father's death she went out very little; after her sweetheart went away, people hardly saw her at all. A few of the ladies had the temerity to call, but were not received, and the only sign of life about the place was the Negro man—a young man then—going in and out with a market basket.

"Just as if a man—any man—could keep a kitchen properly," the ladies said; so they were not surprised when the smell developed. It was another link between the gross, teeming world and the high and mighty Griersons.

A neigher, a woman, complained to the mayor, Judge Stevens, eighty years old.

"But what will you have me do about it, madam?" he said.

"Why, send her word to stop it," the woman said. "Isn't there a law?"

"I'm sure that won't be necessary," Judge Stevens said. "It's probably just a snake or a rat that nigger of hers killed in the yard. I'll speak to him about it."

The next day he received two more complaints, one from a man who came in diffident deprecation. "We really must do something about it, Judge. I'd be the last one in the world to bother Miss Emily, but we've got to do something." That night the Board of Aldermen met - three gray-beards and one younger man, a member of the rising generation.

"It's simple enough," he said. "Send her word to have her place cleaned up. Give her a certain time to do it in, and if she don't ..."

"Dammit, sir," Judge Stevens said, "will you accuse a lady her face of smelling bad?"

So the next night, after midnight, four men crossed Miss Emily's lawn and slunk about the house like burglars, sniffing along the base of the brickwork and at the cellar openings while one of them performed a regular sowing motion with his hand out of a sack slung from his shoulder. They broke open the cellar door and sprinkled lime there, and in all the outbuildings. As they recrossed the lawn, a window that had been dark was lighted and Miss Emily sat in it, the light behind her, and her upright torso motionless as that of an idol. They crept quietly across the lawn and into the shadow of the locusts that lined the street. After a week or two the smell went away.

That was when people had begun to feel really sorry for her. People in our town, remembering how old lady Wyatt, her great-aunt, had gone completely crazy at last, believed that the Griersons held themselves a little too high for what they really were.

None of the young men were quite good enough for Miss Emily and such. We had long thought of them as a tableau; Miss Emily a slender figure in white in the back-ground, her father a spraddled silhouette in the foreground, his back to her and clutching a horsewhip, the two of them framed by the back-flung front door. So when she got to be thirty and was still single, we were not pleased exactly, but vindicated; even with insanity in the family she wouldn't have turned down all of her chances if they had really materialized.

When her father died, it got about that the house was all that was left to her; and in a way, people were glad. At last they could pity Miss Emily. Being left alone, and a pauper, she had become humanized. Now she too would know the old thrill and the old despair of a penny more or less.

The day after his death all the ladies prepared to call at the house and offer condolence and aid, as is our custom. Miss Emily met them at the door, dressed as usual and with no trace of grief on her face. She told them that her father was not dead. She did that for three days, with the ministers calling on her, and the doctors, trying to persuade her to let them dispose of the body. Just as they were about to resort to law and force, she broke down, and they buried her father quickly.

We did not say she was crazy then. We believed she had to do that. We remembered all the young men her father had driven away, and we knew that with nothing left, she would have to cling to that which had robbed her, as people will.

III

She was sick for a long time. When we saw her again, her hair was cut short, making her look like a girl, with a vague resemblance to those angels in colored church windows-sort of tragic and serene.

The town had just let the contracts for paving the sidewalks, and in the summer after her father's death they began to work. The construction company came with niggers and mules and machinery, and a foreman named Homer Barron, a Yankee-a big, dark, ready man, with a big voice and eyes lighter than his face. The little boys would follow in groups to hear him cuss the niggers, and the niggers singing in time to the rise and fall of picks. Pretty soon he knew everybody in town. Whenever you heard a lot of laughing anywhere about the square, Homer Barron would be in the center of the group. Presently we began to see him and Miss Emily on Sunday afternoons driving in the yellow-wheeled buggy and the matched team of bays from the livery stable.

At first we were glad that Miss Emily would have an interest, because the ladies all said, "Of course a Grierson would not think seriously of a Northerner, a day laborer." But there were still others, older people, who said that even grief could not cause a real lady to forget *noblesse oblige*-without calling it *noblesse oblige.* They just said, "Poor Emily. Her kinsfolk should come to her." She had some kin in Alabama; but years ago her father had fallen out with them over the estate of old lady Wyatt, the crazy woman, and there was no communication between the two families. They had not even been represented at the funeral.

And as soon as the old people said, "Poor Emily," the whispering began. "Do you suppose it's really so?" they said to one another. "Of course it is. What else could..." This behind their hands; rustling of craned silk and satin behind jalousies closed upon the sun of Sunday afternoon as the thin, swift clop-clop-clop of the matched team passed: "Poor Emily."

She carried her head high enough—even when we believed that she was fallen. It was as if she demanded more than ever the recognition of her dignity as the last Grierson; as if it had wanted that touch of earthiness to reaffirm her imperviousness. Like when she bought the rat poison, the arsenic. That was over a year after they had begun to say "Poor Emily," and while the two female cousins were visiting her.

"I want some poison," she said to the druggist. She was over thirty then, still a slight woman, though thinner than usual, with cold, haughty black eyes in a face the flesh of which was strained across the temples and about the eyesockets as you imagine a lighthouse-keeper's face ought to look. "I want some poison," she said.

"Yes, Miss Emily. What kind? For rats and such? I'd recom—"

"I want the best you have. I don't care what kind."

The druggist named several. "They'll kill anything up to an

elephant. But what you want is —"

"Arsenic," Miss Emily said. "Is that a good one?"

"Is...arsenic? Yes ma'am. But what you want —"

"I want arsenic."

The druggist looked down at her. She looked back at him, erect, her face like a strained flag. "Why, of course," the druggist said. "If that's what you want. But the law requires you to tell what you are going to use it for."

Miss Emily just stared at him, her head tilted back in order to look him eye for eye, until he looked away and went and got the arsenic and wrapped it up. The Negro delivery boy brought her the package; the druggist didn't come back. When she opened the package at home there was written on the box, under the skull and bones: For rats."

IV

So the next day we all said, "She will kill herself"; and we said it would be the best thing. When she had first begun to be seen with Homer Barron, we had said, "She will marry him." Then we said. "She will persuade him yet," because Homer himself had remarked — he liked men, and it was known that he drank with the younger men in the Elk's Club — that he was not a marrying man. Later we said, "Poor Emily," behind the jalousies as they passed on Sunday afternoon in the glittering buggy, Miss Emily with her head high and Homer Barron with his hat cocked and a cigar in his teeth, reins and whip in a yellow glove.

Then some of the ladies began to say that it was a disgrace to the town and a bad example to the young people. The men did not want to interfere, but at last the ladies forced the Baptist minister-Miss Emily's people were Episcopal-to call upon her. He would never divulge what happened during that interview, but he refused to go back again. The next Sunday they again drove about the streets, and the following day the minister's wife wrote to Miss Emily's relations in Alabama.

So she had blood-kin under her roof again and we sat back to watch developments.n At first nothing happened. Then we were sure that they were to be married. We learned that Miss Emily had been to the jeweler's and ordered a man's toilet set in silver, with the letters H.B. on each piece. Two days later we learned that she had bought a complete outfit of men's clothing, including a nightshirt, and we said, "They are married." We were really glad. We were glad because the two female cousins were even more Grierson than Miss Emily had ever been.

So we were not surprised when Homer Barron-the streets had been finished some time since-was gone. We were a little disappointed that there was not a public blowing-off, but we believed that he had gone on to prepare for Miss Emily's coming, or to give her a chance to get rid of the cousins. (By that time it was a cabal, and we were all Miss Emily's allies to help circumvent the cousins.) Sure enough, after another week they departed. And, as we had expected all along, within three days Homer Barron was back in town. A neighbor saw the Negro man admit him at the kitchen door at dusk one evening.

And that was the last we saw of Homer Barron. And of Miss Emily for some time. The Negro man went in and out with the market basket, but the front door remained closed. Now and then we would see her at a window for a moment, as the men did that night when they sprinkled the lime, but for almost six months she did not appear on the streets. Then we knew that this was to be expected too; as if that quality of her father which had thwarted her woman's life so many times had been too virulent and too furious to die.

When we next saw Miss Emily, she had grown fat and her hair was turning gray. During the next few years it grew grayer and grayer until it attained an even pepper-and-salt iron-gray, when it ceased turning. Up to the day of her death at seventy-four it was still that vigorous iron-gray, like the hair of an active man.

From that time on her front door remained closed, save for a period of six or seven years, when she was about forty, during which she gave lessons in china-painting. She fitted up a studio in one of the down-stairs rooms, where the daughters and grand-daughters of Colonel Sartoris' contemporaries were sent to her with the same regularity and in the same spirit that they were sent on Sundays with a twenty-five cent piece for the collection plate. Meanwhile her taxes had been remitted.

Then the newer generation became the backbone and the spirit of the town, and the painting pupils grew up and fell away and did not send their children to her with boxes of color and tedious brushes and pictures cut from the ladies' magazines. The front door closed upon the last one and remained closed for good. When the town got free postal delivery Miss Emily alone refused to let them fasten the metal numbers above her door and attach a mailbox to it. She would not listen to them.

Daily, monthly, yearly we watched the Negro grow grayer and more stooped, going in and out with the market basket. Each December we sent her a tax notice, which would be returned by the post office a week later, unclaimed. Now and then we would see her in one of the downstairs windows—she had evidently shut up the top floor of the house—like the carven torso of an idol in a niche, looking or not looking at us, we could never tell which. Thus she passed from generation to generation—dear, inescapable , impervious, tranquil, and perverse.

And so she died. Fell ill in the house filled with dust and shadows, with only a doddering Negro man to wait on her. We did not even know she was sick; we had long since given up trying to get any information from the Negro. He talked to no one, probably not even to her, for his voice had grown harsh and rusty, as if from disuse.

She died in one of the downstairs rooms, in a heavy walnut bed with a curtain, her gray head propped on a pillow yellow and moldy with age and lack of sunlight.

V

The Negro met the first of the ladies at the front door and let them in, with their hushed, sibilant voices and their quick, curious glances, and then he disappeared. He walked right through the house and out the back and was not seen again.

The two female cousins came at once. they held the funeral on the second day, with the town coming to look at Miss Emily beneath a mass of bought flowers, with the crayon face of her father musing profoundly above the bier and the ladies sibilant and macabre; and the very old men-some in their brushed Confederate uniforms-on the porch and the lawn, talking of Miss Emily as if she had been a contemporary of theirs, believing that they had danced with her and courted her perhaps, confusing time with its mathematical progression, as the old do, to whom all the past is not a diminishing road, but, instead, a huge meadow which no winter ever quite touches, divided from them now by the narrow bottleneck of the most recent decade of years.

Already we knew that there was one room in that region above stairs which no one had seen in forty years, and which would have to be forced. They waited until Miss Emily was decently in the ground before they opened it.

The violence of breaking down the door seemed to fill this room with pervading dust. A thin, acrid pall as of the tomb seemed to lie everywhere upon this room decked and furnished as for a bridal: upon the valance curtains of faded rose color, upon the rose-shaded lights, upon the dressing table, upon the delicate array of crystal and the man's toilet things backed with tarnished silver, silver so tarnished that the monogram was obscured. Among them lay a collar and tie, as if they had just been removed, which, lifted, left upon the surface a pale crescent in the dust. Upon a chair hung the suit, carefully folded; beneath it the two mute shoes and the discarded socks.

The man himself lay in the bed.

For a long while we just stood there, looking down at the profound and fleshless grin. The body had apparently once lain in the attitude of an embrace, but now the long sleep that outlasts love, that conquers even the grimace of love, had cuckolded him. What was left of him, rotted beneath what was left of the nightshirt, had become inextricable from the bed in which he lay; and upon him and upon the pillow beside him lay that even coating of the patient and biding dust.

Then we noticed that in the second pillow was the indentation of a head. One of us lifted something from it, and leaning forward, that faint and invisible dust dry and acrid in the nostrils, we saw a long strand of iron-gray hair.

The Snow of Kilimanjaro
— by Earnest Hemingway

Kilimanjaro is a snow-covered mountain 19,710 feet high, and is said to be the highest mountain in Africa. Its western summit iscalled the Masai "Ngaje Ngai," the House of God. Close to the western summit there is the dried and frozen carcass of a leopard. No one has explained what the leopard was seeking at the altitude.

"The marvellous thing is that it's painless," he said. "That's hoe you know when it starts."

"Is it really?"

"Absolutely. I'm awfully sorry about the odor, though. That must bother you."

"Don't! Please don't."

"Look at them," he said. "Now is it sight or is it scent that brings them like that?"

The cot the man lay on was in the wide shade of a mimosa tree and as he looked out past the shade on to the glare of the plain there were three of the big birds squatted obscenely, while in the sky a dozen more sailed, making quick-moving shadows as they passed.

"They've been there since the day the truck broke down," he said. "Today's the first time any have lit on the ground. I watched the way they sailed very carefully at first in case I ever wanted to use them in a story. That's funny now."

"I wish you wouldn't," she said.

"I'm only talking," he said. "It's much easier if I talk. But I don't want to bother you"

"You know it doesn't bother me," she said. "It's that I've gotten so very nervous not being able to do anything. I think we might make it as easy as we can until the plane comes."

"Or until the plane doesn't come."

"Please tell me what I can do. There must be something I can do."

"You can take the leg off and that might stop it, though I doubt it. Or you can shoot me. You're a good hot now. I taught you to shoot, didn't I?"

"Please don't talk that way. Couldn't I read to you?"

"Read what?"

"Anything in the book bag that we haven't read."

"I can't listen to it," he said. "Talking is the easiest. We quarrel and that makes the time pass."

"I don't quarrel. I never want to quarrel. Let's not quarrel any more. No matter how nervous we get. Maybe they will be back with another truck today. Maybe the plane will come."

"I don't want to move," the man said. "There is no sense in moving now except to make it easier for you."

"That's cowardly."

"Can't you let a man die as comfortably as he can without calling him names? What's the use of slanging me?"

"You're not going to die."

"Don't be silly. I'm dying now. Ask those bastards."

He looked over to where the huge, filthy birds sat, their naked heads sunk in the hunched feathers. A fourth planed down to run quicked-legged and then waddle slowly toward the others.

"They are around every camp. You never notice them. You can't die if you don't give up."

"Where did you read that? You're such a bloody fool."

"You might think about some one else."

"For Christ's sake," he said, "that's been my trade"

He lay then and was quiet for a while and looked across the heat shimmer of the plain to the edge of the bush. There were a few Tommies that showed minute and white against the yellow and, far off, he saw a herd of zebra, white against the green of the bush. This was a pleasant camp under big trees against a hill, with good water, and close by, a nearly dry water hole where sand grouse flighted in the mornings.

"Wouldn't you like me to read?" she asked. She was sitting on a canvas chair beside his cot. "There's a breeze coming up."

"No thanks."

"Maybe the truck will come."

"I don't give damn about the truck."

"I do."

"You give a damn about so many things that I don't"

"Not so many, Harry."

"What about a drink?"

"It's supposed to be bad for you. It said in Black's to avoid all alcohol. You shouldn't drink."

"Molo!" he shouted.

"Yes, Bwana."

"Bring whiskey-soda."

"You shouldn't," she said. "That's what I mean by giving up. It says it's bad for you. I know it's bad for you."

"No," he said. "It's good for me."

So now it was all over, he was thought. So now he would never have a chance to finish it. So this was the way it ended in a bickering over a drink. Since the gangrene started in his right leg he had no pain and with the pain the horror had gone and all he felt now was a great tiredness and anger that this was the end of it. For this, that now was coming, he had very little curiosity. For years it had obsessed him ; but now it meant nothing in itself. It was strange how easy being tired enough made it.

Now he would never write the things that he had saved to write until he knew enough to write them well. Well, he would not have to fail at trying to write them either. Maybe you could never write them, and that was why you put them off and delayed the starting. Well, he would never know, now.

"I wish we'd never come," the woman said. She was looking at him holding the glass and biting her lip. "You never would have gotten anything like this in Paris. You always said you loved Paris. We could have stayed in Paris or gone anywhere. I'd have gone anywhere. I said. I'd go anywhere you wanted. If you wanted to shoot we could have gone shooting in Hungary and been comfortable."

"Your bloody money," he said.

"That's not fair," she said. "It was always yours as much as mine. I left everything and I went wherever you wanted to go and I've done what you wanted to do. But I wish we'd never come here."

"You said you loved it."

"I did when you were all right. But now I hate it. I don't see why that had to happen to your leg. What have we done to have that happen to us?"

"I suppose what I did was to forget to put iodine on it when I first scratched it. Then I didn't pay any attention to it because I never infect. Then, later, when it got bad, it was probably using that weak carbolic solution when the other antiseptics ran out that paralyzed the minute blood vessels and started the gangrene." He looked at her, "What else?"

"I don't mean that."

"If we would have hired a good mechanic instead of a half-baked kikuyu driver, he would have checked the oil and never burned out that bearing in the truck."

"I don't mean that."

"If you hadn't left your own people, your god-damned Old Westbury, Saratoga, Palm Beach people to take me on—"

"Why, I loved you. That's not fair. I love you now. I'll always love you. Don't you love me?"

"No," said the man. "I don't think so. I never have."

"Harry, what are you saying? You're out of your head."

"No. I haven't any head to go out of."

"Don't drink that," she said. "Darling, please don't drink that. We have to do everything we can."

"You do it," he said. "I'm tired."

Now in his mind he saw a railway station at Karagatch and he was standing with his pack and that was the headlight of the Simplon-Orient cutting the dark now and he was leaving Thrace then after the retreat. That was one of the things he had saved to write, with, in the morning at breakfast, looking out the window and seeing snow on the mountains in Bulgaria and Nansen's Secretary asking the old man if it were snow and the old man looking at it and saying, No, that's not snow. It's too early for snow. And the Secretary repeating to the other girls, No, you see. It's not snow and them all saying. It's not snow, we were mistaken. But it was the snow all right and he sent them on into it when he evolved the exchange of populations. And it was snow they tramped along in until they died that winter.

It was snow too that fell all Christmas week that year up in the Gauertal, that year they lived in the wood-cutter's house with the big square porcelain stove that filled half the room, and they slept on mattresses filled with beech leaves, the time the deserter came with his feet bloody in the snow. He said the police were right behind him and they gave him wooden socks and held the gendarmes talking until the tracks had drifted over.

In Schrunz, on Christmas day, the snow was so bright it hurt your eyes when you looked out from the Weinstube and saw every one coming from church. That was where they walked up the sleigh-smoothed urine-yellowed road along the river with steep pine hills, skis heavy on the shoulder, and where they ran that great run down the glacier above the Madlener-haus, the snow as smooth to see as cake frosting and as light as powder and he remembered the noiseless rush the speed made as you dropped down like a bird.

They were snow-bound a week in the Madlener-haus that time in the blizzard playing cards in the smoke by the lantern light and the stakes were higher al the time as Herr Lent lost more. Finally he lost it all. Everything, the skischule money and all the season's profit and then his capital. He could see him with his long nose, picking up the cards and then opening, "Sans Voir." There was always gambling then. When there was no snow you snow you gambled and when there was too much you gambled. He thought of all the time in his life he had spent gambling.

But he had never written a line of that, nor of that cold, bright Christmas day with the mountains showing across the plain that Barker had flown across the lines to bomb the Austrian officers' leave train, machine-gunning them as they scattered and ran. He remembered Barker afterwards coming into the mess and starting to tell about it. And how quiet it got and then somebody saying, "You bloody murderous bastard."

Those were the same Austrians they killed then that he skied with later. No, not the same. Hans, that he skied with all that year, had been in the Kaiser-Jasers and when they went hunting hares together up the little valley above the saw-mill they had *talked of the fighting on Pasubio and of the attack on Pertica and Asalone and he had never written a word of that. Nor of Mont Corno, nor the Siete Commum, nor of Arsiedo.*

How many winters had he lived in the Voralberg and the Arlberg? It was four and then he remembered the man who had the fox to sell when they had walked into Bludenz, that time to buy presents, and the cherry-pip taste of good kirsch, the fast-slipping rush of running powder-snow on crust, singing "Hi! Ho! said Rolly!" as you ran down the last stretch to the steep drop, taking it straight, then running the orchard in three turns and out across the ditch and on to the icy road behind the inn. Knocking your bindings loose, kicking ihe skis free and leaning them up against the wooden wall of the inn, the lamplight coming from the window, where inside, in the smoky, new-wine smelling warmth, they were playing the accordion.

"Where did we stay in Paris?" he asked the woman who was sitting by him in a canvas chair, now, in Africa.

"At the Crillon. You know that."

"Why do I know that?"

"That's where we always stayed."

"No. not always."

"There and at the Pavilion Henri-Quatre in St. Germain. You said you loved it there."

"Love is a dunghill," said Harry. "And I'm the cock that gets on it to crow."

"If you have to go away," she said. "is it absolutely necessary to kill off everything you leave behind? I mean do you have to take away everything? Do you havr to kill your horse, and your wife and burn your saddle and your Armour?"

"Yes," he said. "Your damned money was my armour. My Swift and my armour."

"Don't."

"All right. I'll stop that. I don't want to hurt you."

"It's a little bit late now."

"All right then. I'll go on hurting you. It's more amusing. The only thing I ever really liked to do with you I can't do now."

"No, that's not true. You liked to do many things and every thing you wanted to do I did."

"Oh, for Christ sake stop bragging, will you?"

He looked at her and saw her crying.

"Listen," he said. "Do you think that it is fun to do this? I don't know why I'm doing it. It's trying to kill to keep yourself alive, I imagine. I was all right when we started talking. I didn't mean to start this, and now I'm crazy as a coot and being as cruel to you as I can be. Don't pay any attention, darling, to what I say. I love you, really. You know I love you. I've never loved anyone else the way I love you."

He slipped into the familiar lie he made his bread and butter by.

"You're sweet to me."

"You bitch," he said. "You rich bitch. That's poetry. I'm full of poetry now. Rot and poetry. Rotten poetry."

"Stop it. Harry, why do you have to turn into a devil now?"

"I don't like to leave anything," the man said. "I don't like to leave thimgs behind."

It was evening now and he had been asleep. The sun was gone behind the hill and there was a shadow all across the plain and the small animals were feeding close to camp; quick dropping heads and switching tails, he watched them keeping well out away from the bush now. The birds no longer waited on the ground. They were all perched heavily in a tree. There were many more of them. His personal boy was sitting by the bed.
"Memsahib's gone to shoot," the boy said. "Does Bwana want?"
"Nothing."
She had gone to kill a piece of meat and, knowing how he liked to watch the game, she had gone well away so she would not disturb this little pocket of the plain that he could see. She was always thoughtful, he thought. On anything she knew about, or had read, or that she had ever heard.

It was not her fault that when he went to her he was already over. How could a woman know that you meant nothing that you said ; that you spoke only from habit and to be comfortable? After he no longer meant what he said, his lies were successful with women than when he had told them the truth.

It was not so much that he lied as that there was no truth to tell. He had had his life and it was over and then he went on living it again with different people and more money, with the best of the same places, and some new ones.

You kept from thinking and it was all marvellous. You were

equipped with good insides so that you did not go to pieces that way, the way most of them had, and you made an attitude that you cared nothing for the work you used to do, now that you could no longer do it. But, in yourself, you said that you would write about these people ; about the very rich ; that you were really not of them but a spy in their country ; that you would leave it and write of it and for once it would be written by some one who knew what he was writing of. But he would never do it, because each day of not writing, of comfort, of being that which he despised, dulled his ability and softened his will to work so that, finally, he did no work at all. The people he knew now were all much more comfortable when he did not work. Africa was where he had been happiest in the good time of his life, so he had come out here to start again. They had made this safari with the minimum of comfort. There was no hardship ; but there was no luxury and he had thought that he could get back into training that way. That in some way he could work the fat off his soul the way a fighter went into the mountains to work and train in order to burn it out of his body.

She had liked it. She said she loved it. She loved anything that was exciting, that involved a change of scene, where there were new people and where things were pleasant. And he had felt the illusion of returning strength of will to work. Now if this was how it ended, and he knew it was, he must not turn like some snake biting itself because its back was broken. It wasn't this woman's fault. If it had not been she it would have been another. If he lived by a lie he should try to die by it. He heard a shot beyond the hill.

She shot very well, this good, this rich bitch, this kindly caretaker and destroyer of his talent. Nonsense. He had destroyed his talent himself. Why should he blame this woman because she kept him well? He had destroyed his talent by not using it, by betrayals of himself and what he believed in, by drinking so much that he blunted the edge of his perceptions, by laziness, by sloth, and by snobbery, by pride and by prejudice, by hook and by crook. What was this? A catalogue of old books? What was his talent anyway? It was a talent all right but, instead of using it, he had traded on it. It was never what he had done, but always what he could do. And he had chosen to make his living with something else instead of a pen or a pencil. It was strange, too, wasn't it, that when he fell in love with another woman, that woman should always have more money than the last one? But when he no longer was in love, when he was only lying, as to this woman, now, who had the most money of all, who had all the money there was, who had had a husband and children, who had taken lovers and been dissatisfied with them, and who loved him dearly as a write, as a man, as a companion, and as a proud possession; it was a strange that when he did not love her at all and was lying, that he should be able to give her more for her money than when he had really loved.

We must all be cut out for what we do, he thought. However you make your living is where your talent lies. He had sold vitality, in one form or another, all his life, and when your affections are not too involved you give much better value for the money. He had found that out but he would never write that, now, either. No, he would not write that, although it was well worth writing.

Now she came in sight, walking across the open toward the camp. She was wearing jodhpurs and carrying her rifle. The two boys had a Tommie slung and they were coming along behind her. She was still a good-looking woman, he thought, and she had a pleasant body. She had a great talent and appreciation for the bed, she was not pretty, but he liked her face, she read enormously, liked to ride and shoot and, certainly, she drank too much. Her husband had died when she was still a comparatively young woman and for a while she had devoted herself to her two just-grown children, who did not need her and were embarrassed at having her about, to her stable of horses, to books, and to bottles. She liked to read in the evening before dinner and she drank Scotch and soda while she read. By dinner she was fairly drunk and after a bottle of wine at dinner she was usually drunk enough to sleep.

That was before the loves. After she had the lovers she did not drink so much because she did not have to be drunk to sleep. But the lovers bored her. She had been married to a man who had never bored her and these people bored her very much.

Then one of her two children was killed in a plane crash and after that was over she did not want the lovers, and drink being no an anaesthetic she had to make another life. Suddenly, she had been acutely frightened of being alone. But she wanted some one that she respected with her.

It had begun, very simply. She liked what he wrote and she had always envied the life he led. She thought he did exactly what he wanted to. The steps by which she had acquired him and the way in which she had finally fallen in love with him were all part of a regular progression in which she had built herself a new life and he had traded away what remained of his old life.

He had traded it for security, for comfort too, there was no denying that, and for what else? He did not know. She would have bought him anything he wanted. He knew that. She was a damned nice woman too. He would as soon be in bed with her as any one ; rather with her, because she was richer, because she was very pleasant and appreciative and because she never made scenes. And now thislife that she had built again was coming to a term because he had not used iodine two weeks ago when a thorn had scratched his knee as they moved forward trying to photograph a herd of waterbuck standing, their heads up, peering while their nostrils searched the air, their ears spread wide to hear the first noise that would send them rushing into the bush. They had bolted, too, before he got the picture.

Here she came now.

He turned his head on the cot to look toward her.

"Hello," he said.

"I shot a Tommy ram," she told him. "He'll make you good broth and I'll have them mash some potatoes with the Klim. How do you feel?"

"Much better."

"Isn't that lovely? You know I thought perhaps you would. You were sleeping when I left."

"I had a good sleep. Did you walk far?"

"No. Just around behind the hill. I made quite a good shot on the Tommy."

"You shoot marvellously, you know."

"I love it. I've loved Africa. Really. If you're all right it's the most fun that I've ever had. You don't know the fun it's been to shoot with you. I've loved the country."

"I love it too."

"Darling, you don't know how marvellous it is to see you feeling better. I couldn't stand it when you felt that way. You won't talk to me like that again, will you? Promise me?"

"No," he said. "I don't remember what I said."

"You don't have to destroy me. Do you? I'm only a middle-aged woman who loves you and wants to do what you want to do. I've been destroyed two or three times already. You wouldn't want to destroy me again, would you?"

"I'd like to destroy you a few times in bed," he said.

"Yes. That's the good destruction. That's the way we're made to be destroyed. The plane will be here tomorrow."

"How do you know?"

"I'm sure. It's bound to come. The boys have the wood all ready and the grass to make the smudge. I went down and looked at it again today. There's plenty of room to land and we have the smudges ready at both ends."

"What makes you think it will come tomorrow?"

"I'm sure it will. It's overdue now. Then, in town, they will fix up your leg and then we will have some good destruction. Not that dreadful talking kind."

"Should we have a drink? The sun is down."

"Do you think you should?"

"I'm having one."

"We'll have one together. *Molo, letti dui whiskeysoda!*" she called.

"You'd better put on your mosquito boots," he told her.

"I'll wait till I bathe....?"

While it grew dark they drank and just before it was dark and there was no longer enough light to shoot, a hyena crossed the open on his way around the hill.

"That bastard crosses there every night," the man said. "Every night for two weeks."

"He's the one makes the noise at night. I don't mind it. They're a filthy animal though."

Drinking together, with no pain now except the discomfort of lying in the one position, the boys lighting a fire, its shadow jumping on the tents, he could feel the return of acquiescence in this life of pleasant surrender. She was very good to him. He had been cruel and unjust in the afternoon. She was a fine woman, marvelous really. And just then it occurred to him that he was going to die.

It came with a rush; not as a rush of water nor of wind; but of a sudden evil-smelling emptiness and the odd thing was that the hyena slipped lightly along the edge of it.

"What is it, Harry?" she asked him.

"Nothing," he said. "You had better move over to the other side. To windward."

"Did Molo change the dressing?"

"Yes. I'm just using the boric now."

"How do you feel?"

"A little wobbly."

"I'm going in to bathe," she said. "I'll be right out. I'll eat with you and then we'll put the cot in."

So, he said to himself, we did well to stop the quarrelling. He had never quarreled much with this woman, while with the woman that he loved he had quarreled so much they had finally, always, with the corrosion of the quarrelling, killed what they had together. He had loved too much, demanded too much, and he wrote it all out.

He thought about alone in Constantinople that time, having quarrelled in Paris before he had gone out. He had whored the whole time and then, when that was over, and he had failed to kill his loneliness, but only made it worse, he had written her, the first one, the one who left him, a letter telling her how he had never been able to kill it.... How when he thought he saw her outside the Regence one time it made him go all faint and sick inside, and that he would follow a woman who looked like her in some way, along the Boulevard, afraid to see it was not she, afraid to lose the feeling it gave him. How every one he had slept with had only made him miss her more. How what she had done could never matter since he knew he could not cure himself of loving her. He wrote this letter at the Club, cold sober, and mailed it to New York asking her to write him at the office in Paris. That seemed safe. And that night missing her so much it made him feel hollow sick inside, he wandered up past Taxim's, picked a girl up, and took her out to supper. He had gone to a place to dance with her afterward, she danced badly, and left her for a hot Armenian slut, that swung her belly against him so it almost scalded. He took her away from a British gunner subaltern after a row. The gunner asked him outside and they fought in the street on the cobbles in the dark. He'd hit him twice, hard, on the side of the jaw and when he didn't go down he knew he was in for a fight. The gunner hit him in the body, then beside his eye. He swung with his left again and landed and gunner fell on him and grabbed his coat and tore the sleeve off and he clubbed him twice behind the ear and then smashed him with his right as he pushed him away. When the gunner went down his head hit first and he ran with the girl because they heard the M.P.'s coming. They got into a taxi and drove out to Rimmily Hissa along the Bosphorus, and around, and back in he cool night and went to bed and she felt as over-ripe as she looked but smooth, rose-petal, syrupy, smooth-bellied, big-breasted and needed no pillow under her buttocks, and he left her before she was awake looking blousy enough in the first daylight and turned up at the Pera Palace with a black eye, carrying his coat because one sleeve was missing.

That same night he left for Anatolia and he remembered, later on that trip, riding all day through fields of the poppies that they raised for opium and how strange it made you feel, finally, and all the distances seemed wrong, to where they had made the attack with the newly-arrived Constantine officers, that did not know a god-damned thing, and the artillery had fired into the troops and the British observer had cried a child.

That was the day he'd first seen dead men wearing white ballet skirts and upturned shoes with pompons on them. The Turks had come steadily and lumpily and he had seen the skirted men running and the officers shooting into them and running then themselves and he and the British observer had run too until his lungs ached and his mouth was full of the taste of pennies and they stopped behind some rocks and there were the Turks coming as lumpily as ever. Later he had seen the things that he could never think of and later still he had seen much worse. So when he got back to Paris that time he could not talk about it or stand to have it mentioned. And there in the caf as he passed was that American poet with a pile of saucer in front of him and a stupid look on his potato face talking about the Dada movement with a Roumanian who said his name was Tristan Tzara, who always wore a monocle and had a headache, and, back at the apartment with his wife that now he loved again, the quarrel all over, the madness all over, glad to be home, the office sent his mail up to the flat. So then the latter in answer to the one he'd written came in on a platter one morning and when he saw the hand writing he went cold all over and tried to slip the letter underneath another. But his wife said,

"Who is that letter from, dear?" and that was the end of the beginning of that.

He remembered the good times with them all, and the quarrels. They always picked the finest places to have the quarrels. And why had they always quarrelled when he was feeling best? He had never written any of that because, at first, he never wanted to hurt any one and then it seemed as though there was enough to write without it. But he had always thought that he would write it finally. There was so much to write. He had seen the world change; not just the events; although he had seen many of them and had watched the people, but he had seen the subtler change and he could remember how the people were at different times. He had been in it and he had watched it and it was his duty to write of it; but now he never would.

"How do you feel?" she said. She had come out from the tent now after her bath.

"All right."

"Could you eat now?" He saw Molo behind her with the folding table and the other boy with the dishes.

"I want to write," he said.

"You ought to take some broth to keep your strength up."

"I'm going to die tonight," he said. "I don't need my strength up."

"Don't be melodramatic, Harry, please," she said.

"Why don't you use your nose? I'm rotted halfway up my thigh now. What the hell should I fool with broth for? Molo, bring whiskey-soda."

"Please take the broth," she said gently.

"All right."

The broth was too hot. He had to hold it in the cup until it cooled enough to take it and then he just got it down without gagging.

"You're a fine woman," he said. "Don't pay any attention to me."

She looked at him with her well-known, well-loved face from *Spur* and *Town and Country*, only a little the worse for drink, only a little the worse for bed, but *Town and Country* never showed those good breasts and those useful things and those lightly small-of-back-caressing hands, and as he looked and saw her well-known pleasant smile, he felt death come again. This time there was no rush. It was a puff, as of a wind that makes a candle flicker and the flame go tall.

"They can bring my net out later and hang it from the tree and build the fire up. I'm not going in the tent tonight. It's not worth moving. It's a clear night. There won't be any rain."

So this was how you died, in whispers that you did not hear. Well, there would be no more quarrelling. He could promise that. The one experience that he had never had he was not going to spoil now. He probably would. You spoiled everything. But perhaps he wouldn't.

"You can't take dictation, can you?"

"I never learned," she told him.

"That's all right."

There wasn't time, of course, although, it seemed as though it telescoped so that you might put it all into one paragraph if you could get it right.

There was a log house, chinked while with mortar, on a hill above the lake. There was a bell on a pole by the door to call the people in to meals. Behind the house were fields and behind the fields was timber. A line of Lombardy poplars ran from the house to the dock. Other poplars ran along the point. A road went up to the hills along the edge of the timber and along that road he picked blackberries. Then that log house was burned down and all the guns that had been on deer foot racks above the open fire place were burned and afterwards their barrels, with the lead melted in the magazines, and the stocks burned away, lay out on the heap of ashes that were used to make lye for the big iron soap kettles, and you asked Grandfather if you could have them to play with, and he said, no. you see they were his guns still and he never bought any others. Nor did he hunt any more. The house was rebuilt in the same place out of lumber now and painted white and from its porch you saw the poplars and the lake beyond; but there were never any more guns. The barrels of the guns that had hung on the deer feet on the wall of the log house lay out there on the heap of ashes and no one ever touched them.

In the Black Forest, after the war, we rented a trout stream and there were two ways to walk to it. One was down the valley from Triberg and around the valley road in the shade of the trees that bordered the white road, and then up a side road that went up through the hills, past many small farms, with the big Schwarzwald houses, until that road crossed the stream. That was where our fishing began.

The other way was to climb steeply up to the edge of the woods and then go across the top of the hills through the pine woods, and then out of the edge of a meadow and down across this meadow to the bridge. There were birches along the stream and it was not big, but narrow, clear and fast, with pools where it had cut under the roots of the birches. At the Hotel in Triberg the proprietor had a fine season. It was very pleasant and we were all great friends. The next year came the inflation and the money he had made the year before was not enough to buy supplies to open the hotel and he hanged himself.

You could dictate that, but you could not dictate the Place Contrescarpe where the flower sellers dyed their flowers in the street and the dye ran over the paving where the autobus started and the old men and the women, always drunk on wine and bad marc; and the children with their noses running in the cold; the smell of dirty sweat and poverty and drunkenness at the Cafe des Amateurs and the whores at the Bal Musette they lived above. The Concierge who entertained the trooper of the Garde Republicaine in her loge, his horse-hair-plumed helmet on a chair. The locataire across the hall whose husband was a bicycle racer and her joy that morning at the Cremerie when she had opened L'Auto and seen where he placed third in Paris-Tours, his first big race. She had blushed and laughed and then gone upstairs crying with the yellow sporting paper in her hand. The husband of the woman who ran the Bal Musette drove a taxi and when he, Harry, had to take an early plane the husband knocked upon the door to wake him and they each drank a glass of white wine at the zinc of the bar before they started. He knew his neighbors in that quarter then because they all were poor.

Around that Place there were two kinds; the drunkards and the sportifs. The drunkards killed their poverty that way; the sportifs took it out in exercise. They were the descendants of the Communards and it was no struggle for them to know their politics. They knew who had shot their fathers, their relatives, their brothers, and their friends, when the Versailles troops came in and took the town after the Commune and executed any one they could catch with calloused hands, or who wore a cap, or carried any other sign he was a working man. And in that poverty, and in that quarter across the street from a Boucherie Chervaline and a wine co-operative he had written the start of all he was to do. There never was another part of Paris that he loved like that, the sprawling trees, the old white plastered houses painted brown below, the one long green of the autobus in that round square, the purple flower dye upon the paving, the sudden drop down the hill of the rue Cardinal Lemoine to the River and the other way the narrow crowded world of the rue Mouffetard. The street that ran up toward the Pantheon and the other that he always took with the bicycle, the only asphalted street in all that quarter, smooth under the tires, with the high narrow houses and the cheap tall hotel where Paul Verlaine had *died. There were only two rooms in the apartments where they lived and he had a room on the top floor of that hotel that cost him sixty francs a month where he did his writing, and from it he could see the roofs and chimney pots and all the hills of Paris.*

From the apartment you could only see the wood and coal man's place. He sold wine too, bad wine. The golden horse's head outside the Boucherie Chevaline where the carcasses hung yellow gold and red in the open window, and the green painted co-operative where they bought their wine; good wine and cheap. The rest was plaster walls and the windows of the neighbors. The neighbors, who at night, when some one lay drunk in the street, moaning and groaning in that typical French ivresse that you were propaganded to believe did not exist, would open their window and then the murmur of talk.

"Where is the policeman? When you don't want him the bugger is always there. He's sleeping with some concierge. Get the Agent." Till some one threw a bucket of water from a window and the moaning stopped. "What's that? Water. Ah, that's intelligent." And the windows shutting. Marie, his femme de meage, protesting against the eight-hour day saying, "If a husband works until six he gets only a little drunk on the way home and does not waste too much. If he works only until five he is drunk every night and one has no money. It is the wife of the working man who suffers from this shortening of hours."

"Wouldn't you like some more broth?" the woman asked him now.

"No, thank you very much. It is awfully good."

"Try just a little."

"I would like a whiskey-soda."

"It's not good for you."

"No. It's bad for me. Cole Poter wrote the words and misic. This knowledge that you're going mad for me."

"You know I like you to drink."

"Oh, yes. Only it's bad for me."

When she goes, he thought. I'll have all I want. Not all I want but all there is. Ayee he was tired. Too tired. He was going to sleep a little while. He lay still and death was not there. It must have gone around another street. It went in pairs, on bicycles, and moved absolutely silently on the pavements.

No, he had never written about Paris. Not the Paris that he cared about. But what about the rest that he had never written?

What about the ranch and the silvered gray of sage brush, the quick, clear water in the irrigation ditches, and the heavy green of the alfalfa. The trail went up into the hills and the cattle in the summer were shy as deer. The bawling and the steady noise and slow moving mass raising a dust as you brought them down in the fall. And behind the mountains, the clear sharpness of the peak in the evening light and, riding down along the trail in the moonlight, bright across the valley. Now he remembered coming down through the timber in the dark holding the horse's tail when you could not see and all the stories that he meat to write.

About the half-wit chore boy who was left at the ranch that time and told not to let any one get any hay, and that old bastard from the Forks who had beaten the boy when he had worked for him stopping to get some feed. The boy refusing and the old man saying he would beat him again. The boy got the rifle from the kitchen and shot him when he tried to come into the barn and when they came back to the ranch he'd been dead a week, frozen in the corral, and the dogs had eaten part of him. But what was left you packed on a sled wrapped in a blanket and roped on and you got the boy to help you haul it, and the two of you took it out over the road on skis, and sixty miles down to town to turn the boy over. He having no idea that he would be arrested. Thinking he had done his duty and that you were his friend and he would be rewarded. He'd helped to haul the old man in so everybody could know how bad the old man had been and how he's tried to steal some feed that didn't belong to him, and when the sheriff put the handcuffs on the boy he couldn't believe it. Then he'd started to cry. That was one story he had saved to write. He knew at least twenty good stories from out there and he had never written one. Why?

"You tell them why," he said.
"Why what, dear?"
"Why nothing."
"She didn't drink so much, now, since she had him. But if lived he would never write about her, he knew that now. Nor about any of them. The rich were dull and they drank too much, or they played too much backgammon. They were dull and they

were repetitious. He remembered poor Julian and his romantic awe of them and how he had started a story once that began, "The very rich are different from you and me." And how some one had said to Julian, Yes, they have more money. But that was not humorous to Julian. He thought they were a special glamorous race and when he found they weren't it wrecked him just as much as any other thing that wrecked him.

He had been contemptuous of those who wrecked. You did not have to like it because you understood it. He could beat anything, he thought, because no thing could hurt him if he did not care.

All right. Now he would not care for death. One thing he had always dreaded was the pain. He could stand pain as well as any man, until it went on too long, and wore him out, but here he had something that had hurt frightfully and just when he had felt it breaking him, the pain had stopped.

He remembered long ago when Williamson, the bombing officer, had been hit by a stick bomb some one in a German patrol had thrown as he was coming in through the wire that night and, screaming, had begged every one to kill him. He was a fat man, very brave, and a good officer, although addicted to fantastic shows. But that night he was caught in the wire, with a flare lighting him up and his bowels spilled out into the wire, so when they brought him in, alive, they had to cut him loose. Shoot me, Harry. For Christ sake shoot me. They had had an argument one time about our Lord never sending you anything you could not bear and some one's theory had been that meant that at a certain time the pain passed you out automatically. But he had always remembered Williamson, that night. Nothing passed out Williamson until he gave him all his morphine tablets that he had always saved to use himself and then they did not work right away.

Still this now, that he had, was very easy; and if it was no worse as it went on there was nothing to worry about. Except that he would rather be in better company.

He thought a little about the company that he would like to have.

No, he thought, when everything you do, you do too long, and do too late, you can't expect to find the people still there. The people all are gone. The party's over and you are with your hostess now.

I'm getting as bored with dying as with everything else, he thought.

"It's a bore," he said out loud.

"What is, my dear?"

"Anything you do too bloody long"

He looked at her face between him and the fire. She was leaning back in the chair and the firelight shone on her pleasantly lined face and he could see that she was sleepy. He heard the hyena make a noise just outside the range of the fire.

"I've been writing," he said. "But I got tired."

"Do you think you will be able to sleep?"

"Pretty sure. Why don't you turn in?"

"I like to sit here with you."

"Do you feel anything strange?" he asked her.

"No. Just a little sleepy."

"I do," he said.

He had just felt death come by again.

"You know the only thing I've never lost is curiosity," he said to her.

"You've never lost anything. You're the most complete man I've ever known."

"Christ," he said. "How little a woman knows. What is that? Your intuition?"

Because, just then, death had come and rested its head on the foot of the cot and he could smell its breath.

"Never believe any of that about a scythe and a skull," he told her. "It can be two bicycle policemen as easily, or be a bird. Or it can have a wide snout like a hyena."

It had moved up on him now, but it had no shape any more. It simply occupied space.

"Tell it to go away."

It did not go away but moved a little closer.

"You've got a hell of a breath," he told it, "You stinking bastard."

It moved up closer to him still and now he could not speak to it, and when it saw he could not speak it came a little closer, and now he tried to send it away without speaking, but it moved in on him so its weight was all upon his chest, and while it crouched there and he could not move, or speak, he heard the woman say, "Bwana is asleep now. Take the cot up very gently and carry it into the tent,"

He could not speak to tell her to make it go away and it crouched now, heavier, so he could not breathe. And then, while they lifted the cot, suddenly it was all right and the weight went from his chest.

It was morning and had been morning for some time and he heard the plane. It showed very tiny and then made a wide circle and the boys ran out and lit the fires, using kerosene, and piled on grass so there were two big smudges at each end of the level place and the morning breeze blew them toward the camp and the plane circled twice more, low this time, and then glided down and leveled off and landed smoothly and, coming walking toward him, was old Compton in slacks, a tweed jacket and a brown felt hat.

"What's the matter, old cock?" Compton said.

"Bad leg," he told him. "Will you have some breakfast?"

"Thanks. I'll just have some tea. It's the Puss Moth you know. I won't be able to take the Memsahib. There's only room for one. Your lorry is on the way."

Helen had taken Compton aside and was speaking to him. Compton came back more cheery than ever. "We'll get you right in," he said. "I'll be back for the Mem. Now I'm afraid I'll have to stop at Arusha to refuel. We'd better get going."

"What about the tea?"

"I don't really care about it you know."

The boys had picked up the cot and carried it around the green tents and down along the rock and out onto the plain and along past the smudges that were burning brightly now, the grass all consumed, and the wind fanning the fire, to the little plane. It was difficult getting him in, but once in he lay back in the leather seat, and the leg was stuck straight out to one side of the seat where Compton sat. Compton started the motor and got in. he waved to Helen and to the boys and, as clatter moved into the old familiar roar, they swung around with Compie watching for wart-hog holes and roared, bumping, along the stretch between the fires and with the last bump rose and he saw them all standing below, waving, and the camp beside the hill, flattening now, and the plain spreading, clumps of trees, and the bush flattening, while the game trails ran now smoothly to the dry waterholes, and there was a new water that he had never known of. The zebra, small rounded backs now, and the wildebeeste, big-headed dots seeming to climb as they moved in long fingers across the plain, now scattering as the shadow came toward them, they were tiny now, and the movement had no gallop, and the plain as far as you could see, gray-yellow now and ahead old Compie's tweed back and the brown felt hat. Then they were over the first hills and the wildebeeste were trailing up them, and then they were over mountains with sudden depths of green-rising forest and the solid bamboo slopes, and then the heavy forest again, sculptured into peaks and hollows until they crossed, and hills slopes down and then another plain, hot now, and purple brown, bumpy with heat and Compie looking back to see how he was riding. Then there were other mountains dark ahead.

And then instead of going on to Arusha they turned left, he evidently figured that they had the gas, and looking down he saw a pink sifting cloud, moving over the ground, and in the air, like the first snow in a blizzard, that comes from nowhere, and he knew the locusts were coming up from the South. Then they beganto climb and they were going to the East it seemed, and then it darkened and they were in a storm, the rain so thick it seemed like flying through a waterfall, and then they were out and Compie turned his head and grinned and pointed and there, ahead, all he cloud see, as wide as all the world, great, high, and unbelievably white in the sun, was the square top of Kilimanjaro. And then he knew that there was where he was going.

Just then the hyena stopped whimpering in the night and started to make a strange, human, almost crying sound. The woman heard it and stirred uneasily. She did not wake. In her dream she was at the house on Long Island and it was the night before her daughter's debut. Somehow her father was there and he had been very rude. Then the noise the hyena made was so loud she woke and for a moment she did not know where she was and she was very afraid. Then she took the flashlight and shone it on the other cot that they carried in after Harry had gone to sleep. She could see his bulk under the mosquito bar but somehow he had gotten his leg out and it hung down alongside the cot. The dressings had all come down and she could not look at it, "Molo," she called, "Molo! Molo!"

Then she said. "Harry, Harry!" Then her voice rising, "Harry! Please, Oh Harry!"

There was no answer and she could not hear him breathing.

Outside that tent the hyena made the same strange noise that had awakened her. But she did not hear him for the beating of her heart.

Red

—by Somerset Maugham

THE skipper thrust his hand into one of his trouser pockets and with difficulty, for they were not at the sides but in front and he was a portly man, pulled out a large silver watch. He looked at it and then looked again at the declining sun. The Kanaka at the wheel gave him a glance, but did not speak. The skipper's eyes rested on the island they were approaching. A white line of foam marked the reef. He knew there was an opening large enough to get his ship through, and when they came a little nearer he counted on seeing it. They had nearly an hour of daylight still before them. In the lagoon the water was deep and they could anchor comfortably. The chief of the village which he could already see among the coconut trees was a friend of the mate's, and it would be pleasant to go ashore for the night. The mate came forward at that minute and the skipper turned to him.

'We'll take a bottle of booze along with us and get some girls in to dance,' he said.

'I don't see the opening,' said the mate.

He was a Kanaka, a handsome, swarthy fellow, with somewhat the look of a later Roman emperor, inclined to stoutness; but his face was fine and clean-cut.

'I'm dead sure there's one right here,' said the captain, looking through his glasses. 'I can't understand why I can't pick it up. Send one of the boys up the mast to have a look.'

The mate called one of the crew and gave him the order. The captain watched the Kanaka climb and waited for him to speak. But the Kanaka shouted down that he could see nothing but the unbroken line of foam. The captain spoke Samoan like a native, and he cursed him freely.

'Shall he stay up there?' asked the mate.

'What the hell good does that do?' answered the captain.

'The blame fool can't see worth a cent. You bet your sweet life I'd find the opening if I was up there.'

He looked at the slender mast with anger. It was all very well for a native who had been used to climbing up coconut trees all his life. He was fat and heavy.

'Come down,' he shouted. 'You're no more use than a dead dog. We'll just have to go along the reef till we find the opening.'

It was a seventy-ton schooner with paraffin auxiliary, and it ran when there was no head wind, between four and five knots and hour. It was a bedraggled object; it had been painted white a very long time ago, but it was now dirty, dingy, and mottled. It smelt strongly of paraffin, and of the copra which was its usual cargo. They were within a hundred feet of the reef now and the captain told the steersman to run along it till they came to the opening. But when they had gone a couple of miles he realized that they had missed it. He went about and slowly worked back again. The white foam of the reef continued without interruption and now the sun was setting. With a curse at the stupidity of the crew the skipper resigned himself to waiting till next morning.

'Put her about,' he said. 'I can't anchor here.'

They went out to sea a little and presently it was quite dark. They anchored. When the sail was furled the ship began to roll a good deal. They said in Apia that one day she would roll right over; and the owner, a German-American who managed one of the largest stores, said that no money was big enough to induce him to go out in her. The cook, a Chinese in white trousers, very dirty and ragged, and a thin white tunic, came to say that supper was ready, and when the skipper went into the cabin he found the engineer already seated at table. The engineer was a long, lean man with a scraggy neck. He was dressed in blue overalls and a sleeveless jersey which showed his thin arms tattooed from elbow to wrist.

'Hell, having to spend the night outside,' said the skipper.

The engineer did not answer, and they ate their supper in silence. The cabin was lit by a dim oil-lamp. When they had eaten the canned apricots with which the meal finished the Chink brought them a cup of tea. The skipper lit a cigar and went on the upper deck. The island now was only a darker mass against the night. The stars were very bright. The only sound was the ceaseless breaking of the surf. The skipper sank into a deck-chair and smoked idly. Presently three or four members of the crew came up and sat down. One of them had a banjo and another a concertina. They began to play, and one of them sang. The native song sounded strange on these instruments. Then to the singing a couple began to dance. It was a barbaric dance, savage and primeval, rapid, with quick movements of the hands and feet and contortions of the body; it was sensual, sexual even, but sexual without passion. It was very animal, direct, weird without mystery, natural in short, and one might almost say childlike. At last they grew tired. They stretched themselves on the deck and slept, and all was silent. The skipper lifted himself heavily out of his chair and clambered down the companion. He went into his cabin and got out of his clothes. He climbed into his bunk and lay there. He panted a little in the heat of the night.

But next morning, when the dawn crept over the tranquil sea, the opening in the reef which had eluded them the night before was seen a little to the east of where they lay. The schooner entered the lagoon. There was not a ripple on the surface of the water. Deep down among the coral rocks you saw little coloured fish swim. When he had anchored his ship the skipper ate his breakfast and went on deck. The sun shone from an unclouded sky, but in the early morning the air was grateful and cool. It was Sunday, and there was a feeling of quietness, as though nature were at rest, which gave him a peculiar sense of comfort. He sat, looking at the wooded coast, and felt lazy and well at ease. Presently a slow smile moved his lips and he threw the stump of his cigar into the water.

'I guess I'll go ashore,' he said. 'Get the boat out.'

He climbed stiffly down the ladder and was rowed to a little cove. The coconut trees came down to the water's edge, not in rows, but spaced out with an ordered formality. They were like a ballet of spinsters, elderly but flippant, standing in affected attitudes with the simpering graces of a bygone age. He sauntered idly through them, along a path that could be just seen winding its tortuous way, and it led him presently to a broad creek. There was a bridge across it. but a bridge constructed of single trunks of coconut trees, a dozen of them, placed end to end and supported where they met by a forked branch driven into the bed of the creek. You walked on a smooth, round surface, narrow and slippery, and there was no support for the hand. To cross such a bridge required sure feet and a stout heart. The skipper hesitated. But he saw on the other side, nestling among the trees, a white man's house; he made up his mind and, rather gingerly, began to walk. He watched his feet carefully, and where one trunk joined on to the next and there was a difference of level, he tottered a little. It was with a gasp of relief that he reached the last tree and finally set his feet on the firm ground of the other side. He had been so intent on the difficult crossing that he never noticed anyone was watching him, and it was with surprise that he heard himself spoken to.

'It takes a bit of nerve to cross these bridges when you're not used to them,'

He looked up and saw a man standing in front of him. He had evidently come out of the house which he had seen.

'I saw you hesitate,' the man continued, with a smile on his lips, 'and I was watching to see you fall in.'

'Not on your life,' said the captain, who had now recovered his confidence.

'I've fallen in myself before now. I remember, one evening I came back from shooting, and I fell in, gun and all. Now I get a boy to carry my gun for me.'

He was a man no longer young, with a small beard, bow somewhat grey, and a thin face. He was dressed in a singlet, without arms, and a pair of duck trousers. He wore neither shoes nor socks. He spoke English with a slight accent.

'Are you Neilson?' asked the skipper.

'I am.'

'I've heard about you. I thought you lived somewheres round here.'

The skipper followed his host into the little bungalow and sat down heavily in the chair which the other motioned him to take. While Neilson went out to fetch whisky and glasses he took a look round the room. It filled him with amazement. He had never seen so many books. The shelves reached from floor to ceiling on all four walls, and they were closely packed. There was a grand piano littered with music, and a large table on which books and magazines lay in disorder. The room made him feel embarrassed. He remembered that Neilson was a queer fellow. No one know very much about him, although he had been in the islands for so many years, but those who know him agreed that he was queer. He was a Swede.

'You've got one big heap of books here,' he said, when Neilson returned.

'They do no harm,' answered Neilson with a smile.

'Have you read them all?' asked the skipper.

'Most of them.'

'I'm a bit of a reader myself. I have the *Saturday Evening Post* sent me regler.'

Neilson poured his visitor a good stiff glass of whisky and gave him a cigar. The skipper volunteered a little information.

'I got in last night, but I couldn't find the opening, so I had to anchor outside. I never been this run before, but my people had some stuff they wanted to bring over here. Gray, d'you know him?'

'Yes, he's got a store a little way along.'

'Well, there was a lot of canned stuff that he wanted over, an' he's got some copra. They thought I might just as well come over as lie idle at Apia. I run between Apia and Pago-Pago mostly, but they've got smallpox there just now, and there's nothing stirring.'

He took a drink of his whisky and lit a cigar. He was a taciturn man, but there was something in Neilson that made him nervous, and his nervousness made him talk. The Swede was looking at him with large dark eyes in which there was an expression of faint amusement.

'This is a tidy little place you've got here.'

'I've done my best with it.'

'You must do pretty well with your trees. They look fine. With copra at the price it is now. I had a bit of a plantation myself once, in Upolu it was, but I had to sell it.'

He looked round the room again, where all those books gave him a feeling of something incomprehensible and hostile.

'I guess you must find it a bit lonesome here though,' he said.
'I've got used to it. I've been here for twenty-five years.'

Now the captain could think of nothing more to say, and he smoked in silence. Neilson had apparently no wish to break it. He looked at his guest with a meditative eye. He was a tall man, more than six feet high, and very stout. His face was red and blotchy, with a network of little purple veins on the cheeks, and his features were sunk into its fatness. His eyes were bloodshot. His neck was buried in rolls of fat. But for a fringe of long curly hair, nearly white, at the back of his head, he was quite bald; and that immense, shiny surface of forehead, which might have given him a false look of intelligence, on the contrary gave him one of peculiar imbecility. He wore a blue flannel shirt, open at the neck and showing his fat chest covered with a mat of reddish hair, and a very old pair of blue serge trousers. He sat in his chair in a heavy ungainly attitude, his great belly thrust forward and his fat legs uncrossed. All elasticity had gone from his limbs. Neilson wondered idly what sort of man he had been in his youth. It was almost impossible to imagine that this creature of vast bulk had ever been a boy who ran about. The skipper finished his whisky, and Neilson pushed the bottle towards him.

'Help yourself.'

The skipper leaned forward and with his great hand seized it.

'And how come you in these parts anyways?' he said.

'Oh, I came out to the islands for my health. My lungs were bad and they said I hadn't a year to live. You see they were wrong.'

'I meant, how come you to settle down right here?'

'I am a sentimentalist.'

'Oh!'

Neilson knew that the skipper had not an idea what he meant, and he looked at him with an ironical twinkle in his dark eyes. Perhaps just because the skipper was so gross and dull a man the whim seized him to talk further.

'You were too busy keeping your balance to notice, when you crossed the bridge, but this spot is generally considered rather pretty.'

'It's a cute little house you've got here.'

'Ah, that wasn't here when I first came. There was a native hut, with its beehive roof and its pillars, overshadowed by a great tree with red flowers; and the croton bushes, their leaves yellow and red and golden, made a pied fence around it. And then all about were the coconut trees, as fanciful as women, and as vain. They stook at the water's edge and spent all day looking at their reflections. I was a young man then—good heavens, it's a quarter of a century ago—and I wanted to enjoy all the loveliness of the world in the short time allotted to them before I passed into the darkness. I thought it was the most beautiful spot I had ever seen. The first time I saw it I had a catch at my heart, and I was afraid I was going to cry. I wasn't more than twenty-five, and though I put the best face I could on it, I didn't want to die. And somehow it seemed to me that the very beauty of this place made it easier for me to accept my fate. I felt when I came here that all my past life had fallen away, Stockholm and its

University, and then Bonn : it all seemed the life of somebody else, as though now at last I had achieved the reality which our doctors of philosophy-I am one myself, you know-had discussed so much. "A year," I cried to myself. "I have a year. I will spend it here and then I am content to die."

'We are foolish and sentimental and melodramatic at twenty-five, but if we weren't perhaps we should be less wise at fifty.

'Now drink, my friend. Don't let the nonsense I talk interfere with you.'

He waved his thin hand towards the bottle, and the skipper finished what remained in his glass.

'You ain't drinking nothin',' he said, reaching for the whisky.

'I am of sober habit,' smiled the Swede. 'I intoxicate myself in ways which I fancy are more subtle. But perhaps that is only vanity. Anyhow, the effects are more lasting and the results less deleterious.'

'They say there's a deal of cocaine taken in the States now,' said the captain.

Neilson chuckled.

'But I do not see a white man often,' he continued, 'and for once I don't think a drop of whisky can do me any harm.'

He poured himself out a little, added some soda, and took a sip.

'And presently I found out why the spot had such an unearthly loveliness. Here love had tarried for a moment like a migrant bird that happens on a ship in mid-ocean and for a little while folds its tired wings. The fragrance of a beautiful passion hovered over it like the fragrance of hawthorn in May in the meadows of my home. It seems to me that the place where men have loved or suffered keep about them always some faint aroma of something that has not wholly died. It is as though they had acquired a spiritual significance which mysteriously affects those who pass. I wish I could make myself clear.' He smiled a little. 'Though I cannot imagine that if I did you would understand.'

He paused.

'I think this place was beautiful because here for a period the ecstasy love had invested it with beauty.' And now he shrugged his shoulders. 'But perhaps it is only that my aesthetic sense is gratified by the happy conjunction of young love and a suitable setting.'

Even a man less thick-witted than the skipper might have been forgiven if he were bewildered by Neilson's words. For he seemed faintly to laugh at what he said. It was as though he spoke from emotion which his intellect found ridiculous. He had said himself that he was a sentimentalist, and when sentimentality is joined with scepticism there is often the devil to pay.

He was silent for an instant and looked at the captain with eyes in which there was a sudden perplexity.

'You know, I can't help thinking that I've seen you before somewhere or other,' he said.

'I couldn't say as I remember you,' returned the skipper.

'I have a curious feeling as though your face were familiar to me. It's been puzzling me for some time. But I can't situate my recollection in any place or at any time.'

The skipper massively shrugged his heavy shoulders.

'It's thirty years since I first come to the islands. A man can't figure on remembering all the folk he meets in a while like that.'

The Swede shook his head.

'You know how one sometimes has the feeling that a place one has never been to before is strangely familiar. That's how I seem to see you,' He gave a whimsical smile. 'Perhaps I knew you in some past existence. Perhaps, perhaps you were the master of a galley in ancient Rome and I was a slave at the oar. Thirty years have you been here?'

'Every bit of thirty years.'

'I wonder if you knew a man called Red?'

'Red?'

'That is the only name I've ever known him by. I never knew him personally. I never even set eyes on him. And yet I seem to see him more clearly than many men, my brothers, for instance, with whom I passed my daily life for many years. He lives in my imagination with the distinctness of a Paolo Malatesta or a Romeo. But I dare say you have never read Dante or Shakespeare?'

'I can't say as I have,' said the captain.

Neilson, smoking a cigar, leaned back in his chair and looked vacantly at the ring of smoke which floated in the still air. A smile played on his lips, but his eyes were grave. Then he looked at the captain. There was in his gross obesity something extraordinarily repellent. He had the plethoric self-satisfaction of the very fat. It was an outrage. It set Neilson's nerves on edge.

But the contrast between the man before him and the man he had in mind was pleasant.

'It appears that Red was the most comely thing you ever saw. I've talked to quite a number of people who knew him in those days, white men, and they all agree that the first time you saw him his beauty just took your breath away. They called him Red on account of his flaming hair. It had a natural wave and he wore it long. It must have been of that wonderful colour that the pre-Raphaelites raved over. I don't think he was vain of it, he was much too ingenuous for that, but no one could have blamed him if he had been. He was tall, six feet and an inch or two — in the native house that used to stand here was the mark of his height cut with a knife on the central trunk that supported the roof — and he was made like a Greek god, broad in the shoulders and thin in the flanks; he was like Apollo, with just that soft roundness which Praxiteles gave him, and that suave, feminine grace which has in it something troubling and mysterious. His skin was dazzling white, milky, like satin; his skin was like a woman's.'

'I had kind of a white skin myself when I was a kiddie,' said the skipper, with a twinkle in his bloodshot eyes.

But Neilson paid no attention to him. He was telling his story now and interruption made him impatient.

'And his face was just as beautiful as his body. He had large blue eyes, very dark, so that some say they were black, and unlike most red-faired people he had dark eyebrows and long dark lashes. His features were perfectly regular and his mouth was like a scarlet wound. He was twenty.

On these words the Swede stopped with a certain sense of the dramatic. He took a sip of whisky.

'He was unique. There never was anyone more beautiful. There was no more reason for him than for a wonderful blossom to flower on a wild plant. He was a happy accident of nature.

'One day he landed at that cove into which you must have put this morning. He was an American sailor, and he had deserted from a man-of-war in Apia. He had induced some good-humoured native to give him a passage on a cutter that happened to be sailing from Apia to Safoto, and he had been put ashore here in a dug-out. I do not know why he deserted. Perhaps life on a man-of-war with its restrictions irked him, perhaps he was in trouble, and perhaps it was the South Seas and these romantic islands that got into his bones. Every now and then they take a man strangely, and he finds himself like a fly in a spider's web. It may be that there was a softness of fiber in him, and these green hills with their soft airs, this blue seas, took the northern strength from him as Delilah took the Nazarite's. Anyhow, he wanted to hide himself, and he thought he would be safe in this secluded nook till his ship had sailed from Samoa.

'There was a native hut at the cove and as he stood there, wondering where exactly he should turn his steps, a young girl came out and invited him to enter. He knew scarcely two words of the native tongue and she as little English. But he understood well enough what her smiles meant, and her pretty gestures, and he followed her. He sat down on a mat and she gave him slices of pineapple to eat. I can speak of Red only from hearsay, but I saw the girl three years after he first met her, and she was scarcely nineteen then. You cannot imagine how exquisite she was. She had the passionate grace of the hibiscus and the rich colour. She was rather tall, slim, with the delicate features of her race, and large eyes like pools of still water under the palm trees; her hair, black and curling, fell down her back, and she wore a wreath of scented flowers. Her hands were lovely. They were so small, so exquisitely formed, they gave your heart-strings a wrench. And in those days she laughed easily. Her smile was so delightful that it made your knees shake. Her skin was like a field of ripe corn on a summer day. Good heavens, how can I describe her? She was too beautiful to be real.

'And these two young things, she was sixteen and he was twenty, fell in love with one another at first sight. That is the real love, not the love that comes from sympathy, common interests, of intellectual community, but love pure and simple. That is the love that Adam felt for Eve when he awoke and found her in the garden gazing at him with dewy eyes. That is the love that draws the beasts to one another, and the Gods. That is the love that makes the world a miracle. That is the love which gives life its pregnant meaning. You have never heard of the wise, cynical French duke who said that with t재 lovers there is always one who loves and one who lets himself be loved; it is bitter truth to which most of us have to resign ourselves; but now and then there are two who love and two who let themselves be loved. Then one might fancy that the sun stands still as it stood when Joshua prayed to the God of Israel.

'And even now after all these years, when I think of these two, so young, so fair, so simple, and of their love, I feel a pang. It tears my heart just as my heart is torn when on certain nights I watch the full moon shining on the lagoon from an unclouded sky. There is always pain in the contemplation of perfect beauty.

'They were children. She was good and sweet and kind. I know nothing of him, and I like to think that then at all events he was ingenuous and frank. I like to think that his soul was as comely as his body. But I dare say he had no more soul than the creatures of the woods and forests who made pipes from reeds and bathed in the mountain streams when the world was young, and you might catch sight of little fawns galloping through the glade on the back of a bearded centaur. A soul is a troublesome possession and when man developed it he lost the Garden of Eden.

'Well, when Red came to the island it had recently been visited by one of those epidemics which the white man brought to the South Seas, and one third of the inhabitants had died. It seems that the girl had lost all her near kin and she lived now in the house of distant cousins. The household consisted of two ancient crones, bowed and wrinkled, two younger women, and a man and a boy. For a few days he stayed there. But perhaps he felt himself too near the shore, with the possibility that he might fall in with white men who would reveal his hiding-place; perhaps the lovers could not bear that the company of others should rob them for an instant of the delight of being together. One morning they set out, the pair of them, with the few things that belonged to the girl, and walked along a grassy path under the coconuts, till they came to the creek you see. They had to cross the bridge you crossed, and the girl laughed gleefully because he was afraid. She held his hand till they came to the end of th first tree, and then his courage failed him and he had to go back. He was obliged to take off all his clothes before he could risk it, and she carried them over for him on her head. They settled down in the empty hut that stood there. Whether she had any rights over it(land tenure is a complicated business in the islands), or whether the owner had died during the epidemic, I do not know, but anyhow no one questioned them, and they took possession. Their furniture consisted of a couple of grass mats on which they slept, a fragment of looking-glass, and a bowl or two. In this pleasant land that is enough to start housekeeping on.

'They say that happy people have no history, and certainly a happy love had none. They did nothing all day long and yet the days seemed all too short. The girl had a native name, but Red called her Sally. He picked up the easy language very quickly, and he used to lie on the mat for hours while she chattered gaily to him. He was a silent fellow, and perhaps his mind was lethargic. He smoked incessantly the cigarettes which she made him out of the native tobacco and pandanus leaf, and he watched her while with deft fingers she made grass mats. Often natives would come in and tell long stories of the old days when the island was disturbed by tribal wars. Sometimes he would go fishing on the reef, and bring home a basket full of coloured fish.

Sometimes at night he would go out with a lantern to catch lobster. There were plantains round the hut and Sally would roast them for their frugal meal. She knew how to make delicious messes from coconuts, and the breadfruit tree by the side of the creek gave them its fruit. On feast-days they killed a little pig and cooked it on hot stones. They bathed together in the creek; and in the evening they went down to the lagoon and paddled about in a dug-out, with its great outrigger. The sea was deep blue, wine-coloured at sundown, like the sea of Homeric Greece; but in the lagoon the colour had an infinite variety, aquamarine and amethyst and emerald; and the setting sun turned it for a short moment to liquid gold. Then there was the colour of the coral, brown, white, pink, red, purple; and the shapes it took were marvellous. It was like a magic garden, and the hurrying fish were like butterflies. It strangely lacked reality. Among the coral were pools with a floor of white sand and here, where the water was dazzling clear, it was very good to bathe. Then, cool and happy, they wandered back in the gloaming over the soft grass road to the creek, walking hand in hand, and now the mynah birds filled the coconut trees with their clamour. And then the night, with that great sky shining with gold, that seemed to stretch more widely than the skies of Europe, and the soft airs that blew gently through the open hut, the long night again was all too short. She was sixteen and he was barely twenty. The dawn crept in among the wooden pillars of the hut and looked at those lovely children sleeping in one another's arms. The sun hid behind the great tattered leaves of the plantains so that it might not disturb them, and then, with playful malice, shot a golden ray, like the outstretched paw of a Persian cat, on their faces. They opened their sleepy eyes and they smiled to welcome another day. The weeks lengthened into months, and a year passed. They seemed to love one another as — I hesitate to say passionately, for passion has in it always a shade of sadness, a touch of bitterness or anguish, but as wholeheartedly, as simply and naturally as on that first day on which, meeting, they had recognized that a god was in them.

'If you had asked them I have no doubt that they would have thought it impossible to suppose their love could ever cease. Do we not know that the essential element of love is a belief in its own eternity? And yet perhaps in Red there was already a very little seed, unknown to himself and unsuspected by the girl, which would in time have grown to weariness. For one day one of the natives from the cove told them that some way down the coast at the anchorage was a British whaling-ship.

"Gee," he said, "I wonder if I could make a trade of some nuts and plantains for a pound or tow of tobacco."

'The pandanus cigarettes that Sally made him with untiring hands were strong and pleasant enough to smoke, but they left him unsatisfied; and he yearned on a sudden for real tobacco, hard, rank, and pungent. He had not smoked a pipe for many months. His mouth watered at the thought of it. One would have thought some premonition of harm would have made Sally seek to dissuade him, but love possessed her so completely that it never occurred to her any power on earth could take him from her. They went up into the hills together and gathered a great basket of wild oranges, green, but sweet and juicy; and they picked plantains from around the hut, and coconuts from their trees, and breadfruit and mangoes; and they carried them down to the cove. They loaded the unstable canoe with them, and Red and the native boy who had brought them the news of the ship paddled along outside the reef.

'It was the last time she ever saw him.

'Next day the boy came back alone. He was all in tears. This is the story he told. When after their long paddle they reached the ship and Red hailed it, a white man looked over the side and told them to come on board. They took the fruit they had brought with them and Red piled it up on the deck. The white man and he began to talk, and they seemed to come to some agreement. One of them went below and brought up tobacco. Red took some at once and lit a pipe. The boy imitated th zest with which he blew a great cloud of smoke from his mouth. Then they said something to him and he went into the cabin. Through the open door the boy, watching curiously, saw a bottle brought out and glasses. Red drank and smoked. They seemed to ask him something, for he shook his head and laughed. The man, the first man who had spoken to them, laughed too, and he filled Red's glass once more. They went on talking and drinking, and presently, growing tired of watching a sight that meant nothing to him, the boy curled himself up on the deck and slept. He was awakened by a kick; and jumping to his feet, he saw that the ship was slowly sailing out of the lagoon. He caught sight of Red seated at the table, with his head resting heavily on his arms, fast asleep. He made a movement towards him, intending to wake him, but a rough hand seized his arm, and a man, with a scowl and words which he did not understand, pointed to the side. He shouted to Red, but in a moment he was seized and flung overboard. Helpless, he swam round to his canoe, which was drifting a little way off, and pushed it on to the reef. He climbed in and, sobbing all the way, paddled back to shore.

'What had happened was obvious enough. The whaler, by desertion or sickness, was short of hands, and the captain when Red came aboard had asked him to sign on; on his refusal he had made him drunk and kidnapped him.

'Sally was beside herself with grief. For three days she screamed and cried. The natives did what they could to comfort her, but she would not be comforted. She would not eat. And then, exhausted, she sank into a sullen apathy. She spent long days at the cove, watching the lagoon, in the vain hope that Red somehow or other would manage to escape. She sat on the white sand, hour after hour, with the tears running down her cheeks, and at night dragged herself wearily back across the creek to the little hut where she had been happy. The people with whom she had lived before Red came to the island wished her to return to them, but she would not; she was convinced that Red would come back, and she wanted him to find her where he had left her. Four months later she was delivered of a still-born child, and the old woman who had come to help her through her confinement remained with her in the hut. All joy was taken from her life. If her anguish with time became less intolerable it was replaced by a settled melancholy. You would not have thought that among these people, whose emotions, though so violent, are very transient, a woman could be found capable of so enduring a passion. She never lost the profound conviction that sooner or later Red would come back. She watched for him, and every time someone crossed this slender little bridge of coconut trees she looked. It might at last be he.

Neilson stopped talking and gave a faint sigh.

'And what happened to her in the end?' asked the skipper.

Neilson smiled bitterly.

'Oh, three years afterwards she took up with another white man.'

The skipper gave a fat, cynical chuckle.

'That's generally what happens to them,' he said.

The Swede shot him a look of hatred. He did not know why that gross, obese man excited in him so violent a repulsion. But his thoughts wandered and he found his mind filed with memories of the past. He went back five-and-twenty years. It was when he first came to the island, weary of Apia, with its heavy drinking, its gambling and coarse sensuality, a sick man, trying to resign himself to the loss of the career which had fired his imagination with ambitious thought. He set behind him resolutely all his hopes of making a great name for himself and strove to content himself with the few poor months of careful life which was all that he could count on. He was boarding with a half-caste trader who had a store a couple of miles along the coast at the edge of a native village; and one day, wandering aimlessly along the grassy paths of the coconut groves, he had come upon the hut in which Sally lived. The beauty of the spot had filled him with a rapture so great that it was almost painful, and then he had seen Sally. She was the loveliest creature he had ever seen, and the sadness in those dark, magnificent eyes of hers affected him strangely. The Kanakas were a handsome race, and beauty was not rare among them, but it was the beauty of shapely animals. It was empty. But those tragic eyes were dark with mystery, and you felt in them the bitter complexity of the groping, human soul. The trader told him the story and it moved him.

'Do you think he'll ever come back?' asked Neilson.

'No fear. Why, it'll be a couple of years before the ship is paid off, and by then he'll have forgotten all about her. I bet he was pretty mad when he woke up and found he'd been shang-haied, and I shouldn't wonder but he wanted to fight somebody. But he'd got to grin and bear it, and I guess in a month he was thinking it the best thing that had ever happened to him that he got away from the island.'

But Neilson could not get the story out of his head. Perhaps because he was sick and weakly, the radiant health of Red appealed to his imagination. Himself an ugly man, insignificant of appearance, he prized very highly comeliness in others. He had never passionately in love, and certainly he had never been passionately loved. The mutual attraction of those two young things gave him a singular delight. It had the ineffable beauty of the Absolute. He went again to the little hut by the creek. He had a gift for languages and an energetic mind, accustomed to work, and he had already given much time to the study of the local tongue. Old habit was strong in him and he was gathering together material for a paper on the Samoan speech. The old crone who shared the hut with Sally invited him to come in and sit down. She gave him *kava* to drink and cigarettes to smoke. She was glad to have someone to chat with and while she talked he looked at Sally. She reminded him of the Psyche in the museum at Naples. Her features had the same clear purity of line, and though she had borne a child she had still a virginal aspect.

It was not till he had seen her two or three times that he induced her to speak. Then it was only to ask him if he had seen in Apia a man called Red. Two years had passed since his disappearance, but it was plain that she still thought of him incessantly.

It did not take Neilson long to discover that he was in love with her. It was only by an effort of will now that he prevented himself from going every day to the creek, and when he was not with Sally his thoughts were. At first, looking upon himself as a dying man, he asked only to look at her, and occasionally hear her speak, and his love gave him a wonderful happiness. He exulted in its purity. He wanted nothing from her but the opportunity to weave around her graceful person a web of beautiful fancies. But the open air, the equable temperature, the rest, the simple fare, began to have an unexpected effect on his health. His temperature did not soar at night to such alarming heights, he coughed less and began to put on weight; six months passed without his having a haemorrhage; and on a sudden he saw the possibility that he might live. He had studied his disease carefully, and the hope dawned upon him that with great care he might arrest its course. It exhilarated him to look forward once more to the future. He made plans. It was evident that any active life was out of the question, but he could live on the islands, and the small income he had, insufficient elsewhere, would be ample to keep him. He could grow coconuts; that would give him an occupation; and he would send for his books and a piano; but his quick mind saw that in all this he was merely trying to conceal from himself the desire which obsessed him.

He wanted Sally. He loved not only her beauty, but that dim soul which he divined behind her suffering eyes. He would intoxicate her with his passion. In the end he would make her forget. And in an ecstasy of surrender he fancied himself giving her too the happiness which he had thought never to know again, but had now so miraculously achieved.

He asked her to live with him. She refused. He had expected that and did not let it depress him, for he was sure that sooner or later she would yield. His love was irresistible. He told the old woman of his wishes, and found somewhat to his surprise that she and the neighbours, long aware of them, were strongly urging Sally to accept his offer. After all, every native was glad to keep house for a white man, and Neilson according to the standards of the island was a rich one. The trader with whom he boarded went to her and told her not to be a fool; such an opportunity would not come again, and after so long she could not still believe that Red would ever return. The girl's resistance only increased Neilson's desire, and what had been a very pure love now became an agonizing passion. He was determined that nothing should stand in his way. He gave Sally no peace. At last, worn out by his persistence and the persuasions, by turns pleading and angry, of everyone around her, she consented. But the day after, when exultant he went to see her he found that in the night she had burnt down the hut in which she and Red had lived together. The old crone ran towards him full of angry abuse of Sally, but he waved her aside; it did not matter; they would build a bungalow on the place where the hut had stood. A European house would really be more convenient if he wanted to bring out a piano and a vast number of books.

And so the little wooden house was built in which he had now lived for many years, and Sally became his wife. But after the first few weeks of rapture, during which he was satisfied with what she gave him, he had known little happiness. She had yielded to him, through weariness, but she had only yielded what she set no store on. The soul which he had dimly glimpsed escaped him. He knew that she cared nothing for him. She still loved Red, and all the time she was waiting for his return. At a sign from him, Neilson knew that, notwithstanding his love, his tenderness, his sympathy, his generosity, she would leave him without a moment's hesitation. She would never give a thought to his distress. Anguish seized him and he battered at that impenetrable self of hers which sullenly resisted him. His love became bitter. He tried to melt her heart with kindness, but it remained as hard as before; he feigned indifference, but she did not notice it. Sometimes he lost his temper and abused her, and then she wept silently. Sometimes he thought she was nothing but a fraud, and that soul simply an invention of his own, and that he could not get into the sanctuary of her heart because there was no sanctuary there. His love became a prison from which he longed to escape, but he had not the strength merely to open the door-that was all it needed-and walk out into the open air. It was torture and at last he became numb and hopeless. In the end the fire burnt itself out and, when he saw her eyes rest for an instant on the slender bridge, it was no longer rage that filled his heart but impatience. For many years now they had lived together bound by the ties of habit and convenience, and it was with a smile that he looked back on his old passion. She was an old woman, for the women on the islands age quickly, and if he had no love for her any more he had tolerance. She left him alone. He was contented with his piano and his books.

His thoughts led him to a desire for words.

'When I look back now and reflect on that brief passionate love of Red and Sally, I think that perhaps they should thank the ruthless fate that separated them when their love seemed still to be at its height. They suffered, but they suffered in beauty. They were spared the real tragedy of love.'

'I don't know exactly as I get you,' said the skipper.

'The tragedy of love is not death or separation. How long do you think it would have been before one or other of them ceased to care? Oh, it is dreadfully bitter to look at a woman whom you have loved with all your heart and soul, so that you felt you could not bear to let her out of your sight, and realize that you would not mind if you never saw her again. The tragedy of love is indifference.'

But while he was speaking a very extraordinary thing happened. Though he had been addressing the skipper he had not been talking to him, he had been putting his thoughts into words for himself, and with his eyes fixed on the man in front of him he had not seen him. But now an image presented itself to them, an image not of the man he saw, but of another man. It was as though he were looking into one of those distorting mirrors that make you extraordinarily squat or outrageously elongate, but here exactly the opposite took place, and in the obese, ugly old man he caught the shadowy glimpse of a stripling. He gave him now a quick, searching scrutiny. Why had a haphazard stroll brought him just to this place? A sudden tremor of his heart made him slightly breathless. An absurd suspicion seized him. What had occurred to him was impossible, and yet it might be a fact.

'What is your name?' he asked abruptly.

The skipper's face puckered and he gave a cunning chuckle. He looked then malicious and horribly vulgar.

'It's such a damned long time since I heard it that I almost forget it myself. But for thirty years now in the islands they've always called me Red.'

His huge from shook as he gave a low, almost silent laugh. It was obscene. Neilson shuddered. Red was hugely amused, and from his bloodshot eyes tears ran down his cheeks.

Neilson gave a gasp, for at that moment a woman came in. She was a native, a woman of somewhat commanding presence, stout without being corpulent, dark, for the natives grow darker with age, with very grey hair. She wore a black Mother Hubbard, and its thinness showed her heavy breasts. The moment had come.

She made an observation to Neilson about some household matter and he answered. He wandered if his voice sounded as unnatural to her as it did to himself. She gave the man who was sitting in the chair by the window an indifferent glance, and went out of the room. The moment had come and gone.

Neilson for a moment could not speak. He was strangely shaken. Then he said:

'I'd be very glad if you'd stay and have a bit of dinner with me. Pot luck.'

'I don't think I will,' said Red. 'I must go after this fellow Gray. I'll give him his stuff and then I'll get away. I want to be back in Apia tomorrow.'

'I'll send a boy along with you to show you the way.'

'That'll be fine.'

Red heaved himself out of his chair, while the Swede called one of the boys who worked on the plantation. He told him where the skipper wanted to go, and the boy stepped along the bridge.

Red prepared to follow him.

'Don't fall in,' said Neilson.

'Not on your life.'

Neilson watched him make his way across and when he had disappeared among the coconuts he looked still. Then he sank heavily in his chair. Was that the man who had prevented him from being happy? Was that the man whom Sally had loved all these years and for whom she had waited so desperately? It was grotesque. A sudden fury seized him so that he had an instinct to spring up and smash everything around him. He had been cheated. They had seen each other at last and had not known it. He began to laugh, mirthlessly, and his laughter grew till it became hysterical. The Gods had played him a cruel trick. And he was old now.

At last Sally came in to tell him dinner was ready. He sat down in front of her and tried to eat. He wondered what she would say if he told her now that the fat old man sitting in the chair was the lover whom she remembered still with the passionate abandonment of her youth. Years ago, when he hated her because she made him so unhappy, he would have been glad to tell her. He wanted to hurt her then as she hurt him, because his hatred was only love. But now he did not care. He shrugged his shoulders listlessly.

'What did that man want?' she asked presently.

He did not answer at once. She was too old, a fat old native woman. He wondered why he had ever loved her so madly. He had laid at her feet all the treasures of his soul, and she had cared nothing for them. Waste, what waste! And now, when he looked at her, he felt only contempt. His patience was at last exhausted. He answered her question.

'He's the captain of a schooner. He's come from Apia.'

'Yes.'

'He brought me news from home. My eldest brother is very ill and I must go back.'

'Will you be gone long?'

He shrugged his shoulders.

The Black Cat
—by Adgar Allan Poe

FOR the most wild, yet most homely narrative which I am about to pen, I neither expect nor solicit belief. Mad indeed would I be to expect it, in a case where my very senses reject their own evidence. Yet, mad am I not – and very surely do I not dream. But tomorrow I die, and today I would unburthen my soul. My immediate purpose is to place before the world, plainly, succinctly, and without comment, a series of mere household events. In their consequences, these events have terrified – have tortured–have destroyed me. Yet I will not attempt to expound them. To me, they have presented little but Horror – to many they will seem less terrible than **baroques**. Hereafter, perhaps, some intellect may be found which will reduce my phantasm to the common-place – some intellect more calm, more logical, and far less excitable than my own, which will perceive, in the circumstances I detail with awe, nothing more than an ordinary succession of very natural causes and effects.

From my infancy I was noted for the docility and humanity of my disposition. My tenderness of heart was even so conspicuous as to make me the jest of my companions. I was especially fond of animal, and was indulged by my parents with a great variety of pets. With these I spent most of my time, and never was so happy as when feeding and caressing them. This peculiarity of character grew with my growth, and in my manhood, I derived from it one of my principal sources of pleasure. To those who have cherished an affection for a faithful and sagacious dog, I need hardly be at the trouble of explaining the nature or the intensity of the gratification thus derivable. There is something in the unselfish and self-sacrificing love of a brute, which goes directly to the heart of him who has had frequent occasion to test the paltry friendship and gossamer fidelity of mere **Man**.

I married early, and was happy to find in my wife a disposition not uncongenial with my own. Observing my partiality for domestic pets, she lost no opportunity of procuring those of the most agreeable kind. We had birds, gold fish, a fine dog, rabbits, a small monkey, and **a cat**.

This latter was a remarkably large and beautiful animal, entirely black, and sagacious to an astonishing degree. In speaking of his intelligence, my wife, who at heart was not a little tinctured with superstition, made frequent allusion to the ancient popular notion, which regarded all black cats as witches in disguise. Not that she was ever **serious** upon this point—and I mention the matter at all for no better reason than that it happens, just now, to be remembered.

Pluto—this was the cat's name—was my favourite pet and playmate. I alone fed him, and he attended me wherever I went about the house. It was even with difficulty that I could prevent him from following me through the streets.

Our friendship lasted, in this manner, for several years, during which my general temperament and character—through the instrumentality of the Fiend Intemperance-had (I blush to confess it) experienced a radical alteration for the worse. I grew, day by day, more moody, more irritable, more regardless of the feelings of others. I suffered myself to use intemperate language to my wife. At length, I even offered her personal violence. My pets, of course, were made to feel the change in my disposition. I not only neglected, but ill-used them. For Pluto, however, I still retained sufficient regard to restrain me from maltreating him, as I made no scruple of maltreating the rabbits, the monkey, or even the dog, when by accident, or through affection, they came in my way. But my disease grew upon me-for what disease is like Alcohol!-and at length even Pluto, who was now becoming old, and consequently somewhat peevish-even Pluto began to experience the effects of my ill temper.

One night, returning home, much intoxicated, from one of my haunts about town, I fancied that the cat avoided my presence. I seized him; when, in his fright at my violence, he inflicted a slight wound upon my hand with his teeth. The fury of a demon instantly possessed me. I knew myself no longer. My original soul seemed, at once, to take its flight from my body; and a more than fiendish malevolence, gin-nurtured, thrilled every fibre of my frame. I took from my waistcoat-pocket a pen-knife, opened it, grasped the poor beast by the throat, and deliberately cut one of its eyes from the socket! I blush, I burn, I shudder, while I pen the damnable atrocity.

When reason returned with the morning-when I had slept off the fumes of the night's debauch-I experienced a sentiment half of horror, half of remorse, for the crime of which I had been guilty; but it was, at best, a feeble and equivocal feeling, and the soul remained untouched. I again plunged into excess, and soon drowned in wine all memory of the deed.

In the meantime the cat slowly recovered. The socket of the lost eye presented, it is true, a frightful appearance, but he no longer appeared to suffer any pain. He went about the house as usual, but, as might be expected, fled in extreme terror at my approach. I had so much of my old heart left, as to be at first grieved by this evident dislike on the part of a creature which had once so loved me. But this feeling soon gave place to irritation. And then came, as if to my final and irrevocable overthrow, the spirit of PERVERSENESS. Of this spirit philosophy takes no account. Yet I am not more sure that my soul lives, than I am that perverseness is one of the primitive impulses of the human heart—one of the indivisible primary faculties, or sentiments, which gives direction to the character of Man. Who has not, a hundred times, found himself committing a vile or a silly action, for no other reason than because he knows he should **not**? Have we not a perpetual inclination, in the teeth of our best judgment, to violate that which is **Law**, merely because we understand it to be such? This spirit of perverseness, I say, came to my final overthrow. It was this unfathomable longing of the soul **to vex itself**—to offer violence to its own nature—to do wrong for the wrong's sake only—that urged me to continue and finally to consummate the injury I had inflicted upon the unoffending brute. One morning, in cool blood, I slipped a noose about its neck and hung it to the limb of a tree;-hung it with the tears streaming from my eyes, and with the bitterest remorse at my heart;-hung it **because** I knew that it had loved me, and **because** I felt it had given me no reason of offence;-hung it **because** I knew that in so doing I was committing a sin -a deadly sin that would so jeopardize my immortal soul as to place it-if such a thing were possible-even beyond the reach of the infinite mercy of the Most Merciful and Most Terrible God.

On the night of the day on which this cruel deed was done, I was aroused from sleep by the cry of fire. The curtains of my bed were in flames. The whole house was blazing. It was with great difficulty that my wife, a servant, and myself, made our escape from the conflagration. The destruction was complete. My entire worldly wealth was swallowed up, and I resigned myself thenceforward to despair.

I am above the weakness of seeking to establish a sequence of cause and effect, between the disaster and the atrocity. But I am detailing a chain of facts-and wish not to leave even a possible link imperfect. On the day succeeding the fire, I visited the ruins. The walls, with one exception, had fallen in. This exception was found in a compartment wall, not very thick, which stood about the middle of the house, and against which had rested the head of my bed. The plastering had here, in great measure, resisted the action of the fire-a fact which I attributed to its having been recently spread. About this wall a dense crowd were collected, and many persons seemed to be examining a particular portion of it with very minute and eager attention. The words "strange!" "singular!" and other similar expressions, excited my curiosity. I approached and saw, as if graven in **bas-relief** upon the white surface, the figure of a gigantic **cat**. The impression was given with an accuracy truly marvellous. There was a rope about the animal's neck.

When I first beheld this apparition—for I could scarcely regard it as less—my wonder and my terror were extreme. But at length reflection came to my aid. The cat, I remembered, had been hung in a garden adjacent to the house. Upon the alarm of fire, this garden had been immediately filled by the crowd—by some one of whom the animal must have been cut from the tree and thrown, through an open window, into my chamber. This had probably been done with the view of arousing me from sleep. The falling of the other walls had compressed the victim of my cruelty into the substance of the freshly-spread plaster; the lime of which, with the flames, and the **ammonia** from the carcass, had then accomplished the portraiture as I saw it.

Although I thus readily accounted to my reason, if not altogether to my conscience, for the startling fact just detailed, it did not the less fall to make a deep impression upon my fancy. For months I could not rid myself of the phantasm of the cat; and, during this period, there came back into my spirit a half-sentiment that seemed, but was not, remorse. I went so far as to regret the loss of the animal, and to look about me, among the vile haunts which I now habitually frequented, for another pet of the same species, and of somewhat similar appearance, with which to supply its place.

One night as I sat, half stupefied, in a den of more than infamy, my attention was suddenly drawn to some black object, reposing upon the head of one of the immense **hogsheads of Gin, or of Rum**, which constituted the chief furniture of the apartment. I had been looking steadily at the top of this hogshead for some minutes, and what now caused me surprise was the fact that I had not sooner perceived the object thereupon. I approached it, and touched it with my hand. It was a black cat—a very large one—fully as large as Pluto, and closely resembling him in every respect but one. Pluto had not a white hair upon any portion of his body; but this cat had a large, although indefinite splotch of white, covering nearly the whole region of the breast.

Upon my touching him, he immediately arose, purred loudly, rubbed against my hand, and appeared delighted with my notice. This, then, was the very creature of which I was in search. I at once offered to purchase it of the landlord; but this person made no claim to it—knew nothing of it—had never seen it before.

I continued my caresses, and, when I prepared to go home, the animal evinced a disposition to accompany me. I permitted it to do so; occasionally stooping and patting it as I proceeded. When it reached the house it domesticated itself at once, and became immediately a great favorite with my wife.

For my own part, I soon found a dislike to it arising within me. This was just the reverse of what I had anticipated; but I know not how or why it was—its evident fondness for myself rather disgusted and annoyed. By slow degrees, these feelings of disgust and annoyance rose into the bitterness of hatred. I avoided the creature; a certain sense of shame, and the remembrance of my former deed of cruelty, preventing me from physically abusing it. I did not, for some weeks, strike, or otherwise violently ill use it; but gradually-very gradually-I came to look upon it with unutterable loathing, and to flee silently from its odious presence, as from the breath of a pestilence.

What added, no doubt, to my hatred of the beast, was the discovery, on the morning after I brought it home, that, like Pluto, it also had been deprived of one of its eyes. This circumstance, however, only endeared it to my wife, who, as I have already said, possessed, in a high degree, that humanity of feeling which had once been my distinguishing trait, and the source of many of my simplest and purest pleasures.

With my aversion to this cat, however, its partiality for myself seemed to increase. It followed my footsteps with a pertinacity which it would be difficult to make the reader comprehend. Whenever I sat, it would crouch beneath my chair, or spring upon my knees, covering me with its loathsome caresses. If I arose to walk it would get between my feet and thus nearly throw me down, or, fastening its long and sharp claws in my dress, clamber, in this manner, to my breast. At such times, although I longed to destroy it with a blow, I was yet withheld from so doing, partly by a memory of my former crime, but chiefly-let me confess it at once-by absolute dread of the beast.

This dread was not exactly a dread of physical evil-and yet I should be at a loss how otherwise to define it. I am almost ashamed to own-yes, even in this felon's cell, I am almost ashamed to own-that the terror and horror with which the animal inspired me, had been heightened by one of the merest chimaeras it would be possible to conceive. My wife had called my attention, more than once, to the character of the mark of white hair, of which I have spoken, and which constituted the sole visible difference between the strange beast and the one I had destroyed. The reader will remember that this mark, although large, had been originally very indefinite; but, by slow degrees-degrees nearly imperceptible, and which for a long time my Reason struggled to reject as fanciful-it had, at length, assumed a rigorous distinctness of outline. It was now the representation of an object that I shudder to name-and for this, above all, I loathed, and dreaded, and would have rid myself of the monster **had I dared**-it was now, I say, the image of a hideous-of a ghastly thing-of the GALLOWS!-oh, mournful and terrible engine of Horror and of Crime-of Agony and of Death!

And now was I indeed wretched beyond the wretchedness of mere Humanity. And a brute beast-whose fellow I had contemptuously destroyed-a **brute beast to work** out for **me**-for me, a man, fashioned in the image of the High God-so much of insufferable **woe**! Alas! neither by day nor by night knew I the blessing of rest any more! During the former the creature left me no moment alone; and, in the latter, I started, hourly, from dreams of unutterable fear, to find the hot breath of **the thing** upon my face, and its vast weight-an incarnate nightmare that I had no power to shake off-incumbent eternally upon my **heart**!

Beneath the pressure of torments such as these, the feeble remnant of the good within me succumbed. Evil thoughts became my sole intimates — the darkest and most evil of thoughts. The moodiness of my usual temper increased to hatred of all things and of all mankind; while, from the sudden, frequent, and ungovernable outbursts of a fury to which I now, blindly abandoned myself, my uncomplaining wife, alas! was the most usual and the most patient of sufferers.

One day she accompanied me, upon some household errand, into the cellar of the old building which our poverty compelled us to inhabit. The cat followed me down the steep stairs, and, nearly throwing me headlong, exasperated me to madness. Uplifting an axe, and forgetting, in my wrath, the childish dread which had hitherto stayed my hand, I aimed a blow at the animal which, of course, would have proved instantly fatal had it descended as I wished. But this blow was arrested by the hand of my wife. Goaded, by the interference, into a rage more than demoniacal, I withdrew my arm from her grasp and buried the axe in her brain. She fell dead upon the spot, without a groan.

This hideous murder accomplished, I set myself forthwith, and with entire deliberation, to the task of concealing the body. I knew that I could not remove it from the house, either by day or by night, without the risk of being observed by the neighbors. Many projects entered my mind. At one period I thought of cutting the corpse into minute fragments, and destroying them by fire. At another, I resolved to dig a grave for it in the floor of the cellar. Again, I deliberated about casting it in the well in the yard-about packing it in a box, as if merchandize, with the usual arrangements, and so getting a porter to take it from the house. Finally I hit upon what I considered a far better expedient than either of these. I determined to wall it up in the cellar-as the monks of the middle ages are recorded to have walled up their victims.

For a purpose such as this the cellar was well adapted. Its walls were loosely constructed, and had lately been plastered throughout with a rough plaster, which the dampness of the atmosphere had prevented from hardening. Moreover, in one of the walls was a projection, caused by a false chimney, or fireplace, that had been filled up, and made to resemble the rest of the cellar. I made no doubt that I could readily displace the at this point, insert the corpse, and wall the whole up as before, so that no eye could detect anything suspicious.

And in this calculation I was not deceived. By means of a crowbar I easily dislodged the bricks, and, having carefully deposited the body against the inner wall, I propped it in that position, while, with little trouble, I re-laid the whole structure as it originally stood. Having procured mortar, sand, and hair, with every possible precaution, I prepared a plaster which could not be distinguished from the old, and with this I very carefully went over the new brick-work. When I had finished, I felt satisfied that all was right. The wall did not present the slightest appearance of having been disturbed. The rubbish on the floor was picked up with the minutest care. I looked around triumphantly, and said to myself-"Here at least, then, my labor has not been in vain."

My next step was to look for the beast which had been the cause of so much wretchedness; for I had, at length, firmly resolved to put it to death. Had I been able to meet with it, at the moment, there could have been no doubt of its fate; but it appeared that the crafty animal had been alarmed at the violence of my previous anger, and forebore to present itself in my present mood. It is impossible to describe, or to imagine, the deep, the blissful sense of relief which the absence of the detested creature occasioned in my bosom. It did not make its appearance during the night—and thus for one night at least, since its introduction into the house, I soundly and tranquilly slept; aye, **slept** even with the burden of murder upon my soul!

The second and the third day passed, and still my tormentor came not. Once again I breathed as a freeman. The monster, in terror, had fled the premises forever! I should behold it no more! My happiness was supreme! The guilt of my dark deed disturbed me but little. Some few inquiries had been made, but these had been readily answered. Even a search had been instituted—but of course nothing was to be discovered. I looked upon my future felicity as secured.

Upon the fourth day of the assassination, a party of the police came, very unexpectedly, into the house, and proceeded again to make rigorous investigation of the premises. Secure, however, in the inscrutability of my place of concealment, I felt no embarrassment whatever. The officers bade me accompany them in their search. They left no nook or corner unexplored. At length, for the third or fourth time, they descended into the cellar. I quivered not in a muscle. My heart beat calmly as that of one who slumbers in innocence. I walked the cellar from end to end. I folded my arms upon my bosom, and roamed easily to and fro. The police were thoroughly satisfied and prepared to depart. The glee at my heart was too strong to be restrained. I burned to say if but one word, by way of triumph, and to render doubly sure their assurance of my guiltlessness.

"Gentlemen," I said at last, as the party ascended the steps, "I delight to have allayed your suspicions. I wish you all health, and a little more courtesy. By the bye, gentlemen, this-this is a very well constructed house," (In the rabid desire to say something easily, I scarcely knew what I uttered at all.)-"I may say an **excellently** well constructed house. These walls-are you going, gentlemen?-these walls are solidly put together"; and here, through the mere phrenzy of bravado, I rapped heavily, with a cane which I held in my hand, upon that very portion of the brick-work behind which stood the corpse of the wife of my bosom.

But may God shield and deliver me from the fangs of the Arch-Fiend! No sooner had the reverberation of my blows sunk into silence, than I was answered by a voice from within the tomb!-by a cry, at first muffled and broken, like the sobbing of a child, and then quickly swelling into one long, loud, and continuous scream, utterly anomalous and inhuman-a howl-a wailing shriek, half of horror and half of triumph, such as might have arisen only out of hell, conjointly from the throats of the damned in their agony and of the demons that exult in the damnation.

Of my own thoughts it is folly to speak. Swooning, I staggered to the opposite wall. For one instant the party upon the stairs remained motionless, through extremity of terror and of awe. In the next, a dozen stout arms were tolling at the wall. It fell bodily. The corpse, already greatly decayed and clotted with gore, stood erect before the eyes of the spectators. Upon its head, with red extended mouth and solitary eye of fire, sat the hideous beast whose craft had seduced me into murder, and whose informing voice had consigned me to the hangman. I had walled the monster up within the tomb!

The Real Thing   —by Henry James

I

When the porter's wife, who used to answer the house-bell, announced "A gentleman and a lady, sir," I had, as I often had in those days - the wish being father to the thought - an immediate vision of sitters. Sitters my visitors in this case proved to be; but not in the sense I should have preferred. There was nothing at first however to indicate that they might n't have come for a portrait. The gentleman, a man of fifty, very high and very straight, with a moustache slightly grizzled and a dark grey walking-coat admirably fitted, both of which I noted professionally - I don't mean as a barber or yet as a tailor - would have struck me as a celebrity if celebrities often were striking. It was a truth of which I had for some time been conscious that a figure with a good deal of frontage[1] was, as one might say, almost never a public institution. A glance at the lady helped to remind me of this paradoxical law: she also looked too distinguished to be a "personality." Moreover one would scarcely come across two variations together.

Neither of the pair immediately spoke - they only prolonged the

---

1) 인상적인 앞모습.

preliminary gaze suggesting that each wished to give the other a chance. They were visibly shy; they stood there letting me take them in—which, as I afterwards perceived, was the most practical thing they could have done. In this way their embarrassment served their cause. I had seen people painfully reluctant to mention that they desired anything so gross as to be represented on canvas; but the scruples of my new friends appeared almost insurmountable. Yet the gentleman might have said "I should like a portrait of my wife," and the lady might have said "I should like a portrait of my husband." Perhaps they were n't husband and wife—this naturally would make the matter more delicate. Perhaps they wished to be done together—in which case they ought to have brought a third person to break the news.

"We come from Mr. Rivet," the lady finally said with a dim smile that had the effect of a moist sponge passed over a "sunk"[2] piece of painting, as well as of a vague allusion to vanished beauty. She was as tall and straight, in her degree, as her companion, and with ten years less to carry. She looked as sad as a woman could look whose face was not charged with expression; that is her tinted oval mask showed waste as an exposed surface shows friction. The hand of time had played over her freely, but to an effect of elimination. She was slim and stiff, and so well-dressed, in dark blue cloth, with lappets[3] and pockets and buttons, that it was clear she employed the same

---

2) 낡은, 즉 'Faded'의 뜻.
3) 늘어진 부분이나 주름. 'folds' 혹은 'flaps'.

tailor as her husband. The couple had an indefinable air of prosperous thrift-they evidently got a good deal of luxury for their money. If I was to be one of their luxuries it would behove me to consider my terms.

"Ah Claude Rivet recommended me?" I echoed; and I added that is was very kind of him, though I could reflect that, as he only painted landscape, this was n't a sacrifice.

The lady looked very hard at the gentleman, and the gentleman looked round the room. Then staring at the floor a moment and stroking his moustache, he rested his pleasant eyes on me with the remark: "He said you were the right one."

"I try to be, when people want to sit."

"Yes, we should like to," said the lady anxiously.

"Do you mean together?"

My visitors exchanged a glance. "If you could do anything with me I suppose it would be double," the gentleman stammered.

"Oh yes, there's naturally a higher charge for two figures than for one."

We should like to make it pay," the husband confessed.

"That's very good of you," I returned, appreciating so unwonted a sympathy-for I supposed he meant pay the artist.

A sense of strangeness seemed to dawn on the lady. "We mean for the illustrations-Mr. Rivet said you might put one in."

"Put in-an illustration?" I was equally confused.

"Sketch her off, you know," said the gentleman, colouring.

It was only then that I understood the service Claude Rivet had rendered me; he had told them how I worked in black-and-white, for magazines, for storybooks, for sketches of contemporary life, and consequently had copious employment for models. These things were true, but it was not less true — I may confess it now; whether because the aspiration was to lead to everything or to nothing I leave the reader to guess — that I could n't get the honours, to say nothing of the emoluments, of a great painter of portraits out of my head. My "illustrations" were my pot-boilers; I looked to a different branch of art — far and away the most interesting it had always seemed to me — to perpetuate my fame. There was no shame in looking to it also to make my fortune; but that fortune was by so much further from being made from the moment my visitors wished to be "done" for nothing. I was disappointed; for in the pictorial sense I had immediately *seen* them. I had seized their type — I had already settled what I would do with it. Something that would n't absolutely have pleased them, I afterwards reflated.

"Ah you're — you're — a — ?" I began as soon as I had mastered my surprise. I could n't bring out the dingy word "models" : it seemed so little to fit the case.

"We have n't had much practice," said the lady.

"We've got to *do* something, and we've thought that an artist in your line might perhaps make something of us," her husband threw off. He further mentioned that they did n't know many artists and that they had gone first, on the off-chance — he painted views of course, but sometimes put in figures; perhaps I remembered — to Mr. Rivet, whom they had met a few years before at a place in Norfolk where he was sketching.

"We used to sketch a little ourselves," the lady hinted.

"It's very awkward, but we absolutely *must* do something," her husband went on.

"Of course we're not so *very* young," she admitted with a wan smile.

With the remark that I might as well know something more about them the husband had handed me a card extracted from a neat new pocket-book — their appurtenances were all of the freshest — and inscribed with the words "Major Monarch." Impressive as these words were they did n't carry my knowledge much further; but my visitor presently added: "I've left the army and we've had the misfortune to lose our money. In fact our means are dreadfully small."

"It's awfully trying — a regular strain," said Mrs. Monarch.

They evidently wished to be discreet — to take care not to swagger because they were gentlefolk. I felt them willing to recognise this as something of a drawback, at the same time that I guessed at an underlying sense — their consolation in adversity — that they *had* their points. They certainly had; but these advantages struck me as preponderantly social; such for instance as would help to make a drawing-room look well. However, a drawing-room was always, or ought to be, a picture.

In consequence of his wife's allusion to their age Major Monarch observed: "Naturally it's more for the figure that we thought of going in. We can still hold ourselves up." On the instant I saw that the figure was indeed their strong point. His "naturally" did n't sound vain, but it lighted up the question.

"*She* has the best one," he continued, nodding at his wife with a pleasant after-dinner absence of circumlocution. I could only reply, as if we were in fact sitting over our wine, that this did n't prevent his own from being very good; which led him in turn to make answer: "We thought that if you ever have to do people like us we might be something like it. *She* particularly – for a lady in a book, you know."

I was so amused by them that, to get more of it, I did my best to take their point of view; and though it was an embarrassment to find myself appraising physically, as if they were animals on hire or useful blacks, a pair of whom I should have expected to meet only in one of the relations in which criticism is tacit, I looked at Mrs. Monarch judicially enough to be able to exclaim after a moment with conviction: "Oh yes, a lady in a book!" She was singularly like a bad illustration.

"We'll stand up, if you like," said the Major; and he raised himself before me with a really grand air.

I could take his measure at a glance – he was six feet two and a perfect gentleman. It would have paid any club in process of formation and in want of a stamp to engage him at a salary to stand in the principal window. What struck me at once was that in coming to me they had rather missed their vocation; they could surely have been turned to better account for advertising purposes. I could n't of course see the thing in detail, but I could see them make somebody's fortune – I don't mean their own. There was something in them for a waistcoat-maker, an hotel-keeper or a soap-vendor. I could imagine "We always use it" pinned on their bosoms with the greatest effect; I had a vision of the brilliancy with which they would launch a table d'hote.[4]

Mrs. Monarch sat still, not from pride but from shyness, and presently her husband said to her: "Get up, my dear, and show how smart you are." She obeyed, but she had no need to get up to show it. She walked to the end of the studio and then came back blushing, her fluttered eyes on the partner of her appeal. I was reminded of an incident I had accidently had a glimpse of in Paris-being with a friend there, a dramatist about to produce a play, when an actress came to him to ask to be entrusted with a part. She went through her paces before him, walked up and down as Mrs. Monarch was doing. Mrs, Monarch did it quite as well, but I abstained from applauding. It was very odd to see such people apply for such poor pay. She looked as if she had ten thousand a year. Her husband had used the word that described her: she was in the London current jargon essentially and typically "smart." Her figure was, in the same order of ideas, conspicuously and irreproachably "good." For a woman of her age her waist was surprisingly small; her elbow moreover had the orthodox crook. She held her head at the conventional angle, but why did she come to *me*? She ought to have tried on jackets at a big shop. I feared my visitors were not only destitute but "artistic"-which would be a great complication. When she sat down again I thanked her, observing that what a draughtsman most valued in his model was the faculty of keeping quiet.

---

4) 즉 식당, 'a restaurant'을 뜻함.

"Oh *she* can keep quiet," said Major Monarch. Then he added jocosely: "I've always kept her quiet."

"I'm not a nasty fidget, am I?" It was going to wring tears from me, I felt, the way she hid her head, ostrich-like, in the other broad bosom.

The owner of this expanse addressed his answer to me. "Perhaps it is n't out of place to mention – because we ought to be quite business-like, ought n't we? – that when I married her she was known as the Beautiful Statue."

"Oh dear!" said Mrs. Monarch ruefully.

"Of course I should want a certain amount of expression," I rejoined.

"Of *course!*" – and I had never heard such unanimity.

"And then I suppose you know that you'll get awfully tired."

"Oh, we *never* get tired!" they eagerly cried.

"Have you had any kind of practice?"

They hesitated – they looked at each other. "We've been photographed – *immensely*," said Mrs. Monarch.

"She means the fellows have asked us themselves," added the Major.

"I see – because you're so good-looking."

"I don't know what they thought, but they were always after us."

"We always got our photographs for nothing," smiled Mrs. Monarch.

"We might have brought some, my dear," her husband remarked.

"I'm not sure we have any left. We've given quantities away," she explained to me.

"With our autographs and that sort of thing," said the Major.

"Are they to be got in the shops?" I enquired as a harmless pleasantry.

"Oh yes, *hers*—they used to be."

"Not now," said Mrs. Monarch with her eyes on the floor.

II

I could fancy the "sort of thing" they put on the presentation copies of their photographs, and I was sure they wrote a beautiful hand. It was odd how quickly I was sure of everything that concerned them. If they were now so poor as to have to earn shillings and pence they could never have had much of a margin. Their good looks had been their capital, and they had good-humouredly made the most of the career that this resource marked out for them. It was in their faces, the blankness, the deep intellectual repose of the twenty years of country-house visiting that had given them pleasant intonations. I could see the sunny drawing-rooms, sprinkled with periodicals she didn't read, in which Mrs. Monarch had continuously sat; I could see the wet shrubberies in which she had walked, equipped to admiration for either exercise. I could see the rich covers[1] the Major had helped to shoot and the wonderful garments in which, late at night, he repaired to the smoking-room to talk about them. I could imagine

---

1) 사냥꾼들을 위해 경기가 이루어지는 숲과 덤불(Woods and thickets from which game is driven for hunters).

their leggings and waterproofs, their knowing tweeds and rugs, their rolls of sticks and cases of tackle and neat umbrellas; and I could evoke the exact appearance of their servants and the compact variety of their luggage on the platforms of country stations.

They gave small tips, but they were liked; they did n't do anything themselves, but they were welcome. They looked so well everywhere; they gratified the general relish for stature, complexion and "form." They knew it without fatuity or vulgarity, and they respected themselves in consequence. They were n't superficial; they were thorough and kept themselves up − it had been their line. People with such a taste for activity had to have some line. I could feel how even in a dull house they could have been counted on for the joy of life. At present something had happened − it did n't matter what, their little income had grown less, it had grown least − and they had to do something for pocket-money. Their friends could like them, I made out, without liking to support them. There was something about them that represented credit − their clothes, their manners, their type; but if credit is a large empty pocket in which an occasional chink reverberates, the chink at least must be audible. What they wanted of me was to help to make it so. Fortunately they had no children − I soon divined that. They would also perhaps wish our relations to be kept secret: this was why it was "for the figure" − the reproduction of the face would betray them.

I liked them − I felt, quite as their friends must have done − they were so simple; and I had no objection to them if they would suit. But somehow with all their perfections I did n't easily believe in them. After all they were amateurs, and the ruling passion of my life was the detestation of the amateur. Combined with this was another perversity-an innate preference for the represented subject over the real one: the defect of the real one was so apt to be a lack of representation. I liked things that appeared; then one was sure. Whether they *were* or not was a subordinate and almost always a profitless question. There were other considerations, the first of which was that I already had two or three recruits in use, notably a young person with big feet, in alpaca from Kilburn, who for a couple of years had come to me regularly for my illustrations and with whom I was still-perhaps ignobly-satisfied. I frankly explained to my visitors how the case stood, but they had taken more precautions than I supposed. They had reasoned out their opportunity, for Claude Rivet had told them of the projected *edition de luxe* of one of the writers of our day-the rarest of the novelists-who, long neglected by the multitudinous vulgar and dearly prized by the attentive (need I mention Philip Vincent?) had had the happy fortune of seeing, late in life, the dawn and then the full light of a higher criticism; an estimate in which on the part of the public there was something really of expiation. The edition preparing, planned by a publisher of taste, was practically an act of high reparation; the wood-cuts with which it was to be enriched were the homage of English art to one of the most independent representatives of English letters. Major and Mrs. Monarch confessed to me they had hoped I might be able to work them into my branch of the enterprise. They knew I was to do the first of the books, "Rutland Ramsay," but I had to make clear to them that my participation in the rest of the affair—this first book was to be a test—must depend on the satisfaction I should give. If this should be limited my employers would drop me with scarce common forms. It was therefore a crisis for me, and naturally I was making special preparations, looking about for new people, should they be necessary, and securing the best types. I admitted however that I should like to settle down to two or three good models who would do for everything.

"Should we have often to—a—put on special clothes?" Mrs. Monarch timidly demanded.

"Dear yes—that's half the business."

"And should we be expected to supply our own costumes?"

"Oh no; I've got a lot of things. A painter's models put on—or put off—anything he likes."

"And you mean—a—the same?"

"The same?"

Mrs. Monarch looked at her husband again.

"Oh she was just wondering," he explained, "if the costumes are in *general* use." I had to confess that they were, and I mentioned further that some of them—I had a lot of genuine greasy last-century things—had served their time, a hundred years ago, on living world-stained men and women; on figures not perhaps so far removed, in that vanished world, from their type, the Monarchs', *quoi*!2) of a breeched and bewigged age. "We'll put on anything that *fits*," said the Major.

"Oh I arrange that-they fit in the pictures."

"I'm afraid I should do better for the modern books. I'd come as you like," said Mrs. Monarch.

"She has got a lot of clothes at home: they might do for contemporary life," her husband continued.

"Oh I can fancy scenes in which you'd be quite natural." And indeed I could see the slipshod rearrangements of stale properties -the stories I tried to produce pictures for without the exasperation of reading them-whose sandy tracts the good lady might help to people. But I had to return to the fact that for this sort of work-the daily mechanical grind-I was already equipped: the people I was working with were fully adequate.

"We only thought we might be more like *some* characters," said Mrs. Monarch mildly, getting up.

Her husband also rose; he stood looking at me with a dim wistfulness that was touching in so fine a man. "Would n't it be rather a pull sometimes to have-a-to have-?" He hung fire; he wanted me to help him by phrasing what he meant. But I could n't-I did n't know. So he brought it out awkwardly: "The *real* thing; a gentleman, you know, or a lady." I was quite ready to give a general assent-I admitted that there was a great deal in that. This encouraged Major Monarch to say, following up his appeal with an unacted gulp: "It's awfully hard-we've tried everything." The gulp was communicative; it proved too much for his wife. Before I knew it Mrs. Monarch had dropped again upon

---

2) 불어로 'what!'의 뜻이다.

a divan and burst into tears. Her husband sat down beside her, holding one of her hands; whereupon she quickly dried her eyes with the other, while I felt embarrassed as she looked up at me. "There is n't a confounded job I have n't applied for — waited for — prayed for. You can fancy we'd be pretty bad first. Secretaryships and that sort of thing? You might as well ask for a peerage. I'd be *anything* — I'm strong; a messenger or a coalheaver. I'd put on a gold-laced cap and open carriage-doors in front of the haberdasher's; I'd hang about a station to carry portmanteaux;[3] I'd be a postman. But they won't *look* at you; there are thousands as good as yourself already on the ground. *Gentlemen,* poor beggars, who've drunk their wine, who've kept their hunters!"

I was as reassuring as I knew how to be, and my visitors were presently on their feet again while, for the experiment, we agreed on an hour. We were discussing it when the door opened and Miss Churm came in with a wet umbrella. Miss Churm had to take the omnibus to Maida Vale and then walk half a mile. She looked a trifle blowsy and slightly splashed. I scarcely ever saw her come in without thinking afresh how odd it was that, being so little in herself, she should yet be so much in others. She was a meagre little Miss Churm, but was such an ample heroine of romance. She was only a freckled cockney,[4] but she could represent everything, from a fine lady to a shepherdess; she had the faculty as she might have had a fine voice or long hair. She could n't spell and she loved beer, but she had two or three

---

3) 큰 가방들(Large suitcases)을 뜻함.
4) 런던의 East End 지역에 사는 빈민가 주민. 따라서 하층계급의 일원이다.

"points," and practice, and a knack, and mother-wit, and a whimsical sensibility, and love of the theatre, and seven sisters, and not an ounce of respect, especially for the *h.* The first thing my visitors saw was that her umbrella was wet, and in their spotless perfection they visibly winced at it. The rain had come on since their arrival.

"I'm all in a soak; there *was* a mess of people in the bus. I wish you lived near a styition," said Miss Churm. I requested her to get ready as quickly as possible, and she passed into the room in which she always changed her dress. But before going out she asked me what she was to get into this time.

"It's the Russian princess, don't you know?" I answered; "the one with the 'golden eyes,' in black velvet, for the long thing in the *Cheapside.*"5)

"Golden eyes? I *say!*" cried Miss Churm, while my companions watched her with intensity as she withdrew. She always arranged herself, when she was late, before I could turn round; and I kept my visitors a little on purpose, so that they might get an idea, from seeing her, what would be expected of themselves. I mentioned that she was quite my notion of an excellent model — she was really very clever.

"Do you think she looks like a Russian princess?" Major Monarch asked with lurking alarm.

"When I make her, yes."

"Oh if you have to *make* her—!" he reasoned, not without

---

5) 런던의 상업지역 거리를 위해 이름을 붙인 잡지이다.

point.

"That's the most you can ask. There are so many who are not makeable."

"Well now, *here's* a lady"—and with a persuasive smile he passed his arm into his wife's—"who's already made!"

"Oh I'm not a Russian princess," Mrs. Monarch protested a little coldly. I could see she had known some and did n't like them. There at once was a complication of a kind I never had to fear with Miss Churm.

This young lady came back in black velvet—the gown was rather rusty and very low on her lean shoulders and with a Japanese fan in her red hands. I reminded her that in the scene I was doing she had to look over some one's head. "I forget whose it is; but it does n't matter. Just look over a head."

"I'd rather look over a stove," said Miss Churm; and she took her station near the fire. She fell into position, settled herself into a tall attitude, gave a certain backward inclination to her head and a certain forward droop to her fan, and looked, at least to my prejudiced sence, distinguished and charming, foreign and dangerous. We left her looking so while I went downstairs with Major and Mrs. Monarch.

"I believe I could come about as near as that," said Mrs. Monarch.

"Oh you think she's shabby, but you must allow for the alchemy of art."

However, they went off with an evident increase of comfort founded on their demonstrable advantage in being the real thing. I could fancy them shuddering over Miss Churm. She was very droll about them when I went back, for I told her what they wanted.

"Well, if *she* can sit I'll tyke to bookkeeping," said my model.

"She's very ladylike," I replied as an innocent form of aggravation.

"So much the worse for *you*. That means she can't turn round."

"She'll do for the fashionable novels."

"Oh yes, she'll *do* for them!" my model humorously declared. "Ain't they bad enough without her?" I had often sociably denounced them to Miss Churm.

III

It was for the elucidation of a mystery in one of these works that I first tried Mrs. Monarch. Her husband came with her, to be useful if necessary – it was sufficiently clear that as a general thing he would prefer to come with her. At first I wondered if this were for "propriety's" sake – if he were going to be jealous and meddling. The idea was too tiresome, and if it had been confirmed it would speedily have brought our acquaintance to a close. But I soon saw there was nothing in it and that if he accompanied Mrs. Monarch it was – in addition to the chance of being wanted – simply because he had nothing else to do. When they were separate his occupation was gone and they never *had* been separate. I judged rightly that in their awkward situation their close union was their main comfort and that this union had no weak spot. It was a real marriage, an encouragement to the hesitating, a nut for pessimists to crack. Their address was humble – I remember afterwards thinking it had been the only thing about them that was really professional – and I could fancy the lamentable lodgings in which the Major would have been left alone. He could sit there more or less grimly with his wife – he could n't sit there anyhow without her.

He had too much tact to try and make himself agreeable when he could n't be useful; so when I was too absorbed in my work to talk he simply sat and waited. But I liked to hear him talk – it made my work, when not interrupting it, less mechanical, less special. To listen to him was to combine the excitement of going out with the economy of staying at home. There was only one hindrance – that I seemed not to know any of the people this brilliant couple had known. I think he wondered extremely, during the term of our intercourse, whom the deuce I *did* know. He had n't a stray sixpence of an idea to fumble for, so we did n't spin it very fine; we confined ourselves to questions of leather and even of liquor – saddlers and breeches-makers and how to get excellent claret cheap – and matters like "good trains" and the habits of small game. His lore on these last subjects was astonishing – he managed to interweave the stationmaster with the ornithologist. When he could n't talk about greater things he could talk cheerfully about smaller, and since I could n't accompany him into reminiscences of the fashionable world he could lower the conversation without a visible effort to my level.

So earnest a desire to please was touching in a man who could so easily have knocked one down. He looked after the fire and had an opinion on the draught of the stove without my asking him, and I could see that he thought many of my arrangements not half knowing. I remember telling him that if I were only rich I'd offer him a salary to come and teach me how to live. Sometimes he gave a random sigh of which the essence might have been: "Give me even such a bare old barrack as *this*, and I'd do something with it!" When I wanted to use him he came alone; which was an illustration of the superior courage of women. His wife could bear her solitary second floor, and she was in general more discreet; showing by various small reserves that she was alive to the propriety of keeping our relations markedly professional-not letting them slide into sociability. She wished it to remain clear that she and the Major were employed, not cultivated, and if she approved of me as a superior, who could be kept in his place, she never thought me quite good enough for an equal.

She sat with great intensity, giving the whole of her mind to it, and was capable of remaining for an hour almost as motionless as before a photographer's lens. I could see she had been photographed often, but somehow the very habit that made her good for that purpose unfitted her for mine. At first I was extremely pleased with her ladylike air, and it was a satisfaction, on coming to follow her lines, to see how good they were and how far they could lead the pencil. But after a little skirmishing I began to find her too insurmountably stiff; do what I would with it my drawing looked like a photograph or a copy of a photograph. Her finger had no variety of expression-she herself had no sense of variety. You may say that this was my business and was only a question of placing her. Yet I placed her in every conceivable position and she managed to obliterate their differences. She was always a lady certainly, and into the bargain was always the same lady. She was the real thing, but always the same thing. There were moments when I rather writhed under the serenity of her confidence that she *was* the real thing. All her dealings with me and all her husband's were an implication that this was lucky for *me*. Meanwhile I found myself trying to invent types that approached her own, instead of making her own transform itself — in the clever way that was not impossible for instance to poor Miss Churm. Arrange as I would and take the precautions I would, she always came out, in my pictures, too tall — landing me the dilemma of having represented a fascinating woman as seven feet high, which (out of respect perhaps to my own very much scantier inches) was far from my idea of such a personage.

The case was worse with the Major — nothing I could do would keep *him* down, so that he became useful only for the representation of brawny giants. I adored variety and range, I cherished human accidents, the illustrative note; I wanted to characterise closely, and the thing in the world I most hated was the danger of being ridden by a type. I had quarrelled with some of my friends about it; I had parted company with them for maintaining that one *had* to be, and that if the type was beautiful — witness Raphael and Leonardo — the servitude was only a gain. I was neither Leonardo nor Raphael — I might only be a presumptuous young modern searcher; but I held that everything was to be sacrificed sooner than character. When they claimed that the obsessional form could easily *be* character I retorted, perhaps superficially, "Whose?" It could n't be everybody's-it might end in being nobody's.

"After I had drawn Mrs. Monarch a dozen times I felt surer even than before that the value of such a model as Miss Churm resided precisely in the fact that she had no positive stamp, combined of course with the other fact that what she did have was a curious and inexplicable talent for imitation. Her usual appearance was like a curtain which she could draw up at request for a capital performance. This performance was simply suggestive; but it was a word to the wise-it was vivid and pretty. Sometimes even I thought it, though she was plain herself, too insipidly pretty; I made it a reproach to her that the figures drawn from her were monotonously (*betement*,[1] as we used to say) graceful. Nothing made her more angry: lt was so much her pride to feel she could sit for characters that had nothing in common with each other. She would accuse me at such moments of taking away her "reputytion."

It suffered a certain shrinkage, this queer quantity, from the repeated visits of my new friends. Miss Churm was greatly in demand, never in want of employment, so I had no scruple in putting her off occasionally, to try them more at my ease. It was certainly amusing at first to do the real thing-it was amusing to do Major Monarch's trousers. They *were* the real thing, even if

---

1) 불어로 'stupidly'의 뜻이다.

he did come out colossal. It was amusing to do his wife's back hair-it was so mathematically neat-and the particular "smart" tension of her tight stays. She lent herself especially to positions in which the face was somewhat averted or blurred; she abounded in ladylike back views and *profils perdus*.[2] When she stood erect she took naturally one of the attitudes in which court-painters represent queens and princesses; so that I found myself wondering whether, to draw out this accomplishment, I could n't get the editor of the *Cheapside* to publish a really royal romance, "A Tale of Buckingham Palace." Sometimes however the real thing and the make-believe came into contact; by which I mean that Miss Churm, keeping an appointment or coming to make one on days when I had much work in hand, encountered her invidious rivals. The encounter was not on their part, for they noticed her no more than if she had been the housemaid; not from intentional loftiness, but simply because as yet, professionally, they did n't know how to fraternise, as I could imagine they would have liked-or at least that the Major would. They could n't talk about the omnibus-they always walked; and they did n't know what else to try-she was n't interested in good trains or cheap claret. Besides, they must have felt-in the air-that she was amused at them, secretly derisive of their ever knowing how. She wasn't a person to conceal the limits of her faith if she had had a chance to show them. On the other hand Mrs. Monarch did n't think her tidy; for why else did she take pains to say to me-

---

[2] 불어로 '없어진 옆얼굴 모습들'. 옆얼굴 모습보다 나의 머리의 뒤를 더 많이 보여주는 자세들.

it was going out of the way, for Mrs. Monarch-that she did n't like dirty women?

One day when my young lady happened to be present with my other sitters-she even dropped in, when it was convenient, for a chat-I asked her to be so good as to lend a hand in getting tea, a service with which she was familiar and which was one of a class that, living as I did in a small way, with slender domestic resources, I often appealed to my models to render. They liked to lay hands on my property, to break the sitting, and sometimes the china-it made them feel Bohemian. The next time I saw Miss Churm after this incident she surprised me greatly by making a scene about it-she accused me of having wished to humiliate her. She had n't resented the outrage at the time, but had seemed obliging and amused, enjoying the comedy of asking Mrs. Monarch, who sat vague and silent, whether she would have cream and sugar, and putting an exaggerated simper into the question. She had tired intonations-as if she too wished to pass for the real thing-till I was afraid my other visitors would take offence.

Oh they were determined not to do this, and their touching patience was the measure of their great need. They would sit by the hour, uncomplaining, till I was ready to use them; they would come back on the chance of being wanted and would walk away cheerfully if it failed. I used to go to the door with them to see in what magnificent order they retreated. I tried to find other employment for them-I introduced them to several artists. But they didn't "take," for reasons I could appreciate, and I became rather anxiously aware that after such disappointments they fell back upon me with a heavier weight. They did me the honour to think me most *their* form. They were n't romantic enough for the painters, and in those days there were few serious workers in black-and-white. Besides, they had an eye to the great job I had mentioned to them – they had secretly set their hearts on supplying the right essence for my pictorial vindication of our fine novelist. They knew that for this undertaking I should want no costume-effects, none of the frippery of past ages – that it was a case in which everything would be contemporary and satirical and presumably genteel. If I could work them into it their future would be assured, for the labour would of course be long and the occupation steady.

One day Mrs. Monarch came without her husband – she explained his absence by his having had to go to the City.[3] While she sat there in her usual relaxed majesty there came at the door a knock which I immediately recognised as the subdued appeal of a model out of work. It was followed by the entrance of a young man whom I at once saw to be a foreigner and who proved in fact an Italian acquainted with no English word but my name, which he uttered in a way that made it seem to include all others. I had n't then visited his country, nor was I proficient in his tongue; but as he was not so meanly constituted – what Italian is? – as to depend only on that member of expression he conveyed to me, in familiar but graceful mimicry,

---

3) 런던의 금융과 상업 중심지.

that he was in search of exactly the employment in which the lady before me was engaged. I was not struck with him at first, and while I continued to draw I dropped few signs of interest or encouragement. He stood his ground however－not importunately, but with a dumb dog-like fidelity in his eyes that amounted to innocent impudence, the manner of a devoted servant－he might have been in the house for years－unjustly suspected. Suddenly it struck me that this very attitude and expression made a picture; whereupon I told him to sit down and wait till I should be free. There was another picture in the way he obeyed me, and I observed as I worked that there were others still in the way he looked wonderingly, with his head thrown back, about the high studio. He might have been crossing himself in Saint Peter's. Before I finished I said to myself "The fellow's a bankrupt orange－monger, but a treasure."

When Mrs. Monarch withdrew he passed across the room like a flash to open the door for her, standing there with the rapt pure gaze of the young Dante spellbound by the young Beatrice. As I never insisted, in such situations, on the blankness of the British domestic, I reflected that he had the making of a servant－and I needed one, but could n't pay him to be only that－as well as of a model; in short I resolved to adopt my bright adventurer if he would agree to officiate in the double capacity. He jumped at my offer, and in the event my rashness－for I had really known nothing about him－wasn't brought home to me. He proved a sympathetic though a desultory ministrant, and had in a wonderful degree the *sentiment de la pose*.[4] It was uncultivated, instinctive, a part of the happy instinct that had guided him to my door and helped him to spell out my name on the card nailed to it. He had had no other introduction to me than a guess, from the shape of my high north window, seen outside, that my place was a studio and that as a studio it would contain an artist. He had wandered to England in search of fortune, like other itinerants, and had embarked, with a partner and a small green hand-cart, on the sale of penny ices. The ices had melted away and the partner had dissolved in their train. My young man wore tight yellow trousers with reddish stripes and his name was Oronte. He was sallow but fair, and when I put him into some old clothes of my own he looked like an Englishman. He was as good as Miss Churm, who could look, when requested, like an Italian.

IV

I thought Mrs. Monarch's face slightly convulsed when, on her coming back with her husband, she found Oronte installed. It was strange to have to recognise in a scrap of a lazzarone[5] a competitor to her magnificent Major. It was she who scented danger first, for the Major was anecdotically unconscious. But Oronte gave us tea, with a hundred eager confusions—he had never been concerned in so queer a process—and I think she thought better of me for having at last an "establishment." They

---

4) 불어로 '자세를 취하는 본능'을 뜻함.
5) 이탈리아어로 거지(beggar)의 뜻임.

saw a couple of drawings that I had made of the establishment, and Mrs. Monarch hinted that it never would have struck her he had sat for them. "Now the drawings you make from *us*, they look exactly like us," she reminded me, smiling in triumph; and I recognised that this was indeed just their defect. When I drew the Monarchs I could n't anyhow get away from them - get into the character I wanted to represent; and I hadn't the least desire my model should be discoverable in my picture. Miss Churm never was, and Mrs. Monarch thought I hid her, very properly, because she was vulgar; whereas if she was lost it was only as the dead who go to heaven are lost - in the gain of an angel the more.

By this time I had got a certain start with "Rutland Ramsay," the first novel in the great projected series; that is I had produced a dozen drawings, several with the help of the Major and his wife, and I had sent them in for approval. My understanding with the publishers, as I have already hinted, had been that I was to be left to do my work, in this particular case, as I liked, with the whole book committed to me; but my connexion with the rest of the series was only contingent. There were moments when, frankly, it *was* a comfort to have the real thing under one's hand; for there were characters in "Rutland Ramsay" that were very much like it. There were people presumably as erect as the Major and women of as good a fashion as Mrs. Monarch. There was a great deal of country house life - treated, it is true, in a fine fanciful ironical generalised way - and there was a considerable implication of knickerbockers[6] and kilts. There were certain things I had to settle at the outset; such things for instance as the exact appearance of the hero and the particular bloom and figure of the heroine. The author of course gave me a lead, but there was a margin for interpretation. I took the Monarchs into my confidence, I told them frankly what I was about, I mentioned my embarrassments and alternatives. "Oh take *him*!" Mrs. Monarch murmured sweetly, looking at her husband; and "What could you want better than my wife?" the Major enquired with the comfortable candour that now prevailed between us.

I was n't obliged to answer these remarks—I was only obliged to place my sitters. I was n't easy in mind, and I postponed a little timidly perhaps the solving of my question. The book was a large canvas, the other figures were numerous, and I worked off at first some of the episodes in which the hero and the heroine were not concerned. When once I had set *them* up I should have to stick to them—I could n't make my young man seven feet high in one place and five feet nine in another. I inclined on the whole to the latter measurement, though the Major more than once reminded me that *he* looked about as young as any one. It was indeed quite possible to arrange him, for the figure, so that it would have been difficult to detect his age. After the spontaneous Oronte had been with me a month, and after I had given him to understand several times over that his native exuberance would presently constitute an insurmountable barrier to our further

---

[6] 무릎에서 모여지는 바지(knickers).

intercourse, I waked to a sense of his heroic capacity. He was only five feet seven, but the remaining inches were latent. I tried him almost secretly at first, for I was really rather afraid of the judgment my other models would pass on such a choice. If they regarded Miss Churm as little better than a snare what would they think of the representation by a person so little the real thing as an Italian street-vendor of a protagonist formed by a public school?

If I went a little in fear of them it was n't because they bullied me, because they had got an oppressive foothold, but because in their really pathetic decorum and mysteriously permanent newness they counted on me so intensely. I was therefore very glad when Jack Hawley came home: he was always of such good counsel. He painted badly himself, but there was no one like him for putting his finger on the place. He had been absent from England for a year; he had been somewhere - I don't remember where - to get a fresh eye. I was in a good deal of dread of any such organ, but we were old friends; he had been away for months and a sense of emptiness was creeping into my life. I had n't dodged a missile for a year.

He came back with a fresh eye, but with the same old black velvet blouse, and the first evening he spent in my studio we smoked cigarettes till the small hours. He had done no work himself, he had only got the eye; so the field was clear for the production of my little things. He wanted to see what I had produced for the *Cheapside*, but he was disappointed in the exhibition. That at least seemed the meaning of two or three comprehensive groans which, as he lounged on my big divan, his leg folded under him, looking at my latest drawings, issued from his lips with the smoke of the cigarette.

"What's the matter with you?" I asked.

"What's the matter with *you?*"

"Nothing save that I'm mystified."

"You are indeed. You're quite off the hinge. What's the meaning of this new fad?" And he tossed me, with visible irreverence, a drawing in which I happened to have depicted both my elegant models. I asked if he did n't think it good, and he replied that it struck him as execrable, given the sort of thing I had always represented myself to him as wishing to arrive at; but I let that pass—I was so anxious to see exactly what he meant. The two figures in the picture looked colossal, but I supposed this was *not* what he meant, inasmuch as, for aught he knew to the contrary, I might have been trying for some such effect. I maintained that I was working exactly in the same way as when he last had done me the honour to tell me I might do something some day. "Well, there's a screw loose somewhere," he answered; "wait a bit and I'll discover it." I depended upon him to do so: where else was the fresh eye? But he produced at last nothing more luminous than "I don' t know—I don't like your types." This was lame for a critic who had never consented to discuss with me anything but the question of execution, the direction of strokes and the mystery of values.

"In the drawings you've been looking at I think my types are very handsome."

"Oh, they won't do!"

"I've been working with new models."

"I see you have. *They* won't do."

"Are you very sure of that?"

"Absolutely – they're stupid."

"You mean *I* am – for I ought to get around that."

"You *can't* – with such people. Who are they?"

I told him, so far as was necessary, and he concluded heartlessly: "*Ce sont des gens qu'il faut mettre a la porte.*"7)

"You've never seen them; they're awfully good" – I flew to their defence.

"Not seen them? Why all this recent work of yours drops to pieces with them. It's all I want to see of them."

"No one else has said anything against it – the *Cheapside* people are pleased."

"Every one else is an ass, and the *Cheapside* people the biggest asses of all. Come, don't pretend at this time of day to have pretty illusions about the public, especially about publishers and editors. It's not for *such* animals you work – it's for those who know, *coloro che sanno*,"8) so keep straight for *me* if you can't keep straight for yourself. There was a certain sort of thing you used to try for – and a very good thing is was. But this twaddle is n't *in* it." When I talked with Hawley later about "Rutland

---

7) 불어로 "They are people one must show to me door,"의 뜻인데, 다시 말해 'get rid of'를 뜻한다.
8) 이탈리아어로 "those who know,"의 뜻이며, 단테의『신곡』제1부 '지옥편'의 4장, 131행에서 인용함.

Ramsay" and its possible successors he declared that I must get back into my boat again or I should go to the bottom. His voice in short was the voice of warning.

I noted the warning, but I did n't turn my friends out of doors. They bored me a good deal; but the very fact that they bored me admonished me not to sacrifice them—if there was anything to be done with them—simply to irritation. As I look back at this phase they seem to me to have pervaded my life not a little. I have a vision of them as most of the time in my studio, seated against the wall on an old velvet bench to be out of the way, and resembling the while a pair of patient courtiers in a royal antechamber. I'm convinced that during the coldest weeks of the winter they held their ground because it saved them fire. Their newness was losing its gloss, and it was impossible not to feel them objects of charity. Whenever Miss Churm arrived they went away, and after I was fairly launched in "Rutland Ramsay" Miss Churm arrived pretty often. They managed to express to me tacitly that they supposed I wanted her for the low life of the book, and I let them suppose it, since they had attempted to study the work—it was lying about the studio—without discovering that it dealt only with the highest circles. They had dipped into the most brilliant of our novelists without deciphering many passages. I still took an hour from them, now and again, in spite of Jack Hawley's warning; it would be time enough to dismiss them, if dismissal should be necessary, when the rigour of the season was over. Hawley had made their acquaintance—he had met them at my fireside—and thought them a ridiculous pair. Learning that he was a painter they tried to approach him, to show him too that they were the real thing; but he looked at them, across the big room, as if they were miles away; they were a compendium of everything he most objected to in the social system of his country. Such people as that, all convention and patent-leather, with ejaculations that stopped conversation, had no business in a studio. A studio was a place to learn to see, and how could you see through a pair of feather-beds?

The main inconvenience I suffered at their hands was that at first I was shy of letting it break upon them that my artful little servant had begun to sit to me for "Rutland Ramsay." They knew I had been odd enough - they were prepared by this time to allow oddity to artist - to pick a foreign vagabond out of the streets when I might have had a person with whiskers and credentials; but it was some time before they learned how high I rated his accomplishments. They found him in an attitude more than once, but they never doubted I was doing him as an organ-grinder. There were several things they never guessed, and one of them was that for a striking scene in the novel, in which a footman briefly figured, it occurred to me to make use of Major Monarch as the menial. I kept putting this off, I did n't like to ask him to don the livery - beside the difficulty of finding a livery to fit him. At last, one day late in the winter, when I was at work on the despised Oronte, who caught one's idea on the wing, and was in the glow of feeling myself go very straight, they came in, the Major and his wife, with their society laugh about nothing (there was less and less to laugh at); came in like country-callers - they always reminded me of that - who have walked across the park after church and are presently persuaded to stay to luncheon. Luncheon was over, but they could stay to tea - I knew they wanted it. The fit was on me, however, and I could n't let my ardour cool and my work wait, with the fading daylight, while my model prepared it. So I asked Mrs. Monarch is she would mind laying it out - a request which for an instant brought all the blood to her face. Her eyes were on her husband's for a second, and some mute telegraphy passed between them. Their folly was over the next instant; his cheerful shrewdness put an end to it. So far from pitying their wounded pride, I must add, I was moved to give it as complete a lesson as I could. They bustled about together and got out the cups and saucers and made the kettle boil. I know they felt as if they were waiting on my servant, and when the tea was prepared I said: "He'll have a cup, please - he's tired." Mrs. Monarch brought him one where he stood, and he took it from her as if he had been a gentleman at a party squeezing a crush-hat with an elbow.

Then it came over me that she had made a great effort for me - made it with a kind of nobleness - and that I owed her a compensation. Each time I saw her after this I wondered what the compensation could be. I could n't go on doing the wrong thing to oblige them. Oh it *was* the wrong thing, the stamp of the work for which they sat - Hawley was not the only person to say it now. I sent in a large number of the drawings I had made for "Rutland Ramsay," and I received a warning that was more to the point than Hawley's. The artistic adviser of the house for which I was working was of opinion that many of my illustrations were not what had been looked for. Most of these illustrations were the subjects in which the Monarchs had figured. Without giving into the question of what *had* been looked for, I had to face the fact that at this rate I should n't get the other books to do. I hurled myself in despair on Miss Churm -I put her through all her paces. I not only adopted Oronte publicly as my hero, but one morning when the Major looked in to see if I did n't require him to finish a *Cheapside* figure for which he had begun to sit the week before, I told him I had changed my mind-I'd do the drawing from my man. At this my visitor turned pale and stood looking at me. "Is *he* your idea of an English gentleman ?" he asked.

I was disappointed, I was nervous, I wanted to get on with my work; so I replied with irritation: "Oh my dear Major-I can' t be ruined for *you!*"

It was a horrid speech, but he stood another moment-after which, without a word, he quitted the studio. I drew a long breath, for I said to myself that I should n't see him again. I had n't told him definitely that I was in danger of having my work rejected, but I was vexed at his not having felt the catastrophe in the air, read with me the moral of our fruitless collaboration, the lesson that in the deceptive atmosphere of art even the highest respectability may fail of being plastic.

I did n't owe my friends money, but I did see them again. They reappeared together three days later, and, given all the other facts, there was something tragic in that one. It was a clear proof they could find nothing else in life to do. They had threshed the matter out in a dismal conference-they had digested the bad news that they were not in for the series. If they were n't useful to me even for the *Cheapside* their function seemed difficult to determine, and I could only judge at first that they had come, forgivingly, decorously, to take a last leave. This made me rejoice in secret that I had little leisure for a scene; for I had placed both my other models in position together and I was pegging away at a drawing from which I hoped to derive glory. It had been suggested by the passage in which Rutland Ramsay, drawing up a chair to Artemisia's piano-stool, says extraordinary things to her while she ostensibly fingers out a difficult piece of music. I had done Miss Churm at the piano before-it was an attitude in which she knew how to take on an absolutely poetic grace. I wished the two figures to "compose" together with intensity, and my little Italian had entered perfectly into my conception. The pair were vividly before me, the piano had been pulled out; it was a charming show of blended youth and murmured love, which I had only to catch and keep. My visitors stood and looked at it, and I was friendly to them over my shoulder.

They made no response, but I was used to silent company and went on with my work, only a little disconcerted-even though exhilarated by the sense that *this* was at least the ideal thing- at not having got rid of them after all. Presently I heard Mrs. Monarch's sweet voice beside or rather above me; "I wish her hair were a little better done." I looked up and she was staring with a strange fixedness at Miss Churm, whose back was turned to her. "Do you mind my just touching it?" she went on-a question which made me spring up for an instant as with the instinctive fear that she might do the young lady a harm. But she quieted me with a glance I shall never forget-I confess I should like to have been able to paint *that*-and went for a moment to my model. She spoke to her softly, laying a hand on her shoulder and bending over her; and as the girl, understanding, gratefully assented, she disposed her rough curls, with a few quick passes, in such a way as to make Miss Churm's head twice as charming. It was one of the most heroic personal services I've ever seen rendered. Then Mrs. Monarch turned away with a low sigh and, looking about her as if for something to do, stooped to the floor with a noble humility and picked up a dirty rag that had dropped out of my paint-box.

The Major meanwhile had also been looking for something to do, and, wandering to the other end of the studio, saw before him my breakfast-things neglected, unremoved. "I say, can't I be useful here?" he called out to me with an irrepressible quaver. I assented with a laugh that I fear was awkward, and for the next ten minutes, while I worked, I hear the light clatter of china and the tinkle of spoons and glass. Mrs. Monarch assisted her husband-they washed up my crockery, they put it away. They wandered off into my little scullery, and I afterwards found that they had cleaned my knives and that my slender stock of plate had an unprecedented surface. When it came over me, the latent eloquence of what they were doing, I confess that my drawing was blurred for a moment—the picture swam. They had accepted their failure, but they could n't accept their fate. They had bowed their heads in bewilderment to the perverse and cruel law in virtue of which the real thing could be so much less precious than the unreal; but they did n't want to starve. If my servants were my models, then my models might be my servants. They would reverse the parts—the others would sit for the ladies and gentlemen and *they* would do the work. They would still be in the studio—it was an intense dumb appeal to me not to turn them out. "Take us on," they wanted to say—"we'll do *anything*."

My pencil dropped from my hand; my sitting was spoiled and I got rid of my sitters, who were also evidently rather mystified and awestruck. Then, alone with the Major and his wife I had a most uncomfortable moment. He put their prayer into a single sentence: "I say, you know—just let *us* do for you, can't you?" I could n't—it was dreadful to see them emptying my slops, but I pretended I could, to oblige them, for about a week. Then I gave them a sum of money to go away, and I never saw them again. I obtained the remaining books, but my friend Hawley repeats that Major and Mrs. Monarch did me a permanent harm, got me into false ways. If it be true I'm content to have paid the price—for the memory.

1892, 1909

The Lightening-Rod Man   —by Herman Melville

WHAT grand irregular thunder, thought I, standing on my hearth-stone among the Acroceraunian hills, as the scattered bolts boomed overhead, and crashed down among the valleys, every bolt followed by zigzag irradiations, and swift slants of sharp rain, which audibly rang, like a charge of spear-points, on my low shingled roof. I suppose, though, that the mountains hereabouts break and churn up the thunder, so that it is far more glorious here than on the plain. Hark!–some one at the door. Who is this that chooses a time of thunder for making calls? And why don't he, man-fashion, use the knocker, instead of making that doleful undertaker's clatter with his fist against the hollow panel? But let him in. Ah, here he comes. "Good day, sir:" and entire stranger. "Pray be seated." What is that strange-looking walking-sick he carries: "A fine thunder-storm, sir."

"Fine? –Awful!"

"You are wet. Stand here on the hearth before the fire."

"Not for worlds!"

The stranger still stood in the exact middle of the cottage, where he had first planted himself. His singularity impelled a closer scrutiny. A lean, gloomy figure. Hair dark and lank, mattedly streaked over his brow. His sunken pitfalls of eyes were ringed by indigo halos, and played with an innocuous sort of lighting : the gleam without the bolt. The whole man was dripping. He stood in a puddle on the bare oak floor: his strange walking-stick vertically resting at his side.

It was a polished copper rod, four feet long, lengthwise attached to a neat wooden staff, by insertion into two balls of greenish glass, ringed with copper bands. The metal rod terminated at the top tripodwise, in three keen tines, brightly gilt. He held the thing by the wooden part alone.

"Sir," said I, bowing politely, "have I the honor of a visit from that illustrious god, Jupiter Tonans? So stood he in the Greek statue of old, grasping the lightning-bolt. If you be he, or his viceroy, I have to thank you for this noble storm you have brewed among our mountains.

Listen: That was a glorious peal. Ah, to a lover of the majestic, it is a good thing to have the Thunderer himself in one's cottage. The thunder grows finer for that. But pray be seated. This old rush-bottomed arm-chair, I grant, is a poor substitute for your evergreen throne on Olympus: but, condescend to be seated."

While I thus pleasantly spoke, the stranger eyed me, half in wonder, and half in a strange sort of horror: but did not move a foot.

"Do, sir, be seated, you need to be dried ere going forth again."

I planted the chair invitingly on the broad hearth, where a little fire had been kindled that afternoon to dissipate the dampness, not the cold; for it was early in the month of September.

But without heeding my solicitation, and still standing in the middle of the floor, the stranger gazed at me portentously and spoke.

"Sir," said he, "excuse me; but instead of my accepting your invitation to be seated on the hearth there, I solemnly warn you, that you had best accept *mine*, and stand with me in the middle of the room. Good heavens!" he cried, starting—"there is another of those awful crashes. I warn you, sir, quit the hearth."

"Mr. Jupiter Tonans," said I, quietly rolling my body on the stone, "I stand very well here."

"Are you so horridly ignorant, then," he cried, "as not to know, that by far the most dangerous part of a house, during such a terrific tempest as this, is the fire-place?"

"Nay, I did not know that," involuntarily stepping upon the first board next to the stone.

The stranger now assumed such an unpleasant air of successful admonition, that—quite involuntarily again—I stepped back upon the hearth, and threw myself into the erectest, proudest posture I could command. But I said nothing.

"For Heavens' sake," he cried, with a strange mixture of alarm and intimidation—"for Heavens's sake, get off the hearth! Know you not, that the heated air and soot are conductors;—to say nothing of those immense iron fire-dogs? Quit the spot—I conjure —I command you."

"Mr. Jupiter Tonans, I am not accustomed to be commanded in my own house."

"Call me not by that pagan name. You are profane in this time of terror."

"Sir, will you be so good as to tell me your business? If you seek shelter form the storm, you are welcome, so long as you be civil; but if you come on business, open it forthwith. "Who are you?"

"I am a dealer in lightning-rods," said the stranger, softening his tone; "my special business is – Merciful heaven! what a crash! – Have you ever been struck – your premises, I mean? No? It's best to be provided;" – significantly rattling his metallic staff on the floor; – "by nature, there are no castles in thunder-storms; yet, say but the word, and of this cottage I can make a Gibraltar by a few waves of this wand. Hark, what Himalayas of concussions!"

"You interrupted yourself; your special business you were about to speak of."

"My special business is to travel the country for orders for lightning-rods. This is my specimen-rod." tapping his staff; "I have the best of references" – fumbling in his pockets. "In Criggan last month, I put up three-and-twenty rods on only five building."

"Let me see. Was it not at Criggan last week, about midnight on Saturday, that the steeple, the big elm, and the assembly-room cupola were struck? Any of your rods there?"

"Not on the tree and cupola, but the steeple."

"Of what use is your rod, then?"

"Of life-and-death use. But my workman was heedless. In fitting the rod at top to the steeple, he allowed a part of the metal to graze the tin sheeting. Hence the accident. Not my fault, but his. Hark!"

"Never mind. That clap burst quite loud enough to be heard without finger-pointing. Did you hear of the event at Montreal last year? A servant girl struck at her bed-side with a rosary in her hand; the beads being metal. Does your beat extend into the Canadas?"

"No. And I hear that there, iron rods only are in use. They should have *mine*, which are copper. Iron is easily fused. Then they draw out the rod so slender, that it has not body enough to conduct the full electric current. The metal melts; the building is destroyed. My copper rods never act so. Those Canadians are fools. Some of them knob the rod at the top, which risks a deadly explosion, instead of imperceptibly carrying down the current into the earth, as this sort of rod does. *Mine* is the only true rod. Look at it. Only one dollar a foot."

"This abuse of your own calling in another might make one distrustful with respect to yourself."

"Hark! The thunder becomes less muttering. It is nearing us, and nearing the earth, too. Hark! One crammed crash! All the vibrations made one by nearness. Another flash. Hold!"

"What do you?" I said, seeing him now, instantaneously relinquishing his staff, lean intently forward towards the window, with his right fore and middle fingers on his left wrist.

But ere the words had well escaped me, another exclamation escaped him.

"Crash! only three pulses—less than a third of a mile off—yonder, somewhere in that wood. I passed three stricken oaks there, ripped out new and glittering. The oak draws lightning more than other timber, having iron in solution in its sap. Your floor here seems oak."

"Heart-of-oak. From the peculiar time of your call upon me, I suppose you purposely select stormy weather for your journeys. When the thunder is roaring, you deem it an hour peculiarly favorable for producing impressions favor able to your trade."

"Hark! – Awful!"

"For one who would arm others with fearlessness, you seem unbeseemingly timorous yourself. Common men choose fair weather for their travels: you choose thunderstorms; and yet – "

"That I travel in thunder-storms, I grant; but not without particular precautions, such as only a lightning-rod man may know. Hark! Quick – look at my specimen rod. Only one dollar a foot."

"A very fine rod, I dare say. But what are these particular precautions of yours? Yet first let me close yonder shutters; the slanting rain is beating through the sash. I will bar up."

"Are you mad? Know you not that yon iron bar is a swift conductor? Desist."

"I will simply close the shutters, then, and call my boy to bring me a wooden bar. Pray, touch the bell-pull there."

"Are you frantic? That bell-wire might blast you. Never touch bell-wire in a thunder-storm, nor ring a bell of any sort."

"Nor those in belfries? Pray, will you tell me where and how one may be safe in a time like this? Is there any part of my house I may touch with hopes of my life?"

"There is; but not where you now stand. Come away from the wall. The current will sometimes run down a wall, and – a man being a better conductor than a wall – it would leave the wall and run into him. Swoop! That must have fallen very nigh. That must have been globular lightening."

"Very probably. Tell me at one, which is, in your opinion, the safest part of this house?"

"This room, and this one spot in it where I stand. Come hither."

"The reasons first."

"Hark!–after the flash the gust–the sashes shiver–the house, the house!–Come hither to me!"

"The reasons, if you please."

"Come hither to me!"

"Thank you again, I think I will try my old stand–the hearth. And now, Mr. Lightning-rod man, in the pauses of the thunder, be so good as to tell me your reasons for esteeming this one room of the house the safest, and your own one stand-point there the safest spot in it."

There was now a little cessation of the storm for a while. The Lightning-rod man seemed relieved, and replied:–

"Your house is a one-storied house, with an attic and a cellar; this room is between. Hence its comparative safety. Because lightning sometimes passes from the clouds to the earth, and sometimes form the earth to the clouds. Do you comprehend?–and I choose the middle of the room, because, if the lightning should strike the house at all, it would come down the chimney or walls; so, obviously, the further you are from them, the better. Come hither to me, now."

"Presently. Something you just said, instead of alarming me, has strangely inspired confidence."

"What have I said?"

"You said that sometimes lightning flashes from the earth to the clouds."

"Aye, the returning-stroke, as it is called; when the earth, being overcharged with the fluid, flashes its surplus upward."

"The returning-stroke; that is, from earth to sky. Better and better. But come here on the hearth and dry yourself."

"I am better here, and better wet."

"How?"

"It is the safest thing you can do – Hark, again! – to get yourself thoroughly drenched in a thunder-storm. Wet clothes are better conductors than the body; and so, if the lightning strike, it might pass down the wet clothes without touching the body. The storm deepens again. Have you a rug in the houses? Rugs are non-conductors. Get one, that I may stand on it here, and you, too. The skies blacken – it is dusk at noon. Hark! – the rug, the rug!"

I gave him one; while the hooded mountains seemed closing and tumbling into the cottage.

"And now, since our being dumb will not help us," said I, resuming my place, "let me hear you precautions in traveling during thunder-storms."

"Wait till this one is passed."

"Nay, proceed with the precautions. You stand in the safest possible place according to your own account. Go on."

"Briefly, then. I avoid pine-trees, high houses, lonely barns, upland pastures, running water, flocks of cattle and sheep, a crowd of men. If I travel on foot – as to-day – I do not walk fast;

if in my buggy, I touch not its back or sides; if on horseback, I dismount and lead the horse. But of all things, I avoid tall men."

"Do I dream? Man avoid man? and in danger-time, too."

"Tall men in a thunder-storm I avoid. Are you so grossly ignorant as not to know, that the height of a six-footer is sufficient to discharge an electric cloud upon him? Are not lonely Kentuckians, ploughing, smit in the unfinished furrow? Nay, if the six-footer stand by running water, the cloud will sometimes *select* him as its conductor to that running water. Hark! Sure, yon black pinnacle is split. Yes, a man is a good conductor. The lightning goes through and through a man, but only peels a tree. But sir, you have kept me so long answering your questions, that I have not yet come to business. Will you order one of my rods? Look at this specimen one? See: it is of the best of copper. Copper's the best conductor. Your house is low; but being upon the mountains, that lowness does not one whit depress it. You mountaineers are most exposed. In mountainous countries the lightning-rod man should have most business. Look at the specimen, sir. One rod will answer for a house so small as this. Look over these recommendations. Only one rod, sir; cost, only twenty dollars. Hark! There go all the granite Taconics and Hoosics dashed together like pebbles. By the sound, that must have struck something. An elevation of five feet above the house, will protect twenty feet radius all about the rod. Only twenty dollars, sir - a dollar a foot. Hark! - Dreadful! - Will you order? Will you buy? Shall I put down your name? Think of being a heap of charred offal, like a haltered horse burnt in his stall; and all in one flash!"

"You pretended envoy extraordinary and minister plenipotentiary to and from Jupiter Tonans," laughed I; "you mere man who come here to put you and your pipestem between clay and sky, do you think that because you can strike a bit of green light from the Leyden jar, that you can thoroughly avert the supernal bolt? Your rod rusts, or breaks, and where are you? Who has empowered you, you Tetzel, to peddle round your indulgences from divine ordinations? The hairs of our heads are numbered, and the days of our lives. In thunder as in sunshine, I stand at ease in the hands of my God. False negotiator, away! See, the scroll of the storm is rolled back; the house is unharmed; and in the blue heavens I read in the rainbow, that the Diety will not, of purpose, make war on man's earth."

"Impious wretch!" foamed the stranger, blackening in the face as the rainbow beamed, "I will publish your infidel notions."

The scowl grew blacker on his face; the indigo-circles enlarged round his eyes as the storm-rings round the mid-night moon. He sprang upon me; his tri-forked thing at my heart.

I seized it; I snapped it; I dashed it; I trod it; and dragging the dark lightning-king out of my door, flung his elbowed, copper sceptre after him.

But spite of my treatment, and spite of my dissuasive talk of him to my neighbors, the Lightning-rod man still dwells in the land; still travels in storm-time, and drives a brave trade with the fears of man.

현대 영미 에세이

What Statesmen Must Know —by Oswald Spengler

Oswald Spengler(1880-1936) was born in Blankenburg, Germany, of a fairly wealthy family. He attended the Gymnasium in Halle, and majored in mathematics and philosophy at the universities of Halle, Munich, and Berlin. After receiving his Ph.D. he taught for a time, but retired in 1911 to read and write. He finished the first draft of his two-volume interpretation of history, *The Decline of the West*, in 1914, and carried it with him on army duty, publishing the first volume in 1918. The second volume was published in 1922, filling out his thesis that under cover of a superficial Western political philosophy a new Dark Age was stirring, that the power-state of Caesarism would supersede the democracies, and that the sword would ultimately triumph. After the rise of Hitler, Spengler took an active interest in politics, while the expanding Nazi party found his work an invaluable guide in formulating its program. However, Spengler did not look with great favor on naziism, differing sharply with party policy on its race theories, despite *the ironic fact that his own concepts of "fact-race theories, despite the ironic fact that his own concepts of "fact-men" and truth and power-politics provided leaves for the Nazi book. He was finally denounced and killed in the thirties.*

How is politics done? The born statesman is above all a valuer – a valuer of men, situations, and things. He has the "eye" which unhesitatingly and inflexibly embraces the round of possibilities, as the judge of horses takes in an animal with one glance and knows what prospects it will have in a race. To do the correct thing without knowing it, to have the hands that imperceptibly tighten or ease the bit – this talent is the very opposite to that of the man of theory.

There are born destiny-men and causality-men. A whole world separates them. The purely living man is peasant and warrior, statesman and general, man of the world and man of business, everyone who wills to prosper, to rule, to fight, and to dare, the organizer or entrepreneur, the adventurer or bravo or gambler. Opposed is the man who is destined either by the power of his mind or the defect of his blood to be an "intellectual" – the saint, priest, savant, idealist, or ideologue.

Even the foot-fall of the fact-man sounds different from, sounds more planted than, that of the thinker, in whom the pure microcosmic can acquire no firm relation with earth.

Destiny has made the man so or so – subtle and fact-shy, or active and contemptuous of thought. The man of the active category is a whole man. Whereas in the contemplative man a single organ can operate without (and even against) the body. All the worse, then, when this organ tries to master actuality as well as its own world. For then we get all those ethico-politico-social reform-projects which demonstrate, unanswerably, how things ought to be and how to set about making them so – theories that, without exception, rest on the hypothesis that all men are as rich in ideas and as poor in motives as the author is (or thinks he is). Such theories, even when they have taken the field armed with the full authority of a religion or the prestige of a famous name, have not in one single instance effected the slightest alteration in life. They have merely caused us to think otherwise than before about life.

And this, precisely, is the doom of the "late" ages of a culture, the ages of much writing and much reading. They perpetually confuse the opposition of life and thought with the opposition between thought-about-life and thought-about-thought. All world-improvers, priests, and philosophers are unanimous in holding that life is a fit object for the nicest meditation; but the life of the world goes its own way and cares not in the least what is said about it. And even when a community succeeds in living "according to rule," all that it achieves is, at best, a note on itself in some future history of the world – if there is space left after the proper and only important subject-matter has been dealt with.

For, in the last resort, only the active man, the man of destiny, lives in the actual world of political, military, and economic decisions – in which concepts and systems do not figure or count.

Here a shrewd conclusion. And there is sense in the contempt with which statesmen and soldiers of all times have regarded the "ink-slinger" and the "bookworm," who think that world-history exists for the sake of the intellect or science or even art.

Men of theory commit a huge mistake in believing that their place is at the head of and not in the train of great events. They misunderstand completely the role played, for example, by the political Sophists in Athens, or by Voltaire and Rousseau in doing, but that does not prevent him from following with confidence just the one path that leads to success. The political doctrinaire, on the contrary, always knows what should be done, and yet his activity, once it ceases to be limited to paper, is the least successful and therefore the least valuable in history. These intrusions happen only too frequently in times of uncertainty, like that of the Attic enlightenment, or the French or the German revolutions, when the ideologue of word or pen is eager to be busy with the actual history of the people instead of with systems. He mistakes his place. He belongs with his principles and programs to no history but the history of a literature. Real history passes judgment on him not by controverting the theorist, but by leaving him and all his thoughts to himself.

A Plato or a Rousseau – not to mention the smaller intellects – could build up abstract political structures, but for Alexander, Scipio, Caesar, and Napoleon, with their schemes and battles and settlements, they were entirely without importance. The thinker could discuss destiny if he liked; it was enough for these men to be destiny.

The fact-man is immune from the risk of practising sentimental or program politics. He does not believe in the big words. Pilate's question is constantly on his lips – truths? The born statesman stands beyond true and false. He does not confuse the logic of events with the logic of systems. "Truths" or "errors" – which here amount to the same – only concern him as intellectual currents, and in respect to workings. He surveys their potency, durability, and direction, and duly books them in his calculations for the destiny of the power that he directs.

He has convictions, certainly, that are dear to him. But he has them as a private person; no real politician ever felt himself tied to them when in action. "The doer is always conscienceless; no one has a conscience except the spectator," said Goethe. It is equally true of Sulla and Robespierre as it is of Bismarck and Pitt.

The great Popes and the English party-leaders, so long as they had still to strive for the mastery of things, acted on the same principles as the conquerors and upstarts of all ages. Take the dealings of Innocent III, who very nearly succeeded in creating a world-dominion of the Church, and deduce therefrom the catechism of success; it will be found in the extremest contradiction with all religious moral. Yet without it there could have been no bearable existence for any Church, not to mention the English Colonies, American fortunes, victorious revolutions, or, for that matter, states or parties or peoples in general. It is life, not the individual, that is conscienceless.

The essential, therefore, is to understand the time for which one is born. He who does not sense and understand its most secret forces-who does not feel in himself something cognate that drives him forward on a path neither hedged nor defined by concepts-who believes in the surface, public opinion, large phrases and ideals of the day-he is not of the stature for its events. He is in their power, not they in his.

Look not back to the past for measuring-rods. Still less sideways for some system or other! There are times, like our own present and the Gracchan age, in which there are two most deadly kinds of idealism, the reactionary and the democratic. The one believes in the reversibility of history, the other in a teleology of history. It makes no difference, to the inevitable failure with which both burden a nation over whose destiny they have power, whether it is to a memory or to a concept that they sacrifice it.

The genuine statesman is incarnate history, its directedness expressed as individual will and its organic logic as character. The true statesman must be, in a large sense of the word, an educator-not the representative of a moral or a doctrine, but an exemplar in doing.

It is a patent fact that a religion never yet altered the style of an existence. It penetrated the waking-consciousness, the intellectual man; it threw new light on another world; it created an immense happiness by way of humanity, resignation, and patience unto death. But over the forces of life it possessed no power. In the sphere of the living only the great personality-the "it," the race, the cosmic force bound up in that personality-has been creative. Only this has effectively modified the type of entire classes and peoples.

It is not "the" truth or "the" good or "the" upright; but "the" Roman or "the" Puritan or "the" Prussian, that is a fact. The sum of honour and duty, discipline, resolution, is a thing not learned from books, but awakened in the stream of being by a living exemplar, That is why Frederick William I was one of those educators, great for all time, whose personal race-forming conduct does not vanish in the course of the generations.

The genuine statesman is distinguished from the "mere politician" - the player who plays for the pleasure of the game, the arriviste on the heights of history, the seeker after wealth and rank - as also from the schoolmaster of an ideal, by one fact: He dares to demand sacrifices - and obtains them, because his feeling that he is necessary to the time and the nation is shared by thousands; transforms them to the core; and renders them capable of deeds to which otherwise they could never have risen.

Highest of all, is not action, but the ability to command. It is this that takes the individual up out of himself and makes him the centre of a world of action.

There is one kind of commanding that makes obedience a proud, free, and noble habit. That kind Napoleon, for example, did not possess. A residue of subaltern outlook in him prevented him from training men to be men and not bureau-personnel, and led him to govern through edicts instead of through personalities. As he did not understand this subtlest act of command, and therefore was obliged to do everything really decisive himself, he slowly collapsed from inability to reconcile the demands of his position with the limit of human capacities.

But one who, like Caesar or Frederick the Great, possesses this last and highest gift of complete humanity, feels-on a battle-evening when operations are sweeping to a willed conclusion, and the victory is turning out to be conclusive of the campaign; or when the last signature is written that rounds off a historical epoch-a wondrous sense of power that the man of truths can never know. There are moments-and they indicate the maxima of cosmic flowings-when the individual feels himself to be identical with Destiny, the centre of the world. And his own personality seems to him almost as a covering in which the history of the future is about to clothe itself.

The first problem is to make oneself somebody. The second-less obvious, but harder and greater in its ultimate effects-is to create a traditional to bring on others so that one's work may be continued with one's own pulse and spirit; to release a current of like activity that does not need the original leader to maintain it in form.

And here the statesman rises to something that in the Classical world would doubtless have been called divinity. He becomes the creator of a new life, the spirit-ancestor of a young race. He himself, as a unit, vanishes from the stream after a few years. But a minority called into being by him takes up his course and maintains it indefinitely. This cosmic something, this soul of a ruling stratum, an individual can generate and leave as a heritage, and throughout history it is this that has produced the durable effects.

The great statesman is rare. Whether he comes, or wins through, too soon or too late, incident determines. Great individuals often destroy more than they have built up-by the gap that their death makes in the flow of happening. But the creation of tradition means the elimination of the incident.

A tradition breeds a high average, with which the future can reckon-no Caesar, but a Senate; no Napoleon, but an incomparable officer-corps. A strong tradition attracts talents from all quarters, and out of small gifts produces great results. The schools of painting of Italy and Holland are proof of this, no less than the Prussian army and the diplomacy of the Roman Curia.

It was the great flaw in Bismarck, as compared with Frederick William I, that he could achieve, but could not form, a tradition. He did not parallel Moltke's officer-corps by a corresponding race of politicians who would identify themselves in feeling with his State and its new tasks; who would constantly take up good men from below, and so provide for the continuance of the Bismarckian action-pulse forever.

If this creation of a tradition does not come off, then instead of a homogeneous ruling stratum we have a congeries of heads that are helpless when confronted by the unforeseen. If it does, we have a Sovereign People in the one sense of the phrase worthy of a people and possible in the world of fact-a highly trained, self-replenishing minority with sure and ripened traditions; a minority which attracts every talent into the charmed circle and uses it to the full, and *ipso facto* keeps itself in harmony with the remainder of the nation that it rules.

Such a minority slowly develops into a true "breed," even when it had begun merely as a party. And the sureness of its decisions comes to be that of blood, not of reason. This means that what happens in it happens "of itself" and does not need the Genius. *Great politics,* so to put it, *takes the placed of the great politician.*

What, then, *is* politics? It is the art of the possible – an old saying, and almost an all-inclusive saying. The gardener can obtain a plant from the seed, or he can improve its stock. He can bring to bloom, or let languish, the dispositions hidden in it, its growths and colour, its flower and fruit. On his eye for possibilities – and, therefore, necessities – depends its fulfillment, its strength, its whole Destiny. But the basic form and direction of its being, the stages and tempo and direction thereof, are *not* in his power. It must accomplish them or it decays.

The same is true of the immense plant that we call a "Culture," and the being-streams of human families that are bound up in its form-world. The great statesman in the gardener of a people.

Every doer is born in a time and for a time, and thereby the ambit of *his* attainable achievement is fixed. For his grandfather, for his grandson, the data, and therefore the task and the object, are not the same. The circle is further narrowed by the limits of his personality, the properties of his people, the situation and the men with who, he has to work. It is the hall-mark of the high politician that he is rarely caught out in a misappreciation of this limit, and equally rarely overlooks anything realizable within it.

With this goes a sure discrimination between what "ought" to be and what *will* be. The basic forms of the state and of political life, the direction and degree of their evolution, are give values unalterably dependent on the given time. They are the track of political success, and not its goal.

The worshippers of political ideals create out of nothing. Their intellectual freedom is astounding, but their castles of the mind, built of airy concepts like wisdom and righteousness, liberty and equality, are in the end all the same; they are built from the top storey downwards. The master of fact, for his part, is content to direct imperceptibly that which he sees and accepts as plain reality. This does not seem very much, yet it is the very starting point of freedom, in a grand sense of the word.

The art of the statesman consists not only in a clear idea of the main lines drawn undeviably before him, but also in the sure handling of the single occurrences and the single persons, encountered along those lines, which can turn an impending disaster into a decisive success. An adept in the game can, like Talleyrand, go to Vienna as ambassador of the vanquished party and make himself master of the victor. At the Lucca meeting, Caesar, whose position was well nigh desperate, not only made Pompey's power serviceable to his own ends, but undermined in at the same time, and without his opponent's becoming aware of the fact.

A revolution that reaches explosion-point is always a proof of the lack of the political pulse in the governors *and* in their opponents. The necessary must be done *opportunely*- namely, while it is a present wherewith the governing power can buy confidence in itself. If it has to be conceded as a sacrifice, it discloses a weakness and excites contempt. Political forms are living forms whose changes inexorably follow a definite direction. To attempt to prevent this course or to divert it towards some ideal is to confess oneself "out of condition." The Roman nobility possessed this congruence of pulse, the Spartan did not. In the period of mounting democracy we find again and again (as in France in 1789 and Germany before 1918) the arrival of a fatal moment when it is too late for the necessary reform to be given as a free gift. *Then* that which should be refused with the sternest energy is given as a *sacrifice*, and so becomes the sign of dissolution. But those who fail to detect the first necessity in good time will all the more certainly fail to misunderstand the second situation. Even a journey to Canossa can be made too soon or too late-the timing may settle the future of whole peoples, whether they shall be Destiny for others, or themselves the objects or another's Destiny.

The declining democracy also repeats the same error of trying to hold what was the ideal of yesterday. This is the danger of our twentieth century. On the path towards Caesarism there is ever a Cato to be found.

The influence that a statesman-ever one in an exceptionally strong position-possesses over the methods of politics is very small, and it is one of the characteristics of the high-grade statesman that he does not deceive himself on this matter. His task is to work in and with the historical form that he finds in existence. Is is only the theorist who enthusiastically searches for more ideal forms.

But to be politically "in form" means necessarily, amongst other things, an unconditional command of the most modern means. There is no choice about it. The means and methods are premises pertaining to the time and belong to the inner form of the time. One who grasps at the inapposite, who permits his taste or his feelings to overpower the pulse in him, loses at once his grip of realities.

The danger of an aristocracy is that of being conservative in its means; the danger of democracy is the confusion of formula and form. The means of the present are, and will be for many years, parliamentary-elections and the press. He may think what he pleases about them, he may respect them or despise them, but he must command them-as Bach and Mozart commanded the musical means of their times. This is the hall-mark of mastery in any and every field. And statecraft is no exception.

Now, the publicly visible outer form thereof is not the essential but merely the disguise. It may be altered, rationalized, and brought down to constitutional texts-without its actualities being necessarily affected in the slightest. The ambitions of all revolutionaries expend themselves in playing the game of rights, principles, and franchises on the surface of history. But the statesman knows that the extension of a franchise is quite unimportant in comparison with the technique-Athenian or Roman, Jacobin or American or German-of operating the votes. How the English constitution reads is a matter of small import, compared with the fact that it is managed by a small stratum of high families - so that an Edward Ⅶ is simply a minister of his Ministry. As for the modern Press, the sentimentalist may beam with contentment when it is constitutionally "free" - but the realist merely asks at whose disposal it is.

Politics, lastly, is the form in which is accomplished the history of a nation within a plurality of nations.

The great art is to maintain one's own nation inwardly "inform" for events outside. This is the natural relation of home and foreign politics - holding not only for People and States and Estates, but for living units of every kind, down to the simplest animal swarms and into the individual bodies. As between the two, the first exists exclusively for the second, and not vie versa. The true democrat is accustomed to treat home politics as an end in itself; the rank and file of diplomats think solely of foreign affairs; just because of this, the individual successes of either "cut no ice."

No doubt, the political master exhibits his powers most obviously in the tactics of home reform; in his economic and social activities; in his cleverness in maintaining the "rights and liberties" in tune with the tastes of the period and at the same time effective; and in the education of those feelings without which it is impossible for a people to be "in condition" - namely, trust, respect for the leadership, consciousness of power, contentment, and (when necessary) enthusiasm.

But the value of all this depends upon its relation to this basic fact of higher history - a people is not alone in the world, and its future will be decided by its force-relationships towards other peoples and powers and not by its mere internal ordering. And, since the ordinary man is not so long-sighted, it is the ruling minority that must possess this quality on behalf of the rest. Not unless there is such a minority does the statesman find the instrument wherewith he can carry his purposes into effect.

The social Responsibilities of Scientists
— by Bertrand Russell

Bertrand Russell (1872–) was born at Trelleck, Monmouthshire, England, and educated at Cambridge, where he remained for a rime as Fellow and Lecturer in Mathematical Logic. He has since taught at Harvard, the University of Chicago, and the University of California, in addition to continuing his post at Cambridge. Accounted by many as one of the world's foremost living philosophers, Russell has written about everything from mathematics, manners and morals, and religion, to politics, economics, and education. He is perhaps best known for Principia Mathematica (1910), which he wrote with Alfred North Whitehead, Mysticism and Logic (1918), The ABC of Relativity (1925), and The History of Western Philosophy (1945). He was awarded a Nobel Prize for literature in 1950. A rebellious spirit, who likes to provoke discussion, Russell recently led protest movements in England against atomic weapons and has been sentenced to jail more than once during his long career as a crusader and reformer.

Science, ever since it first existed, has had important effects in matters that lie outside the purview of pure science. Men of science have differed as to their responsibility for such effects. Some have said that the function of the scientist in society is to supply knowledge, and that he need not concern himself with the use to which this knowledge is put.

I do not think that this view is tenable, especially in our age. The scientist is also a citizen; and citizens who have any special skill is utilized in accordance with the public interest.

Historically, the functions of the scientist in public life have generally been recognized. The Royal Society was founded by Charles II as an antidote to "fanaticism" which had plunged England into a long period of civil strife. The scientists of that time did not hesitate to speak out on public issues, such as religious toleration and the folly of prosecutions for witchcraft.

But although science has, in various ways at various times, favored what may be called a humanitarian outlook, it has from the first had an intimate and sinister connection with war. Archimedes sold his skill to the Tyrant of Syracuse for use against the Romans; Leonardo secured a salary from Duke of Milan for his sill in the art of fortification; and Galileo got employment under the Grand Duke of Tuscan because he could calculate the trajectories of projectiles. In the French Revolution the scientist who were not guillotined were set to making new explosives, but Lavoisier was not spared, because he was only discovering hydrogen which, in those days, was not a weapon of war.

There have been some honorable exceptions to the subservience of scientists to warmongers. During the Crimean War the British Government consulted Faraday as to the feasibility of attack by poisonous gases. Faraday replied that it was entirely feasible, but that it was entirely feasible, but that it was inhuman and he would have nothing to do with it.

Modern democracy and modern methods of publicity have made the problem of affection public opinion quite different from what it used to be. The knowledge that the public possesses on any important issue is derived from vast and powerful organizations; the press, radio, and above all, television.

The knowledge that governments possess is more limited. They are too busy to search out the facts for themselves, and consequently they know only what their underlings thick good for them unless there is such a powerful movement in a different sense that politicians cannot ignore it. Facts which ought to guide the decisions of statesmen-for instance, as to the possible lethal qualities of fallout-do not acquire their due importance if they remain buried in scientific journals. They acquire their due importance only when become known to so many voters that they affect the course of the elections.

In general, there is an opposition to widespread publicity for such fact. This opposition springs from various sources, some sinister, some comparatively respectable. At the bottom of the moral scale there is the financial interest of the various industries connected with armaments. Then there are various effects of a somewhat thoughtless patriotism which believes in secrecy and in what is called "toughness."

But perhaps more important than either of these is the unpleasantness of the facts, which makes the general public turn aside to pleasanter topics such as divorce and murders. The consequence is that what ought to be known widely throughout the general public will not be known unless great efforts are made by disinterested persons to see that the information reaches the minds and hearts of vast numbers of people.

I do not think this work can be successfully accomplished except by the help of men of science. They, alone, can speak with the authority that is necessary to combat the misleading statements of those scientists who have permitted themselves to become merchants of death. If disinterested scientists do not speak out, the others will succeed in conveying a distorted impression, not only to the public but also to the politicians.

It must be admitted that there are obstacles to individual action in our age which did not exist at earlier times. Galileo could make his own telescope. But one when I was talking with a very famous astronomer he explained that the telescope upon which his work depended owed its existence to the benefactions of enormously rich men, and , if he had not stood well with them, his astronomical discoveries would have been impossible.

More frequently, a scientist only acquires access to enormously expensive equipment if he stands well with the government of his country. He knows that if he adopts a rebellious attitude he and his family are likely to perish along with the rest of civilized mankind. It is a tragic dilemma, and I do not think that one should censure a man whatever his decision; but I do think – and I think men of science should realize – that unless something rather drastic is done under the leadership or through the inspiration of some part of the scientific world, the human race, like the Gadarene swine, will rush down a steep place to destruction in blind ignorance of the fate that scientific skill has prepared for it.

It is impossible in the modern world for a man of science to say with any honesty, "My business is to provide knowledge, and what use is made of the knowledge is not my responsibility." The knowledge that a man of science, or even a large body of men of science, can altogether prevent this but they can diminish the magnitude of the evil.

There is another direction in which men of science can attempt to provide leadership. They can suggest and urge in many ways the value of those branches of science of which the important practical uses are beneficial and not harmful. Consider what might be done if the money at present spent on armaments were spent on increasing and distributing the food supply of the world and diminishing the population pressure. In a few decades, poverty and malnutrition, which now afflict more than half the population of the globe, could be ended.

But at present almost all the governments of great states consider that it is better to spend money on killing foreigners than on keeping their own subjects alive. Possibilities of a hopeful sort in whatever field can best be worked out and stated authoritatively by men of science; and, since they can do this work better than others, it is part of their duty to do it.

As the world becomes mere technically unified, life in an ivory tower becomes increasingly impossible. Not only so; the man who stands out against the powerful organizations which control most of human activity is apt to find himself no longer in the ivory tower, with a wide outlook over a sunny landscape, but the dark and subterranean dungeon upon which the ivory tower was erected. To risk such a habitation demands courage. It will not be necessary to inhabit the dungeon if there are many who are willing to risk it, for everybody knows that the modern world depends upon scientists, and, if they are insistent, they must be listened to. We have it in our power to make a good world ; and, therefore, with whatever labor and risk, we must make it.

Six Typical Americans

—by Alistair Cooke

(Alfred) Alistair Cooke(1908–   ) was born in Manchester, England, educated at Cambridge, and also attended Yale and Harvard. In 1938 he was appointed commentator on American affairs for the British Broadcasting Corporation, and in 1948 also became chief United States correspondent for the Manchester Guardian, thereby serving as a cultural and reporterial middleman between the two great English-speaking civilizations. Since 1946 he has been a familiar figure in both British and American radio and television, both in dramatic roles and as matter of ceremonies. His essays and talks on current affairs have been collected in several books, nearby A Generation on Trial (1950), and One Man's America (1952). A disciple of H. L. Mencken, he edited The Vintage Mencken in 1955.

Before I left to go off on a trip around this continent an old friend turned up in New York. He is a metallurgist, from Cambridge (England), and he was making his first visit to the United States. I had not seen him in sixteen or seventeen years. Back in those days my own interest in metals was not exactly raging, but this man had been, in the brisk days of our youth, the treasure of a college dramatic society I had something do to with. He is still the treasurer. You might think that that is a slender thread by which to hold a friendship. But having become a reporter since I last saw him, I had cone to be interested in lots of things that would have bored me stiff twenty years ago. It is one of the rewards of a reporter's life that he is always meeting people who are experts in fascinating things he never knew existed. I have become, down the years, interested in metals, especially light metals, And so at our first reunion in seventeen years we had the odd and refreshing experience of two old friends talking madly about the only thing that in the interest of friendship was always politely ignored.

Then we parted. He to go off on a round of factories-Buffalo, Toledo, Pittsburgh, looking for the English equivalents of his specialty ; I to take a train south and look for no equivalents. It is necessary for reporters to do this everywhere, lest they get too confident about the nation and the people they are reporting. It is essential in the United States, where the mere size of the country encourages you for your self-respect to think of the other regions of the country in terms of what we call types: the typical Southerner, the typical Californian the typical steelworker, New Englander, and so on. but it is not a reporter's job to tell you what are the correct generalizations. It is to report what he sees, and if it doesn't fit into generalizations no harm is done. And the great good that you reap from going thousands of miles to discover the typical American is that you don't find him. You simply marvel again, as you do on any other continent, at the variety and richness of God's creatures. For America is not a bigger Britain. It is a bigger Europe.

So what I am going to do is to tell you briefly about six Americans I met on the road. The only thing they have in common is that they are Americans and that they came my way. But they are all typical. And I shall leave it to you to write the moral, if any.

And who were these fascinating creatures? The first I met when I went abroad a train in Richmond, Virginia, for the trip to New Orleans. I looked quickly around the car, or carriage, to pick out somebody who might be fun to talk to. First thing I saw was a clergyman. The seat by his side was empty. So I plumped down. He was, I should think, in his late thirties or early forties. He had a soft, pale face, with steely-blue eyes, and many wrinkles around them. He was a placid urban type. I figured, and when he spoke, and there was no Southern accent, I knew him for a Midwesterner. I thought to myself, he runs a church in a fashionable suburb of Cleveland or Cincinnati. Well, he came from Pittsburgh. And he was a priest. I might have known that from his collar in reverse, for there are about sixty denominations in the United States that dress like you and me. The chances are that a reverse collar means a priest. this man had been visiting his parents in Pittsburgh for the first time in four years. He was going back "hone," as he said. And where was home? Home was in the extreme south of Arizona, in the middle of the desert and the wilderness. He was a missionary priest on the reservation of the Papago Indians near Ajo. He lived, as they did, in a mud ut braced with cactus ribs and ministered—as priest, doctor, builder, sports coach—to several hundred Indians. there are about seven thousand Indians on this reservation, but it is a big one, running north from the Mexican border for about a hundred miles. He worked in one of the parent villages and was far from any other white man. He nursed then and in many ways helped them make the best of a poor life, sustained mostly by growing beans (Papago means "the bean people") in a barren land to which the hardier whites-had forced them. His pale face came not from a fashionable suburb but from always going covered in the blazing sun. The wrinkles around his eyes also. Before we settled in for the night, he reached in his pocket and took out a little pack. "Gum?" he said.

 The next two were a boy and a girl. A soldier and a girl. We stood in the hot dry night air at one in the morning, waiting for a train at an Arizona station. nothing but the purple arc of shy and at the end of the platform the silhouette of a cottonwood tree lapped by a hot breeze. The stars big as sunflowers. The yellow cabs dozed in formation like enormous wasps. A colored porter sat propped against the stanchions of an express truck. His arms were folded and his cap titled over his eyes. There was no movement anywhere except for the gasping reflection of an unseen neon sign. A mexican in a blue coat padded by and went off to the end of the world. The ling tracks glistening in the moonlight seemed to bisect the earth.

 On a bench was a girl sitting upright with the sleeping head of a soldier in her lap. She was nit a pretty girl, but as she sat there with her legs out at a wide angle to leave a friendly lap for the head and shoulders, she was a Madonna, beautifully self-contained—wife, mother, mistress, guardian angel. She smoked a cigarette. And all around her was such a still and inoffensive world that the glowing ash of her cigarette was the only human aggression. And then the train light bristled in the horizon and it cae snorting across the desert and in about five minutes it was in the station. the porter came to life again. The soldier soke up with a start, looked up and wildly at the girl for a moment, assembled his sprawling, limb, fixed his cap his cap. "Pardon me, and thank you, ma'am," he said. The girl dusted the ash off her skirt with the back of her hand and without rising said, with a small smile, "You're welcome, soldier." He boarded the train and she sat back to wait for her friend or mother, or whoever, due on another train coming the other way.

The fourth America was a big man, sitting opposite me on the way up from San Francisco to Portland, Oregon. He was about six feet five, with a weathered face and fingers fat as baseball bats. He was gloomy about something. He turned out to be a lumberman, a big lumberman, from Portland. He'd been talking to shipbuilders in San Francisco. They needed more and more wood for cargo-ships. His problem was that the great forests of the Cascade Mountains— the last remaining stand of forest primeval in America—were beginning to give out. They couldn't replant enough to replace what they cut down. The shipbuilders had said they were very short of wood for dunnage—for the protective covering they use very cheap wood. They hadn't enough. They dared to suggest the great and beautiful monarch of the Northwest forests—the Douglas fir that rises like thousands of Cathedral spires on mountainsides carpeted with lupines. The lumberman , a businessman out for a dollar after all, and no sentimentalist about chopping down trees-this man leaned over and tapped the fat tips of his fingers and shook his head and groaned. "Douglas fir," he kept saying, "Douglas fir for dunnage. No, sir."

The fifth man was Chicago meat-packer. A prosperous Chicago meat-packer. I'm sure you know the type, everybody does. Well, this man was typical, in his queer way, of many a prosperous Midwestern businessman. His grandfather had bee an Irish immigrant who came to work on the railroads. His father had slaughtered cattle and later came to see that what ambles into Chicago in the hoof can, with the proper care, go out as steak or a tennis racket. This observation has been the basis of several Midwestern fortunes, and he passed it to on to his son, who prudently let other people handle the gut and himself was content to pack the steaks. He was now about sixty, and very wealthy.

One day at the age of about forty-five, when he had had a heavy competitive morning, he sat back at his de나 and told himself, "I simply have to take an afternoon off." He took it there and then. He went out and by chance into the Art Institute in Chicago, which by expert consent houses the finest collection anywhere of French impressionist painting. The meat-packer was in there for four hours and came out in a terrified glow. He had discovered to his rising astonishment that he liked pictures. Liking is the wrong word. The man made the guilty discovery that he was an unwitting slave of good painting waiting only to be needled into a hopeless addiction. He was not a man who lay around contemplating his passions. He was a man with several telephones. He picked one up – he later, by the way, had a special line put in to take care of his hobby – and called the University. "Who've you got there," he asked, "Who can teach me about art?" What sort of art, they asked, fine art, archaeology, Oriental art, frescoes . . . ? "Fine art, rough art – any art," he said.

He started with a university lecturer in modern painting. He soon employed almost a small faculty of his own. He traveled to every museum and private collection in the United States. He did the same in Europe. He talked to artists, to portrait-painters and landscape-painters, and miniature-painters, and curators, and buyers. He went into paint-manufacturing works. He talked to brush-makers and frame-makers. He saw the country and studied the light throughout the day over the landscapes his favorite men had painted. He read all their memoirs and notes. Today in his chicago home he has the most exquisitely chosen collection – that has everything to do with his taste rather that his learning – of the minor works of a generation of great Frenchmen. One of the greatest of modern art critics has said that nobody alive has a finer flair for assessing the quality of disputed French moderns than this same hale, sixty-year-old, and still unretired Chicago meat-packer.

The last American of my half-dozen–and I put him last because it would be impossible to talk about anybody else after him–was a tattooist in San Die해, California. A sleek, foxy-looking little man in his early fifties with a bow tie, an Adolphe Menjou mustache, and his shirt-sleeves rolled high, his arms blue with writhing snakes, cooch dancers, patterns of lacework, and assorted nicknames. The moment I asked him to open up about his work, he adopted the manner of the government people in charge of defense in the last war. Deliberate, but not so that you could get a word in. Defiant, lest you dared to think that anyone in America was in a better position to feel the people's pulse. He announced, choosing his words with great weight, that "no trade or business in these United States is a better barometer, you might say," of the American mood and economy. In the first war, he said, "sailors used to come in here and ask for hearts, and their girl's names. No more," he said. "It's a very different picture. Now they seem to want their mothers, just the word 'Mother.'" He sighed. Tattooing, it seemed, wasn't what it used to be in the good old days of private enterprise. "I mean from the medical angle. I never had a customer yet get blood-poisoning. But in the last twenty years the doctors start hornin' in and settin' up what they call standards. Tattoing today's what you might call a scientific, surgical operation. Sterile needles and all that stuff. That sorta thing makes you pretty leery. They don't encourage tattooing on some parts of the body no more. I have to take it easy. Girls used to come in here, they didn't give a damn what you tattooed on 'em or where. They just want it to hurt, get it? Most guys who get tattooed do it on a dare, just to show they're tough. Sure it hurts. That's the psychology of it. If it didn't hurt, I'd a been outa business thirty-five years ago. But don't forget there are ethics in this game. I don't want to harm nobody. I charge five dollars a square inch for the forearm, teen dollars in the upper arm. I wouldn't touch a chest for fifty bucks."

I asked him what was the weirdest assignment he'd ever had. He looked me over and shut the door and lit a cigarette. He had obviously told this many times before, but he had to set the stage.

"Well, a soman about two years ago was sick some place up north, Los Angeles-Glendale, I guess. But I mean sick. Had some sort of stomach trouble. And seems the doctor wanted to operate. Well, this guy-a brother- phones here around one in the morning. Wanted to know how much I'd charge to get the way out to Glendale and tattoo her stomach. Now, I mean, I told him that was a tough thing to figure. You see, somebody asks a price on a job and you gotta know where it's gonna be. When I was young at this game I used to quote 'em so much a square inch, thinkin' it'd be a forearm or lower leg or some place where the skin's thin and tight. Hell, if you fix the price, then you have to go to work on a flabby leg. By the time you stretched it so's you can keep the needle goin' smooth, you'd cover an acre. So I figured she was a middle-aged dame and anyway I didn't wanna drive a hundred some odd miles out there. So I says a hundred and twenty bucks. Okay, says the guy, and charge the cab. Honest.

"So I collect the dyes and needles and stuff and I'm on my way. I get out there- to this house, I mean- and go up to the bedroom. It was like a morgue in there. Dark and everythin' and this dame lyin' across the bed screamin' about bein' cut up. Seems she was goin' in the hospital the next day for you know what they call it- observation? She was scared they'd operate on her, and me not get there. Well, I took one look at her and, brother, I gypped myself on the deal. She was enormous. It took me three hours. She'd a been a whole lot more comfortable having' the operation. I sure was glad to get outa that place. How's that?-What did I write? I wrote what she told me, sort of a note to the surgeon. Clear across her middle. 'Do not violate this Body.'" to attack us and that sooner or later they intend to strike. Both are wrong. Each side, so far as the masses are concerned, is desirous of peace. Both dread war. But the constant acceleration of preparation may, without specific intent, ultimately precipitate a kind of spontaneous combustion.

Many will tell you, with mockery and ridicule, that the abolition of war can be only a dream, that it is but the vague imaginings of a visionary. But we must go on or we will go under. And criticism is that the world has no plan which will enable us to go on. We have suffered the blood and the sweat and the tears. Now we week the wat and the truth and the light. We are in a new era. The old methods and solutions for this vital problem no longer suffice. We must have new thoughts, new ideas, new concepts. We must break out of the strait-jacket of the past. We must have sufficient imagination and moral courage to translate this universal wish- which is rapidly becoming a universal necessity-into actuality. And until then we must be fully prepared, whatever the cost or sacrifice, lest we perish.

The Present Human Condition —by Erich Fromm

*E*rich Fromm (1990–) was born in Frankfurt, Germany, and educated at Heidelberg, Munich, and the Psychoanalytic Institute of Berlin. He taught and lectured on psychology and psychoanalysis at Frankfurt, and in 1934 came to the United States to New York's International Institute of Social Research. Since that time he has lectured and taught at many of the nation's major colleges and universities; he is currently Professor of Psychology at the National University of Mexico and at Michigan State University. His writings on psychoanalysis, philosophy, religion, literature, and current affairs have had a great impact on contemporary social thinking. Among his most influential books are Psychoanalysis and Religion (1950), The Forgotten Language (1951), and The Sane Society (1955).

At the close of the Middle Ages, Western man seemed to be headed for the final fulfillment of his keenest dreams and visions. He freed himself from the authority of a totalitarian church, the weight of traditional thought, the geographical limitations of our but half-discovered globe. He built a new science which eventually led to the release of hitherto unheard-of productive powers, and to the complete transformation of the material world. He created political systems which seem to guarantee the free and productive growth of the individual; he so reduced the time of work that man could enjoy hours of leisure to an extent his forefathers had hardly dreamed of.

Yet where are we today? The danger of an all-destructive are hangs over humanity, a danger which is by no means overcome by the spirit of Geneva prevalent at the time of this writing. But even of man's political representatives have enough sanity left to avoid a war, man's condition is far from the fulfillment of the hopes of the sixteenth, seventeenth, and eighteenth centuries.

Man's character has been molded by the demands of the world he has built with his won hands. Un the eighteenth and nineteenth centuries, man's character orientation was essentially exploitative and hoarding. His course through life was determined by the desire to exploit others and to save his earnings to make further profit from them. In the twentieth century, man's character orientation is essentially a receptive and a marketing one. He is receptive in most of his leisure time. He is the eternal consumer; he :takes in" drink, food, cigarettes, lectures, sights, books, movies-all are consumed, swallowed. The world is one great object for his appetite, a big bottle, a big apple, a big breast. Man has become the suckler, the eternally expectant-and the eternally disappointed one.

It "privately," individually, modern man is a consumer, he is "publicly," in his active participation in his society, a trader. Our economic system is centered around the function of the market as determining the value of all commodities, and as the regulator of each one's share in the social product. Neither force nor tradition, as in previous periods of history, nor fraud or trickery govern man's economic activities. He is free to produce and to sell; market day is judgment day for the success of his efforts. Now only are commodities offered and sold on the market; labor itself has become a commodity, sold on the labor market under the same conditions of fair competition. But the market system has reached out farther than the economic sphere of commodities and labor. Man has transformed himself into a commodity, experiences his life as capital to be invested profitably; if he succeeds in this, he is "successful," and his life has meaning; if not, "he is a failure." His "value" lies in his salability, not in his human qualities of love and reason or in his artistic capacities. Hence, his sense of his own value depends on extraneous factors, his success, the judgement of others. Hence, he is dependent on these others, and his security lies in conformity, in never being more than two feet away from the herd.

However, It is not only the market that determines modern man's "public" character. Another factor, closely related to the market function, is the mode of industrial production. Enterprises become bigger and bigger; the number of people employed by these enterprises as workers or clerks grows incessantly; ownership is separated from management, and the industrial giants are governed by a professional bureaucracy which is mainly interested in the smooth functioning and in the expansion of their enterprise, rather than in profit per se.

What kind of man, then, does our society need in order to function smoothly? It needs men who co-operate smoothly in large groups; who want to consume more and more, and whose tastes are standardized and can be easily influenced and anticipated. It needs men who feel free and independent who do not feel subject to any authority or principle or conscience, yet are willing to be commanded, to do what is expected, to fit into the social machine without friction-men who can be guided without force, led without leaders, be prompted without an aim except the aim to be on the move, to function, to go ahead. Modern capitalism has succeeded in producing this kind of man; he is the automaton, the alienated man. He is alienated in the sense that his acts and forces have become estranged from him; they stand above and against him, and rule him rather than being ruled by him. His life forces have flowed into things and institutions, and these things, having become idols, are not experienced as the result of his own efforts, but as something apart from him which he worships and to which he submits. Alienated man bows down before the works of his own hands. His idols represent his own life forces in an alienated form. Man does nor experience himself as the active bearer of his own forces and riches, but as an impoverished "thing," dependent on other things-things outside himself, into which he has projected his living substance.

Man's social feelings are projected in the state. Just because he has made the state the embodiment of his own social feelings, he worships it and its symbols. He projects his sense of power, wisdom, and courage into his leaders, and he worships them as his idols. As a worker, clerk of manager, modern man is alienated from his work. The worker has become an economic atom that dances to the tune of automatized management. He has no part in planning the work precess, in its outcome; he is hardly ever in touch with the whole product. The manager, on the other hand, is in touch with the whole product, but he is alienated from it as something concrete and useful. His aim is to employ profitably the capital invested by others; the commodity is the abstractified embodiment of capital, not something which, as a concrete entity, matters to him. The manager has become a bureaucrat who handles things, figures, and human beings as mere objects of his activity. Their manipulation is considered to be a concern with human relations when actually one deals with the most inhuman relations–those between abstractified automatons.

Our consumption is equally alienated. It is determined by the advertising slogans, rather than by our palates, eyes, or ears.

As a citizen, then, modern man is willing even to give his life for his fellow men; as a private individual, he is filled with an egotistical concern for himself. The meaninglessness and alienation of work result in a longing for complete laziness. Man hates his working life because it makes him feel a prisoner and a fraud. His ideal becomes absolute laziness, in which he will not have to make a move, where everything goes according to the Kodak slogan: "You press the button; we do the rest." This tendency is reinforced by the type of consumption necessary for the expansion of the inner market, leading to a principle which Huxley has very succinctly expressed in his Brave New World. One might epitomize the way many of us today have been conditioned from childhood with: "Never put off till tomorrow the fun you can have today." If I do not postpone the satisfaction of my wish (and I am conditioned only to wish for what I can get), I have no conflicts, no doubts; no decision has to be made; I am never alone with myself because I am always busy - either working of having fun. I have no need to be aware of myself as myself because I am constantly absorbed with consuming. I am a system of desires and satisfactions; I have to work in order to fulfill my desires, and these very desires are constantly stimulated and directed by the economic machine.

We claim that we pursue the aims of the Judaeo-Christian tradition, the love of God and of our neighbor. We are even told that we are going through a period of a promising religious renaissance. Nothing could be farther from the truth. We use symbols belonging to a genuinely religious tradition, and transform them into formulas serving the purposes of alienated man. Religion becomes a self-help device for increasing one's own powers for success. God becomes a partner in business. The "Power of Positive Thinking" is the successor of "How to Make Friends and Influence People."

Love of man is rare phenomenon too. Automatons do not love; alienated men do not care. What is praised by love experts and marriage counselors is a team relationship between two people who manipulate watch other with the right techniques, and whose love is essentially a haven from an otherwise unbearable aloneness, and egotism a deux.

What, then, can be expected from the future? If one ignores those thoughts produced by our wishes, one has to admit, I am afraid, that the most likely possibility is still that the discrepancy between technical intelligence and reason will lead the world into an atomic war. The most likely outcome of such a war is the destruction of industrial civilization abd the regression of the world to a primitive agrarian level. Or, if the destruction should not prove to be as thorough as many specialists in the field believe, the result will be the necessity for the victor to organize and dominate the whole world. This could be realized only by a centralize state based on force, and it would make little difference whether Moscow or Washington would be the seat of government.

But, unfortunately, even the avoidance of war does not in itself promise a bright future. In the development of both capitalism and communism as we can visualize them in the next fifty or a hundred years, the process of automatization and alienation will proceed. Both these systems are developing managerial societies in which inhabitants are well fed and well clad, having their wishes satisfied, and not having wishes that cannot be satisfied; automatons, who follow without force, who are guided without leaders, who make machines that act like men and produce men who act like machines; men whose reason deteriorates while their intelligence rises, thus creating the dangerous situation of equipping man with the greatest material power without the wisdom to use it.

In spite of increasing production and comfort, man loses more and more the sense of self, feels that his life is meaningless, even though such feeling is largely unconscious. In the nineteenth century the problem was that God is dead; in the twentieth century the problem is man is dead. In the nineteenth century inhumanity meant cruelty; in the twentieth it means schizoid self-alienation. The danger of the past was that men became slaves. The danger of the future is that men may become robots. True, robots do not rebel. But given man's nature, robots cannot live and remain same. They become "golems"; they will destroy their world and themselves because they can no longer stand the boredom of a meaningless life.

What is the alternative to war and robotism? Most fundamentally, perhaps, the answer could be given by reversing. Emerson's phrase; "Things are in the saddle and ride making," and saying: "Put mankind in the saddle so that it rides things." This is another way of saying that man must overcome the alienation which makes him an impotent and irrational worshiper of idols. This means, if we remain in the psychological sphere, that he must overcome the marketing and receptive orientation which dominates him now, and emerge into the mature, productive orientation. He must acquire again a sense of self, he must be capable of loving and of making his work a meaningful and concrete activity. He must emerge from a materialistic orientation and arrive at a level where spiritual values, love, truth, and justice, truly become of ultimate concern to him. But any attempt to change only one section of life, the human or spiritual one, will fail. In fact, progress occurring only in one sphere is destructive of progress in all spheres. The gospel concerned only with spiritual salvation led to the establishment of the Roman Catholic Church; the French Revolution, with its exclusive concern with political reform, led to Robespierre and Napoleon; socialism, insofar as it was only concerned with economic change, led to Stalinism

Applying this principle of simultaneous change to all spheres of life, we must think of those economic and political changes which are necessary in order to overcome the psychological fact of alienation We must retain the industrial method. But we muse decentralize work and the state so as to give them human proportions, and permit centralization only to an optimal point which is necessary because of the requirements of industry. In the economic sphere we need comanagement of all who work in an enterprise to permit their active and responsible participation. The new forms for such participation can be found. In the political sphere, we must return to the town meeting by creating thousands of small face-to-face groups which are well informed, which are integrated in a new "lower house." A cultural renaissance must combine work education for the young, adult education, and a new system of popular art, and secular system throughout the whole nation.

Just as primitive man was helpless before the natural forces, modern man is helpless before the social and economic forces created by himself. He worships the works of his own hands, bowing to the new idols, yet swearing by the name of the God who commanded him to destroy all idols. Man can protect himself from the consequences of his own madness only by creating a sane society which conforms with the needs of man, needs which are rooted in the very conditions of his existence: a society in which man relates to man lovingly, in which he is rooted in bonds of brotherliness and solidarity, rather than in the ties of blood and soil; a society which gives him the possibility of transcending nature by creating rather than by conformity; one in which a system of orientation and devotion exists without man's needing to distort reality and to worship idols.

Building such a society means taking the nest step; it means the end of "humanoid" history, the phase in which man has not become fully human. It does not meat the "end of days," the "completion," the state of perfect harmony in which no conflicts or problems confront man. On the contrary, it is man's fate that his existence is beset by contradictions which he is impelled to solve without ever solving them. When he has overcome the primitive state of human sacrifice, be it in the ritualistic form of the Aztec or in the secular form of war; when he has been able to regulate his relationship with become his servants rather than his idols – he will be confronted with the truly human conflicts and problems. He will have to be adventuresome, courageous, imaginative, capable of suffering and of joy, but his powers will be in the service of life, and not in the service of death. The new phase of human history, if it comes to pass, will be a beginning, not an end.

My View of History   ―by Arnold Toynbee

*A*rnold J. Toynbee(1889–)was born in England, and educated at Winchester and Oxford, later becoming a tutor at Oxford until the outbreak of World War I. He worked in a government office during the war, and was a member of the British delegation to the Paris Peace Conference. From 1919 to 1924 he was Professor of Greek Literature at the University of London, and since 1925 has been Director of Study at the Royal Institute of International Affairs and Research Professor of International History at the University of London.

His first historical work, Nationality and the War(1915), was followed by many other volumes. However, his six-volume A Study of History(1934-1939) laid down the thesis of historical interpretation which has been the basis of his reputation as the most distinguished historian of this generation. A one-volume abridgement of this work appeared in 1947, and a book of essays, Civilization on Trial(1948), further explains his philosophical interpretations of history. Toynbee's view of history, and especially his theory of challenge and response in the rise and fall of civilizations, have been attacked and defended by various scholars; but his optimistic hope that through faith mankind may yet emerge from its confusion, places him at the opposite pole from Spengler, who saw only doom in his study of the past.

My view of history is itself a tiny piece of history; and this mainly other people's history and not my own; for a scholar's life-work is to add his bucketful of water to the great and growing river of knowledge fed by countless bucketfuls of the kind. If my individual view of history is to be made at all illuminating, or indeed intelligible, it must be presented in its origin, growth, and social and personal setting.

There are many angles of vision from which human minds peer at the universe. Why am I a historian, not a philosopher or a physicist? For the same reason that I drink tea and coffee without sugar. Both habits were formed at a tender age by following a lead from my mother. I am a historian because my mother was one before me; yet at the same time I am conscious that I am of a different school from hers. Why did I not exactly take my mothers's cue?

First, because I was born by my mother into the next generation to hers, and my mind was, therefore, not yet set hard when history took my generation by the throat in 1914; and, secondly, because my education was more old-fashioned than my mother's had been. My mother-belonging as she did to the first generation, in England, of university women-had obtained an up-to-date education in modern Western history, with the national history of England itself as the principal guide-line. Her son, being a boy, went to an old-fashioned English public school and was educated, both there and at Oxford, almost entirely on the Greek and Latin classics.

For any would-be historian-and especially for one born into

these times-a classical education is, in my belief, a priceless boon. As a training-ground, the history of the Graeco-Roman world has its conspicious merits. In the first place, Graeco-Roman history is visible to us in perspective and can be seen by us as a whole, because it is over-in contrast to the history of our own Western world, which is a still-unfinished play of which we do not know the eventual ending and cannot even see the present general aspect from our own position as momentary actors on its crowded and agitated stage.

In the second place, the field of Graeco-Roman history is not encumbered and obscured by a surfeit of information, and so we can see the wood-thanks to a drastic thinning of the trees during the interregnum between the dissolution of the Graeco-Roman society and the emergence of our own. Moreover, the conveniently manageable amount of evidence that has survived is not overweighted by the state papers of parochial principalities, like those which, in our Western world, have accumulated, ton upon ton, during the dozen centuries of its pre-atomic-bomb age. The surviving materials for a study of Graeco-Roman history are not only manageable in quantity and select in quality; they are also well-balanced in their character. Statues, poems, and works of philosophy count here for more than the texts of laws and treaties; and this breeds a sense of proportion in the mind of a historian nursed on Graeco-Roman history; for-as we can see in the perspective given by lapse of time more easily than we can see it in the life of our own generation-the works of artists and men of letters outlive the deeds of business men, soldiers and statesmen. The poets and the philosophers outrange the historians; while the prophets and the saints overtop and outlast them all. The ghosts of Agamemnon and Pericles haunt the living world of to-day by grace of the magic words of Homer and Thucydides; and, when Homer and Thucydides are no longer read, it is safe to prophesy that Christ and the Buddha and Socrates will still be fresh in the memory of (to us) almost inconceivably distant generations of men.

The third, and perhaps greatest, merit of Graeco-Roman history is that its outlook is oecumenical rather than parochial. Athens may have eclipsed Sparta and Rome Samnium, yet Athens in her youth made herself the education of all Hellas, while Rome in her old age made the whole Graeco-Roman world into a single commonwealth. In Graeco-Roman history, surveyed from beginning to end, unity is the dominant note; and, when once I had heard this great symphony, I was no longer in danger of being hypnotized by the lone and outlandish music of the parochial history of my own country, which had once enthralled me when I listened to my mother telling it to me in instalments, night by night, as she put me to bed. The historical pastors and masters of my mother's generation, not only in England but in all Western countries, had been eagerly promoting the study of national history in the mistaken belief that it had a closer bearing on their country-men's lives and was, therefore, somehow more readily accessible to their understanding than the history of other places and times(although it is surely evident that, in reality, Jesus' Palestine and Plato's Greece were more potently operative than Alfred's or Elizabeth's England in the lives of English men and women of the Victorian age).

Yet, in spite of this misguided Victorian canonization — so alien from the spirit of the father of English history, the Venerable Bede — of the history of the particular country in which one happened to have been born, the unconscious attitude of the Victorian Engliahman towards history was that of someone living outside history altogether. He took it for granted — without warrant — that he himself was standing on trra firma, secure against being engulfed in that ever-rolling stream in which Time had borne all his less privileged sons away. In his own privileged state of being emancipated, as he supposed, from history, the Victorian Englishman gazed with curiosity, condescension, and a touch of pity, but altogether without apprehension, at the spectacle of less fortunate denizens of other places and periods struggling and foundering in history's flood — in much the same way as, in a mediaeval Italian picture, the saved lean over the balustrade of Heaven to look down complacently at the torments of the damned in Hell. Charles the First — worse luck for him — had been in history, but Sir Robert Walpole, though threatened with impeachment, had just managed to scramble out of the surf, while we ourselves were well beyond high-water mark in a snug coign of vantage where nothing could happen to us. Our more backward contemporaries might, perhaps, still be waist-high in the now receding tide, but what was that to us?

I remember, at the beginning of a university term during the Bosnian crisis of 1908-9, Professor L. B. Namier, then an undergraduate at Balliol and back from spending a vacation at his family home just inside the Galician frontier of Austria, saying to us other Balliol men, with (it seemed to us) a portentous air: "Well, the Austrian army is mobilized on my father's estate and the Russian army is just across the frontier, half-an-hour away." It sounded to us like a scene from The Chocolate Solder, but the lack of comprehension was mutual, for a lynx-eyed Central European observer of international affairs found it hardly credible that these English undergraduates should not realize that a stone's-throw away, in Galicia, their own goose, too, was being cooked.

Hiking round Greece three years later on the trail of Epaminondas and Philopoemen and listening to the talk in the village cafes, I learnt for the first time of the existence of something called the foreign policy of Sir Edward Grey. Yet, even then, I did not realize that we too were still in history after all. I remember feeling acutely homesick for the historic Mediterranean as I walked, one day in 1913, along the Suffolk coast of a grey and uneventful North Sea. The general war of 1914 overtook me expounding Thucydides to Balliol undergraduates reading for Litera Humaniores, and then suddenly my understanding was illuminated. The experience that we were having in our world now had been experienced by Thucydides in his world already. I was re-reading him now with a now perception - perceiving meanings in his words, and feelings behind his phrases, to which I had been insensible until I, in my turn, had run into that historical crisis that had inspired him to write his work.

Thucydides, it now appeared, had been over this ground before. He and his generation had been ahead of me and mine in the stage of historical experience that we had respectively reached; in fact, his present had been my future. But this made nonsense of the chronological notation which registered my world as "modern" and Thucydides' world as "ancient." Whatever chronology might say, Thucydides' world and my world had now proved to be philosophically contemporary. And, if this were the true relation between the Graeco-Roman and the Western civilizations, might not the relation between all the civilizations known to us turn out to be the same?

This vision-new to me-of the philosophical contemporaneity of all civilizations was fortified by being seen against a background provided by some of the discoveries of our modern Western physical science. On the time-scale now unfolded by geology and cosmogony, the five or six thousand years that had elapsed since the first emergence of representatives of the species of human society that we label "civilizations" were an infinitesimally brief span of time compared to the age, up to date, of the human race, of life on this planet, of the planet itself, of our own solar system, of the galaxy in which it is one grain of dust, or of the immensely vaster and older sum total of the stellar cosmos. By comparison with these orders of temporal magnitude, civilizations that had emerged in the second millenium B.C. (like the Graeco-Roman), in the fourth millennium B.C.(like the Ancient Egyptian), and in the first millennium of the Christian era (like our own) were one another's contemporaries indeed.

Thus history, in the sense of the histories of the human societies called civilizations, revealed itself as a sheaf of parallel, contemporary, and recent essays in a new enterprise: a score of attempts up to date, to transcend the level of primitive human life at which man, after having become himself, had apparently lain torpid for some hundreds of thousands of years-and was still, in our day, so lying in out-of-the-way places like New Guinea, Tierra del Fuego and the north-eastern extremity of Siberia, where such primitive human communities had not yet been pounced upon and either exterminated or assimilated by the aggressive pioneers of other human societies that, unlike these sluggards, had now, though this only recently, got on the move again. The amazing present difference in cultural level between various extant societies was brought to my attention by the works of Professor Teggart of the University of California. This fargoing differentiation had all happened within these brief last five or six thousand years. Here was a promising point to probe in investigating, sub specie temporis, the mystery of the universe.

What was it that, after so long a pause, had so recently set in such vigorous motion once again, towards some new and still unknown social and spiritual destination, those few societies that had embarked upon the enterprise called civilization? What had roused them from a torpor that the great majority of human societies had never shaken off? This question was simmering in my mind when, in the summer of 1920, Professor Namier-who had already put Eastern Europe on my map for me-placed in my hands Oswald Spengler's Untergang des Abendlandes. As I read those pages teeming with firefly flashes of historical insight, I wondered at first whether my whole inquiry had been disposed of by Spengler before even the questions, not to speak of the answers, had fully taken shape in my own mind. One of my own cardinal points was that the smallest intelligible fields of historical study were whole societies and not arbitrarily insulated fragments of them like the nation-states of the modern West or the city states of the Graeco-Roman world. Another of my points was that the histories of all societies of the species called civilizations were in some sense parallel and contemporary; and both these points were also cardinal in Spengler's system. But when I looked in Spengler's book for an answer to my question about the geneses of civilizations, I saw that there was still work for me to do, for on this point Spengler was, it seemed to me, most unilluminatingly dogmatic and deterministic. According to him, civilizations arose, developed, declined, and foundered in unvarying conformity with a fixed time-table, and no explanation was offered for any of this. It was just a law of nature which Spengler had detected, and you must take it on trust from the master: ipse dixit. This arbitrary fiat seemed disappointingly unworthy of Spengler's brilliant genius; and here I became aware of a difference in national traditions. Where the German a priori method drew blank, let us see what could be done by English empiricism. Let us test alternative possible explanations in the light of the facts and see how they stood the ordeal.

Race and environment were the two main rival keys that were offered by would-be scientific nineteenth-century Western historians for solving the problem of the cultural inequality of various extant human societies, and neither key proved, on trial, to unlock the fast-closed door. To take the race theory first, what evidence was there that the differences in physical race between different members of the genus homo were correlated with differences on the spiritual plane which was the field of history? And, if the existence of this correlation were to be assumed for the sake of argument, how was it that members of almost all the races were to be found among the fathers of one or more of the civilizations? The black race alone had made no appreciable contribution up to date; but, considering the shortness of the time during which the experiment of civilization had been on foot so far, this was no cogent evidence of incapacity; it might merely be the consequence of a lack of opportunity or a lack of stimulus. As for environment, there was, of course, a manifest similarity between the physical conditions in the lower Nile valley and in the lower Tigris-Euphrates valley, which had been the respective cradles of the Egyptian and Sumerian civilizations; but, if these physical conditions were really the cause of their emergence, why had no parallel civilizations emerged in the physically comparable valleys of the Jordan and the Rio Grande? And why had the civilization of the equatorial Andean plateau had no African counterpart in the highlands of Kenya? The breakdown of these would-be scientific impersonal explanations drove me to turn to mythology. I took this turning rather self-consciously and shamefacedly, as though it were a provocatively retrograde step. I might have been less diffident if I had not been ignorant, as I was at that date, of the new ground broken by psychology during the war of 1914-18. If I had been acquainted at the time with the works of C. G. Jung, they would have given me the clue. I actually found it in Goethe's Faust, in which I had fortunately been grounded at school as thoroughly as in Aeschylus' Agamemnon.

Goethe's "Prologue in Heaven" opens with the archangels hymning the perfection of God's creation. But, just because His works are perfect, the Creator has left Himself no scope for any further exercise of His creative powers, and there might have been no way out of this impasse if Mephistopheles-created for this very purpose-had not presented himself before the throne and challenged God to give him a free hand to spoil, if he can, one of the Creator's choicest works. God accepts the challenge and thereby wins an opportunity to carry His work of creation forward. An encounter between two personalities in the form of challenge and response: have we not here the flint and steel by whose mutual impact the creative spark is kindled?

In Goethe's exposition of the plot of the Divina Commedia, Mephistopheles is created to be diddled-as the fiend, to his disgust, discovers too late. Yet if, in response to the Devil's challenge, God genuinely puts His created works in jeopardy, as we must assume that He does, in order to win an opportunity of creating something new, we are also bound to assume that the Devil does not always lose. And thus, if the working of challenge-and-response explains the otherwise inexplicable and unpredictable geneses and growths of civilizations, it also explains their breakdowns and disintegrations. A majority of the score of civilizations known to us appear to have broken down already and a majority of this majority have trodden to the end the downward path that terminates in dissolution.

Our post mortem examination of dead civilizations does not enable us to cast the horoscope of our own civilization or of any other that is still alive. Pace Spengler, there seems to be no reason why a succession of victorious responses ad infinitum. On the other hand, when we make an empirical comparative study of the paths which the dead civilizations have respectively travelled from breakdown to dissolution, we do her seem to find a certain measure of Spenglerian uniformity, and this, after all, is not surprising. Since breakdown means loss of control, this in turn means the lapse of freedom into automatism, and, whereas free acts are infinitely variable and utterly unpredictable, automatic processes are apt to be uniform and regular.

Briefly stated, the regular pattern of social disintegration is a schism of the disintegrating society into a recalcitrant proletariat and a less and less effectively dominant minority. The process of disintegration is a schism of the disintegrating society into a recalcitrant proletariat and a less and less effectively dominant minority. The process of disintegration does not proceed evenly; it jolts along in alternating spasms of rout, rally, and rout, In the last rally but one, the dominant minority succeeds in temporarily arresting the society's lethal self-laceration by imposing on it the peace of a universal state. Within the framework of the dominant minority's universal state the proletariat creates a universal church, and after the next rout, in which the disintegrating civilization finally dissolves, the universal church may live on to become the chrysalis from which a new civilization eventually emerges. To modern Western students of history, these phenomena are most familiar in the Graeco-Roman examples of the Pax Romana and the Christian Church. The establishment of the Pax Romana by Augustus seemed, at the time, to have put the Graeco-Roman world back upon firm foundations after it had been battered for several centuries by perpetual war, misgovernment, and revolution. But the Augustan rally proved, after all, to be no more than a respite. After two hundred and fifty years of comparative tranquillity, the Empire suffered in the third century of the Christian era a collapse from which it never fully recovered, and at the next crisis, in the fifth and sixth centuries, it went to pieces irretrievably. The true beneficiary of the temporary Roman Peace was the Christian Church. The Church seized this opportunity to strike root and spread; it was stimulated by persecution until the Empire, having failed to crush it, decided, instead, to take it into partnership. And, when even this reinforcement failed to save the Empire from destruction, the Church took over the Empire's heritage. The same relation between a declining civilization and a rising religion can be observed in a dozen other cases. In the Far East, for instance, the Ts'in and Han Empire plays the Roman Empire's part, while the role of the Christian Church is assumed by the Mahayana school of Buddhism.

If the death of one civilization thus brings on the birth of another, does not the at first sight hopeful and exciting quest for the goal of human endeavours resolve itself, after all, into a dreary round of vain repetitions of the Gentiles? This cyclic view of the process of history was taken so entirely for granted by even the greatest Greek and Indian souls and intellects-by Aristotle, for instance, and by the Buddha-that they simply assumed that it was true without thinking it necessary to prove it. On the other hand, Captain Marryat, in ascribing the same view to the ship's carpenter of HMS Rattlesnake, assumes with equal assurance that this cyclic theory is an extravaganza, and he makes the amiable exponent of it a figure of fun. To our Western minds the cyclic view of history, if taken seriously, would reduce history to a tale told by an idiot, signifying nothing. But mere repugnance does not in itself account for effortless unbelief. The traditional Christian beliefs in hell fire and in the last trump were also repugnant, yet they continued to be believed for generations. For our fortunate Western imperviousness to the Greek and Indian belief in cycles we are indebted to the Jewish and Zoroastrian contributions to our Weltanschauung.

In the vision seen by the Prophets of Israel, Judah, and Iran, history is not a cyclic and not a mechanical process. It is the masterful and progressive execution, on the narrow stage of this world, of a divine plan which is revealed to us in this fragmentary glimpse, but which transcends our human powers of vision and understanding in every dimension. Moreover, the Prophets, through their own experience, anticipated Aeschylus' discovery that learning comes through suffering-a discovery which we, in our time and circumstances, have been making too.

Shall we opt, then, for the Jewish-Zoroastrian view of history as against the Graeco-Indian? So drastic a choice may not, after all be forced upon us, for it may be that the two views are not fundamentally irreconcilable. After all, if a vehicle is to move forward on a course which its driver has set, it must be borne along on wheels that turn monotonously round and round. While civilizations rise and fall and, in falling, give rise to others, some purposeful enterprise, higher than theirs, may all the time be making headway, and, in a divine plan, the learning that comes through the suffering caused by the failures o'f civilizations may be the sovereign means of progress. Abraham was an emigre from a civilization in extremis; the Prophets were children of another civilization in disintegration; Christianity was born of the sufferings of a disintegrating Graeco-Roman world. Will some comparable spiritual enlightenment be kindled in the "displaced persons" who are the counterparts, in our world, of those Jewish exiles to whom so much was revealed in their painful exile by the waters of Babylon? The answer to this question, whatever the answer may be, is of greater moment than the still inscrutable destiny of our world-encompassing Western civilization.

참고문헌

Brantlinger, Patrick(1990). *Crusoe's Footprints: Cultural Studies in Britain and America.* New York: Routledge, Chapman and Hall, Inc.

Carol, Gilles & Mary Bixby, Paul Crowley, Shirley R. Crenshaw, Margaret Henrichs, Frances E. Reynolds, Donelle Pyle. ed.(1988). *Whole Language Strategies for Secondary Students.* New York: Richard C. Owen Publishers, Inc.

Harris, A. J.(1962). *Effective Teaching of Reading.* New York: David Mckay Company, Inc.

Harris, D. P.(1966). *Reading Improvement Exercises for Students of English as a Second Language.* New Jersey: Prentice-Hall, Inc.

Maley, Alan. & Alan Duff(1989). *The Inward Ear: Poetry in the Language Classroom.* Cambridge: Cambridge Univ. Press.

Muller, Gilbert H. & Harvey S.(2009). *The Short Prose Reader.* Boston: Mc Graw Hill Company Inc.

Nye, Russel(1963). *Modern Essays.* Chicago: Scott, Foreman and Company.

Slater, Stephen. and Joanne Collie(1987). *Literature in the Language Classroom.* Cambridge: Cambridge Univ. Press.

강인애(2003). 『왜 구성주의인가』. 서울: 문음사.

권오현(1997). "독일 문학교육에서의 행위지향 패러다임". 한국문학교육학회,『문학교육학』창간호. 서울: 태학사.
김옥순·주옥 옮김(2001). Bruno Betteheim.『옛이야기의 매력 1』. 서울: 시공사.
_____(2000). Bruno Betteheim.『옛이야기의 매력 2』. 서울: 시공사.
김용규·전봉철·정병언 옮김(2000). Patrick Brantlinger.『영미문화 연구-로빈슨크루소의 발자국』. 서울: 문화과학사.
김정섭·강승희·강순희(2004).『동화를 통한 창의성 교육』. 경기도 고양시: 서현사.
김종문 외(2002).『구성주의 교육학』. 서울: 교육과학사.
김창원(1999). "제 2 언어 교육을 위한 아동문학",『문학과 교육』제8호. 서울: 한국교육 미디어.
박경수(2000).『영어교육론』. 서울: 형설출판사.
부산광역시교육과학연구원(2001).『인터넷으로 만나는 신나는 영어수업』. 부산: 부산인쇄정보산업협동조합.
손정표(2005).『신독서지도방법론』. 서울: 태일사.
송영희(2006). 속독 훈련이 영어 독해력에 미치는 영향에 대한 연구. 부산대학교 교육대학원 석사학위 논문.
송정숙 외(2005). 어린이 독서지도-이론과 실제. 부산대학교 평생교육원 어린이 독서지도사 과정(I·II). 부산: 대진문화사.
신헌재 외(2001).『학습자 중심의 국어과 수업방안』. 서울: 박이정.
신헌재·이재성(2001).『학습자 중심의 국어교육』. 서울: 박이정.
어도선 번역 및 편집(1998).『영미문학과 중등 영어교육』. *Teaching English Literature in ESL/EFL Context: A complete guide for English teachers*(인터넷자료집 http://bmh.hs.kr/~aaaa1320/english/cyberclassroom/poetry/eur.htm).
안정효(1997).『안정효의 영어 길들이기』. 서울: 현암사.

양재한·김수경·김석임(2005).『어린이 독서지도론』. 서울: 태일사.
양재한·이경민·황금숙(2004).『독서치료와 어린이 글쓰기 지도』. 서울: 태일사.
이경우(1998).『총체적 언어 - 문학적 접근을 중심으로』. 서울: 창지사.
이성은(1988).『총체적 언어교육』. 서울: 창지사.
인터넷 자료. http://www.tellingtales.com.
정동빈(2002).『유아 영어 의사소통 교육론』. 서울: 한국문화사.
조영식(2000).『창조적 독서교육』. 서울: 인간과 자연사.
조일제 번역(2002). Joanne Collie and Stephen Slater.『영어교사를 위한 영문학 작품 지도법』. 서울: 한국문화사.
주강식(1998). 읽기의 자기주도적 학습력 신장방안. 부산대학교 교육연구소, 부산교육대학교 초등교육연구소 공동 주최 학술발표회 『구성주의와 교과교육』발표자료.
한국독서학회(2003).『독서연구』제 10호. 서울: 박이정.
한국독서학회(2004).『독서연구』제 11호. 서울: 박이정.
한철우·김명순·박영민(2001).『문학중심 독서지도』. 서울: 대한교과서주식회사.
한철우·박진용·김명순·박영민(2001).『과정 중심 독서지도』. 서울: 교학사.
황적륜 외(1984).『영어교수법』. 서울: 신아사.
황정현(2001).『창의력 계발을 위한 동화교육 방법론』. 서울: 열린교육.
황정현 옮김(1998). Nancy King.『창조적인 언어사용 능력을 위한 교육연극방법』. 서울: 평민사.

저자 조일제

부산대학교 사범대 영어교육과 교수
부산대학교 사범대 영어교육과 졸업, 동대학원에서 문학 석사 및 문학 박사
영국 Univ. of Nottingham 객원교수
미국 Fordham Univ. 및 Univ. of Hawaii 객원교수
부산대학교 국제교류교육원 원장
부산대학교 교육대학원 부원장
부산대학교 국제전문실무인력양성 특성화사업단 운영위원
부산대학교 평생교육원 어린이영어도자교실 및 TESOL INTERNATIONAL CLASS 주임교수
교과부 한국연구재단 우수인력양성대학 교육역량강화사업 컨설팅 및 성과평가 위원
한국로렌스학회 회장, 부회장, 편집이사, 총무이사
새한영어영문학회 부회장, 총무이사
한국영어영문학회 상임이사, 일반이사, 감사
부산광역시 교육청 협동장학사
부산녹색연합 창립위원, 운영위원, 자문위원

| 저서

D.H. 로렌스 연구(1995 한국문화사)
원초적 실재의 탐색-D.H. 로렌스문학과 어둠의 자아(1995 신아사)
한국과 세계를 잇는 문화소통-영어 문화소통 능력 향상 방안과 문화정보(1998 한국문화사)
영국문화의 이해와 탐방-영어교육을 위한 문화정보(2000 우용출판사)
D.H.로렌스문학 연구의 고대적 동양적 접근(2000 우용출판사)
영국문학과 사회(2001 우용출판사)
영어로 진행하는 영어수업의 교실영어와 수업모형(2001 우용출판사)
영미문화의 이해와 탐방-영어교육을 위한 문화정보(2002 우용출판사)
타자의 타자성과 그 담론적 전략들(2004 부산대학교 출판부 공저)
틈새 공간의 시학과 실제(2005 부산대학교 출판부 공저)
물질·물질성의 담론과 영미소설 읽기(2007 도서출판 동인, 공저)
채털리 부인의 사랑-성스럽고 경이로운 성의 체험(2006 살림출판사)
창의성 개발을 위한 활동 중심 독서지도법(2006 한국문화사)
창조적 생명의 실현(2008 한국학술정보)
영어교육을 위한 영어문학텍스트 활용법(2009 우용출판사)
영어 산문텍스트의 문체론적 분석-외국어 교육의 한 가지 접근법(2010 한국문화사) 외 다수

| 역서

영어교사를 위한 영문학 작품 지도법(1997 한국문화사)
외국어 교사를 위한 언어습득론(1999 한국문화사)
학습자 활동 중심의 (영)시 지도법과 언어교육(2005 한국문화사)
한영대역 불교성전 THE TEACHING OF BUDDHA(2005 보진재)

| 수상

제 45회 눌원문화상(인문과학 부문 2009)